Changing LEARNING Changing LIVES

A HIGH SCHOOL WOMEN'S STUDIES CURRICULUM FROM THE GROUP SCHOOL

By Barbara Gates, Susan Klaw, and Adria Steinberg

THE FEMINIST PRESS

The Clearinghouse on Women's Studies
Old Westbury, New York

Library of Congress Cataloging in Publication Data

Gates, Barbara, 1946–
   Changing learning, changing lives.

   Bibliography: p.
   1. Women's studies—United States—Curricula.   2. High
schools—United States—Curricula.   3. Feminism—Study and
teaching (Secondary)—United States.   I. Klaw, Susan, joint author.
II. Steinberg, Adria, joint author.   III. The Group School.
IV. Title.
HQ1426.G28   375'.301 41'20973   78–11912
ISBN 0–912670–47–9

The photographs in this book are of Group School students and staff.
They were contributed by students and teachers participating in
the school's photography program.

TABLE OF CONTENTS

UNIT I
MESSAGES FROM SOCIETY

UNIT II
EARLY SOCIALIZATION

UNIT III
GROWING UP FEMALE

UNIT VI

MEAN STREETS

UNIT VII

WOMEN AND WORK

UNIT VIII

WOMEN ORGANIZING THEMSELVES

UNIT IX

WOMEN'S NEWS

BIBLIOGRAPHY

ACKNOWLEDGMENTS

The students and staff at The Group School (past and present) made this book possible by creating together a wonderful environment for teaching and learning.

In particular, we'd like to thank the young women and men who contributed the poetry and essays which illuminate this book. They are: Annie Bithoney, Cheryl Burke, Cynthia Byrne, Linda M. Cabral, Pat Connolly, Janet Ferreira, Deborah L. Gillespie, Donna Gillespie, Teresé T. Gray, Cheryl Greene, Deborah Stewart Hedges, Billy Igo, Colleen Long, Robbin Luzaitis, Beth McCombe, Jane Reale, Julie Scanlon, Kenny Stewart, John Sullivan, Judi Teeter, Diane Tomaino Arsenault, Lisa Allison Weinberg.

All of the photographs in this book are of Group School students and staff. They were contributed by students and teachers participating in the school's photography program: Larry Aaronson, Colleen Long, Robbin Luzaitis, Janice Rogovin, and Wayne Sharnock. Special thanks are due to Janice Rogovin, who volunteered so many of her hours teaching photographic skills.

A number of young women and men gave life to our lesson plans by participating in the courses described in this book when they were first being developed. For their part in that work, we offer our thanks to: Priscilla Aylward, Janice Brown, Brian Burke, Carole Burke, Jacqui Burke, Joan Carpinella, Stacy Croucher, Marilyn Cieuzo, Francis Currier, Elena Dilando, Mark Donahue, Lyz Etter, Ann Farino, Donna Farino, Pauline Farino, Beverly Ferreira, Terry Gray, Cindy Graham, Marie Lange, Sandy Ledwell, Jimmy Long, Kathy Maxwell, Debby McCarthy, Kevin O'Rourke, Michael Pearson, Michael Pelham, Nancy Potember, Alylia Pugh, Elaine Ravanis, Denise Robicheau, Diane Robicheau, Jeannie Sullivan, Donna Sullivan, Kathy Sullivan, Theresa Sullivan, Kathy Teeter, Sean Tevlin, Mark Thomas, Henry Tomasczewski, Kathy Vincent, Linda Walsh.

Special acknowledgments are due to other individuals at The Group School. Staff members who encouraged us, who read, tested, and commented on the materials, who put up with our absence from teaching while we worked on the manuscript include: Larry Aaronson, Paul Atwood, Patricia Collinge, Marion Gillon, David Kelston, Bob McManus, Rose Monroe, Rudi Petersons, Judy Remcho, Michael Riley, Steve Seidel, Judy Tharinger. The volunteer teachers who helped develop units of the curriculum are Christina Barnes, Ernie Brooks, Janine Fay, and Jim Shine.

There are also many persons outside of The Group School who contributed a great deal to this project. Friends who gave helpful criticism and comments all along the way are Sandy Clifford, Jack De Long, Peter del Tredici, Henry Grunebaum, Dick Kravitz, and Steve Seidel. Many teachers and friends in Massachusetts read and tested units from the curriculum. In particular, we'd like to thank Barbara Beckwith, Kay Doherty, Evelyn Goldman, Debbie Kuhn, Lynn Miller, June Namias, Carolyn Ricker, Nan Stein, and Diane Tabor for giving us a great deal of feedback and for suggesting new ideas and approaches. The typists who spent many hours laboring over our manuscript in its various stages are Carole Lippman and Gale Halpern. The Institute of Open Education generously gave office space to the project.

We are indebted to The Feminist Press for encouraging us to seek funding for the book, accompanied by The Press's commitment to assume responsibility for its editing and production. We are especially grateful for the educational vision of Florence Howe and for the assistance of Corrine Lucido, beginning with the earliest stages of the project's development. Our thanks are due also to our capable editors, Sue Davidson and Merle Froschl; to Susan Trowbridge, who designed the book and oversaw its production; to Jim Anderson and Mary Mulrooney, who assisted in the book's production; to Wendy Wolf, who supervised the typesetting; and to Helen W. Wallace, who proofread the galleys.

Finally, we offer special thanks to the Rockefeller Family Fund and to the Shaw Foundation for believing in our work enough to award us supporting grants. The Massachusetts Department of Education made it possible for us to offer workshops for Cambridge public school teachers and to accomplish final revisions of the curriculum.

Changing
LEARNING
Changing
LIVES

**I learned a lot about myself, to respect myself more.
I'm no longer ashamed of who I am and where I'm coming from.
I know now I have to accept my history and make it better.**

[From a student evaluation of "Women and Society," 1972]

INTRODUCTION

The growth of feminist consciousness in American society has been accompanied by increasingly serious attempts to bring these ideas into the secondary schools. Starting with the adaptations of college women's studies programs into some of the more advanced classes in suburban, middle-class high schools, curricula related to women's issues have been allowed or encouraged in more and more school systems throughout the country.

The curriculum presented on these pages extends these efforts toward a population not generally reached by women's issues or women's courses—working-class young women. Anyone teaching high school in an urban community or working-class suburb has witnessed the school problems experienced by this group of students. Tracked into business or homemaking courses; labeled as slow, or unmotivated, or underachieving; given textbooks with strong sex, class, and race biases; many working-class young women feel that school is irrelevant to their lives. Their attitude becomes one of "serving time"; a debilitating passivity sets in. It is our belief and our experience that a high school women's program can begin to turn that process around. These young women need courses that help them realize their strengths and confront the personal and societal obstacles before them; that relate directly to their histories, experiences, and futures. They need a pedagogy that encourages them to be active, to teach each other, to share, to develop new skills and competencies.

The materials in this book have been designed to speak to these needs. This curriculum was developed over a period of five years by teachers and students at The Group School, a certified, alternative high school for students from working-class and low income backgrounds in Cambridge, Massachusetts. The school is small, with sixty-five to eighty students. Staff and students work closely together—both in the classes, which range in size from eight to fifteen, and in committees and meetings, where all decisions are made. Students come voluntarily. Most have dropped out from the public schools, having experienced failures there. They come to The Group School because it is outside the public system, where they felt defeated, and because of its reputation as a school where working-class Cambridge youth can learn something about themselves and the world while working towards a certified, high school diploma.

The Group School setting is obviously not typical of most schools or youth programs. But the teaching approaches and materials we have developed at the school can be useful to other people, in other settings, who are working with students from low-income backgrounds. In the atmosphere of trust and mutuality of the school, students have been able to suspend their suspicions and doubts about a women's program and we, as teachers, have learned which feminist issues resonate for them and how best to approach these issues.

When we started teaching women's courses at The Group School, in 1971, we had a great deal of positive energy that came from our own emotional involvement in the women's movement. But we had very few relevant teaching materials and only very general teaching ideas. The women's movement that was our political context at that point was mainly comprised of college-educated, middle-class women; the literature, ideas, and structure of that movement were thus largely inappropriate for our students.

The situation forced us to be creative in our search for materials and, whenever possible, to develop our own. With constant feedback from the students, over a period of years, we have been able to translate the political commitment with which we started our program into a women's studies curriculum for working-class high school women.

The goals, methodology, and content of the curriculum reflect what we have learned about our students' lives. In working at The Group School, we have gotten to know the students beyond their school personalities and achievements. A description of some of the characteristic attitudes, problems, and strengths of working-class young women is thus an important part of any introduction to these materials. On the following pages, we present three individual profiles designed to portray some of the nuances, complexities, and tensions within the lives of low-income young women we have known. So as not to single out any one student, we have drawn each profile from a number of different people. The three taken together form a composite picture of the many students who have helped to shape this curriculum, and whose voices are heard throughout this book.

PROFILES OF STUDENTS

Marsha. Marsha's ideas are in a period of great flux. Within the past two months, she's accepted a ring from Frank, the boyfriend she's been going with since she was twelve; written for an application to the State Art College; and, with the help of a teacher, started to develop a portfolio for admission. Marsha is also seriously thinking about getting an apartment with a girlfriend and looking for a job to bring in the rent money.

Marsha is confused right now about which of these directions to move in. Before last year, she never thought of herself as someone who could go to college. Her early school history was unhappy; she felt out of place at her parochial school. Many of the students were from middle-class families, whereas Marsha was of the working class. They always seemed to talk better, to get along better with the teachers, and to know all the answers. Marsha can remember only one

or two teachers who seemed to notice her at all; who could understand why it might be hard for her to get all the homework done or speak up more in class. Her conclusion, reinforced at different points by low grades and directly disparaging comments from teachers and counselors, was, "I'm really pretty dumb in school." She certainly didn't feel smart enough for future schooling. That was for those "other kids."

The only thing Marsha knows she can do is run a household. For a number of years, she has helped take care of her younger brothers and sisters after school, cleaned the house, done the laundry, and often made dinner. Marsha's father is a disabled veteran; unable to work, he receives a small government pension. Her mother has a steady job as a cafeteria worker for a local university. When her older sister left home to be married, Marsha took over a lot of the responsibility for managing the household.

Although very devoted and close to her family, Marsha has been having increasingly bitter conflicts with her mother. As a result, she has been thinking seriously about moving out of the house. Marsha's role in the family makes her feel like an adult, in spite of her young age; for several years now she has felt capable of making her own decisions about such important issues as schooling and sexuality. Her mother, up until very recently, has seen Marsha as a young girl, just entering adolescence. She still is upset about Marsha's decision to leave parochial school for an unknown alternative school and about how much time Marsha spends with her boyfriend, who is four years older than Marsha, lives in the projects, has long hair, and uses bad language frequently.

As this rift has widened, Marsha has come to depend more and more on her boyfriend for feelings of closeness and support. Several years older than Marsha, he tends to dominate their relationship and reinforce her image of herself as passive and confused. They have been having a sexual relationship since she was fourteen. The combination of her age and inexperience, her parochial schooling, and her mother's inability to accept her maturation has led to feelings of confusion about birth control. For a long time, Marsha was ashamed of having sex and afraid to seek out information for fear her mother would find out. She is still not sure she wants to prevent a baby. At times, her relationship with Frank seems like a way out of an increasingly tense family situation.

It was her boyfriend who brought Marsha into The Group School and convinced her to attend—in spite of her mother's objections. Although Marsha originally attended largely to spend more time with her boyfriend, she quickly began to utilize the school in good ways for herself.

Now Marsha sees that there may be some real options for herself, but she is confused about her priorities. She knows she wants to go to art college, but she's not sure why or where it could lead. She's very attached to her boyfriend, but not sure she's ready to make a permanent commitment—especially since he has made it clear that he is threatened by the whole idea of her going to college and meeting new people. She knows that she wants to move out of her family's house. With eight brothers and sisters, she desperately feels the need for more space—both physical and emotional. But she is afraid to move out on her own and would feel guilty about leaving her family. In addition, rents are high, and, in order to afford even to share an apartment, she does need to get a job. Taking on a job might very well undercut her portfolio and college hopes; she would not be able to concentrate on finishing high school or to prepare her material for admission to college.

Carole. Carole has just missed her third straight day of school. Worse than that, she has managed to miss the second appointment this week that she had set up with Joan, the college counselor at The Group School. When questioned about her attitudes toward school, Carole insists that she really likes school and, furthermore, needs it to reach her future goal of becoming a nurse. But the late hours she keeps with her friend Joey and the other young people at the neighborhood park tire her out and distract her from her responsibilities and goals. Joey goes to the public high school—or rather, he's enrolled, but usually doesn't go, if he can help it. He is not very supportive of Carole's attending school regularly.

Ever since the city ran out of funds for the neighborhood teen center, Carole and Joey and their friends have been out on the street much more and getting into more trouble with the police. Carole has to go to court soon on a charge of assault and battery on a police officer, for an incident that happened at the park last week. She has a fierce temper, which is especially set off by police authority. Carole wouldn't be worried, except that it is the second arrest this month —the first was for shoplifting and "resisting arrest." "All I did was clip a knit cap and then tell the cop to get his hands off me. But then they make it such a big deal, 'A and B on a P.O.' "

Carole does not like going to court, especially when she is one of the few young women there. Most of her life she has gotten along with and trusted males more than females. The males have seemed more interesting to Carole, and she feels they have been more accepting of her. But she does not like being one of the only females sitting on the bench at court with other young people who are clearly heading *down*. That's not the direction Carole is planning to go.

Carole's stepfather does not accept her differentiation between herself and the other young people in court, whom he calls "young hoodlums." In the three years he has been in the family, he has never adjusted to the fact that Carole hangs out with males on street corners and comes home late at night, without even bothering to explain herself to her mother. His feeling is that young women should be at home more than Carole is, helping around the house. Carole's habits consistently infuriate him and cause strains in his relationship with his wife.

Although upset about Carole's arrests, her mother has been feeling much better about her recently. For a few years, they had not communicated at all—a period which culminated with Carole's decision to quit school. Her mother couldn't understand Carole; she had never had such problems with Carole's two older brothers or with her younger sister, for that matter. By the time they actually had their final argument about school, her reaction to Carole's cavalier, "Hey, I'm sixteen. I can quit school if I want," was a resigned, "It's your life. You can mess it up if you want to."

She was distrustful when Carole said she had
found an alternative school to attend, but extremely grateful when, in fact, Carole started to
go. The combination of Carole's getting older
and her going back to school relieved some of
the worst tensions in their interaction. Carole's
mother doesn't give serious credence to Carole's
plans to go into nursing—an attitude which in-
furiates Carole because it touches on her own
doubts about the project. Her mother keeps urging Carole to study something "practical" like
typing. Secretaries make good money, and the
job is something "you can do easily enough part-
time when you're raising a family."

Sometimes even Joey makes fun of her, with
her plans to become a nurse. That really gets her
mad. "Just wait till I really become somebody;
you'll wish you still knew me." More often, he
just seems to ignore the fact that those are her
plans. And too often she forgets, herself.

Carole has wanted to be a nurse ever since
two summers ago when she had a Neighborhood
Youth Corps job in the hospital as a nurse's aide.
It was her first exposure to a social service sort
of job, and she liked it a great deal. "It's interesting, taking care of people, more interesting
than being a machine." One of Carole's problems is that she really isn't too clear about how
one becomes a nurse. And, although publicly
full of bravado about her chosen career, privately, she's not at all sure that she can "make it" into nursing. On the first "Futures" form she filled
out at The Group School, when she indicated her
interest in nursing, she commented: "It seems
that you need some credentials to work in a
hospital. To do something like that you have to
show people you have the credentials. That's
what scares me. I don't know anything about
how you become a nurse really. I think you can
go into training when you're sixteen. I don't
know if I'll be able to do it—getting through all
those years of college and following the rules.
And I'm sort of weak in the stomach."

This ambivalence is reflected in Carole's recent actions. She sets up appointments with the
college counselor, then misses them. She asks
her mother and stepfather to treat her like an
adult and support her in her career goals, but
then defies them in her street life. She signs up

for difficult courses at school, then fails to attend. She talks responsibly about her future,
then risks arrest and court involvement.

Bonnie. Bonnie feels that she's at an awkward
time in her life—caught between being a child
and being an adult. Although only sixteen, she
has a one and one-half-year-old child, Billy.
Because of being a mother, Bonnie feels much
more mature than her sixteen years. She takes
care to dress and act older, too. But in some
ways, having the child has forced her to be more
dependent on her own mother.

With Billy's father in no position to marry or
support her, and Bonnie just fifteen at the time of
the birth, Bonnie's mother did what she thought
was required of her. She took both mother and
child in—and integrated Billy into her own
family of five children. She, herself, had been
through a similar experience growing up. It was
the last thing she wanted for her oldest daughter.
Throughout Bonnie's childhood and early adolescence, her mother tried to keep her close and
protected. Bonnie experienced this protection as
restrictive and punitive. She sought retribution
through doing exactly what her mother most
feared—getting pregnant at fourteen.

In a way, this situation has drawn Bonnie and
her mother closer together. Pregnancy and
childbirth are women's experiences that they
can share. Bonnie's mother knows how to support her in this situation. And Bonnie, for the
first time, has begun to understand some of her
mother's difficulties. She had always resented
her mother for having so many children and for
never being able to hold onto a man long enough
to get any financial help from him. The in-
dignities of being on welfare seemed somehow
connected to her mother's failings. Now, being
forced into this same situation herself, she can
empathize with her mother and can appreciate
her mother's amazing strength in holding the
family together.

Although grateful to her mother, Bonnie also
resents being in such a dependent position and
fears repeating all of her mother's mistakes. She
wants to show her mother and Billy that she is a
separate person, that she can stand on her own
two feet, that she is someone deserving of

respect. That's why she found a high school to attend after Billy's birth. "I'll be the first one in this family to graduate high school," she points out to her mother whenever she gets down on Bonnie for not helping out more at home.

Right now she's not too sure of what will happen after high school. She knows she wants to have money—money to buy things for Billy, money for clothes, money to keep her skin clear and her hair shaped. Bonnie has thought about taking up modeling. At a store where she buys most of her clothes, there's a poster for a modeling school that promises "glamorous employment" and "good opportunities for attractive young Black women." But this school costs a lot of money, and Bonnie has no idea where she'll get it.

One way or another, Bonnie plans to leave home when she graduates from high school. "I'm too old to be listening to my mama," she says. If worst comes to worst, she knows she can get support from Aid for Dependent Children (AFDC) for a while—enough for her own apartment and clothes and food for Billy. It would mean independence, but not in the style Bonnie would like. In the back of her mind, she also toys with the idea of getting married.

Ever since Billy was born, Bonnie has only been interested in dating older men. She enjoys dressing up and going out to a club with a date. Mark, the man she is seeing most frequently now, is twenty-four and has a steady job as a car salesperson. They enjoy going out together every week in different cars he borrows from the showroom. Sometimes they joke about getting married and "bringing up that kid right"—and, as Mark always adds, "giving him some brothers and sisters to play with." And sometimes Bonnie feels really tempted to do just that. Getting married just might be the answer to some of her problems. She could leave home without going on welfare. She could stop wondering about her future for a while. But then, it's hard for Bonnie to imagine herself as a housewife. And she certainly doesn't want to have any more children as yet. The fantasy she keeps returning to is the mature Bonnie—making lots of money as a model, living on her own, dating a number of different men.

DISCUSSION OF THE PROFILES

The profiles of Marsha, Carole, and Bonnie focus on the dramatic moments of transition in their lives—and the choices, issues, and tensions of those moments. While useful in conveying a sense of the identity of these young women, this approach runs the risk of reducing the larger framework—the institutions and socio-economic conditions—to the level of a personal dilemma. It is important to know that Marsha, Carole, or Bonnie have a number of decisions to make regarding family, boyfriends, future plans. But it is also important to understand their decisions in the context of the inequalities and discrimination of a class system. Too great an emphasis on the personal problems and struggles of low-income people can lead to seeing causes and solutions primarily in terms of individuals or families. Bonnie is confused because she comes from a "truncated family." Carole or Marsha's problems stem from their "low self-image." All three young women suffer from "cultural deprivation."

These labels draw attention away from the systematic inequalities of the social and economic institutions, they have the effect of "blaming the victim." The approach we want to take acknowledges the personal choices and struggles of the individuals, but also focuses on the ways their lives emerge from and are affected by the broader socioeconomic framework. In the discussion that follows, we will draw from the experiences of Marsha, Carole, and Bonnie. We will emphasize the ways in which factors of social class, race, sex, and age interact to influence their lives and the lives of the other young women we have known.

Relationships with Families

Like most adolescents, the young women represented by these profiles feel the need to define themselves as separate individuals and to assert their independence from their families. Yet because of their social class and poor economic circumstances, they often experience the outside world as hostile or indifferent and draw closer to their families for mutual support and protection. Marsha wants to move out on her own, but cannot afford to do so without getting a job and forgetting about her college plans for a while. And she is intensely aware of how much her mother depends on her to manage the household. Carole has developed a pattern of defiant behavior that gets her into trouble, but clearly needs those close to her to support her attempts to take positive steps. Bonnie is furious at her mother for being on welfare and for not having the money to bring her up right. But, in her time of need, she depends on and trusts her mother. And when the social worker or any other authority harasses her mother, Bonnie becomes fiercely protective and expresses great pride in her mother's strengths in the face of adverse circumstances.

Relationships with Boyfriends

The intimate relationships these young women form outside of their families are marked by deeply ambivalent feelings. Once again, their social class and low income influences the quality of the personal interactions. Marsha and her boyfriend Frank have been intimate for a long time. Older and more experienced, Frank helped Marsha grow up. Now, their relationship seems precarious. Marsha has the opportunity to continue growing, but to do so may involve leaving Frank behind. Laid off for the second time this year, unable to afford nice things for himself or his girlfriend, Frank feels doomed to repeat the patterns of his parents' lives. He is deeply threatened by Marsha's plan to go on to college, where she may become "too good" for him or may meet new men who will replace him. Thus, they have trouble supporting each other at a difficult moment for both.

Carole and Joey also end up hurting each other when they both want and need support. Put down in school, seeing no future for himself in the job market, Joey derives his sense of identity and self-importance largely from being "big" and "bad" in the eyes of his girlfriend and others on the street. It is exactly this kind of bravado that draws Carole to Joey, yet makes her want to leave him and the others behind. She wants to find new ways to prove herself—but street-wise behavior and defiance of authority

are the most direct ways available to her to achieve a sense of identity and status.

Bonnie's history is typical of many other young women. Reaching puberty early, she was pursued by a number of males—none of whom made any real commitment to her or took any responsibility for birth control. She became pregnant. The father, in no position to provide support, promptly withdrew from the scene. Even though she has a boyfriend now, who cares for her and her child, Bonnie cannot trust the situation. With a steady job and income, he feels ready to get married and have a family. Bonnie is worried that she is not ready to get "tied down" at this point with any one "old man," but she is also afraid of being on her own with a child to support.

Plans for the Future

Although caught up in the relationships with family and close friends, all of the young women represented in the profiles also feel concerned about the future. After previous unpleasant experiences or failures in school, they all sought out and found an alternative high school at which to pursue their education. Some, like Carole or Marsha, have plans that go beyond high school; others, like Bonnie, feel more lost about what will come next. Common to most of the young women is a lack of self-confidence that is reinforced by very real economic and social obstacles. Even Marsha, who has a goal in mind and has started working toward it, finds she has immediate family and financial needs and issues to contend with that undercut her plans.

Many young women find themselves in a situation similar to Carole's. Although very attracted to a professional or semiprofessional social service vocation in which they might help other people, they cannot believe that this is a feasible career goal. They know enough about the way the world works to expect these jobs to be connected to future schooling. As Carole says, "You need to show the Establishment you have the credentials." And that involves difficult training programs or college, which many of the students lack the grades, academic background, or money to enter or complete. While some young women have enough confidence to imagine themselves being good at the work, few can imagine themselves making it through the college program.

This disparity of aspirations and school achievement throws the young women back on the jobs they know they do not want.

> I've always been taught that if I don't go to college, I'm not going to get a good job. I'll end up in a job where you're in a factory all day and you're working on a very routine type thing, which has nothing to do except with your physical self. I sort of experienced that this year. It was a candy factory, you know, I was doing a bunch of different things. I was running the machine some of the time and packing some of the time. I didn't feel needed; I did it for the money.
>
> I've only had one job—stuffing envelopes and packing stuff—this summer. I didn't like it at all. If worst comes to worst, I guess I can get a filing job. It's really hard to get a job now that's interesting. You just have to take anything, 'cause, you know, it's no career.

While middle-class women see careers as a way of gaining personal satisfaction, of fulfilling themselves through doing productive work, working-class young women know that the jobs available to them tend to be boring, frustrating, often physically demanding, and with no chance of promotion.

All of these factors enhance the other readily available choice, which both Marsha and Bonnie are tempted to take—to have children, to marry, to set up and maintain a household. To most of the students we have worked with, this is always an option. In some cases, so much of their young energy has gone toward maintaining their families that they have difficulty imagining any other future for themselves. Home is their sphere of competence. They have already "practiced" being mothers by taking care of younger brothers and sisters.

There are also pressures on them to become wives and/or mothers. In communities where college and careers are distant dreams, the accepted way for females to grow up and leave home is to marry young and immediately start raising a family. Some young women find

themselves pressured into sexual relations before they know anything about, or can deal emotionally with, birth control. Combined with indecision and a tendency to be passive, this can lead—as in Bonnie's case—to early, unplanned pregnancies. Although less respectable, this is still a route to adulthood. With AFDC payments, the young woman can set up her own household. For a while, this may mean a new independence, but often it turns out to be a trap. Once dependent on AFDC for income, it is very hard to find other means of support. To get training, to find a decent job that pays more than AFDC, to find inexpensive babysitters or day care, all present enormous obstacles.

Carole, feeling these kinds of pressures and feeling ambivalent about herself, turns to her street life for escape. A small but increasing number of low-income young women are doing the same. Although satisfying and diverting for the moment, the street is only a temporary escape for them. Spending most of their energy finding places to congregate with friends, protecting those places from the intrusions of other groups, getting high, arguing with police or parents, these women can fall into a kind of resigned passivity about the important issues of their lives. Feeling little responsibility for their own actions, they may initiate or go along with schemes that are sure to get them into trouble. If these acts of delinquency lead to involvement with the juvenile justice system, the feelings of passivity and powerlessness are reinforced. When Carole has to go to court, she adopts a tone of bravado, but in fact feels pretty discouraged about herself and the company she finds herself in at the courthouse. If anything, court involvement lowers the already low self-image of working-class women.

GOALS OF THE CURRICULUM

The young women in these profiles, like all those we have worked with, have amazing strength and resilience. Practically from birth, they have had to struggle for what they want and need. Although their families are often important sources of emotional support and strength, these relationships cannot really protect them from the difficulties of growing up poor, or Black, or working-class in America. They have had to learn for themselves how to handle the dangers of the city streets, the institutional discrimination of the courts and schools toward poor people and minorities, and the more subtle condescensions of the social welfare bureaucracy. In learning to deal with these situations, they gain a maturity incommensurate with their years. They develop survival skills.

In the process, however, they may suffer damages. Some adopt a hardened or cynical facade. Many turn their anger against themselves and people close to them. They blame themselves for their situation and feel inadequate to do anything about it. They feel stupid because they went to school for all those years and never learned to read or write adequately. Most lack basic confidence in themselves. The very ideology being taught in the schools reinforces these feelings of personal failure and inadequacy. Young people are encouraged to believe that any talented individual who works hard will gain influence, wealth, power, and prestige. In short, "you can make it if you really try." Class, race, and sex inequalities are obscured or ignored. Since working-class and poor young people are from families who, in some sense, did not "make it," this obfuscation of the socioeconomic system can only make them ashamed of their backgrounds and discouraged about their own prospects for the future.

A major goal of this curriculum is to help working-class young women gain pride in the strengths and skills they and their families have developed. This involves counteracting the traditional ideology that leads them to turn their anger and despair inward and to blame themselves. We approach this curriculum from the political viewpoint that wealth and opportunity are unevenly and unfairly distributed in this society. There are systematic, as well as personal, reasons why some people are rich and others poor, why some people succeed and others fail. The socioeconomic structures have to change in order for the quality of the lives of most people to improve.

In communicating that point of view to our students, we are aware that we run the risk of reinforcing their fatalism. If the institutions and structures of "the system" are to blame, how can anyone ever find a way to make her life better? How can we, as teachers, make any difference? If we are to be effective teachers, we must be able to answer these questions—for ourselves, as well as for our students. It is our belief that an understanding of the real obstacles and inequities of the system, rather than blocking students, can help them take pride in the struggles of their own families and help them strengthen their determination to develop the skills to make things better for themselves and their communities. With enormous effort on their parts, and help and support from us, these young women can feel a new appreciation for and sense of their own strengths, develop new competencies, and realize their individual and collective potential to be productive human beings. It is certainly important that they try, and that we help them.

The goals of The Group School Women's Curriculum reflect these assumptions and beliefs. We attempt to combine our political viewpoints with a concern for the personal growth of students and a sensitivity to issues in their lives.

GOALS STATEMENT

To help students:

—Recognize their strengths and build self-confidence and self-esteem;
—Learn new skills and develop competency in areas in which they feel inadequate or insecure;
—Broaden their sense of their own options for the future;
—Believe in the legitimacy and importance of their own feelings, perceptions, and experiences as young working-class women;
—See that many of their concerns as young women are shared concerns;
—Overcome feelings of competition among themselves and realize there are a range of legitimate ways to act and feel as a woman;
—Become aware of and examine sex-role stereotyping—in the society and as it has become internalized;
—Understand the inequities of the social system,

in regard to sex, class, and race, and how these inequities affect them;

—Turn their misplaced anger away from themselves toward the institutions that oppress them;

—Become aware of struggles to bring about changes in an inequitable social system.

PEDAGOGICAL APPROACH

In this curriculum, we have tried to develop a pedagogy that supports our goals. The nine thematic units are built around a variety of structured exercises, calling for active participation from the students and the teacher. Students make collages that express their views of the world; they go out and interview people about their experiences and opinions; they make a film or publish a newspaper. Sometimes students are the experts; at other times, they are the investigators. Always, there is an emphasis given to the development of basic academic skills. We have found the generally low level of academic skill among the young women who come into our program to be a major contributing factor in their feelings of inadequacy and their lack of self-confidence. Although they have previously rejected school—both in words and actions—they have internalized the institutional values and evaluations. They think of themselves as "slow" or "stupid."

It is our belief that the integration of academic skills with thematic content strengthens the learning of both. The students' interest in the issues and ideas under exploration in the curriculum—and the relevance of the material to their lives and experiences—motivates them to work on their academic skills. They want to be able to read and understand books about other young women growing up; they want to be able to write about their own childhood experiences, to write a paper expressing their ideas on topics like women's prisons. They want to learn new words to help them express these ideas and feelings.

Furthermore, learning new skills influences the way students approach the thematic content of the curriculum. As these young women see themselves learning and becoming more compe-

tent, as they improve their reading and comprehension levels, as they begin to express themselves in writing, they feel a surge of energy and hope. Believing more in their own potential to change and grow, they are less discouraged by material dealing with the limiting effects of sex-role socialization and institutional discrimination, less disheartened by explorations of the particular obstacles to working-class women from social and economic pressures. They are more able to connect to sections of the curriculum emphasizing individual and collective attempts to bring about changes.

Classroom activities, like role-playing, speakers, trips, and interviews, play an important part in the integration of skills with thematic content. Participating in these kinds of exercises, students with different learning styles, interests, or skills levels can find entry points into the material. Students who have difficulty writing may be able to express their feelings and thoughts in role-plays. Students who read slowly, with little comprehension, may learn a great deal through interviewing people with interesting and varied experiences. Furthermore, having done a role-play well or conducted a good interview, a student may feel more motivated and open to try something that is harder for her—like writing or reading.

Trips, speakers, interviews, and role-plays add to the curriculum in several other important ways. In role-playing other people, like the characters in books or historical personages, students grasp the material in a personal way. By playing themselves in different situations, students have a chance to try out different responses and see how they feel. Trips, speakers, and interviews help broaden the context by connecting the readings and personal accounts to people, institutions, and events outside the classroom. Students can learn a great deal from a speaker who has overcome personal and societal obstacles to find work unusual for women or who is working collectively with other people to bring about changes in her community or workplace. A trip to a prisoners' rights program or a rape crisis center familiarizes students with organizations and services in the community and introduces them to people doing important social service work. Traveling to Newton or another suburban community to talk to high school women gives them a chance to compare their experiences to those of other people, thus, they strengthen their own sense of identitu and gain some perspective on their lives. On the whole, these activities help students build a sense of what is positive in their own experiences and backgrounds; they provide students with models of how to move ahead.

THE CONTENTS OF THE BOOK

In the first chapter, we present specific techniques for teaching skills in reading, writing, and vocabulary. We discuss ways to successfully utilize methods like role-plays, speakers, trips, and interviews. Rather than describe the "how-to's" of doing a vocabulary exercise or a role-play every time these appear in the curriculum, we have organized all of these suggestions into the chapter, "Techniques of Teaching and Learning." Here you can find detailed comments on how to make these activities and exercises successful The methodological suggestions are cross-referenced with the exercises that are generally described in the units.

The remainder of the book is divided into nine teaching units, which are organized thematically. They draw on ideas and experiences from the first modest Group School offering of a two-day -a-week course, "Women and Society," in 1971, to our more recent program that includes at least one four-day-a-week English/social studies course every term and a women's discussion group on sex education. Sifting through five years' worth of lesson plans, student papers, teacher and student evaluations, we have tried to present the material in a format useful to other teachers and students, both in similar and very different settings from our own.

Units, or sections of units (two or three activities), can be used to raise women's issues in regular English, history, psychology, anthropology, career education, or health courses. Several of the longer units, like "Women and Work," can stand by themselves as entire semester courses; several units together can comprise a full-year program. The curriculum, in other words, should be viewed as a series of

shapes and colors, temporarily framed in a particular pattern, that can be rearranged in many different configurations. The order in which we have placed the units corresponds roughly to the increasing complexity of the issues raised and the depth of the explorations of these issues.

The first two units, "Messages from Society" and "Early Socialization," contain the most basic consciousness-raising activities. Teachers working with students who have never before considered issues of sex-role socialization might do well to start with these units. The next two units follow facets of "Growing Up Female" through the life cycle: from childhood, to adolescence, to adulthood. These are the units that draw most heavily from literature and probably could be integrated most readily into English courses.

"Sexuality" presents a methodology for handling the more personal concerns of young women—concerns with their appearance, their bodies, their developing sexuality. This material is appropriate to small discussion group settings or to such courses as health. "Mean Streets" focuses students on the particular psychological and sociological concerns of young women in trouble and includes specific explorations of institutions and agencies that come in contact with that population.

"Women and Work" and "Women Organizing Themselves" combine historical material with explorations of current socioeconomic conditions and institutions that affect women. In "Women's News," students consider the range of current issues of concern to women and produce their own newspaper or video news program.

Most of the units end with a section entitled "Notes to the Teacher." These sections discuss problems that may arise for the teacher and for the students in carrying out the activities suggested in the unit. Because the curriculum involves a balancing of personal and academic material, and is cross-disciplinary in approach, teachers may face interesting and sometimes difficult issues—how much to share a point of view, how directive to be, how much to intervene in student interactions. For students, exploring the issues in the curriculum may arouse painful emotions—feelings of insecurity or of shame, fear of success or of change—and these may lead to problems in the classroom dynamic. The "Notes to the Teacher" describe these problems as they have manifested themselves in our classrooms and include suggestions on how, and how not, to handle these situations. Regardless of which units seem appropriate to your teaching situation, we recommend that you read all of the "Notes to the Teacher" sections. Although the particular notes refer specifically to the unit in which they appear, they all discuss problems that might arise anywhere in the curriculum.

ADAPTATIONS OF THE CURRICULUM

The thematic content of the curriculum, the teaching techniques, the "Notes to the Teacher," all come directly out of our experiences at The Group School. We have described the activities as they occurred, including the details of what was said and how students responded. This approach sets the curriculum apart from most classroom materials that are available. Although there are objectives, units, and daily activities, these are not written in a standard, daily lesson-plan outline format. Our style is more anecdotal—falling somewhere in between a step-by-step outline of what to do and a descriptive narrative of life in the classroom. Our hope is that teachers, recognizing their students in ours, will be inspired to try these materials and approaches. In order to facilitate the task for teachers of adapting the curriculum to their own students, we have included explanations of our pedagogical assumptions, outlines of our teaching techniques, and descriptions of how and why we taught each lesson. The students with whom we developed these materials, and whose voices are heard in this book, were primarily white, working-class young women. It is our belief that the lessons we developed for this group, as well as the lessons we learned from this group, are applicable to other, more diverse student populations.

During the school year 1975-1976, forty teachers in the Boston area read and tested the curriculum. Although in a wide variety of settings, with differing student populations, all found they could teach from the materials. From their accounts, differences in class size and length of period did not create problems. Teachers with thirty students and forty-five minute periods, and teachers with twelve to fifteen students meeting in a two-hour, once-a-week discussion group situation, all found ways to utilize the same activities. To our surprise, several teachers chose to use the curriculum with older women, in "mothers" groups. They found several units of the curriculum to be useable almost exactly as they are written.

Teachers of coeducational classes report that they were able to revise and expand the exercises in the curriculum dealing with female identity and sex-role issues to include males. In one school, "Growing Up Female" became "Growing Up Female and Male." The teacher reports positive results from using the books suggested in that unit with mixed classes. Most of the students had never before in their schooling been presented with the opportunity to read and discuss books by women authors and from a distinctively female viewpoint. Although male students were initially resistant, they eventually enjoyed reading the books and comparing male and female experiences in growing up. Other teachers, who had a chance to compare single-sex to mixed classes, feel that something was lost in a coeducational situation. In their view, the atmosphere became less personal, and the women students shared less of themselves.

Teachers working with racially-integrated classes found they could use the units from the curriculum successfully with few revisions, but in some cases the activities led to very different responses and discussions from those described in the narrative. For instance, in the "Messages from Society" unit, one class spent as long talking about media images of Blacks and discrimination against Black people as they did about women. The teacher expanded the activities to include discussions of the ways the issues or themes might be different for Black and white females.

The feedback from all of these teachers, in their many different educational settings, confirms our hypothesis that although the curriculum is not immediately transferable, it is translatable. We hope you enjoy using it.

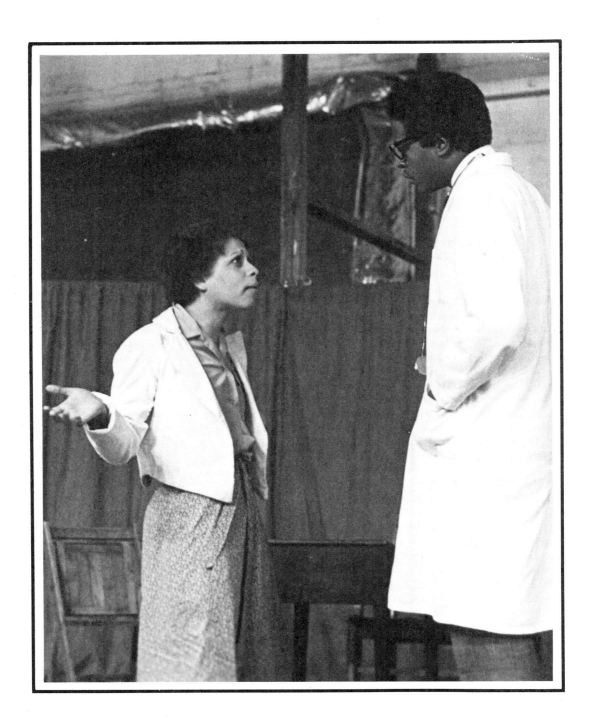

TECHNIQUES OF TEACHING AND LEARNING

OVERVIEW

Throughout the units of the curriculum, there are specific ideas for reading, writing, and vocabulary assignments. These are interspersed with other kinds of classroom activities, particularly role-plays, speakers, trips, and interviews. Within the units, emphasis is on the thematic content—we describe how to utilize particular assignments and activities to explore certain themes and ideas. In this chapter, emphasis is on the technique—we describe how to structure reading, writing, and vocabulary lessons; how to maximize the effectiveness of role-plays, speakers, trips, and interviews.

The suggestions outlined in this chapter are intended to supplement the more descriptive presentations of activities within the units. When the class is ready to read their first book together or do their first role-play, the teacher can turn to this chapter and get specific ideas on how to motivate the class to read, or sustain their interest in the readings, or set up the role-play. The teacher can also make use of this chapter to create new classroom activities. In describing the thinking and planning that has gone into creating our activities, we hope to facilitate the process of curriculum development for other teachers who want to integrate new material into the units.

READING

I did a lot more reading than I ever did before, and that was really good for me. I've really gained confidence in myself around reading. I notice now while I'm reading *Wuthering Heights*. It's not an easy book. I'm reading faster and I comprehend easier. [From a student evaluation]

Objectives:
—To improve students' reading levels, building comprehension and vocabulary skills;
—To inspire students to read more, by showing them they can find support, new ideas, and experiences through books.

Selecting Readings

> *Look for relatively easy, high interest readings that are rich in teaching material.*

We look for materials that are highly readable, enrich students' understandings, open their imaginations, and stretch their skills. It's not easy to find readings which fulfill all of these criteria, but we believe that they are all important; we never give up on our quest for new materials.

Readability is a key consideration for students who rarely read and have low basic skills. We don't want readings which turn students off because of the difficulty of the words, the complexity of the sentences, or the sheer number of pages. We are looking for books our students will finish; finishing a book can be a significant experience for a student. She may never have thought she could read a whole book, never realized reading could be an enjoyable alternative to evening TV.

To inspire our students to read, we look for materials about subjects of high interest to them. Our students are most likely to begin reading through novels, short stories, or plays about young people similar to themselves. Some are excited by reading biographies or first-hand accounts by famous people from the popular-rock culture, like Janis Joplin, or colorful political figures, such as "Mother" Mary Jones. Short articles can also stimulate interest when the subjects directly touch on the students' own lives or raise controversy—for example, articles on such topics as abortion or men raising children.

Novels and Biographies

We select novels, autobiographies, and biographies written in a lively style, preferably with a fair amount of dialogue and without dense sections of descriptive detail. It's important that they have a recognizable story line; otherwise our students confront us with, "I can't get into it. Nothin' happens in that book." The books we chose for Unit III, "Growing Up Female"—*Anne Frank: The Diary of a Young Girl*, *Daddy Was a Number Runner*, *I Know Why the Caged Bird Sings*, and *A Tree Grows In Brooklyn*—all meet these criteria in varying degrees. (See pp. 56–57 for comparative summaries of the books.)

Plays

Students can usually handle more sophisticated material when it is in the form of a play. They may not understand everything that is going on in the play, but in acting out the different parts, they develop a good sense of the characters and the areas of dramatic tension. Although there may be words they have never heard, there are no long descriptive passages to bore or frustrate them. The two plays we have used most frequently are *A Taste of Honey* and *A Doll's House*.

Articles, Pamphlets, Nonfiction Books

Sociological, historical, or anthropological materials provide new viewpoints and new information. Unfortunately, much of this kind of writing is too detailed or too technical for high school students with fairly low levels of skills. However, students can be given enough exposure to this material to realize its potential as a tool in helping them to understand their society.

We suggest you look for fairly short pieces, most or all of which could be read in a class period. Students are most likely to be able to read magazine articles. On their own, many students read popular magazines, like *Cosmopolitan* or *Seventeen*. We do not discourage this reading. Rather, we try to build on these interests and skills by introducing into the class some more difficult and serious articles found, for example, in *Ms.* or *Women: A Journal of Liberation*. The magazine articles, pamphlets, and nonfiction essays and book chapters we have found usable with students are listed in the "Bibliography" as well as in the units.

Give students a choice among books to read.

Choosing a book is more fun than being assigned one. Particularly for new readers, the very process of figuring out what book to read can be educational. One method for presenting a choice is to xerox short, fairly representative selections from each of three or four possible books. Reading these aloud together and briefly discussing each passage will give students some sense of what to expect from each of the books. By the end of the class they can vote for their favorite. This method works especially well when the whole class is going to read the same novel, and when they can select from three or four different novels with similar themes.

When you are presenting students with a choice among books on a variety of topics, it might be better to give students brief written summaries of each of the books, rather than actual selections. The summaries will present the differences in theme more cogently than short selections. In indicating which book they want to read, the class will also be making a choice as to the thematic direction of the course.

> *Encourage students to select books to read on their own.*

Once a student has finished her first book and enjoyed it, she often develops a thirst for more. It makes a big difference if there are books around to handle, skim through, borrow for the night. We keep a small paperback library for our students. It's important not to overwhelm new readers with too many books or books which "look boring" or "too long," so we're selective; we keep different books around for a week or so, to see if they have appeal.

In some courses, we encourage students to read by setting the expectation that they will read a book of their own choosing every three weeks. We keep a card file in our classroom library in which students note the books they've read and make comments for reference:

Your Name: **Date:**
Linda Spartichino   5/25/76
Author:
Angelou, Maya
Title:
Gather Together in My Name
Comment:
Pretty interesting—but the girl was kind of messed up in the head.

Teaching Reading

> *Base your reading program on the students' skill levels.*

You can integrate reading into the curriculum in a number of ways, depending on whom you

are teaching, time constraints, the availability of reading materials, and the particular focus of your course.

Many young women from working-class backgrounds have had little opportunity to develop reading skills. Consequently, they are not comfortable with reading—it seems more like a chore than a pleasure. At first, when asked to read something on their own, they may be unable to find the time, space, or energy to accomplish the task. Or, if they do the assignment, their reading may be perfunctory, aimed at finishing rather than understanding or enjoying.

If you are teaching a group of students who are extremely resistant to reading or have rarely read any book through to the end, you might want to start with reading a short play in class. Or you could use an excerpt approach, giving students short excerpts from a number of different books and drawing on the most provocative episodes in each. When excerpts are used, much of the reading can be done in class.

If your group has a somewhat wider range of reading abilities, it is preferable to select one book to read at a time, according to the prevalent reading level and interests of the class. The students who have never read a book before may be inspired by the others to an increased interest in reading. The use of a single book gives the whole class common reference points for discussions and other classroom activities.

When a class includes students with a very wide range of reading abilities, it makes sense to give different members of the class different books to read, depending on reading level and interest. This approach poses different teaching problems. Although it is important for a teacher to acknowledge and teach to skill differences, it is equally important in a women's program to find ways to draw the class together. Much of the success of the program depends on a high level of openness and sharing. If different books are being read, it is very important to find books with similar themes and to structure discussions and activities that draw on issues which come up in all of the books.

> *Read aloud in class.*

Reading aloud in class can help make printed words come alive for students. There are always at least one or two students who will volunteer to read aloud because they enjoy it. After they read, other students may be inspired to try. Students who are embarrassed to read in front of classmates should not be forced to do so, but they should be strongly encouraged. The first experience of reading aloud usually makes the next attempt easier and more fun, and thus encourages further reading. In addition, it's valuable for a teacher to listen to *all* of her students read aloud. Hearing a student read can give a teacher the opportunity to diagnose specific reading problems that she might otherwise not have noted.

Often, reading aloud is a good way to introduce a new book. Rather than assigning the first few pages, which may be slow reading with a lot of descriptive detail, you ask the students to open the book to a particularly interesting or gripping chapter that plunges them into a moment of dramatic tension. As a result, most students will become interested in the characters and inspired to read more about their histories and experiences. Having actually opened the book, turned some pages, and read some of the print, they may also feel less intimidated by it.

Reading aloud provides common reference for discussions and activities based on the reading. Whenever the reading is important to the lesson, we have students read aloud relevant, short selections. (See Unit III, "Growing Up Female," for examples of lessons that begin with excerpts.) This often enlivens the discussion and allows the whole class to participate. Students who have been reading, but not retaining it, can refresh their memories; those who haven't read the book at all will at least have an entry into the discussion—they may even become motivated to delve into the reading later, for themselves.

Most of all, in reading aloud, students have the opportunity to participate actively in what they are reading, to give it their own expression and, by expressing it, to make it their own. Short nonfiction pieces, like magazine articles or chapters from books, are more accessible to students when read aloud in class and discussed along the way. Of course, plays and dramatic short stories lend themselves particularly to expressive reading aloud. Most students really enjoy taking parts. Some seem to be liberated from their usual reading fears or blocks when they assume the voices of new characters.

Occasionally, short stories are written dramatically enough, with enough dialogue or different voices, to be read aloud as if they were plays. Students can take different parts, with perhaps several students and the teacher sharing a narrator role. We discovered recently that Tillie Olsen's story, "O Yes," can be read in this way (p. 86). This same story when simply handed to students to read on their own baffled and frustrated most of them. Few finished it or felt that they understood it. But when we read it dramatically in class, it had a powerful and provocative effect.

> *Utilize varied classroom activities to make the readings come alive for the students.*

Most TV programs and many movies leave little to the imagination; everything is spelled out in vivid detail. Accustomed to these media, students need to learn how to approach books in which a great deal more participation is required of the reader. The routes toward imaginative participation in reading vary with the individual styles of the students. For instance, some students have visual imaginations; others can imagine and create best through their hands, taking things apart or putting them together. Through various classroom activities and projects, such as role-playing, writing, art or music projects, making charts and graphs, perhaps even trips and speakers, diverse students can gain personal access to the reading material; the material "comes off the page."

Through role-playing, students can get to know the characters by getting inside of them. In a simple role-play, the teacher can interview the students taking part as if they were characters in the book, asking how they feel during a particular scene, what they plan to do in the future, what advice they have for young women in the class.

In another type of role-play, students can act out a dramatic situation from the book in order to imagine more fully how it might feel. For instance, when we read *Anne Frank: The Diary of a Young Girl*, we set aside one class period when no one was allowed to speak "because of the danger of the Nazis overhearing." Pairs of students were given specific tasks to communicate to one another without speaking aloud.

These role-plays can be translated into comparable writing assignments. "Imagine you are Francie when. . . ." "What is going on in Maya's head when. . . ." For some students, art projects may provide a better vehicle for imaginative participation in a book. They might make drawings of places or scenes from the book or their conceptions of the major characters. Others might want to make a musical tape or a slide tape to explore a theme or character. Still others might best grasp a reading through making a sculpture, a model of the physical layout, or a board game which represents the dramatic conflicts.

Occasionally, speakers can be found who lived through an experience described in a book. For instance, you might be able to find a Black person in the community who grew up in the South about the same time as Anne Moody, of *Coming of Age in Mississippi*; someone who was in Europe during the period when the Franks went into hiding; or someone who has one of the jobs described in *Working*. In telling the class about their personal experiences, speakers can give students more entry points into the reading.

> *Give your students questions to think about while they are reading.*

To encourage students to take an active approach in their reading, we sometimes give them questions to think about while they are reading. Instead of simply letting it happen to them, they confront the material through their imaginations, their powers of reasoning, and their feelings. As they read, they wonder: "What is it about Katie, as opposed to Johnnie, that allows her to hold the Nolan family together?" or "During her years in the Secret Annex, what were the key turning points in Anne's growing up?"

We suggest limiting the number of "think questions" you give your students to seven, at the most. Too many questions become one more assignment to be filled in perfunctorily "for the teacher." Further, questions should be interpretive or conceptual, not requiring literal recall. ("What were the experiences which most influenced Maya's attitudes toward men?" not "How old was Maya when she spent her vacation with her father and stepmother?")

Finally, to get across the message that the questions are truly meant for the students, as a stimulus to their own thinking, we don't ask the students to hand in "answers"; we suggest that they make their own notes or simply reflect on the questions and come to class prepared to share their ideas and feelings.

> *Help the students to find ways of discussing the readings with one another.*

It's stimulating for the students when they really exchange their responses to, or ideas about, a reading. How do you inspire good discussions? Certainly, all of the techniques already outlined in the reading section prepare the groundwork: selection of interesting materials, choosing common readings or themes as a focus, having students read aloud to raise or dramatize an issue, leading in with creative activities (role-plays, writing, art projects, etc.), preparing with "think questions."

Further, as a teacher, it is your task to facilitate discussion among the students and to keep the discussion interesting and focused. The kinds of questions you choose to ask are crucial. We often begin with recall questions, to establish the facts and remind students of what happened in a reading. ("What events in the lives of the Coffin family led up to their requesting relief from Madame Queen?") Summary questions are important in teaching students skills in conceptualization and in helping them to draw together the main points of a reading. ("How would you describe the relationship between the Coffin family and Madame Queen?")

The heart of a discussion is generated by interpretative questions, which lead students to draw on their own insights and experiences. ("Could the Coffin family have responded any differently to Madame Queen's humiliating treatment?" "Why do you think the relief system was set up in a way which was so unfair to the needs of the poor?")

Good debates can emerge in the discussion of interpretative questions. As teacher, you elicit differing viewpoints from the students. ("Do you agree with Janie that the family had no choice but to submit to the relief bureaucracy?") Students often tend to direct most of their attention and comments to the teacher, rather than to each other. Asking interpretative questions and encouraging students to respond to each other's ideas helps move them to interact more among themselves. (For more suggestions on getting students to share with each other, see "Sexuality," Unit V, pp. 135–36.)

As students become more comfortable in debating with one another about a reading, you should teach them to back up their ideas with specific references to the text or with examples from their own experience. When disagreements are backed by specifics, the discussion will reach a more meaningful level of debate.

WRITING

I really enjoyed doing the paper on being working class and the one on women being executed, because they made me think. [From a student evaluation]

Objectives:

—To help students become more comfortable with writing;
—To encourage students to see writing as a means of expression and communication in their own lives;
—To help students develop writing skills.

> Lead up to writing with inspirational activities.

The first step in teaching writing is to free students from worrying about exactly what they're going to say or how they're going to say it, to help them relax about taking pencil to paper.

We often begin a writing assignment with inspirational activities—activities that touch off students' feelings, imaginations, and thinking, that help them forget their worries about writing. We read a dramatic section from a book, do role-plays, show photographs, handle props, play music, or close our eyes and imagine. When these activities are working best the students are excited about beginning to write. "Ooh! I know what I want to say. Hurry up, I want to start now before I forget."

> Give students just enough structure to get them started.

Getting the first words down on paper is usually the most difficult part of a writing assignment. In formulating writing choices, it's important to give a student as much structure as is required to get her started, but not so much that you restrict her. Here's an example from Unit III, "Growing Up Female," (p. 63):

> Describe a child (yourself if you want) experiencing something for the first time....Examples: going to school, making a first friend, learning to talk, finding out about death.

Specific examples such as the four above help to stimulate students' memories. ("I remember my first time at the doctor....I hated my first shot!") If the assignment had read simply, "Describe a child experiencing something for the first time," some students would have had trouble getting an idea. "I can't think of anything to write about. What do you mean by that assignment anyhow?" is a typical rejoinder.

At the same time, we're careful not to restrict our students by making the assignment too specific. If the assignment were to be, "Write about a child's first experience at school," some students might feel that they couldn't remember, didn't want to remember, or couldn't think of anything. By giving several examples, we provide students with a greater range of options and also communicate to them that there is room for them to create their own topics. A student's memories may release her imagination. For instance, in this assignment she may decide she wants to describe a child's view of her own house burning down, even though it was not included in the examples, because this has been an image in her own fantasies or simply because the subject both frightens and inspires her.

Give students a choice between writing about themselves and writing about other people.

For many students, the best starting point is a personal experience or memory. Others, however, find it very difficult to write directly about themselves. Below is a sample of a writing assignment adapted from "Growing Up Female" (p. 63), containing a range of entry points:

1. Describe an early memory of a time when you were scared, when you were very excited or happy, when you were angry.
2. Write all the things Francie Nolan would like to say to the storekeeper who enjoys pinching her.
3. Write a poem about your own childhood. Begin each line with "I remember...."

Students who love to tell stories about "who's been hanging out at the park" or "how we really gave this teacher a hard time when we were in third grade" will almost certainly be comfortable with choices like 1 or 3. For these students, the most accessible material comes from situations in their own lives—a childhood incident, a recent exciting or frightening experience. They are most likely to find the words to describe something they have personally seen or felt.

Other students may respond better to choices like 2, in which they write about a character in a book, or ones which ask them, more generally, to write about people they have observed or known. They feel protective of their experiences and of the people closest to them; they don't want to remember the past; they are confused by their experiences and unable to clarify them in writing. In writing about other people, students will often include a great deal about their own feelings and experiences, but they will feel less exposed and vulnerable.

Utilize familiar writing forms.

No matter how uncomfortable they may be with writing, most students are familiar with some writing forms. We have found that even the most reluctant writers will respond to assignments calling for letters, diary entries (for themselves or a fictional character), and dialogues.

Examples of letter-writing assignments range from highly structured ones where students respond to actual questions sent into newspaper advice columns (p. 42), to more open-ended assignments where students are asked to write "helping" letters to someone they care about who is in trouble (p. 154). The dialogue form is suggested for students trying to write about "a day in the life of a young woman they have just read about in a case study (p. 153). The sex-roles journal utilizes the diary form, with a specific focus on daily occurrences that pertain to sex-role distinctions (p. 108).

> *Encourage students to try poetry as a means of expression.*

With support and suggested starting points, most students find great pleasure in writing poetry. Many find poetry a freer form of expression than prose. They do not have to be as concerned with a narrative; points do not have to be as logically or fully developed. They can write down images and feelings that result in a meaningful statement.

We have found that a number of our students have already discovered poetry for themselves. After our first poetry activity together, they have shown us journals or albums of pictures and poems—some of which are original, others found and copied. There are also, of course, students who feel intimidated by poetry and have trouble imagining writing their own.

We don't expect any of our students to be able to plunge into writing poems in class. A tone and mood have to be established—and starting points suggested. Particularly interesting or evocative poems written by other people can be used as models to touch off students' imaginations, for example, Kathleen Fraser's poem, "To My Legs" (p. 91). Some students may emulate the form of a poem they like; others may just want to start with a provocative first line, like Diane Wakowski's ' What I want in a husband besides a mustache. . ." (p.113), and take off on their own from there. Finding a starting point through someone else's ideas or structures does not circumscribe the students' creativity. Rather, the effect is to inspire them to develop their own creative ideas and instincts.

> *Leave time for writing assignments to be worked on in class.*

Although the atmosphere in school may not be the most conducive to creativity or concentration, the teacher is there to help and support the students' efforts. For beginning writers, the teacher's supportive presence and well-timed interventions can be crucial. Countless times we have rushed over just in time to stop students from crumpling up the papers they have just written. They are sure "it's terrible," "I did it all wrong." More often than not they have a fine start, perhaps needing a little more focus or direction. With some words of encouragement or comfort from us, they will unfold the paper and set to work again. Also, they sometimes derive inspiration and support from each other's efforts. Hearing somebody else's first line or story idea suggests a new approach or direction. If the writing were to be done at home, the end result might well be an incompleted homework assignment.

More advanced writers, on the other hand, probably should be encouraged to take their work home with them. To keep progressing with their writing skills, they need to take more time and care with their writing than is possible in a class period. They can still make valuable use of class time, however, to plan and perhaps even outline or start the assignment. They are much more likely to complete the assignment at home if they have made a specific commitment in class.

> *Share writing in class.*

Whenever possible, we leave time at the end of a writing exercise for students to read their papers aloud. This period of sharing helps give the class a feeling of individual and group accomplishment. The sharing also reinforces the concept that writing, like talking, is a form of personal expression and communication with others—not just an exercise to do for a teacher, for a grade. Students may be amazed to find out that through their writing they can interest, amuse, and inform other students.

Getting students to share their papers is, of course, not always easy. Many students are so critical of their own writing that they are reluctant to show it to their peers. They prefer it to remain a private matter between themselves and the teacher. Most will respond to encouragement, however, and at least let someone else read their paper aloud, if they are too nervous or embarrassed.

A comfortable, trusting atmosphere is necessary for the sharing to be successful. A basic ground rule is that everyone agree to listen to each other's papers. If the class is too restless that day, it is best to wait for a calmer time. The best way to encourage listening and a mutual give-and-take is to structure into the assignment some concrete reasons for the students to listen to each other. For instance, in the Children's Books activity (p. 51), students are alerted to look for the sex-roles messages in each other's works. The feedback they give each other may lead to revisions or additions.

Another way for students to share their writing, particularly in a large class, is in a regular in-class publication. Every two or three weeks we make dittoed copies of the writing assignments for that period and distribute these to the class. Since the writing is usually directly related to the thematic content of the unit, this can serve as a good review of some of the topics we have been studying. This method of sharing also has the advantage of allowing time for revising and correcting the first draft. If other people are going to see what they have written, students will have more of a stake in improving it. For most students, it is a thrill to see their writing in print, and they enjoy reading other people's as well. Because the publication will stay basically within the class, it is not too threatening, even for beginning writers. As people feel more confident about their writing over the term, they may want to publish some of their writings for wider

distribution in the school. This is easily done, with each student going through her collected writings for the term and picking her favorite piece or pieces. Illustrations and a cover can be added as finishing touches.

For more advanced writers, publishing a regular newspaper or magazine for the rest of the school is a good learning experience. The process of putting out a newspaper is described in detail in Unit IX, "Women's News" (p. 223).

Don't be overly critical of the students' writing.

One of the reasons it is hard for many of our students to write is that they are ashamed of their low skills levels. "I can't spell at all." "I don't even know where to put a period." Although it is very important to work with them on these skills, you have to be careful about when and how you correct their mistakes. The first step is to get students to write at all, to help them see writing as a tool, not as a punishment or obstacle. Next in importance is helping them express what they mean and want to say. Part of achieving that clarity is, of course, correct spelling, punctuation, and word usage. But these skills do not have to be tackled all at once. Once a student feels that the tool of writing is truly hers, learning the skill comes more easily. The more she wants to express, and the more she wants the expression to match the feeling or thought, the more she will work on the skills.

It is very discouraging for a student to get a paper back covered with corrections. Even though your overall comment might be encouraging, they will not be able to see beyond the red marks. A good way to handle corrections is to work on one problem at a time. Thus, we might decide with a student that for the next couple of weeks we will work on writing complete sentences. Whatever she writes during that period will be corrected only for mistakes in sentencing. In addition, we might also give her some pages from a grammar workbook with exercises reinforcing this particular skill. Focusing this way on one skill at a time makes the task of learning to write more manageable.

VOCABULARY

Learning new words was the best thing for me this term. Now I know what you all are talking about when you start in with those big words. [From a student evaluation]

Objectives

—To help students name and express their feelings and ideas;
—To expand students' perceptions and understandings of their experiences and environment;
—To facilitate and enrich their reading and writing.

Choosing Words

Find words that expand students' perceptions and understandings of themselves and their world.

Words give people power. They are the tools that people use to understand and gain control over themselves—their feelings, relationships, and experiences. A paucity of words, or the lack of accurate words, limits both self-understanding and communication with others. For students, being at a loss for words adds to feelings of passivity and helplessness. They want and need to know how to name their feelings and experiences. They want and need to be heard and understood by others.

Words are also tools for seeing personal experiences in a broader perspective. A student may know she feels overworked and used on a job. And she may be able to articulate her feelings about this. But without knowing that there is

such a concept and such a word as "exploitation," she will probably personalize this experience. Learning this word helps her to see her own experiences as part of a larger pattern in the society.

Select words that students are likely to use in their speech or writing.

There is no use in memorizing words, only to forget them a day or so later. The way to remember words is to use them. In selecting words, you have to be careful to find those that will stretch the students' vocabularies, but that are not so obscure that students will never see them, hear them, or be able to incorporate them into their own language.

Make vocabulary lists from words that are somehow related to one another.

The words within a vocabulary list should be related to each other and to the content being explored. Because they refer to a common theme, the words are easier to learn. Students can be encouraged to begin to use them in discussions, and they can be asked to include them in their writing assignments. Two different vocabulary lists we have used illustrate this point. The first is suggested as part of the unit, "Growing Up Female" (p. 60); the second is in the unit "Women Organizing Themselves" (p. 196).

mature	feminism
immature	feminist
supportive	autonomy
protective	independence
permissive	oppressed
console	abolition
authoritarian	status
precocious	sphere
inventive	franchise
spontaneous	suffragist
inhibited	

Learning the Words

> *Read over the new vocabulary list together.*

It is good to give the students a new vocabulary list in two forms: 1) typed out on dittoed sheets, with simple definitions; 2) written large on a newsprint sheet or poster board, which is mounted on the wall (and left there, throughout the term if possible).

We begin by asking students to volunteer to pronounce each of the words on the list. While helping them with this, we ask whether the word is familiar and where they can remember seeing or hearing it. Then we call on students to read the definition for each word, briefly discussing how the word might be used in a sentence. Occasionally, we vary this procedure by giving students new words in sentences without giving the definitions. They then read the sentences and try to figure out from the context what the words mean. This is a good way to proceed if you suspect a number of the words are familiar or if they are easy to figure out from their roots. You should have a dictionary handy so that students can check their definitions with the official ones.

> *Give the students three or four pages of self-guided vocabulary and writing exercises.*

The purpose of these exercises is to help students become more familiar with the new words, their spellings and definitions, and their usage in sentences. Whenever possible, the exercises should relate the words directly to the content of the unit and to the students' experiences.

Below are examples of different types of exercises that can be used to help students learn a new group of words. One vocabulary assignment should only include three or four of these suggested forms. For instance, a typical assignment for us might consist of "Matching," "Fill in the Blanks," four or five questions based on the words, and a choice among three writing assignments using the words.

Matching words and definitions
Connect these words with their synonyms or meanings.

inhibited	unplanned
mature	comfort
immature	bossy
console	juvenile
protective	adult
permissive	shielding, guarding
authoritarian	pushover
spontaneous	shy, held-back

Fill in the blanks
In the following sentences, fill in the blanks with the words from the vocabulary list above which make the most sense to you in the sentence.

She was forced to become quite _____ early in life, in order to take care of younger brothers and sisters while her parents worked.

Worried about what can happen on the streets late at night, Tommy's parents are very _____ and won't let him stay out after ten o'clock.

On the other hand, Jane's mother and father are very _____ and let her come home as late as she wants.

Word squares
Find the words among all these letters.

Simple crossword puzzles

1		2	3	4		5					
		6									7
8						9			10		
			11	12							
		13									
14	15										
16				17	18			19			
20			21				22				
		23				24					
					25						

ACROSS
1. Letting a child do whatever she wants
6. What you use to play baseball
8. Leave out
9. What happened long ago
11. Opposite of down
13. Older than her years
14. What's in the middle of an apple
16. Comes after one
17. What to do when you're hungry
19. Money to get out of jail
20. Clever, creative
23. Finish, stop
24. What to do to elect the President
25. Opposite of old

DOWN
1. Trying to keep all harm away
2. Important fact about baseball sluggers
3. Developed, grown up
4. Darn _____!
5. Helpful, warm
7. Comfort, soothe
10. The number of hands and feet you have
12. The initials for Physical Education
13. _____ it. What your geometry teacher always says
15. Possess, have
17. The _____ of the line; last stop
18. Where it's _____
19. What you do at the races
21. Abbreviation for English

Defining the word from the sentence

Read the following sentences and try to figure out the meaning of the underlined words. Then write a brief definition of the word.

She was so mad at him for getting so drunk and acting so immature at the party.

Immature:

The policeman was sick of being called an authoritarian all the time; all he wanted was to keep the kids off private property.

Authoritarian:

Questions based on the words

Give an example of something an authoritarian teacher might say to a student he was trying to intimidate.

Imagine you are a little kid and upset because your brother broke your toy. What could someone say to console you?

Do you think the mother in *Daddy Was a Number Runner* is a protective or a permissive parent? She is _____ because:

Writing assignments utilizing the words

Choose one of the following assignments to write. Use at least three of the vocabulary words in your paper.

A child gets in trouble with some authority.

Write a dialogue between a parent and a child where the child wants to do something and the parent is being protective.

Pretend you are Junior in *Daddy Was a Number Runner*. Describe what is going through your head when your father is beating you.

Play games with the words.

Periodic review of vocabulary can be accomplished through word games. Most of these games work best with a fairly large pool of words to draw from. The greater the students' mastery of the definitions, the more fun they will have with the games. Below is an annotated list of games our students have particularly enjoyed.

— Charades: Students act out the definitions. This works best using several word lists from different weeks, so students cannot guess easily just by process of elimination. When the words deal primarily with relationships you can use a kind of modified charades where two students act out a word.

— Concentration: Write out each of the words and each of the definitions on a three by five card. Then all cards are placed face downward, the words in one area, the definitions in another. Students take turns turning over two cards, one from the words grouping, one from the definitions. If they turn over a word and its correct definition, they keep the cards and get a point. This game relies on recognizing the definitions and remembering the placement of the cards.

— Password: Divide the class into pairs, each person sitting across the table from her partner. The first person on one side of the table is given one of the vocabulary words. Her partner has to guess which one. She is allowed to say only one word to her partner as a hint. She tries to communicate the vocabulary word to her partner by finding one other word to say that will tip her partner off. If the partner guesses correctly, they get a point and the next team tries another word. If they don't, the next team gets the same word to work on. This game helps students associate the new words with other words they know.

— Circle story: Every student in the class receives one vocabulary word written on a card. The first student begins by making up a few lines of a story, using her word in the process. Each student, in turn, adds to the story, using her own word. This game is good for reinforcing proper word usage. Another variation of this game is for the first student to write a few sentences of a story, including her word. Before passing the paper to the next person she folds it so only the last line of the story is showing. The next student does the same, and so forth. The last student unfolds the paper and reads the whole story, with all of its funny non sequiturs.

> *Review the words periodically throughout the term.*

Keeping the words on the wall throughout the term reinforces the learning and creates a sense of progress and accomplishment. When people speak or write, they can be encouraged to draw from the words on the lists. Every so often, the class can go over the pronunciation and meaning of the words again.

ROLE-PLAYING

> I never really got into role-playing this term. I never thought I could do that in front of people. But I liked it; I could really get a feeling about what was happening and I could also express what I felt about certain things. [From a student evaluation]

Objectives:

—To encourage students to participate imaginatively in a theme, book or issue;
—To help students connect an issue to their own lives and experiences through acting it out;
—To help review information.

Different Types of Role-Playing

> *Two-person role-plays.*

In these role-plays, two (or occasionally three or four) people come together to talk about an issue of importance to at least one of them. The situation might be that one person wants or needs something from the other, or one person is angry at the other and wants a confrontation. Open conflict does not have to be built in, but there should be some kind of dramatic tension.

Family issues and peer relationships lend themselves well to this kind of role-playing. For instance, a role-play could dramatize a parent and child conflict over the issue of parental protection (p. 60), a family situation with the focus on mother/daughter interactions (p. 71), or competition between girlfriends over males (p. 83).

It is often a good idea in these role-plays to stop them after a while, in order to let other people in the class participate—either through advice to the players or through taking on the same roles themselves. Another technique that can be useful when a role-play breaks down into irresolvable conflict is to have the actors try it again, this time trying to reach some other resolution.

> *Panel role-plays.*

In this type of role-playing, the emphasis is more on information sharing than on emotional interaction. Three or four students are given roles describing historical or contemporary figures who have experiences or points of view to share and debate. In their roles, they serve on a panel with a moderator (usually the teacher) present to facilitate the interaction and sharing of the characters. The moderator asks for initial brief presentations from each panelist, and then, as on a TV talk show, helps them interact and debate.

This type of role-playing is especially useful when the objective is to compare and contrast people who have different viewpoints and experiences. It is a good technique for summarizing historical or sociological material the students have been learning. For instance, a TV panel-show format is suggested in Unit VIII (p. 175), to compare the experiences of factory workers in the nineteenth century and today. Based on historical readings and contemporary interviews, two students play women who worked in factories in the nineteenth century and two play women who are working in factories today.

> *Group simulation.*

Some topics lend themselves to group role-plays, involving everyone in the class. A particular situation (time and place) is defined, and everyone in the class becomes a character dealing with that situation. In these role-plays, character development is minimized; rather, what is important is the situation and atmosphere created by the large group. For instance, a role-play can be used to explore the issue of how it feels to be a "new girl" coming into a clannish group (p. 84) or to raise issues of labeling and tracking in schools (p. 87). The class simulates being a class with exaggerated student and teacher roles. In this kind of role-play, there may be certain characters who act as catalysts to the action. In the schooling role-play (p. 87), for example, the "troublemaker" and the "teacher" can create interesting tensions in their interactions with other characters. In this role-play, we decide ahead of time which students would best play these two key roles and make sure to assign them the parts. Another possibility is to ask another teacher to participate and take on one of the key roles.

Facilitating the Role-Playing

> *Explain the concept of role-playing.*

When a class is about to role-play for the first time, the action should be preceded by a brief discussion of what happens in a role-play. A comparison with a written play will clarify several important points. Like a written play, a role-play has characters, or parts to be taken, but unlike a written play, there are no set lines to learn. Rather, the actor has to try to "become" the character she is playing and, out of her own understanding of the character's viewpoint and feelings, do what that person might do, say what that person might say.

To illustrate these points further, you could write a sample role on the board, or hand out copies of one, and then brainstorm together about what that character might be thinking and saying in the particular situation defined by the role-play. This gives students practice in moving from the description on the card to real dialogue in a scene.

> *Give students short, written descriptions of their roles.*

Improvising a part in front of other people is hard, even for experienced actors. To make this a possible—and positive—activity for students, the teacher has to provide a fair amount of structure. We always begin by giving the students a role card that includes specific information on who they are and what they want or need in this situation. We try to make these descriptions simple and concise, with a touch of melodrama (see p. 83). For example:

Joanie: You are fifteen years old. For the past year you haven't had a boyfriend. You've spent a lot of time with your best girlfriend, Sarah. Sometimes you go out and do things with Sarah and her boyfriend, Jack. About a month ago Jack started paying a lot of attention to you. Last week he came by your house by himself. He let you know that he liked you a lot and was interested in going out with you. You agreed to go out with him. You like Sarah a lot and you feel guilty about your decision. You don't want to lose the friendship.

Sarah: You are sixteen years old. You have been going with Jack for a year. Your other close relationship is with your best girlfriend, Joanie. Often you and Jack spend time with Joanie. The three of you go out together, since Joanie doesn't have a boyfriend. This morning at school you heard from another friend that Jack and Joanie are going out. You are hurt and angry. Furthermore, you have a lot of pride about not showing how upset you are. You want to save your friendship with Joanie, but you are mad at her. You confront her about what's going on between her and Jack.

The trick is to give enough information to get the actor started, but not so much that there is no room for her interpretation or imagination. (For other examples see pp. 71–72.)

When students are role-playing characters from a book, we still give them the specific situation for the role-play (either a situation from the book or an imaginary one in which the characters find themselves); but they are expected to define the role, based on the character in the book.

> Interview students in their roles.

Students need a few minutes to read over their role cards and to think about the characters they are playing. To help them make the transformation into this new personage, the teacher can interview each character, in front of the rest of the class. A few, simple questions suffice: What's your name? How old are you? Are you worried about something? The questions will vary according to the information given in the role cards. The point is to help students focus on the information on the card and adopt the mindset of the character. Without the interview, students may tend to skim over the role cards and then not understand what to do or how to play their characters. The interviews should be kept brief, bringing the role-players to the point at which they are ready to interact. If the role-play depends upon keeping the rest of the class in some suspense about the characters or the situations, the interview is obviously not a good idea. In that case, the teacher can speak privately for a moment or two with each role-player.

> Be actively involved in the role-play yourself.

If a group is not used to role-playing, it takes a great deal of encouragement and support to get them going. One concrete way for the teacher to express her enthusiasm for the project is to volunteer to play a role herself. If no one seems willing to take part in a role-play, we take on one of the parts ourselves and then directly ask one of the more verbal students to take the other part. This almost always works to get things started. And once the ice is broken, others will be willing to try. Even if enough students volunteer for the role-play, the teacher should remain very active and present in setting it up and helping it begin. We generally designate an area of the room for the interaction of the players and sometimes even set up a few simple props.

The teacher's role continues throughout the role-play. Giggling is a common expression of the students' nervousness and can undercut the scene. The teacher has to be ready to intervene, telling the actors, for example, "Try to stick with it. Stay in your role," and the class, "Give them a chance. Let them go on." Sometimes the actors will get stuck or frustrated and start to give up. Then the teacher may need to intervene with a suggestion or ask members of the class to give advice to the actors. Finally, the teacher has to be ready to stop the action, after enough interaction has occurred and before it has gone on too long.

INTERVIEWING

> I didn't think I'd ever do that assignment to ask my grandmother all those questions. I thought she'd think I was weird or something. But she really dug it! [From a student evaluation]

Objectives:

— To bring new ideas, experiences, and information into the classroom;
— To learn to do first-hand research on a topic;
— To see a familiar person in a new light;
— To give students more perspective on their own experiences through comparisons with other people's.

Who to Interview

> *People the students already know.*

There are many people in the students' immediate community who have a great deal to share. From interviewing these people, students bring a wealth of new information, first-hand experiences, and ideas into the classroom. For instance, hearing a five- or six-year-old sibling or neighbor talk about what they want to be when they grow up has a greater impact than reading about early sex-role socialization (p. 49). Talking to a family member or neighbor who works in a factory gives students a way of connecting to the historical material about factory work in the nineteenth century (p. 173).

Furthermore, students are most likely to complete an interviewing assignment if they speak with someone who is readily available and familiar to them. Students who seem most reluctant or timid can be encouraged to interview people very close to them, perhaps people in their immediate or extended family, or best friends. Others, who feel a bit more adventurous, can turn to people they see regularly but do not know well; neighbors, parents of friends, shopkeepers, and other teachers make likely subjects for assignments.

An additional benefit of interviewing people within their community is that students establish new connections with people they have known for years. As one young woman said to us, "That was the first time I ever knew what it was like for my mother working in a factory. I never heard her talk about that before."

> *People whose experiences and values provide useful comparisons for the students in the class.*

Through comparing themselves with other young people, students gain perspective on their own lives, experiences, and values. Interviews with other young women from a different social class background (p. 95) or from different ethnic or racial groups, or interviews with young men from their own or different backgrounds (p. 93) provide interesting comparisons.

Preparation for the Interviews

> *Ask the class to develop appropriate questions.*

Although nervous about the impending interviews, students usually enjoy making up questionnaires together. The natural curiosity these young women have about other people translates into interesting and honest questions. Brainstorming together, the class will probably come up with more than enough questions. After collecting all of these ideas, the group should consolidate the list to eight to fifteen questions (see p. 73). Too many questions make an interview cumbersome; on the other hand, if there are too few questions, the interview may be so brief that it reveals little.

While the questionnaire developed through the students' collective work provides the basic approach, in certain cases different students will not be able to use exactly the same questions for the interviews they conduct. For instance, in the unit on "Mean Streets," the objective of the assignment is for each student to be able to hear another young woman talk about a specific problem or set of problems that she is facing. Thus, each student will need to tailor her questions to the specific concerns and experiences of the individual she is interviewing. An interviewing assignment that requires individual students to develop their own questions should only be given in classes that have already had some experience in interviewing with a questionnaire that the class has developed together.

> *Select possible interviewees together.*

Making arrangements for an interview requires a fair amount of initiative on the part of the student. Students are more likely to accomplish this task if they receive a good deal of support in getting started. After they have made up the questionnaires, you should ask students for specific ideas on whom they will try to interview. It might even be a good idea to have them share that information orally, before leaving the classroom. This verbal commitment can help to carry them through the next difficult step of setting up the appointment.

> *Practice interviewing techniques in class.*

Interviewing is a skill. The interviewer not only has to ask good questions, but also has to know how to ask them. Getting the interviewee to share information and experiences is difficult. Practicing on each other in class gives students the opportunity to develop their interviewing styles.

A good way to start a practice session is for you to role-play an interview with one student in front of the class. You could either take on the role of interviewer or a particularly difficult interviewee. Then the class discusses ways the interviewer might have been able to get a better response. Following this, everyone in the class should be allowed to practice by dividing into pairs and interviewing each other.

When we do this practice exercise for the first time, we give students a set of questions on neighborhoods to ask each other. This serves the double purpose of helping the class members to get to know each other and giving them interviewing experience. Possible questions include:

Name
What do you like to be called?
Where do you live?
Where do you hang out?

How do you spend time on a typical day?
What's the best thing about your neighborhood?
What's the worst thing about your neighborhood?
What would you like to see changed in your neighborhood?

> *Set a reasonable due date.*

Students need some time to complete an interviewing assignment, but too much time will dissipate energy. Sometimes several students are excited enough by the assignment to complete it immediately. Each day, you should ask students who have done the assignment to share their results with the rest of the class. This will have the effect of encouraging others who are having trouble getting started. You should ask everyone to bring in their results within three days.

Follow up on the Interviews

> *Encourage students to share interviewing experiences.*

A number of people may have interesting stories to tell about their interviews. The quality of notes people take will vary, but some students may even be able to repeat part of their interviewing session verbatim. In some cases, the specific responses of interviewees may provide lively discussion material for the class. For instance, when we did the interviews with young children (p. 49), the interviews with mothers (p. 73), and the interviews with young men (p. 93), the specific comments of individual interviewees were provocative.

> *Compile the results of the interviews.*

When a whole class has conducted interviews with similar subjects, on the same questions, many interesting patterns may be revealed in the responses. By charting these responses, the patterns can be studied. For instance, having interviewed very young boys and girls on their experiences and future plans (p. 49), or adolescent males and females on their interests and attitudes (p. 41), the class can learn more from seeing the responses of the males and females compared, than they can through the individual interviews. When the class interviews people for the purpose of making comparisons with themselves—as in the case of the suburban young women (p. 95)—the charted results are an easy reference point for the comparisons.

SPEAKERS

I liked it best when women would come and talk with the class. That way we could actually see them and what they are like, and they could see the school. [From a student evaluation]

Objectives:

— To enliven a topic with first-hand experiences;
— To give students exposure to people with new or different experiences and viewpoints.

Selecting a Speaker

> Look for someone who can speak about a topic from first-hand experience.

Students tune in much more quickly to someone who is speaking from experience, than to someone who has developed expertise on a subject from a distance. It is important, however, to find someone with enough perspective on their experience to be able to describe it well and articulate how and why it is significant.

> Try to find someone who is, in some way, connected to a student in the class.

Students are sometimes intimidated by or uninterested in "outsiders." They are more likely to be open to a speaker if she or he has been brought by or is known to a classmate. For instance, we have had good classes with a parent who spoke about a union organizing drive at her workplace (p. 175). Another time, a lawyer who had represented several of our students came to speak about the trials and tribulations of being a woman lawyer (p. 156).

Drawing on people the students know, you are also more likely to find speakers from working-class backgrounds. The similarities in background may serve as a bridge between the speaker and the class, and the speaker may serve as a role model for the students.

Preparing the Class

> Ask the students what kinds of speakers they might like to hear.

A good time to brainstorm about possible speakers is during the first week or so of a new topic or theme. Students may know people who have something to say about the topic, or they may be able to suggest general categories of speakers who would interest them. "How about a woman cop." "I've always wanted to really talk to a nun." Participating in this way helps students to feel that they have a hand in shaping the educational process.

> Have students decide on questions to ask.

Thinking of specific questions will help the class focus on what they expect and want from the impending visit. You should begin by describing (or having the student who knows the speaker describe) who this person is and what she or he could include in a talk. This will give the students a starting point for their questions.

The questions should be preserved—either on the chalkboard or on dittoed sheets. Then, on the day of the visit, if the students become shy or reluctant to speak up, they can refer to their questions. We sometimes ask students to commit themselves ahead of time to at least one question each will ask.

Preparing the Speaker

> *Be clear about the group's expectations.*

From the first contact with potential speakers, you should be clear why you are asking them to come into the class and what you think their contribution can be. In order to decide whether or not to come, speakers need to know who the students are, what their interests are, and what the class is about. You, in turn, should find out from them what they think they would include in the content of a talk. And you need to assess whether this person could, in fact, hold the interest of the class. If your decision is positive, and the person is interested in coming, you can roughly outline with the speaker the content of the talk.

> *Tell the speaker what tone and style work best with your class.*

It takes a special sensitivity to know how to engage a young audience. Many of the people who come in as speakers will not be used to speaking in front of high school groups. Speakers often do not realize how interesting their own experiences can be to others. Some may be shy

about engaging directly with students in the class. A few of the following hints can be helpful to them: talk as personally as possible, try to use simple language, encourage questions from the group, direct questions to individuals in the group, tell anecdotes that relate to the subject.

> *Ask the speaker to arrive early to get acclimated.*

It is hard to walk into a school building, perhaps for the first time in years, and plunge right into a talk. If the speaker can come even fifteen minutes early, she or he will have a chance to meet you and get acclimated to the situation. This is a good time to fill them in again on what the class expects.

The Teacher's Role

> *Direct the speaker toward the more interesting material.*

From talking with speakers ahead of time, you will have a sense of the more interesting things they have to say. If they stray too far from this material, or if the class seems to be going to sleep, you can intervene with a question or comment that will help bring them back to interesting issues and stories.

> *Help connect the class and the speaker.*

Usually, you are the link between the class and the speaker, knowing more about each than they know about each other. A useful role for the teacher is to draw out individuals in the class when you know they have experiences or questions that relate to something the speaker is saying and to draw out the speaker on issues or experiences you know will connect directly to individuals in the class.

TRIPS

My favorite class was when we got together with those kids in Newton. It was fun finding out how they live. [From a student evaluation]

Objectives:

— To give the class more group cohesion through experiencing something new together;
— To familiarize students with resources in the community;
— To give students experience handling themselves in new and unknown situations;
— To build skills of observation and evaluation.

When to Take Trips

Of all the activities a teacher can plan for a class, trips are the hardest to arrange. The coordination of a trip involves such complicating factors as finding a time that is both convenient to your class and to the site, arranging for transportation to and from, covering the costs of the trip. On the whole, however, we have found trips to be well worth the effort. Many of our students have only the most limited experiences with people or places outside of their immediate neighborhood. Experiencing new sights and smells, new ideas and faces, has a powerful impact on these students.

Before we arrange a trip, however, we weigh carefully the possible benefits and problems. First, we consider whether the proposed trip meets any or all of the objectives listed above. In addition, we ask ourselves whether there will be interesting dynamics or activities to observe; whether students will be interested and comfortable as visitors in the situation. If the answers to these questions are largely affirmative, we move into the arrangements.

Preparation for a Trip

> *Ask the students for ideas.*

The class can be asked to brainstorm about trips at the same time that they think of speakers—during the first week or so of a new topic. When we have involved students in planning this way, we have used a blank calendar of all the class days in the term to help focus them on the task. Together the class decides which day(s) would be best to have speakers, which would be a good day for a trip. Our rule of thumb is usually no more than one special event—speaker, trip, film, etc.—in a week. Other days are spent on classroom activities—reading, discussing, role-playing, writing, etc. In putting items on the calendar, people become more clear and specific about their ideas.

> *Involve at least one student in making the arrangements.*

Setting up a trip usually requires a lot of phone-calling back and forth. If a student has indicated particular interest in a trip, you could enlist her help in coordinating it. This is a good experience for the student, a help to you, and a way to keep the class involved beyond the initial brainstorming.

Your enthusiasm, and that of the student who helps you, will be crucial in getting the class ready for the trip. Although some people in the class are always excited at the idea of going somewhere, others are threatened. "This is stupid." "What are we going to do this for?" "I don't want to go." "I'm not going if we have to walk anywhere." If a student has been involved in the arrangements and is excited about the trip, she can help you deal with some of this fear and lethargy. In fact, most of these students, if prodded to come, will enjoy the trip and get a great deal out of it. They are just frightened of the unknown. They may need to complain right up to and even during the trip, in order to get themselves to do it. It certainly helps your peace of mind to have a few student allies to counterbalance the negativism.

Discuss what to look for on the trip.

Visiting a place for the first time, students will find it hard to focus attention on any single objective. On a trip to court, for instance, there are hundreds of people, incidents, events, and other stimuli to absorb and learn from. If you have a specific educational purpose in mind for the trip, you might want to discuss this with the students and help direct their attention to particular areas. Thus, before our trip to court (p. 156), we decided to try to concentrate on all the ways women are involved in the proceedings.

Developing question sheets or charts for students to fill out while on the trip is not recommended. The sheets often hinder students in responding to the stimuli of the trip or from really observing what is going on. Students either lose them or become preoccupied with them to the exclusion of enjoying themselves. Occasionally, however, if a trip is going to involve on-site interviews, the class should develop a questionnaire as part of their preparations. For instance, when we visited social service agencies (p. 159), the students thought of criteria for evaluating the agency and questions to ask of people there. Since a large part of the trip consisted of interviewing clients and staff, the students made good use of these questionnaires.

Arrange to have someone to greet you and be your guide.

When arriving at a new place it is very comforting and helpful to have someone greet you

who has been expecting your visit. The educational purpose of the trip is much more likely to be achieved if someone on-site has been alerted about your objectives. For instance, when we went to a suburban school (p. 95), what made the trip work for us was having spoken to a teacher there about our students and our course. She, in turn, was able to prepare her students for our visit. So, when the two groups met they were ready to talk. This, of course, is not always possible to arrange. Sometimes it works as well to bring someone with you who can serve as a guide. On a trip to court, for example, you could invite along a lawyer to help explain the proceedings (p. 156).

The Teacher's Role

Be clear on guidelines.

Expectations about behavior should be discussed ahead of time. Issues like smoking or going off alone are bound to come up. Tensions around these can be avoided by previous understandings.

Help focus the students in their observations.

Once out of the school building, some students may find it hard to focus at all. You can remind people about the purposes of the trip and the particular theme the class agreed to concentrate its attention on. Since your eyes and ears will probably be sharper instruments of observation than theirs, you may want to keep pointing things out to them as you go along. Engaging students in conversation about what you are seeing and experiencing can help focus their observations.

Follow up to a Trip

> *Bring the trip back into the classroom.*

After a trip, students learn a great deal from recalling their observations in systematic ways. A general discussion of impressions can be followed by a listing or chart exercise in which students categorize what they observed or learned. For instance, after the suburban school visit (p. 95), the class makes a chart of the similarities and differences between growing up in Cambridge and Newton. In some cases, like the visit to a social service agency, this process can be taken one step further. The information, once reviewed and compiled, is written up and published for other people (p. 161).

More imaginative exercises help students apply what they learned to themselves. For instance, students can be asked to write an essay imagining themselves to be someone they met in the place they visited. After our trip to Newton High School many students chose to do the writing assignment that asked them to describe a typical day in the life of a Newton young woman (p. 97).

> *Preserve the trip through a photo album.*

A satisfying way to remember a trip and preserve the sense of enjoyment and excitement is through a class photo album. People never tire of flipping through the pages and remembering "that weird place" or "that nice lady." Because it has been carefully documented, the whole experience of the trip seems more legitimate and important. The pictures also provide the class with a way to share their experiences with others.

With a grant from Polaroid of a few cameras and film, we were able to take pictures on most of our excursions. What is especially nice about the Polaroids is that students can learn to use them and do all of the documenting themselves. And, of course, there are instant results, which enhance the trip even as it is happening. If Polaroids aren't available, you should urge anyone in the class who has a camera to bring it along and be the trip "historian."

I: MESSAGES FROM SOCIETY

OVERVIEW

Everyone is exposed to societal messages about sex roles. Complaints about women drivers, popular songs about how much a woman needs her man, advertisements featuring slinky models with long, thin cigarettes—these are the sounds and images of everyday life. Because these messages are so familiar and accessible, they provide good curriculum materials for the first few weeks of a women's course. Simply by living their lives as young women, the students have become experts on the messages from society. There are entry points for everyone, and the material is relatively impersonal and nonthreatening. The students can share experiences, ideas, and beliefs without revealing too much of themselves. Furthermore, the process of exploring a common set of messages brings the students together as a group.

Although sayings, songs, advertisements, and TV shows are part of every young woman's experiences, the idea that these images and messages might profoundly affect their view of the world is not as obvious. The activities in this unit help the students reach new levels of awareness about the omnipresent societal messages. The young women develop new eyes and ears with which to experience their environment as well as their own thoughts and feelings.

In the first activity, students generate lists of common sayings about women. Next, they get to know each other better, by interviewing each other on the women they most and least admire. In the rest of the unit, they compare their own viewpoints about sex roles with those of their peers and with messages from the media. They make collages of "society's view of women" as compared to their own, interview other teen-agers for their attitudes about sex roles, read and write advice columns, and examine the presentation of sex roles in different kinds of media.

This unit can be used to introduce many of the other themes and issues in this curriculum. If your class meets four or five times a week, you could probably complete the activties in the unit in two or three weeks. If you are not using the unit as a whole, you could incorporate different activities into other units. For instance, students in a women's discussion group focusing on sex education (see unit V, "Sexuality") could think about issues related to their bodies and appearance through making collages. Students exploring themes of "Growing Up Female" (in Unit III) could benefit from surveying the media for sex-role messages to teen-agers. This unit is easily adaptable to mixed male/female classes. Using exactly the same exercises, students could explore societal messages to men about masculinity. In a mixed class, you would probably want to build in time in every activity for comparing the male and female messages.

ACTIVITIES

1: Word Collages

Structuring a "first class" is always difficult. The membership and dynamics of the group, their interests and expectations are all unknown. The goal of this activity is to involve every member of the class in establishing some group reference points. Students share and examine the common vernacular about women; everyone adds a little piece from her own memories to an emerging collage of phrases, sayings, and words that refer to women.

A few simple questions from the teacher can start this process. You can ask: "What are a few common sayings or phrases that have to do with women?" Students can quickly supply two or three—"Women are lousy drivers," "A woman's place is in the home," "A woman's work is never done." With these listed on the chalkboard or on a large piece of paper, the teacher asks for immediate reactions to each: "Does this seem to be true? Do you agree with this? What would be evidence for or against?" Without getting into lengthy debates or disagreements, members of the group can begin to consider what these cliches really mean and whether or not the sayings seem to be true.

Having exhausted common phrases, the class moves on to single words that are often used to describe or define women. Some suggestive questions from the teacher help the process: "What might someone call a woman he or she is mad at? a woman who has lots of relationships with men? a woman who isn't married? a married woman?" The teacher should encourage everyone to contribute at least one word, perhaps by going around in a circle. Students will probably be amazed to see how many words they can think of as a group. When this list has filled out (again, this should be done visually, on the chalkboard or on posterboard), the class tries to find parallel words to describe men. "What is the equivalent to a bitch? a slut, a whore? an old maid?" People may not be able to name male counterparts for some of the words, but they can usually get at least half of them—and the gaps themselves are often more revealing than the counterparts. Again, having generated the list, the class should take a moment to consider it.

When we have done this exercise, the list of "women's" words usually includes more words with negative connotations than the list of "men's" words. At least one or two of the students realize this disparity. "I'd rather be a bachelor than an old maid." The teacher might ask why people think this disparity exists or what the consequences are of having so many negative labels for women. The intent, as before, is to raise interesting issues for consideration, rather than to have a full discussion.

A good way to conclude this exercise is for each student to choose one of the words or common statements about women and write it down on a piece of paper. Then members of the class paste all of these together into a large word collage. This serves as a visual reminder of this exercise throughout the rest of the unit.

2: Interviews—Whom Do You Most and Least Admire?

People popularized by the media are as familiar to students as common words and phrases. In this activity, students reveal more about themselves by expressing their opinions on the women they most and least admire. Since sharing personal opinions can be threatening, especially in a new group, we suggest the class be divided into pairs. This structure insures that everyone will participate, not just those students who are comfortable talking in a larger group. Many students feel freer to give their opinions and impressions when they are talking to one other person. If the pairs are matched carefully, students will have an opportunity to talk with someone they do not already know well.

The exercise involves interviewing and listening skills. The task for each pair is to interview one another on the questions:

1. What is your name?
2. What do you like to be called by your friends?
3. Name the two women you most admire or most want to be like.
4. Name the two women you least admire or least want to be like.
5. Give the reasons for your choices.

Some students may have difficulty thinking of specific women. In this case, encourage them to think of a *type* of woman they admire or do not admire—i.e., a woman who speaks her mind to everyone, or a woman athlete, or a prostitute, or a policewoman. The teacher should "float" during this part of the activity, helping teams over difficult moments. Or, if everything is going smoothly, you could join an interview team and share your opinions on these questions.

After the pairs have completed their interviews, the class comes back together. The members of each pair now have the task of introducing each other to the rest of the group, using what they have learned from their interviews. For example, a student might say of her partner, "This is Nancy, she likes to be called Nancy. She thinks Betty Ford is pretty cool because she speaks her mind. She thinks Cher Bono shows off too much." With the introduction structured in this way, each student can become the focus of the whole group, without the embarrassment of having to describe herself or her own opinions.

After everyone's choices (including your own) have been expressed, ask the class to look for any patterns that have emerged. We have found that in their "leasts" lists, many students have cited women authority figures—like policewomen, truant officers, and probation officers—or they have mentioned women married to unpopular men, or women in very hard or degrading jobs. In their "mosts" lists, many have mentioned women athletes, or media stars, or women married to male media heroes. We have also found that they often have more difficulty thinking of women they admire than of women they distrust or dislike. Students may have difficulty identifying or describing patterns. This is a skill that takes time and work to develop. We encourage students to notice as much as they can about their responses—and then we move on.

3: Picture Collages—Society's Image and Our Own

This activity helps students further clarify their own views by comparing them with societal messages about women. Students make picture collages, first, of society's image of women, then, of their own.

You start this exercise by writing "Feminine" and "Masculine" on the chalkboard. Then, ask students to list all of the words suggested to them by these terms. When we have done this, students have responded to "feminine" with words like "small," "cute," "frilly," "lacy." "Masculine" has called forth "big," "strong," "never cries." Sometimes this listing process has been punctuated by nervous giggles or underlined by a sarcastic tone. "I always think of a little girl with ruffles."

Students may be somewhat embarrassed to admit the images that are conjured up by these words. They may feel that there is something a little wrong about having stereotyped images, especially in a women's course. They may be confused at feeling resentful of the image and also attracted by it. The teacher's role in this can be to point out how the terms "masculine" and "feminine" have changed in their meanings. At one time, "feminine" referred to anything to do with women, "masculine" to anything to do with men. Yet, these terms have come to project certain, somewhat limiting, images. Often, what is focused on or admired about a woman is her "femininity"—which comes down to certain aspects of her appearance and personality.

Students are now ready to look at one of the major sources of this "feminine" image of women—advertisements. Creating a collage together is an active and enjoyable method of surveying magazine advertisements. This activity may also be a relief for some students from the previous day's talking. The resource materials involved are not difficult to find: a pile of old magazines (probably available from a local recycling outlet), three or four pairs of scissors, several sheets of posterboard or cardboard, glue, and magic markers.

We usually get students started by suggesting they cut out pictures for two different collages. The first follows directly from the previous discussion. They should look for society's image of the perfect, "feminine" woman. For the second collage, they should cut out pictures that represent their own image of women. If students need more direction, you can suggest some specifics: "Look for women doing things you like to do; look for women who remind you of people you've met or liked or admire."

Finding pictures that represent the students' images of women is much more difficult than finding the first, stereotypical set, because, of course, you are drawing from magazines (particularly ads) which tend to project society's limited image. Some of this problem can be alleviated by making sure that a few of the magazines do present a wider range of women. Along with women's magazines, bride magazines, etc., you might want to include *Newsweek*, *Time*, or *Ms.*, and perhaps some daily newspapers. Beyond providing a variety of magazines, you can encourage students to look for parts of ads or pictures that they like. For instance, a Tampax ad may include a woman swimming or canoeing. And anyone who draws well could be encouraged to make her own picture.

We have found that the time spent looking through magazines and clipping pictures can be an interesting period of informal comment and interaction. While they may have expressed some anger or embarrassment at society's "feminine" image in the previous discussion, many of the students, when faced with the pictures, will make derogatory comments about themselves or generally compare themselves unfavorably to the images. "Check out her legs." "I wish I could look like that." "See, that's the haircut I wanted." Some of the students' standards about appearance and their feelings about their own bodies start to emerge through these reactions. Specifically, what these comments reveal is the low self-image of many of the young women.

In our students, the negative feelings stem both from the general awkwardness of being adolescent females and from the shame and anger of being poor. On both counts they feel inadequate to live up to society's image and ideals. We feel that it's best at this time to respond on a surface level rather than to the deep feelings underneath. "Oh I like your hair the way it is." "She probably spends hours to look like that." "I like your style of dressing, too." At this point it is enough if the students become more self-conscious about the messages and images surrounding them and more aware of how these are related to their standards and ideals. It's a small step, but a necessary one in working toward dealing with their negative feelings about themselves.

After twenty to thirty minutes of clipping, the students will probably have more than enough pictures for both of the collages. Depending on how much time you wish to spend on this activity, you could have everyone work together on the first collage and then the second, or you could divide the class in half and give each half one of the sets of pictures to work with. (If you are working with a large group, you will probably want three or four collages presenting "Society's Image," and three or four presenting "Our Image," so that every student has a chance to contribute some of her pictures and participate in creating the whole. For the sake of simplicity, here we will refer to two collages only, one of each type.)

The pasting up can be done on large sheets of cardboard or posterboard. If the surface is large enough, the students may enjoy tracing one of their heads and torsos on the posterboard and using this to define the boundaries of the collage. The final collage is then in the shape of a woman.

The differences in the two collages our students have made have been subtle but provocative. "Society's Image" has included pictures of brides; young mothers with children; "sexy women;" women with silky hair, makeup, puckered lips, long fingernails; housewives cleaning, cooking, or knitting. "Our Image" has been focused around more active women—women canoeing, playing tennis, golfing, biking, swimming, waterskiing; women going to work or at work; women traveling; women driving; women marching together for a cause. Although most are still young models from the ads, there are a few pictures of older women or women whose faces and shapes don't conform to the ideal. Generally, students do not like to spend a great deal of time analyzing what they have made. But it is worth taking a few minutes to look for the differences in the finished products.

A good follow-up to this activity is a writing assignment using the pictures. Each student can be asked to choose one picture from either collage or a picture not used in the collages. They can then choose one of the following tasks: "Write about what this woman is really thinking at the moment the picture is snapped; write a little story about this woman, who she is, how she got into this situation; write a poem about the woman that starts with a word or phrase describing who she is."

4: Survey—What Do Other Teen-agers Think?

Through interviewing people of their own age, students can see whether their discoveries and opinions are part of any larger patterns. Students usually enjoy making up questionnaires together (see p. 28 for an overview of how to use interviewing). In fact, they will probably have many more ideas for questions than are needed or appropriate at this point. The focus of this questionnaire is on finding out whether other young people carry around similar messages from society and whether there are differences in the extent to which males and females agree or disagree with these messages.

The questionnaire should be brief, perhaps six to eight questions at most, since the point is to get quick feedback from a number of people. There will be a chance in a later unit for each student to do a lengthier, more in-depth interview with one male, in order to produce a detailed comparison of adolescent males' and females' interests and attitudes (see "Growing Up Female," p. 93, if you are not planning to use that unit and wish to do the longer interview here).

Questions our students have devised for this survey include:

1. What do you think of when you hear feminine? masculine?
2. Do you have times when you feel you'd like to be someone of the opposite sex? If so, when?
3. What do you want in a girlfriend? boyfriend?
4. Who should ask whom out for dates? For boys, what would you think of a girl who asks you out?
5. Who are better drivers—men or women? How do you know?
6. What do you think of a guy who gets in trouble, like for stealing? of a girl?

7. If you're playing a sport with a friend who is the opposite sex, who do you think should win?

Once the questions have been generated, we type them out on a ditto and give everyone a number of copies. We ask each student whom she thinks she will interview. She can choose any four (or more) people of her age (preferably two male and two female). If any student has trouble thinking of potential interviewees, other students can usually help her out. At the top of each questionnaire, there should be a space for the interviewer to write the sex and age of the person interviewed.

As soon as the first responses come in, the class makes a big chart (on the chalkboard or on posterboard) with the questions listed on the left-hand side, and two columns, one headed "males," the other "females." This will have the effect of encouraging other students to do their interviews and add them to the growing list. When most of the responses are charted, the class can consider whether there are, in fact, any patterns apparent. Did the females interviewed agree in their concepts of "feminine" and "masculine"? Did males agree with one another? Were there consistent differences in the way males and females answered the questions?

The search for patterns may be brief. However, reading over the responses made by the young people interviewed will probably evoke some lively discussion within the class. When a number of males' comments showed that they wanted to beat their girlfriends at games, several of our students told stories about purposely losing at ping-pong or pool when they played with young men they liked. The chart, with its variety of answers from males and females, can inspire students to remember experiences they have had with dating, or sports, or getting into trouble. Be sure to provide ample opportunity for these anecdotes to be told. The students' own experiences form a very important part of this curriculum. It is important that they begin to enjoy sharing these experiences and begin to see them as legitimate material for discussion.

5: Advice Columns—Writing Assignment

Most young people are familiar with advice columns for women. These columns, with their question-and-answer format, provide a good jumping-off point for a writing exercise. Just about everyone can get interested enough in a problem described by another female in distress to want to write a response. Even students who don't like to write, or who feel intimidated by having to put pencil to paper, have been able to complete this assignment. The usual problems of how to say what to whom are circumvented. There is a specific letter to be written to a specific person with specific needs (See p. 18 for suggestions on helping students with their writing.)

When you do this exercise, you should bring in for the class copies of two or three sets of advice-column questions from the local newspapers—with the answers removed. Everyone is instructed to choose one of the questions to answer. If there is enough time and energy, it is a good idea to first have students read the questions aloud. This is good practice in reading aloud (and a chance for the teacher to diagnose levels). The whole process, with the inevitable comments made in response to what is being read, helps to generate more enthusiasm among the class for writing their own responses to these questions.

When students have read over all the questions, each chooses one to answer. The class needs twenty or thirty minutes to complete its answers. If anyone finishes early, she could start on a second letter. (The whole assignment could also, of course, be done as homework.)

You should leave time at the end of class for students to read their responses aloud. Even students who lack confidence about their writing will probably be willing to share their "advice to the lovelorn." After each person reads her own answer to a question, she gets a copy of the "official" answer to read aloud to the rest of the class. Then everyone can compare the answers and decide which one, if either, they would be more likely to follow. This discussion helps the students continue the process begun earlier in this unit of clarifying their own values through comparing them to more official messages. Thus, the emphasis in the sharing period will be on the advice given, rather than on the writing styles and spelling mistakes. This will help students participate even if they feel inadequate in their skills, and will set a precedent for sharing writing.

6: Media Survey

In this activity, students continue to explore the messages around them and assess the impact of these messages on themselves and other people. The subjects of their explorations are the popular media—songs, TV programs, funnies, comic books, and magazines.

The very familiarity of these media presents a problem. When students have heard a song four times a day for two weeks, they may find it hard to step back and really hear what it says about women, or dating, or sex; when they have seen a TV show fifty times in the course of a year, it may be difficult to notice the differences between the male and female characters or the ways in which they interact. To the extent that students can gain some perspective on these media, they have taken an important step in gaining some control over their environment. Whether or not they still accept the messages from the media, they are no longer simply passive receptacles.

The first step in this exercise is for each student to think of one or two songs she listens to frequently that have something to do with women or men or both. If possible, the students bring in the record or the lyrics to the next class. When a number of students bring records, the class can be a great deal of fun. Everyone sits back, listens to the music, and tries to think about the message conveyed by the songs. For each song, students fill out a questionnaire.

What is the subject of this song?
What does the song say about women? about men?
What does the song say about the relationship of women and men?
What feelings are being expressed in the song?
Who is expressing them?

When the focus shifts to TV shows, more of the work has to be done at home, since the show itself cannot be brought into class to be shared. Everyone watching TV should be given a simple questionnaire to fill out.

> List all of the females in the show.
> What do they look like?
> What are their personalities like?
> What do they do with their time?
> What are their interests?
> What are their worries?
> Do the same for all the males on the show.

Although everyone cannot watch the show together, most students are familiar with the same TV shows, so the discussion can still be lively and involve everyone in the class. If television is available in the school, the class can watch a soap opera together. Since these are shows specifically directed at a female audience, they reveal a great deal about popular attitudes. This can be a good follow-up to the home viewing assignment.

Often, in carrying out these assignments, students (and teachers) may choose for analysis their media favorites. People become attached to certain songs or TV shows, regardless of whether the message presented is limiting or insulting to women. It is crucial to respect these preferences and to avoid putting them down. Our first tendency was to be disgusted at ourselves (and by implication, at the students) for liking songs like Mick Jagger's "Under My Thumb." We made excuses: "Oh well, probably none of us ever really heard the lyrics." The result was to inhibit the students from sharing more of their culture with us. The point is that many students (and teachers) have deep attachments to rock culture—sexist or not. The overall effect of the music, the group that shares an attachment to it, the style and presentation of the various performers, count for much more than the implicit, or explicit, messages about women.

Our intention is not to ask students to give up their culture. Our hope is that as they become more conscious of their own needs as women, some of the more blatantly sexist aspects of that culture will become obnoxious to them. But this will probably only happen when they are more aware of how they can grow and of what is to be gained for them personally from rejecting these attachments. At the beginning, the focus is on developing the skills to find the messages being conveyed through the media and, then, sharing and discussing some of these messages.

To the extent that the media are changing, there are some alternative messages to consider. Helen Reddy's "I Am Woman" makes the top ten; Lily Tomlin's routines get prime time on TV. Students may know of songs, shows, or performers trying to project a different view of women. Experiencing a few of these attempts together is a good way to end the activity with a sense of progress and change.

NOTES TO THE TEACHER

For many teachers, the decision to teach a woman's course is a personal statement of the importance of being a woman. We approach the course with our own identities involved. This can, of course, have many positive results for the students. A teacher who is personally committed to a course will bring a great deal of energy and enthusiasm to it. This commitment, however, also raises several complicated questions for the teacher. How do we deal with age, class, and race differences between teacher and students? How much of our own approach to women's issues, of our own beliefs and values, should we share with the students? How can we play an active role in the course and yet avoid being the center of attention?

Awareness of Differences

The commonality of our experiences as women is an important bond between the teacher and students. It is also important, however, to be conscious of the differences between us. Developing this awareness can help us to understand more about what students need and expect, what we should share from our own experiences.

The most obvious difference between teacher and students is one of age—and the different levels of experience, sophistication, and consciousness that represents. A fifteen-year-old who is ashamed of her bad skin may very well be more interested than her thirty-five-year-old teacher in an advertisement for make-up, while she probably will be considerably less interested in the problems of balancing a career and marriage. Issues that interest us may be far in the future for students. Our struggles are not necessarily the same as theirs.

But to say this is not to imply that the disparity of needs and interests will disappear as the students grow up and overcome some of the effects of sex-role training. Factors of social class and race must also be considered. The fifteen-year-old from the projects who reacts favorably to a dishwasher ad featuring a glamorous model may be expressing needs that have as much to do with economic deprivation as with narrow sex-role definitions. She may be as interested in the appliance, and all it represents, as the glamour. (More likely, she sees the two as going hand-in-hand.) The sixteen-year-old who wears a lot of make-up may be doing so more out of shame about the color of her skin, or about her bad teeth, than from any deeply held belief that women are supposed to be sex goddesses. In both these cases, the teacher has to tread gently. You cannot assume a general level of cynicism in the class towards the media. The students cannot afford to be cynical about what society wants them to be, because there is much of that image they themselves want. The media largely presents a white middle-class image, as well as a sex-stereotyped one.

Because this is an introductory unit, we do not deal directly with issues of social class and race here. There will be material in much of the rest of the curriculum that addresses itself to the problem of some students' low self-image, or their feelings of inadequacy or shame, and to the way society feeds these feelings. The important thing initially is for the teacher to allow these feelings to emerge.

If students feel comfortable with the teacher, difference in age, class, or race can be positive. At times it may be an advantage to have some distance or separation between the teacher and the students. This allows the teacher to ask questions she really doesn't know the answers to, to be questioned about her life, or to mediate bad feelings among the group. What is crucial is to be aware of these differences from the start and to be sensitive to the students' views of themselves and their world.

The Teacher's Point of View

Explorations of the media and its potentially damaging effects on self-image and self-esteem have been a starting point for many women's groups trying to help each other grow and make changes in their lives. It is also the starting point in this course. Teachers with the experience of consciousness-raising groups behind them may have visceral reactions to seeing one more advertisement featuring a glamorous model washing dishes with a new detergent, or one more TV show picturing an immature housewife trying to please and manipulate her husband. But as teachers, we have to keep these automatic responses in check, giving students an opportunity to share their own opinions and ideas—even when their responses are much more accepting and positive than we expect. The media represent a part of youth culture the students do not necessarily want to reject; the images projected in the media sometimes represent aspirations for the future. Our holding back allows us to hear the complexities of the students' responses, and allows them to express all of their ambivalences, without feeling that they have to give a "right" answer, or that they are being judged.

There are numerous examples of times we have had to relearn this lesson. Just as one of us was about to make a sarcastic remark about Rhoda's getting married on TV, a student said: "Rhoda, I *like* her. She's cute!" Another time, as we started to react to all the "glop" on a model's face in a make-up ad, we noticed that two of the students sitting around the picture with us had similar quantities of make-up on themselves. We caught ourselves just in time to avoid saying something like, "Look at all the make-up on her." Instead, we opened discussion by asking, "Why do you think people like to wear make-up?"

At the beginning, it is tempting to make points during and after each exercise. When students bring in their results from picture-cutting or surveys, there is a great temptation to draw out the implications for them, to summarize their findings in the language of the women's movement. "Notice how most of the women in these ads have been objectified," may be an accurate statement, but it may also bring out bored or hostile reactions from the students. Some of them may previously have been embarrassed or angered by the rhetoric of the women's movement as conveyed through television programs or newspaper accounts. Others may have had bad experiences with women's centers or projects in their neighborhoods, which they see as being full of "libbers" or "lessies." All of them may be nervous about having signed up to take a "woman's class" in the first place. When we speak a language they cannot understand or have heard before in negative circumstances, we may touch off these fears and create an unhealthy separation between us and them.

In deciding when to share a viewpoint, we consider whether our statement will too greatly influence the outcome of the activity. For instance, in the collage activity we will sometimes offer a picture or two that adds to "Our Image of Women," but we will try not to influence the whole content of the collage. Ideally, the teacher's contributions should help to stretch concepts held by the students without inhibiting

the expression of their viewpoints. Holding our own reactions in check is specially valuable at the beginning of the course. What we learn about our students from their responses and comments in these introductory exercises will help us know how to handle more personal and delicate material in the later units.

The Teacher As Participant

This unit (and the curriculum as a whole) develops an activities-centered approach to teaching and learning. Such an approach allows the students to learn independently, without waiting for the teacher to provide them with all their ideas and information. For example, instead of telling students that the media present certain stereotyped and narrow images of women, we give the students tools for investigating the content of the media themselves. Within the structured activities of the unit, students can relax, have fun with the exercises, learn new observation skills, and share some insights. The teacher, too, can relax and often be a participant.

The teacher, of course, is more than an equal participant. Someone has to be enthusiastic at the beginning, to overcome the initial resistance that may greet any activity that strays from a pencil/paper/book format. But once the activity is set up and people have started working, the teacher can take part, always exercising caution that a greater facility with words or familiarity with the issues does not lead her into being a "super participant." The point is to change the dynamic in which the teacher is always the most active member of the class, not to substitute one style of activity for another. At times, it may be better for the teacher not to participate directly in an activity, in order to help students understand and carry out the assignment. For instance, in the interviewing activity, if the teams seem to be having a hard time starting, we "float" rather than joining one of the interviewing teams.

II: EARLY SOCIALIZATION

OVERVIEW

My friends called me a tomboy, because I didn't like to play with silly dolls or dress up like they did. I was different. I played with trucks; played baseball, hockey, and basketball with the boys. When my girlfriends saw me doing this they would yell out in front of everyone, "Robbin, you're a tomboy." I would say, "I don't care. Go and play with your silly dolls." And I would finish off what I was doing.

Then I would go home, eat supper, tell my mother what I did all day. Sometimes she would say, "You're a girl, Robbin, not a boy." I didn't care what she said. I would just walk out the door and look for the boys I played with. [Robbin Luzaitis]

This unit explores the ways in which young children learn to be females and males. By focusing on childhood, students begin to comprehend the process by which people are influenced by societal messages. The concept of socialization is difficult to understand, particularly for adolescents, who do not like to think of themselves as unduly influenced by media messages or peer pressures. "Nobody tells me what to think." "I wear what I want to wear." We hear comments like these frequently from our students. It is easier for them to understand how and why children are susceptible to, and influenced by, these messages. A baby, after all, does not know how to act like a girl or a boy—and somehow it learns to do just that.

Through the activities in this unit, students can learn to recognize the ways in which everyone is influenced to take on male and female roles. We start by reading a short story by Lois Gould, "X: A Fabulous Child's Story." This humorous account of Baby X, who is brought up with no sex-role messages, is a good introduction to the unit. The struggles the parents go through to protect Baby X from societal messages begin to clarify how socialization usually works. Students then fill out charts on their own families' treatment of them and their brothers. Having remembered what they can of their own experiences, they interview children to see whether things have changed at all. A speaker who teaches children and has observed sex-role differences is invited to share her insights as to how and why these differences occur. Finally, the unit ends with students looking at children's books that present traditional sex roles, then, they create their own children's books with new messages.

This unit is brief; it would probably take a class seven to ten meetings to complete the activities. Like the first unit, "Early Socialization" is good introductory material and easily adapted to a coeducational class. It is fun to participate in, and nonthreatening, yet it raises interesting issues. If you are not using the unit as a whole, you could integrate some of the activities into the beginning section of Unit III, "Growing Up Female: Childhood to Adolescence."

ACTIVITIES

1: Bringing Up Baby X

Sex-role messages do not begin with comic books or TV. They affect us from the moment of birth. Students learn this quickly when they read "X: A Fabulous Child's Story," by Lois Gould. This is a humorous and interesting fairy tale about Baby X, who, as part of a 23-billion-dollar experiment, was raised to be a child—not a boy or a girl.

The day the Joneses brought their baby home, lots of friends and relatives came over to see it. None of them knew about the secret experiment, though. So the first thing they asked was what kind of a baby X was. When the Joneses smiled and said, "It's an X," nobody knew what to say. They couldn't say, "Look at her cute little dimples!" And they couldn't say, "Look at his husky little biceps!" And they couldn't even say just plain "kitchy-coo."

The story goes on to outline the difficulties of the Joneses and Baby X in trying to remain free of sex-role restrictions. They outrage store clerks, who want to know if it's a girl or boy; passers-by, who look into the baby carriage with the same question; and, finally, parents and administrators at the school Baby X attends, which is "full of rules for boys and girls" but "there were no rules for Xes."

In following the progress of X, the story reveals many of the ways boys and girls are influenced to develop into very different types of people; it suggests areas for further investigation. What makes this reading an especially good way to introduce aspects of early socialization is that it is not presented in a negative way, as a list of increasingly oppressive limitations. The Joneses and Baby X are always in there trying— and in many cases, succeeding—to overcome the traditional sex-role boundaries.

This story makes good in-class reading. It is quick reading and amusing enough to hold students' interest to the end. When we have read the story in class, some students have immediately shared stories from their own upbringing—aunts who always pinched their cheeks and told them how adorable they were, teachers who always lined up the girls in front because they know how to be quieter. After finishing the story, the teacher can ask everyone in the class to compare their upbringing to Baby X, to think about the ways they learned (or refused to learn) to act like little girls. Encourage the students to be anecdotal, to draw examples from their sisters and brothers, to think back as far as they can.

2: Remembering the Past—Questionnaire on Family and School Influences

Having told a few stories about their early childhood socialization, students fill out a questionnaire and a chart which ask them to think more systematically and in more specific detail about the ways they were brought up.

The questionnaire includes:

1. What did you play with when you were little (toys, games, etc.)? Did you have a bicycle?
2. Whom did you play with?
3. What did you get punished for?
4. Did you learn to cook? sew? clean? If so, who taught you?
5. Did you learn to fix things? take apart motors? etc.?
6. In elementary school, what sports did you participate in? what other games did you play?
7. Did the teachers ever treat boys and girls differently?
8. Now answer all of the above questions as though you were your own brother (or, if you don't have one, any young boy you knew well).

The chart looks like this:

What if you . . .
hit a sister or brother
got dirty
got upset and cried
ran around the house
played quietly by yourself
cut school
got a good mark
got a bad mark

What if your brother . . .

Students may have trouble remembering some of these things. That is to be expected; they should not be made to feel bad about this. Just ask them to fill out as much as they can. If they can't remember things about themselves, ask them to try to fill in with things they've observed about their younger sisters and brothers. When everyone has had a chance to fill out the questionnaire and the chart, the class compares results. You might want to make lists on the board, with "girls" and "boys" as headings.

There is usually some variation in students' responses. A number of people remember childhood as a time when they were allowed more freedom to be "like boys." One student even re-

I wanted to be an astronaut...
but it's "MAN'S CONQUEST OF SPACE!"

I wanted to be a doctor... but it's
"MAN'S FIGHT AGAINST DISEASE!"

I wanted to be the president... but
it's "MAN'S STRUGGLE FOR POWER!"

Now all I want is a
SELF-CLEANING OVEN....

marked, "I *was* a guy when I was a little kid." Up to that point, some of the students in the class had been cold toward her, probably because her direct manner and very casual way of dressing and talking put them off. Seeing this difference in their early socialization helped to explain some of the later style differences and to bring all of the students in the class together.

When we have done this assignment, people have remembered that their parents treated them differently from their brothers with regard to the issues of cleanliness and crying. "When my brother got all dirty, he just had to wash up. When I got dirty, I had to change my clothes. And then my mother would yell at me if I ran out of clothes to change into. She'd keep me in the house." Or, "My mother used to yell at my brother to stop crying and being a sissy." "I could get anything I wanted by crying; I was really spoiled."

It is a good idea to get the students to think about whether this early treatment affects the way people behave later in life. Do they see current effects from their early training to stay clean? Are women generally affected by this need to "keep it clean"? Our students have talked about how their mothers "freak out" at dirt or clutter. A few have mentioned that their mothers do domestic cleaning work for other women. We then ask them to think about jobs that involve getting very dirty and staying dirty —garbage work, mining, ditchdigging. Everyone had seen these jobs as men's work.

A similar discussion about crying led students to admit that they still cry quite a bit, particularly when they want or need sympathy. They were all very aware that this is a general pattern— women tend to cry more readily than men. Because this is such an observable phenomenon, it is a good way to make the connections between early training and adult patterns.

3: Interviews with Young Children

The experience of young children growing up today may be different from the students' own training in sex roles. To see how much things have changed or remained the same, students interview children. The focus is mainly on sex-role socialization, but they may also want to ask a few more general questions to get in touch with present-day childrens' perspectives on the world.

Before students design the questionnaire for the interviews, tell them to try to have a specific child in mind. This will help them to think of questions that children can relate to and answer easily. Students almost always enjoy making up questions, especially when these questions are to be asked of their favorite "little people."

1. What do you want to be when you grow up?
2. What are you scared of?
3. What games and toys do you like playing with?
4. Who are your friends? Do you like playing with girls or boys more?
5. If you had one wish, what would it be?
6. Do you like fighting? Whom do you fight with?
7. What are your chores and rules at home?
8. What do you think of school?
9. Do you have a girlfriend? boyfriend?
10. What do you think of teachers?
11. What do you think of police?
12. What do you do that you're not supposed to do?
13. Do you ever get into trouble? For what?

Students can create a list of questions like these in about twenty minutes. Each should then be asked to think of one girl and one boy under ten she could interview. The names and ages of targeted interviewees are listed on the board. If possible, there should be an age range, with at least one-quarter of the interviewees six years old or under (see "Techniques," p. 29).

If the class did the "Messages from Society" unit, they should now have a reasonably good idea of how to handle interview results. The simplest system is to list the questions on one side of the blackboard, and place the categories "Girls" and "Boys" at the top of the board. We have found that even more interesting comparisons are possible when there are four categories, by age and six; i.e., "Girls under Six," "Boys under Six," "Girls Six to Ten," "Boys Six to Ten."

As each person gives their interview results, there is often a high level of interest in the class. The students like to hear what the little children had to say for themselves; many of the answers are amusing or unexpected. "What are you most scared of?" "My big brother!" "Fish eyes!" "Ghosts!" "One Wish?" "To be able to beat up my older brother." "A Snoopy radio." "All the money in the world."

In looking for girl/boy patterns, it is best to start with the questions regarding the future and chores at home. On the question, "What do you want to be when you grow up?" our students got such results from the girls as: nurse, married, a mother, a teacher; and from the boys: basketball player, cowboy, cop, fireman. Although our students expected to find differences in aspirations between boys and girls, they were surprised by the definitiveness of these results. There wasn't one little girl, under six or over, who thought of herself in a traditionally male role, or one little boy who could imagine himself in a traditionally female role.

A marked differentiation also occurred around household chores. The little girls interviewed (particularly those six and over) all had tasks like setting the table, helping mother clean, making beds, doing dishes. The little boys (under and over six) often had no chores at all—or just taking out the trash. This brought forth a number of angry responses from students who remembered all too well the unfairness of that division of labor in the home.

The questions about school and teachers also elicited sex-differentiated responses, with age an additional factor. The girls of all ages had more favorable attitudes toward school and teachers than the boys, although the younger boys' responses were very similar to those of the girls.

A good summary for this activity is to ask the students whether they were surprised by any of the answers from the children. "Were the children interviewed like you, or different from you, at that age?"

4: Speaker on Sex-Role Patterns

If an appropriate speaker can be found, students might enjoy comparing what they have found from their interviews with the observations of someone who works with young children every day. Through your own personal contacts, or through students or parents who work as aides in day-care centers or kindergartens, you can probably find speakers who have a great deal to say about the differences in behavior of young girls and boys (see "Techniques," p. 31, for advice on how to locate and prepare speakers).

These speakers should be asked to tell about their experiences, focusing on the ways boys and girls act differently, reasons why this might be so, and examples of how they have tried to overcome some of these differences. Specific questions to ask a speaker include:

1. Do boys and girls play with the same kinds of toys?
2. Do boys and girls play more together, or separately?
3. Do boys and girls dress differently? Does this affect their play?
4. Are the teachers closer to the boys or to the girls?
5. Do girls or boys give up faster when something is hard to do?
6. Do girls fight with each other? Do boys? Do girls and boys fight with each other? Who starts fights?
7. Do the girls or boys act any differently when their parents are around?
8. Do any of these patterns change as the kids get older?

In looking for a speaker to answer these and related questions, it is more important to find someone who speaks the students' language and tunes in quickly to their interests, than to find a professional with a great deal of expertise. The point is to bring in someone who has daily classroom experience with young boys and girls, who is aware of the processes of sex-role socialization, and who has ideas about moving beyond traditional role boundaries.

5: Children's Books

In this activity, students move from examining and interpreting sex-role messages to creating their own. This is an important step to take. In the first two units, they see themselves, other people their age, and young children mainly as the passive recipients of these official messages. Now, in designing children's books, they are in the position of influencing other people. They have to figure out what messages they want children to receive.

This activity begins with students briefly looking over some children's books that present traditional sex roles. The teacher can find a sampling of these books in any children's library or school library; students can also be asked to bring such books from their homes. *I'm Glad I'm a Boy, I'm Glad I'm a Girl*, by Whitney Darrow Jr., and the *When I Grow Up* series, by Jean Bethell, are especially suitable for this purpose. There are numerous others that show typical American families divided into the typical male/female roles for adults and children.

The exercise reinforces and reviews some of the skills developed in the "Messages from Society" unit. Each student goes through one or two books, answering the following questions:

1. Is the main character a girl or boy?
2. How does she or he look? What does he or she wear?
3. What does the main character do, or what happens to her/him?
4. What is the main character interested in?
5. What kind of personality does the main character have?
6. Are there adults in the book? If so, who are they?
7. What are the adult women shown doing, saying, thinking, etc.?
8. What are adult men shown doing, saying, thinking, etc.?
9. What messages would a young girl reading this book get? A young boy?

It is possible to use a simpler format. Each student makes four lists: "Boys," "Girls," "Men,"

"Women." Under each heading, the student describes how these characters look, what they are shown doing or thinking, how they behave, etc.

Typical patterns emerge. Often girls are shown sitting, waiting patiently, watching. The more active ones might be playing with their dolls, cooking, helping mommy, or tagging along behind their brothers. Boys are pictured as having a more adventurous, active young life: climbing trees, playing sports, getting into mischief. Women are mostly mothers, housewives, maids, cooks, or occasionally, secretaries or nurses. Men are shown hurrying off to work, coming home at night to enjoy a family life, or taking their children out on the weekend. All of these are easy to pick out, in both the text and the pictures.

By now, none of this is new or surprising to the students. They have looked at enough magazines and TV, and have talked enough about societal messages to know what to expect. But we have found that for many students it was the children's books that drove the point home. Even though they could see sex-role messages in the media, they could not quite comprehend the extent to which they could affect people. It is easier to accept the susceptibility of children to these messages; it is more obvious that children's books are a form of indoctrination. This beginning part of the activity thus helps to bring together the skills that are being developed in the first two units of the curriculum.

Having acquired the skill of finding and labeling sex-role messages, students are now asked to use their imaginations to create their own children's books. We usually start them off with the directive to try to make up a story that will be different from the ones they have read and that will picture different kinds of young girls and boys. We ask them to think about what choices they would like to see open to their younger brothers and sisters. For students with more advanced writing skills, we might suggest changing a familiar fairy tale to make new points.

If anyone has a hard time coming up with an idea, we show her some new, alternative children's books to suggest approaches. (For example, every issue of Ms. has "Stories for Free Children"; The Feminist Press and Lollipop Power have put out series of liberating children's books.) But most people are able to draw upon experiences in their own lives. A student whose mother is a waitress who has taught herself carpentry in her spare time wrote "A Girl's Dream." This is the story of Lisa, who wants to be a carpenter, even though her brothers tell her to "go play with your dolls." With her mother's support, she studies carpentry in school, makes a beautiful bookcase, and wins the first prize in a woodworking contest—her own tool box. Other titles have included: "Melvin Wants to Be a Nurse," "My Only Best Brother," "Little Jack Riding Hood," "Baseball Is My Favorite Sport!" and "Emily Has Nine Wishes."

The students begin by choosing a topic and writing the rough draft of a story. In writing, they should keep in mind that they will want to illustrate it later. The teacher then goes over the draft with each student, trying to make the stories ready for "publication." The desire to produce complete, attractive children's books motivates the students to do careful corrections on their stories. It is a good chance to work with them on common spelling and grammatical mistakes (see "Techniques," p. 18).

The next step in the process is dividing the copy into short sections and then illustrating those sections. Looking at published children's books may help students get ideas for layout and illustrations. They should be reassured that the drawings can be very simple; even stick figures tell the story. Sometimes the students get so attached to their stories that they really want excellent illustrations, and they ask artistic friends to do these. We neither encourage nor discourage this. The point is for the students to use their creativity and to feel good about the finished products.

Reading over the finished books together serves two purposes. First, it gives everyone a sense of pride in their work and a collective sense of accomplishment. Second, each author can receive feedback about the sex-role messages conveyed by her book. After each student shows her book to the class, other students give their impressions of the messages. This gives everyone in the class a reason for listening carefully to each student's writing. Next, the author herself explains what she intended the messages to be. She has a chance to see whether she accomplished what she intended.

This process has resulted in some interesting discussions and, occasionally, in students' changing their stories. "Baseball Is My Favorite Sport" is about Judy, who thought "playing school, house, dolls, and mother were boring." Instead, she wished that "her brother Joey and the rest of the boys would let her play baseball." In the original version of the story, Judy's mother takes her to a psychiatrist (Dr. Elizabeth Reed), who reassures the mother that "this is all right now—that it is just a stage."

In the discussion, the author realized that the message people took away from the story was that girls outgrow their interest in sports. Her intention had been to make readers feel that it's good for girls to play baseball and that parents should support them in that desire.

In the rewritten version, the book concludes:

In fact, she [the psychiatrist] said that it was quite normal for Judy to play baseball and girls should play just as much as boys. So that afternoon, Judy's mother took her downtown to the department store and bought her a ball, bat, and glove to practice in her yard. [Colleen Long]

A good follow-up to this activity is to visit a day-care center or kindergarten where the students will be allowed to read their children's books to the children. They can then see first-hand how children respond to their stories.

III: GROWING UP FEMALE

OVERVIEW

Where Are All Your Heads At?

Let me know "where your head's at," because
I couldn't say where mine is right now.
I feel like it's blowing away.
I don't want that to happen.
  Maybe it don't like me.
  Maybe I don't like having one.
Your head is my head.
I feel like I have two.
  The strange head that's in mine, is really funny.
It's like a mother taking care of a baby,
teaching it what to do and how to talk.
It's like an egg too. You can't drop it because
you'll kill it and spoil everything that was growing.
It plays games with me. To see where I'm at.
It feels bad and tries to help. It laughs.
And tries to teach me what it knows. But I'm afraid
I can't talk to it, I'm only one but I feel like I'm four.
[Linda M. Cabral]

As young people feel themselves "growing up" and changing, they are excited and afraid, proud and ashamed. They experience new strengths, new depths, new conflicts within themselves and in their relationships. They go through personal struggles to understand and accept their physical changes. They deal with opposing pressures to become adults and remain children.

In this unit we explore what it is like to "grow up female"—from the time a child begins to walk, talk, and play, through the years of her puberty and adolescence. Because the scope of the unit is so large, we have divided the material into seven thematic sections, representing different stages, relationships, and institutions that a young woman experiences in her passage into adulthood: Childhood, Becoming a Woman, Family, Friends, School, Self, and Comparisons—Self and Others.

In the process of growing up female themselves, the students are, in a very real sense, experts on the subject matter. The content of the unit is very closely connected to their lives; the activities draw on their personal thoughts, feelings, and experiences. It would, however, be threatening, and somewhat limiting, for the main content of the unit to come entirely from students' own histories and current lives. Unlike many of the other units, where the problem is to make new and somewhat distant material more immediate and personal, the problem here is to help students look with some objectivity at material that is very immediate and personal.

We strongly advocate the use of novels, short stories, autobiographies, and plays to enrich and enlarge the explorations of this unit. The approach is to integrate discussions based on the readings with role-plays, writing assignments, charts, questionnaires, trips, and other activities that draw both on the readings and on personal experiences. The characters in the readings provide the students with mirrors through which they can examine themselves indirectly. Students can identify issues relevant to their lives, without having to acknowledge the parallels unless they want to. When the students learn that they share thoughts and feelings about the characters in the readings, they may feel more relaxed about volunteering stories from their own lives. As they compare responses to the readings, they make deepened discoveries about themselves and one another (see "Techniques," p. 13).

We have found four books to be especially readable and inspirational for a study of growing up female: *Anne Frank: The Diary of a Young Girl*, by Anne Frank; *Daddy Was a Number Runner*, by Louise Meriwether; *I Know Why the Caged Bird Sings*, by Maya Angelou;

and *A Tree Grows in Brooklyn*, by Betty Smith. Each of these books touches on many of the issues and themes of the unit—from the first games and fantasies of childhood to the later struggles of the young women to understand and accept their families and themselves. Any one (or combination) of these books could be selected for students to read during the duration of the unit. With many of the activities, we have provided a brief description of the way each of the books deals with the theme of the activity, along with a listing of the relevant page numbers. We also use a passage from one of the books to illustrate how the reading might enrich the discussion or connect to the suggested activity. In a few cases, where one of the four books explores an important theme especially well, we suggest you use the excerpt we quote from, no matter what book your class might be reading as a whole. For the most part, however, the excerpted passages are there to give you a sense of how to integrate the activity with a reading from any of the four books.

Several activities in the unit are built around additional readings—short stories, a play, chapters from anthropology books, and poems—selected for their pertinence to specific issues or themes. These readings include: "I Stand Here Ironing" and "O Yes" from the collection *Tell Me a Riddle* by Tillie Olsen; two chapters from Margaret Mead's *Growing Up in New Guinea*; and *A Taste of Honey* by Shelagh Delaney. If, because of time constraints, the availability of materials, or the particular focus of your course, you do not want to assign whole books, you could make use of the additional readings, as well as the excerpts from the four books, quoted within the text of the activities. Many of the excerpts describe provocative and relevant experiences that can stand on their own. If you are going to utilize an "excerpt approach," you should try to find one copy of each of the books, in case you want to expand on any of the excerpts we have selected or provide the students with more background on the setting or characters.

The amount of reading you assign, the balance of in-class reading aloud and outside

assignments will depend on your particular situation and educational goals. By dividing the unit into seven major thematic sections, each containing numerous activities and suggested readings, we have tried to make the unit as flexible as possible. If most of the suggested readings are used, this unit could be taught as a semester-long literature course. With the addition of some novels about growing up male (i.e. *Manchild in the Promised Land*, by Claude Brown; *Studs Lonigan*, by James T. Farrell; or *The Autobiography of Malcolm X*), many of the activities could be adapted to a mixed group. Using the material somewhat differently, you could integrate it into a psychology or sociology curriculum. Finally, if you are teaching a discussion group, of the type we describe in Unit V, "Sexuality," you could use many of the activities to spark discussions in that group.

COMPARATIVE SUMMARIES OF THE BOOKS

The four books provide a range in reading level and length as well as immediate relationship to the current lives of the students. A comparative summary of the books follows.

Anne Frank: The Diary of a Young Girl is the actual diary of Anne Frank, a thirteen to fifteen year old hiding from the Nazis. Anne writes with great sensitivity about the process of coming into womanhood. There are entries on her changing relationship with her family, the changes in her body, and her beginning romance with Peter, whose family shares her hiding place. It is an honest and self-conscious exploration of issues that pertain to becoming a woman.

The setting, a secret hideout in Amsterdam, is alien, and might be hard for your students to imagine. While the book is relatively short (258 pages) and the language is not difficult, there are a fair number of unfamiliar words. On the whole, it is on about the same reading level as *A Tree Grows in Brooklyn*. Many of the diary entries can be used on their own to introduce activities or provoke discussions. There is a dramatized version of Anne Frank's story which is short and easy to read aloud.

While it's more accessible, it lacks the power of Anne's own writing.

Daddy Was a Number Runner, by Louise Meriwether, is the story of Francie Coffin, growing up poor and Black in Harlem. Although the setting is in the thirties, the events and characters seem current. Francie has a sensible, hard-working mother, and a charming father who is the neighborhood number runner. Her parents fight continually through her childhood, until finally her father moves out to live with another woman. Her brothers are members of the Ebony Earls, the toughest street gang around.

Written mainly in street language, and only 188 pages long, the book is accessible to students at all reading levels. Many of our students have enjoyed reading and discussing this book. On the whole, however, it presents a more discouraging picture of growing up than any of the others and is also less self-reflective.

I Know Why the Caged Bird Sings is an autobiography of Maya Angelou's childhood and adolescence. The action moves back and forth— from the South, where Maya is brought up by her grandmother, to St. Louis, where she lives with her mother for a while, to San Francisco and Los Angeles, where she rejoins her mother and then her father as she becomes a teen-ager. From the very first page, Maya shares her awareness of what it was to grow up Black, as well as female.

The book is full of vividly described experiences and adventures, from the joys of stealing pickles from her grandmother's store to the trauma of being raped by her mother's boyfriend. There is some vocabulary that will be new to students, but on the whole, the style is direct and the material very interesting and constantly changing. The 246 pages move quickly.

A Tree Grows in Brooklyn, by Betty Smith, recounts the childhood and adolescence of Francie Nolan, a poor Irish girl growing up in Brooklyn, New York at the turn of the century. Even though the setting is not current, many of Francie's experiences are. Her father, Johnny, is a singing waiter whose life disintegrates and comes to an early end through his ever more frequent bouts with alcoholism. Her mother, Katie, is a cleaning woman and manages the household in a struggle to ensure the family's emotional and economic survival. Francie combines her father's imagination with her mother's pragmatism.

There is a romantic cast to the story. Although Francie suffers many harsh experiences, things have a way of working out for the best. While we recommend it strongly, some of our students have had difficulty reading the book because of the descriptive detail. However, once they've made it through the opening chapters, which are particularly rich in description, they are enthralled by the story. It is the longest of the books (430 pages).

CHILDHOOD

INTRODUCTION

My eyes have not awakened yet
to the craziness of your world.

My mind is not yet wide enough
to fill it with your wisdom.

My hands are not yet strong enough
to hold your thoughts and dreams.

My voice is not yet loud enough
so you can't hear me crying.

[Robbin Luzaitis]

Most students enjoy remembering childhood experiences. This thematic section gives them the opportunity to reminisce about their childhoods, while suggesting new ways of looking at the experiences and events of that period in their lives. This exploration of childhood lays the groundwork for the rest of the unit. Because childhood is sufficiently remote, few students feel threatened by sharing personal experiences from this period. This section helps to establish an atmosphere of openness for later sections of the unit, where the material is more connected to their immediate concerns.

This section also helps to launch students in their reading. Both *A Tree Grows in Brooklyn* and *I Know Why the Caged Bird Sings* begin with the childhoods of their main characters. In *Daddy Was a Number Runner*, Francie is twelve, just beginning to move out of her childhood. In all three books evocative childhood episodes are described. *Anne Frank: The Diary of a Young Girl* starts with Anne's "becoming a woman" and, therefore, is best introduced in the next section. The activities in this unit can accompany first assignments in any of the other three books.

In the first activity, students decide "What's Special about Childhood." The second activity focuses on a child's changing feelings about and experiences with her body. Words that describe aspects of childhood, particularly parent/child relationships, are taught in a vocabulary and role-play exercise. In the next activity, students explore first experiences with the inequities and prejudices of the adult world. Finally, students are asked to do a writing assignment that ties together some of the memories and themes of childhood.

ACTIVITIES

1: What's Special about Childhood

Each day in a child's life marks new discoveries about her world and what it means to be a person. In this activity, we recall some of that beginning sense of discovery through reading a poem about childhood and making a chart of *How, Who, and What's Special About Childhood*.

The poem, from *Daughters in High School*, an anthology of high school writings published by Daughters, Inc., edited by Frieda Singer, expresses the author's regret at the loss of her childhood.

I wanted to hold it—
hug it tightly
but they were around and I was afraid
so I picked it up

and ran with it hidden
underneath my shirt
closed the door
and on my bed
carefully took it out—
so limp in my hands—
I brushed the dust off
took my childhood into my hands and wept.
[P. 4]

Most of our students have liked this poem. All of them have been just as sure as the author that childhood was over for them. Reading it over together gives everyone a chance to express some initial general feelings about childhood.

When we asked why the author wept, our students began to talk about themselves. Some shared in her grieving: "She's sad not to be a kid anymore." "Things are more fun when you're little." "You don't have so many responsibilities." "When you're a kid nobody bothers you." Others expressed relief to be finished with childhood. "I like knowing more about what's going on." "Now I can hang around and go out on my own."

The second part of this activity moves students to talk more specifically. Together, the class makes a large chart of *How, Who, and What's Special about Childhood*. A chart, such as the one below, helps students to formulate their ideas:

How, Who, and What's Special About Childhood

HOW does a young child play?
1.
2.
3.

WHO are the important people in her life?
1.
2.
3.

WHAT are the important firsts?
Events:
1.
2.
3.
4.

Things she learns how to do:
1.
2.

3.

4.

Things she learns about life and the world:

1.

2.

3.

4.

This is the kind of listing exercise that the whole class contributes to. You can go around the room getting additions from everyone, including students who don't usually talk up. When you talk about the "important firsts," encourage students to try to remember "firsts" which were the most exciting, most frightening, or firsts that changed them the most. "Being born," "Christmas" and "Getting a First Spanking" have been some of the important first events our students have described. "Things she learns about life and the world" is the hardest to develop, yet the richest list. Our lists have included: "that you can't always get your way," "that a lot of people are prejudiced," and "that everybody dies." Making this chart together serves as a good introduction to the themes and issues of the rest of the Childhood section.

2: A Child's Body, Her Home

Relevant Readings from the Books

Daddy Was A Number Runner: Francie's early sexual experiences are negative. The boys on the street tease her with catcalls (p. 15). Neighborhood merchants offer special prices in exchange for a chance to fondle her (p. 41). A pervert follows her to parks and movies (p. 16).

I Know Why the Caged Bird Sings: Maya's childhood experiences with sex range from a traumatic rape at age eight (pp. 60–74) to embarrassment and delight at receiving her first valentine (pp. 120–123).

A Tree Grows in Brooklyn: Francie's Aunt Sissy is her first positive model of a woman who enjoys sexuality (pp. 39–41, 107–109). Francie's first personal experience is traumatic, however, when she is nearly attacked by a pervert (pp. 213–232).

A child lives comfortably in her body. As she grows up, a girl is often dressed in constraining clothes and discouraged from running, jumping, or building things with her hands. Sometimes her body is treated like an object, and she begins to see it that way, too. In this activity we discuss the way a child lives in her body; we examine the pressures which may cause her to become distant from her body as she gets older. The focus is on a child's early experiences with her own body and sexuality.

We suggest you begin this activity with a short reading from *Our Bodies, Ourselves*, by the Boston Women's Health Book Collective. Although three of the books deal with early sexuality, the negative experiences are not balanced by the positive. To introduce a positive approach to a child's sexuality, we read aloud this description of a young child:

> I watch my daughter. From morning to night her body is her home. She lives in it and with it. When she runs around the kitchen she uses all of herself. Every muscle in her body moves when she laughs, when she cries. When she rubs her crotch, there is no awkwardness, no feeling that what she is doing is wrong. She feels pleasure and expresses it without hesitation. She knows when she wants to be touched and when she wants to be left alone. She doesn't have to think about it—it's a very direct physical asking or responding to someone else. It's beautiful to be with her. I sometimes feel that she is more a model for me than I am for her! Occasionally I feel jealous of the ease with which she lives inside her skin. I want to be a child again! It's so hard to get back that sense of body as home. [P. 24]

Students find this excerpt meaningful; at the same time, it arouses feelings which are not easily discussed. The teacher needs to be aware that she is on sensitive ground, even while encouraging the students to share some of their responses. "Does this description seem accurate?" "How old do you think the child is?" "What does it mean to say 'her body is her home?'" Have the students generate a list together of the ways a child shows that she is "at home in her body." They can draw from the examples in the reading as well as from their own observations.

When, how, and why do young women often lose their early sense of being at home in their bodies? Many females use their bodies less as they get older; their bodies become more foreign to them. The students are encouraged to reflect on their own experiences, particularly on the ways they were influenced by the media, families, and teachers. "I wasn't allowed to get dirty." "They wouldn't let us run in the halls at school." "Girls were supposed to be 'little ladies.' " 'Kids made fun of me because I was strong, and I could lift heavy things."

In the next part of the activity (which may take place the next day), we focus specifically on a child's early experiences of having her body viewed as an object. We point out that some people act as if they have the right to stare at, touch, or comment on a girl's body. The students share memories of hearing, "Oh, isn't she cute," being "chucked under the chin," or "patted on the bottom."

To deepen the discussion, the class could read aloud a passage from whichever of the books they have started. For instance, in *A Tree Grows in Brooklyn*, Francie allows the junk peddler to pinch her cheek, and receives a penny as a reward:

> Carney liked girls better than boys. He would give a girl an extra penny if she did not shrink when he pinched her cheek.
> Because of the possibility of this bonus, Neely stepped aside and let Francie drag the bag into the stable. . . . As she whispered, "thank you," Carney fixed a rusty junked look on her and pinched her cheek hard. She stood her ground. He smiled and added an extra penny. . . .
> Francie went outside to report to her brother. "He gave me sixteen cents and a pinching penny."
> That's your penny," he said, according to an old agreement. [P. 10]

We ask the students how they imagine Francie felt when Carney pinched her cheek or when he gave her the pinching penny. Some insist, "She got one over on him," while others disagree, "It was him who was ripping her off." Important questions are raised: "How does it feel to get a reward for allowing your body to be treated as an object?" "Even if it's in a minor way, does it affect your sense of yourself?" We

suggest that this kind of interaction can make a girl growing up feel less comfortable with her own body, which is rightfully her home.

3: Vocabulary and Parent/Child Role-Play

This vocabulary exercise is designed to give students new words to describe aspects of childhood, particularly relationships between children and parents. The word list we have used has included: inventive, spontaneous, inhibited, precocious, immature, mature, protective, permissive, supportive, authoritarian, console. Many others could be added, depending on the level of your students' current vocabulary.

We usually follow the definitions with two or three short exercises that reinforce learning these new words (see "Techniques," p. 23). The next step is to make up questions that link these words to the preceding activities. For instance:

1. Give three examples of ways that a young child is usually *spontaneous* in her actions.
2. How does an *authoritarian* adult make a child feel?
3. Give some examples of things an *inventive* child might do with her time.

In answering these questions, students are not only learning correct ways to use the new words, but are also gaining new insights into early memories and feelings.

In studying childhood, we explore the question of what a child needs from her parents. In reading *A Tree Grows in Brooklyn*, *I Know Why the Caged Bird Sings*, and *Daddy Was a Number Runner*, we look at the way the adults support or fail to support the children in their growing up. A number of the words we selected for this vocabulary exercise can be used to designate ways in which adults relate to children. The question of the degree to which parents should protect their children is particularly relevant as we explore the dangers for a child of growing up in the city.

We have developed a role-play through which students can explore their own points of view about the issue of parental protection. In doing this role-play, students will reinforce the vocabulary and learn something about their own attitudes.

> You are Anne Smith, ten years old. It is a very hot summer evening, around 7:30 P.M., and you want to go out to a nearby playground with a girlfriend. So you go to tell your mom.

> You are Mrs. Smith. You have five children ranging in age from five to fifteen, and you're always worried about something happening to one of them. You worry that it is dangerous in your neighborhood, particularly at night, and that the other kids will keep yours out late.

One student is assigned the role of Anne, another of Mrs. Smith. Or you might take one of the roles (see "Techniques," p. 27, for a fuller description of how to set up the role-play). Mother and daughter confront each other at the door, as Anne is on her way out.

One of the good things about this role-play is that in discussing the situation the class can be encouraged to use as many of the vocabulary words as possible. Is Mrs. Smith being *protective*? If she lets Anne go out is she *permissive*? Does Anne feel her mother was acting *authoritarian*? Does Anne feel her mother was *supportive*? Was Anne acting *mature*? *immature*?

A good way to end the activity is by having everyone think about what a parent can and should protect a young daughter from. What limits make sense and what don't? Our students choose curfews ranging from 6 P.M., to 9:30 P.M., to none at all. Some had strong feelings that they would want their daughters to learn to protect themselves and stand up for themselves, because, in the long run, that was all that would work. Others had equally strong feelings that a parent who lets her children do whatever they want isn't showing love for them. Everyone agreed that it isn't easy to be a supportive parent—or to figure out what it really means to be supportive. Students came out of the role-play and discussion without answers, but with new words to help them in thinking through the questions.

4: Pride—No More Name-Calling

Relevant Readings from the Books

Daddy Was a Number Runner: The Coffins, living in the Harlem of the Depression, suffer severe hardships: hunger, police harassment, and degrading treatment by "Madame Queen," the social worker from welfare. Their tremendous struggle to hold onto their pride—both in their family and their Black heritage—is most clearly revealed in the father's confrontations with Madame Queen. Their first encounter leaves him furious: "That ain't her goddamn money she's givin' out, you know" (p. 78). The second makes him tired and more resigned (pp. 90-91).

I Know Why the Caged Bird Sings: Growing up in the South in the 1930's, Maya accepts race divisions and racism as a way of life. Her first serious personal confrontation with racism, however, when she is working as a kitchen maid for a white woman, enrages her to the point of revenge (pp. 87–93).

A Tree Grows in Brooklyn: As a poor Irish girl growing up in Brooklyn just after the turn of the century, Francie experiences class prejudice. In school she encounters a teacher who favors the children of the prosperous storekeepers of the neighborhood (pp. 133–141). When she needs a vaccination, she is insulted by the doctor and the nurse at the neighborhood Health Center (pp.128-130).

"Some people are really ignorant." More than one of our students has described patronizing or insulting treatment by the more privileged in this way. In this activity, we talk about a child's early experiences in coping with prejudice.

A good place to begin is with a discussion of name-calling. What are some of the insulting names applied to young people? Students can easily volunteer current insults: "Pea brain," "Dirty slob," "Punk," "Nigger." What are other names for various racial or ethnic groups? Our students, who are primarily Irish and Italian in background, have volunteered "Mick," "Wop," "Polack," "Chink," and "Spick." How does a child feel when she is called a name? Encourage the class to give as many reasons as they can think of for people calling one another names. "To put them down" or "So you can feel you got one over on them" are among the ideas voiced by students. We point out that some name-calling is indirect. For instance, when a teacher continues to send a student to the principal, the teacher may be indirectly naming that student "troublemaker."

Reading aloud a passage from one of the books provides more content for the discussion. Whichever book your class is reading, we suggest reading aloud excerpts from *I Know Why the Caged Bird Sings* and/or *A Tree Grows in Brooklyn.* In both these selections, the young woman insists on regaining her pride when she suffers from race or class discrimination.

For instance, in *I Know Why the Caged Bird Sings*, Maya is enraged when her employer renames her "Mary," discarding her given name, "Marguerite," as "too long," on the suggestion of a "speckle-faced" tea guest.

> Every person I knew had a hellish horror of being "called out of his name." It was a dangerous practice to call a Negro anything that could be loosely construed as insulting because of the centuries of their having been called niggers, jigs, dingos, blackbirds, crows, boots and spooks. [P. 91]

One day Maya takes her revenge on her employer, Mrs. Cullinan. She carefully breaks all of Mrs. Cullinan's favorite glass and tea china.

> Mrs. Cullinan cried..."That clumsy nigger. Clumsy little black nigger."
>
> Old speckled-face [Mrs. Cullinan's tea guest] leaned down and asked, "Who did it, Viola? Was it Mary? Who did it?"
>
> Everything was happening so fast I can't remember whether her action preceded her words, but I know that Mrs. Cullinan said, "Her name's Margaret, goddamn it, her name's Margaret!" And she threw a wedge of broken plate at me....I left the front door open so all the neighbors could hear.
>
> Mrs. Cullinan was right about one thing. My name wasn't Mary. [P. 93]

In the excerpt from *A Tree Grows in Brooklyn*, Francie and her brother, Neely, go to

the Health Center covered with dirt, after spending the morning making mud pies. As Francie receives her shot she listens to the doctor talking to the nurse:

> "Filth, filth, filth, from morning to night. I know they're poor, but they could wash. Water is free and soap is cheap. Just look at that arm, nurse...."
>
> The nurse was a Williamsburg girl....She didn't want anyone to know she had come from the slums....
>
> "I know. Isn't it terrible? I sympathize with you, Doctor. There is no excuse for these people living in filth."
>
> When the needle jabbed, Francie never felt it. The waves of hurt started by the doctor's words were racking her body and drove out all other feeling.... While the nurse was expertly tying a strip of gauze around her arm... Francie spoke up.
>
> "My brother is next. His arm is just as dirty as mine so don't be surprised. And you don't have to tell him. You told me." They stared at this pit of humanity who had become so strangely articulate. Francie's voice went ragged with a sob. "You don't have to tell him. Besides it won't do no good. He's a boy and he don't care if he is dirty." [pp. 129-130]

After reading aloud one of the excerpts, you can relate the incident described to the introductory discussion. Why did Mrs. Cullinan rename Maya (Marguerite) as "Mary?" What attitude did she have towards Maya? How did Maya feel? In *A Tree Grows in Brooklyn*, the doctor's name-calling is less direct. You can ask the students to list some unstated names the doctor might have been giving Francie. Our students have suggested "Filthy slob" or "Cockroach," among others. How did Francie feel about herself and about the doctor and nurse when she heard them talking?

In the last part of the discussion, it is important to explore the ways Maya and Francie regained their pride. How would Maya have felt if she had continued to ignore the slur? How did she probably feel when she broke the dishes, or when she heard Mrs. Cullinan say, "Her name is Margaret, goddamn it"? What were Francie's feelings when she spoke up to the doctor and nurse? How would she have felt if she had pretended not to hear them? Both incidents can lead to a debate about whether you can affect people's attitudes when you stand up to them.

Follow-up activities include teaching related vocabulary (pride, condescend, patronize, defy, offend) or doing related role-plays. One role-play involves a conflict between Maya and Mrs. Cullinan's loyal old housekeeper, Glory (who used to be Halleluia before *she* was renamed). In another role-play, Francie confronts the nurse, who is on her way to pay a visit to her own family in Francie's neighborhood.

5: Writing about Childhood

Memories of childhood make good writing assignments. Students are called upon to recreate a period and a mood; they are asked to describe experiences they now understand better than when they happened. It is a challenging, and yet possible, task. Some students find it difficult to write directly about themselves. But if given the chance to write about a character in a book, or about "a child," they may include a great deal of their own feelings and experiences. Others find it easier to write directly from their own experiences. We always try to give students a choice of entry points in our writing assignments (see "Techniques," p. 19). In this unit, a writing assignment might include choices like these:

> Select one of the following writing assignments. Try to use at least two of the new vocabulary words in writing your paper.
>
> 1. Describe an early memory of a time when you were happy or excited, when you were scared, when you were angry.
> 2. Describe a child (yourself if you want) experiencing something for the first time, learning to do something new, or gaining a new understanding about life. Examples: going to school, making a first friend, learning to talk, finding out about death.
> 3. Imagine you are Maya in the ten minutes before you break the dishes. You are in the kitchen cleaning up. What are all the thoughts that go through your head as you build up to take action?
> 4. Imagine a child "at home in her body." Describe all the ways she uses her body at play during a day. Include details of how she feels as she moves around. Be specific: How does she feel in her toes, in her stomach, in her knees, etc.? What are the sounds, textures, tastes, colors that she notices?

Students should always be given the option of developing their own topics. Sometimes we encourage students to write about topics that they bring up in class. For instance, we asked one student to write a paper starting with the line, "They called me a tomboy," after she had made that statement one day in the class.

BECOMING A WOMAN

INTRODUCTION

> I used to be a cat, but now I'm a tiger.
> I used to be a bike, but now I'm a car.
> I used to be a pebble, but now I'm a rock.
> I used to be garbage, but now I'm a basket.
> I used to be a stove, but now I'm a refrigerator.
> I used to be a heater, but now I'm the Sun.
> I used to be a seed, but now I'm a big Redwood tree.
> I used to be a child, but now I'm a woman.
> [Cheryl Burke]

The transition from being a child to being a woman is exciting and often confusing. Young women experience secret feelings of excitement, pride, and sometimes shame, in their sexuality.

In this section we try to help students explore their ambivalences about "becoming a woman," and gain more awareness of both their positive and negative feelings about their bodies. Most young women do not have the opportunity to share the feelings they experience at puberty. The structured pairing exercise of the first activity gives students a framework in which to reflect on their feelings about themselves, their changed and changing lives and bodies. The second activity focuses directly on menstruation, the shared point of transition into womanhood.

ACTIVITIES

6: Pairing Exercise

The activity begins with students making a list together of the changes they experienced which made them feel they were becoming women. At first students feel awkward in adding to the list, but as they note their commonalities and relax with one another, they begin to enjoy sharing their recollections. "I started spending a lot of time in front of the mirror." "I got a cute little figure." "I got my 'friend' and gained weight." "I started wanting guys to notice me." "I started dressing."

After generating a list, divide the students into pairs, to continue the discussion one-to-one. We usually make an attempt to break down natural friendship groupings. This helps build the class into a closer, more comfortable group. The two people in each pair interview each other, using suggested questions. They are told that the questions should be used to get them started; they don't need to answer them all, and they can add their own.

Either the teacher prepares a list of questions, or the class develops a list together. We use variations on the following list:

1. When are the times in your life when you feel most like a woman?
2. Are there times when you feel unaware of your sex? When?

3. Is it harder or easier to be a child or a young woman? Why?
4. In becoming a woman did your relationships with other females change? How?
5. In becoming a young woman did your relationships with males change? How?
6. Were you more comfortable with boys or girls when you were a child? How about now?
7. In becoming a young woman did your relationship with your family change? How?
8. Has your relationship with yourself changed? How?

The group comes back together for a general discussion based on the questions. If there is time, each member of a pair introduces the other, using some of the information from the interview. This structure encourages the students to listen carefully during interviews. If a class is too large and there isn't enough time for the introductions, the students can still draw on what they learned during their own interviews in the ensuing discussion.

The general discussion flows easily after these interviews. To get started a teacher can ask: "Which questions did you most enjoy discussing?" "Did any of the answers surprise you?" "What are some of the things you seem to have in common?"

When we've done this exercise, students have expressed the full range of feelings about becoming women. "Your parents want you to act responsible and adult, but don't always treat you that way." "I like going out and lookin' good." "I could do without getting my 'friend.' " "I like knowing I can have kids." "I don't feel like a woman when I get drunk, take out the garbage, or when I go to work." "I never forget I'm a woman. Never."

7: Changing Body, Changing Self— A Reading on Menstruation

Relevant Readings from the Books

Anne Frank: The Diary of a Young Girl: Anne turns from a little girl into a young woman in her years in the "secret annex." Privately, she rejoices in getting her period and in her developing breasts (p.117).

Daddy Was a Number Runner: Francie grows up quickly, without many comfortable cushions or explanations. When she gets her period, her mother hands her a torn sheet and two safety pins and tells her, "Francie, this means you're growing up . . . . It means don' let no boys mess around with you. Understand? (pp. 73–74)

A Tree Grows in Brooklyn: Francie's first period is very traumatic for her. On the day that she gets her period, she watches the "good" women in the neighborhood stone a young mother with her illegitimate child. She thinks the bleeding means that she will die for her silent complicity in this act. Her mother rescues her with warmth and understanding (pp. 208–209).

For many young women, menstruation is a mysterious and taboo subject. They may have picked up vague bits of information from older sisters, friends, perhaps from mothers or other older relatives, but usually they acquire little or no understanding of what causes the bleeding, why it stops, or why it sometimes hurts. When they first menstruate, some young women are excited, some embarrassed, and others scared. Because it is an important shared turning point, rarely explained and often misunderstood, we always take time to focus on feelings about beginning menstruation.

Any of the three selections mentioned above provides a good starting point for a discussion of menstruation. We have found that the entry in *Anne Frank: Diary of a Young Girl* is particularly useful for getting at positive feelings not usually expressed about menstruation.

I think that what is happening to me is so wonderful, and not only what can be seen on my body, but all that is taking place inside. I never discuss myself, or any of these things with anybody; that is why I have to talk to myself about them. Each time I have a period—and that has been only three times—I have the feeling that in spite of all the pain, unpleasantness, and nastiness, I have a sweet secret, and that is why, although it is nothing but a nuisance to me in a way, I always long for the time that I shall feel that secret with me again. [P. 117]

After reading aloud this entry the students talk about themselves through discussing Anne Frank. We ask, "Do Anne's feelings seem real to you?" Some identify with her excitement. "I'd been waiting for it. All my friends had it and I was glad." Others reject Anne's description as too positive. "I felt nasty." Often students like to tell stories about the first time they got their periods. "I had to go home from school. There was blood on my pants and everyone could see it." "I freaked out. 'Maaaaaa, what's this?' " "I knew what it was, and I knew where my older sister kept the pads, so I just figured it out myself and didn't tell anyone."

A discussion of first menstruation sometimes evokes an interest in further discussions around the physiology of menstruation and other physical changes during puberty. (For further suggestions on discussion of these topics, see Unit V, "Sexuality," p. 140.) Even if you don't plan to follow up with further discussions of the physiology, we suggest that you prepare yourself for the discussion of first menstruation by reading pages 33-37 in *Our Bodies, Ourselves,* and have a copy available for reference in the classroom. If students air misconceptions, you can counter the myths with facts. Hearing the facts can be very comforting to students.

Some myths surface year after year in our classes. Many students worry that they may be freaks because they menstruated too early or too late, or because they haven't yet begun to menstruate. "I thought I was a boy until I was seventeen. I hung around with the guys and was really into sports. I think that's why I didn't get it 'til last year." They are relieved to learn that it is normal to begin to menstruate any time between nine and eighteen. Some worry that their cycles are abnormal. We assure them that no one is absolutely "normal." While the average is twenty eight days, normal cycles range from twenty to thirty six days. Small fluctuations are to be expected, and big changes can occur when a woman is under a lot of stress. "I didn't get my period for a couple of months one time when I thought I was pregnant," one student agreed. Some students have heard that you can't use tampons until you have had intercourse. We explain to them the hyman has usually been stretched through everyday exercise, and that there is ordinarily an opening where a tampon may be inserted.

There are many myths about the way you are supposed to treat yourself during your period. "When I've got my 'friend' my mother lets me stay home from school." To counter these myths, if they come up in the discussion, we read aloud from *Our Bodies, Ourselves*:

There is no evidence to indicate that you should stay in bed, avoid exercise, refrain from sexual intercourse, or observe any of the other taboos surrounding menstruation. However, if doing something makes you feel bad, it's only common sense to avoid doing it. [P. 19]

FAMILY

INTRODUCTION

Listen to me.
I know I am young and my words they aren't wise
As the words you use
But they are my words
Speak to me.

Not like a mother speaking to her child,
But more like friends,
Or at least equals.

Don't look down on me because you are older.
Look across.

See me as I am.
Love me.
For what I am,
Not what I could be
Not what you want me to be.

[Pat Connolly]

In this section, we try to help students get in touch with the important role of the family in a young person's growing up, we help them to understand both the closeness and the conflicts which characterize family relationships. The activities explore the interaction of the entire family, while focusing on the relationships between a young woman and her mother, her father, and her siblings. A child's first relationships are with her parents and siblings. In part, she learns to be a woman by imitating her mother; learns about men from the first man in her life—her father. As she enters adolescence, however, she often needs to rebel against her mother and/or father in order to become herself.

Adolescence is usually the period when family relationships undergo the most strain. As one of our students described the situation: "They'll say to you: 'You're not a baby anymore; act your age; get a job; do this; do that.' Then, the next minute, it's: 'Don't stay out late; don't get into trouble; don't skip school.' Like you're a little kid, with no mind of your own." For poor and **working-class young women growing up in the** city, the contradiction becomes acute. On the one hand, they experience family pressures to take on more responsibilities, such as caring for younger brothers and sisters, or earning money to contribute to the family. On the other hand, they may find their actions more restricted by parents who are worried about the dangers and temptations of the city streets.

Through making a diagram of family relationships in one of the books, and doing a vocabulary exercise using words that describe relationships, the students gain new tools for examining family interactions. They study mothers and daughters through reading "I Stand Here **Ironing,"** doing mother/daughter role-plays, interviewing their own mothers, reading *A Taste* *of Honey.* They look at father/daughter relation–ships through readings and a questionnaire.

ACTIVITIES

8: Family Chart—What Holds Us Together or Divides Us?

Relevant Readings from the Books

Anne Frank: The Diary of a Young Girl: The Frank family, through cooperation and inventiveness, and despite interpersonal conflicts, is determined to outlive the outrage that imprisons them. The entire book lends itself to an exploration of family unity and division. Anne's description of her family's emergency preparation for a police raid is a good sample (pp. 179–187).

Daddy Was a Number Runner: The Coffins are fiercely loyal to one another, in the midst of ongoing conflicts. Daddy binds the family together through keeping them proud in their Black heritage (pp. 74–77) and reviving family spirits (pp. 61–68). In the end, building pressures (Daddy's bust, the lack of legitimate work, humiliating and unjust treatment from relief, turmoil in the lives of the two sons) divide the family; both James Junior and Daddy have moved out.

I Know Why the Caged Bird Sings: Maya and her brother Bailey are shuttled among various branch-es of the family, from the southern matriarch, Momma, to Grandmother Baxter in Detroit, and finally to California, back and forth between their beautiful mother and father. Each branch takes them in and nurtures them; no one can quite make up for the childhood hurt they experienced, shipped off at ages three and four to their grand-mother's, when their parents' calamitous marriage ended.

The book as a whole raises discussion questions around the responsibility of family members to one another; parents to their children (pp. 42–50, 191–213), grandparents to grandchildren (pp. 21–27, 156–164), and brothers and sisters to each other (pp. 17–19, 218–224).

A Tree Grows in Brooklyn: Francie's mother, Katie, holds the family together in fighting through hard-ships. The Nolans survive their poverty through

tenacity and resourcefulness, pulling in their belts and using every ounce of imagination (pp. 41–43, 48–51, 74–88). Sometimes pressures to make ends meet demand sacrifice and provoke conflicts (pp. 337–341).

This activity sets a context for further discus-sions of family relationships. Drawing on both readings and personal experiences, we explore some fundamental questions about the family as a whole: "What holds a family together?" "What divides a family?" "What does a family gain through solidarity?" "What does a divided fami-ly lose?" Following the initial discussion, the class makes a chart of family relationships and interactions, based on any of the suggested books.

We have used the following excerpt from *Daddy Was a Number Runner* for a discussion about family pride:

That night everybody was home and we sat around the living room. Junior and Sterling were beating each other at checkers and Daddy was playing the piano.

Mother was sewing on a nineteenth century coat her Jewish lady had given her for me. . . . I swore I wouldn't wear it. . . . My protests were loud but useless. We all knew that when the wind got to whipping around those corners I'd be glad to put that coat on to keep my butt from freezing.

Suddenly Daddy swung around on the piano stool. "Y'all listen to me," he said. "The social worker is gonna interview us tomorrow so we can get on relief. Now this ain't nothing to be ashamed of. People all over the country are catching hell, same as we are and . . . Well, what I want to say is never forget where you come from." . . . "Your great-great grandmother Yoruba was the only daughter of Danakil, the tribal king of Madagascar." [P. 74]

After reading this passage aloud, the class is asked to discuss the way Daddy's pride in the Black heritage of the family helps support them through their economic crisis.

In the next part of the activity, we look more specifically at the variety of relationships and feelings within a family. Students are asked to make color-coded charts of relationships within

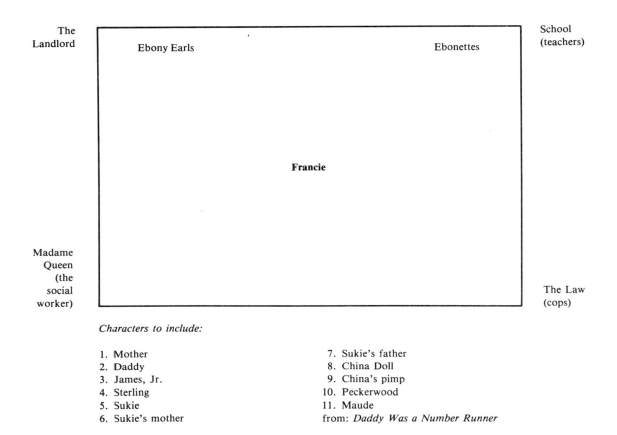

Poverty (depression, no jobs, etc.)

The Landlord

Ebony Earls   Ebonettes

School (teachers)

Francie

Madame Queen (the social worker)

The Law (cops)

Characters to include:

1. Mother
2. Daddy
3. James, Jr.
4. Sterling
5. Sukie
6. Sukie's mother

7. Sukie's father
8. China Doll
9. China's pimp
10. Peckerwood
11. Maude

from: *Daddy Was a Number Runner*

the family, including important family friends or enemies. The chart should be based on the family relationships and friendships in the life of the young woman in the book the class is currently reading. We have found that such a chart provides a valuable visual aid for talking about both the family as a whole and the dynamics between individuals.

The students are given mimeographed sheets on which the basic structure of the chart is clearly drawn [see diagram above].

The task is to fill in the chart according to their own interpretations of the book. Students make individual versions of the chart to keep in their notebooks, while the teacher makes a large chart which is posted and used for reference in future discussions. The basic chart structure sets a framework for drawing in relationships: the name of the hero of the book is circled in the center. The names of the important institutions which affect the life of her family are placed around the edge of the page, forming a square. These might include: the school, the law, the unemployment office, etc. At the bottom of the page, members of her family and other key characters are listed.

The first task is to place the family members and other key characters on the chart at the appropriate distance from one another in order to represent their relative importance in each other's lives. After the students have completed this step in making their charts, they share their interpretations while the teacher makes a big newsprint chart at the front of the room.

The group is now ready to diagram the feelings which characterize these relationships. To make this fun and easy, we hand out red, green, blue, and purple colored pencils to all of the students. We tell the class that *red* represents anger, *green* represents fear, *blue* represents love, and *purple* represents respect. An arrow in one of the colors from one family member to one of the others indicates how the first character feels toward the second; an arrow the other way indicates how the second character feels toward the first. The students are encouraged to make arrows in several colors if they see fit. For example, a given hero might both love (*blue*) and be afraid of (*green*) her mother; the mother might both love (*blue*) and be angry at (*red*) her daughter. Two family members might express their respect (*purple*) for one another by getting angry (*red*).

Once the chart is made, there are many good follow-up activities. One group might use the chart to look at the way outside pressures from a landlord or social worker can affect the relationships among family members. Another group might use the chart to get into a discussion of how and why a person might have conflicting feelings toward a family member or friend at the same time. A third might focus on the relative distances between the hero and different family members. Students might discuss whether the diagram reflects typical family relationships and friendships. For example, as the class reviews the chart, a teacher might ask, "Is the relationship between a sister and her brothers usually so important in their lives?"

When we charted the relationships in *Daddy Was a Number Runner*, we used the chart to explore the reasons various characters got into conflicts with one another. It allowed us to see how pressures from other characters, as well as larger institutions, can shake family unity or inspire the members to draw together in solidarity.

9: Vocabulary—Family and Peer Relationships

Relationships between people are difficult to describe. Learning words that accurately describe family and peer relationships helps students to a better understanding of the people closest to them. Words we have taught include: cooperate, intimidate, manipulate, idolize, placate, soothe, compassionate, sadistic, masochistic, resilient, sibling, peer, scapegoat, and solidarity.

In introducing these words, it can be helpful to refer back to the relationships chart. The teacher might reinforce the meaning of a word by asking: "Using the vocabulary, describe the way the character relates to her father." Or she might clarify a definition by pointing to the chart, "Even though Francie seems to have a lot of pressures on her, she is certainly *resilient*." (For additional help with vocabulary, see "Techniques," p. 22.)

To reinforce the new vocabulary, we use a writing assignment. Students are instructed to use as many words as they can without force-fitting them. The writing choices include:

1. Describe the relationships between someone you know and her/his various family members and friends.
2. Describe the key relationships in the life of the hero of the book you are reading.
3. Select two people who are close to each other. Compare and contrast the way they treat each other.

When we've taught these words, our students have delighted in playing a modified charades game to review meanings. The students divide into teams of two or three members. Each team picks one of the words out of a hat. After a short planning period, the first team pantomimes the meaning of its word while the teacher watches the clock. The first person to guess the correct word gets a point, while the acting team gets points for communicating the meaning quickly. The game continues until each team has acted out several words. There are two winners: the individual who guessed the most words and the team that communicated the fastest. The vocabulary words describing relationships are particularly well suited to this game, as the meanings can be demonstrated easily through the interaction of two or three actors.

10: Mothers and Daughters—
"I Stand Here Ironing"

All of the suggested books raise important discussion topics about mothers and daughters—both the ways they support and share with one another and the ways they come into conflict. (See next page for descriptions and page references for the books.) In addition to these readings, we recommend you use Tillie Olsen's short story, "I Stand Here Ironing." Giving a strong, positive message about a mother/daughter relationship, this story provides a good starting point for a series of activities on mothers and daughters.

In the story, the relationship unfolds through the remembrances of the mother. Feelings of tenderness, rage, pride, guilt, or resignation pass through the mother as she irons; yet she remains clear on what is possible for two humans living their lives as best they can. "Or I will become engulfed with all I did not do, with what I should have been and what cannot be helped."

The story is simple, and at the same time encompasses the contradictions. Upon receiving a note from a teacher requesting that she come in to discuss her daughter, Emily, "who needs help," the mother recalls her daughter's growing up.

> You think because I am her mother I have a key, or that in some way you could use me as a key? She has lived for nineteen years. There is all that life that has happened outside of me, beyond me. [P. 1]

She raised Emily on her own in the "pre-relief, pre-WPA world of the depression." Because she worked during the day, she left Emily with a neighbor and then with Emily's father's family. When she remarried and gave birth to her second child, Emily was very ill, and "they persuaded me at the clinic" to send Emily to a convalescent home, where she stayed for eight months.

As Emily grew up, the family moved a lot, and she never made close friends. Late in high school, she discovered a gift for improvisation and began to perform in high schools and colleges. "You ought to do something about her with a gift like that—but without money or knowing how, what does one do?" As the story closes the mother gathers her thoughts together:

> Let her be. So all that is in her will not bloom—but in how many does it? There is still enough left to live by. Only help her to know—help make it so there is cause for her to know—that she is more than this dress on the ironing board, helpless before the iron. [P. 12]

We recommend reading this twelve-page story aloud in class, stopping often and discussing it along the way. (It can be read and discussed in one class period.) We've found that once our students have been helped to understand that the story is an interior monologue, they are able to follow as it unfolds.

Many students have become very involved with the mother and daughter. In the discussion they have responded to the characters as if they've known them for a long time. "I think Emily's really gonna make it. When somebody like her has talent, she can really go far." "It must have been easier for her mother bringing up the other kids, once she had a husband and they had more money." We ask what they think of the mother, as a mother, or the daughter, as a daughter. In one discussion, two students got into a heated debate. One, from a more privileged background, was angry with the mother, "She was really slow. She didn't pick up on things in time. She shouldn't have left her daughter alone in the apartment, and she should never have sent her to that place!" The other student was outraged, "What else could she do? She did the best she could. She knew her mistakes, but she didn't have a choice."

For many students, reading and discussing this story is both exciting and reassuring. It shows the kinds of things that might go on in a mother's mind, things she wouldn't ordinarily share with her daughter.

11: Mother/Daughter Role-Plays and Readings

Relevant Readings from the Books

Anne Frank: The Diary of a Young Girl: Anne often feels anger toward her mother, a feeling that is intensified in their tiny attic world, where they cannot escape from family interactions. "Mummy and her failings are something I find harder to bear than anything else" (p. 40). Anne writes about her personal struggles to understand her mother and to overcome the tensions between them (pp. 69–70, 114–116).

Daddy Was a Number Runner: Francie is supported by her mother in learning to fight for herself (pp. 17–18) and learning to believe in her own right to a good life. "You don't have to do no domestic work for nobody, Francie.... You finish school and go to college. Somebody in this family got to finish school..." (pp. 170–174).

I Know Why the Caged Bird Sings: As a young child, Maya feels betrayed by her mother's absence (pp. 42–44). In later years, when they live together, Maya is entranced by her mother's vitality and beauty (pp. 49–50, 170–177) and, as she comes into womanhood, she goes to her mother for support (pp. 232–237, 244–246).

A Tree Grows in Brooklyn: Francie's mother Katie works hard to hold the family together. Francie sometimes resents her mother; she feels that her mother favors her brother Neely (pp. 87–88, 337–341). She also loves and respects her mother and comes to realize that her mother needs her (pp. 291–294). Like Maya, she goes to her mother for support when she comes into womanhood (pp. 208–209) and when she has her first experience with a boyfriend (pp. 407–408).

Any number of passages from the book the class is reading aloud could be selected for reading and discussing. For instance, in *I Know Why the Caged Bird Sings,* there is Maya's appeal to her mother for help when she fears that bodily changes signify lesbianism.

"Mother, I've got to talk to you...." It was going to kill me to have to ask her, for in the asking wouldn't it be possible that suspicion would fall on my own normality? I knew her well enough to know that if I committed almost any crime and told her the truth about it she not only wouldn't disown me but would give me her protection. But just suppose I was developing into a lesbian, how would she react?

"Mother...my pocketbook...

"Ritie, do you mean your vagina? Don't use those Southern terms. There's nothing wrong with the word vagina. It's a clinical description. Now, what's wrong with it?" [P. 234]

Maya's mother educates her about her body.

"Sit down, baby. Read this." Her fingers guided my eyes to VULVA. I began to read. She said, "Read it out loud."

It was all very clear and normal-sounding. She drank the beer as I read, and when I had finished she explained it in every-day terms. My relief melted the tears and they liquidly stole down my face.

Mother shot up and put her arms around me. "There's nothing to worry about, baby. It happens to every woman. It's just human nature." [P. 236]

Students enjoy reading this passage—perhaps because they, too, have experienced confusions about their sexual development. To focus the discussion on the interaction of Maya with her mother, you could ask: "What did Maya expect to get from her mother?" "What did she want?" "Did she get what she expected and/or wanted?" "What do you think of the way her mother responded to her?"

In discussing these questions, students will usually begin to bring in their own experiences. "I looked in the mirror and I saw these things growing there and I screamed, 'Ma! I need a brassiere.'" "My mother would have just laughed at me." Some questions to help structure further personal responses are: "Have you ever gone to your mother when you have questions about changes in your body?" "How should a mother respond when her daughter asks her for this kind of help?"

The discussion helps to prepare students for role-plays on the subject of mother/daughter interactions. This is a good subject for role-playing, since most people bring a great deal of experience to it. Without talking directly about themselves, students can express their opinions and feelings in the way they play the situation. (For a complete discussion of role-playing, see "Techniques," p. 26.)

In the first role-play, the daughter talks to her mother about a problem with her boyfriend:

You are Janet, age sixteen. You are in your first serious relationship with a male, Henry. Recently, Henry has been dropping you off at a girlfriend's early in the evening, and going out with the guys. You think he's messing around with other young women. One night your mother asks you where Henry's been lately.

You are Anne, the mother of Janet. At sixteen, Janet is in her first serious relationship with a male, Henry. Lately, you've noticed that Henry hasn't been around very much, and that Janet seems depressed. You approach her and ask her what's happening with Henry.

After the role-play is completed, the mother and daughter should be asked to talk about how they felt during the conversation. Ask the daughter if the mother did or said anything that made her feel better. Did she do or say anything that made the daughter feel angry or withdrawn? Ask the mother if she felt that the daughter was open to her, if the daughter let the mother give to her. If the two people feel very negative about the interaction, have them try it again, with instructions to share more this time. After this second role-play, they can talk about how it felt to share more. Which situation was more familiar? more comfortable? Having specifically discussed the role-play, the class can consider more general questions. Does it make a difference that the mother is a woman, that she has been through these things, too? How does that affect the way the mother relates to the daughter or the way the daughter responds?

On the other side of mother/daughter sharing, we also explore the ways that a mother might need and benefit from her daughter's support.

You are Mary, mother of four. Today at work your boss yelled at you again. Every week or so he comes down hard on you for not working fast enough. You come home, exhausted. You feel lousy about the job and about yourself.

You are Pat, age sixteen. When you come home from school you notice that your mother looks really down. You care a lot about your mother and you want to give her some support. You figure that she's probably feeling bad about work again,

where her boss seems to give her a hard time. You approach her and ask her if there's anything wrong.

Again, the discussion begins with how the mother and daughter felt during the conversation. This time, was the daughter helpful? Was the mother open? Did this situation seem typical? Do daughters support their mothers? In what kinds of situations? When they don't support their mothers, what is it that stops them? When we did this role play, one student became reflective, "I hadn't ever really thought I could help her out that way. I've got problems of my own that take up my time."

The goal of the third mother/daughter role-play is to help students understand a mother's traditional attitudes toward career-choices. It will also help students to gain a deeper understanding of their own attitudes and where they come from. These are the roles:

You are Elaine, age seventeen. Since you were a young girl you have loved taking things apart and putting them back together. During this past year, a friend of yours has been building some furniture for his new apartment and taught you how to use power tools. You've decided that you really love that kind of work and want to become a carpenter when you graduate high school. You tell your mother about your decision. You try to help her understand how being a carpenter will make you happy.

You are Marie. You have always cared a lot about your oldest daughter, Elaine. Now, at the age of seventeen, Elaine is graduating high school. You are hopeful that she will want to go to nursing school. You want her to have a good profession. You want her to have better than you've ever been able to have. She comes to you to tell you she wants to become a carpenter.

This role-play has more potential for conflict than any of the others. We encourage the mother and daughter to try to listen to one another, even if they disagree, because they both value each other's feelings and point of view. In this one, again, we look at the interaction. What did the daughter say that reached the mother? What did the mother say that got through to the daughter? What feelings did she touch off in the daughter? Were there attitudes or feelings that the two had in common? Would it affect their relationship if the daughter took steps toward being "different" and became a carpenter?

12: Mother/Daughter Questionnaire

There are some subjects which mothers and daughters rarely discuss, even though both of them would gain a great deal from the discussion. Our students have eagerly seized the opportunity to learn new things about their mothers when we've done mother/daughter questionnaires. In this activity, the students interview their mothers and share the results.

The class begins by working together to list all the questions they would like to ask their mothers, but have never gotten around to asking. One student records the questions on a ditto master, so that it can be run off before the class is over and taken home while the questions are still fresh in the students' minds.

We made up our questionnaire after discussing "I Stand Here Ironing." Students drew on the discussion of the story, as well as upon their own experiences, in arriving at the following list:

1. What's the most difficult thing about being a mother?
2. Have you ever had a favorite child?
3. What are differences in bringing up daughters and sons?
4. How do you feel when you see your kids grown and on their own?
5. How do you feel about raising your kids alone? (if you do)
6. If you're a housewife are you satisfied?
7. If your daughter has been raped, what do you think should be done to the man?
8. Did you ever want to be a man? Why?
9. What kind of a mother do you think you are?
10. Are you ever jealous of your daughter?
11. Would you rather see your daughter have a career, get married, or both, or become a housewife?

When the questionnaire was drawn up, our students were impatient to go home and try it out. To motherless students, we suggested inter-

viewing an older woman, an aunt, or a neighbor. A number of students brought their completed interviews to school the next day, even though they weren't due for a week. We typed up the questions, with a range of answers under each, on ditto sheets, to facilitate the sharing and comparing of responses.

On the sharing day, take the time to discuss how it felt to ask each question, and to look at the variety of responses. Both students and teachers can learn from the experiences and wisdom of the interviewed mothers. When we did this assignment, it was clear that each mother was struggling to do her best for her children. One mother's response to "What's the most difficult thing about being a mother?" captures the spirit of the others: "Making sure you're bringing up your children the right way. Teaching them the values of life. Being fair—trying to spend the time that is needed with each child and not making the others feel left out."

One mother spoke with particular insight about the differences in bringing up daughters and sons: "A mother was a daughter, so she can understand more what's happening with her daughter. Whereas a mother can't understand boys' feelings; she can only guess. When children are little, boys tend to want their mother more than girls. Then, as they grow older, boys feel that is is childish and immature to listen or do as they're told by their mother. Girls then feel more need for their mother when they get older because they are the same sex and more or less share similar feelings and experiences." The messages we got from the mothers' responses were strong and positive. All hoped that the options would be open for their daughters "Not to be cut off from someday being a doctor, or taking boxing lessons . . . or being a wife and mother with dignity and self respect."

One word of warning. Encourage the students to find the time and space to sit down with their mothers and talk through the questions together. Some of our students handed the questionnaire to their mothers and asked them to fill it out. That missed the point. The most valuable part of the activity was the exchange itself between the mother and daughter, including the parts that never got written down.

13: A Taste of Honey—
Mother/Daughter Conflicts

A Taste of Honey, by Shelagh Delaney, is a short play which centers on the love/hate relationship between Jo, a white working-class English woman and Helen, her saloon-frequenting mother. The dialogue is direct and absorbing and can easily be read aloud in class. Since students almost always enjoy reading a play together, and since this play raises interesting issues about the kinds of problems and conflicts that can arise between mothers and daughters, we recommend using it with your class.

The mother and daughter in *A Taste of Honey* are locked into a negative cycle of hurting one another and protecting themselves from hurt. Shelagh Delaney portrays the mother's destructive manipulation of her daughter without exploring the mother's own pain or looking deeply at causes for the mother's behavior. Because of this, it is crucial to balance a reading of the play with discussions, role-plays, and readings which explore causes of mother/daughter problems, while suggesting positive ways to work on those problems. A reading of *A Taste of Honey* should not be substituted for other activities about mothers and daughters, but discussed in the context of these activities. For instance, it is valuable to compare the mother in "I Stand Here Ironing" with the mother in *A Taste of Honey*; Tillie Olsen gives insight into the mother's point of view, the pressures in her life, and her feelings about having caused her daughter to suffer.

As *Honey* opens, Jo and Helen move into a new flat; here, the entire action takes place over a period of about a year. Helen is involved with a new "fancy man," Peter, who increasingly draws her attention and time. Halfway through the play, Helen moves out on Jo to marry Peter. Excluded, Jo feels competitive. She is jealous both of Peter, for stealing her mother, and of her mother, for being attractive to Peter.

Jo has a brief affair with a Black sailor. She gets pregnant; he disappears. Alone in her pregnancy, she is cynical and flip. Her real support comes, not from her mother, but from her friend Geoff, a homosexual art student, who moves in with her.

Jo's and Helen's relationship is complex. Jo's need for support and love from her mother has been disappointed again and again over the years, as Helen chooses her own life and her relationships with men over her relationship with her daughter. Wanting love, and bitter in her deprivation, Jo acts out her ambivalence by either soliciting her mother's attention or insulting her. Helen alternately needles her daughter, attacks her outright, forgets about her, or insists that she has the right to run her daughter's life. There are moments of closeness between the mother and the daughter, but they quickly provoke more hurt. When Jo tries to reach out by asking about her father, she is pained to hear her mother dismiss him as "retarded." When Helen hears about Jo's pregnancy, and drops by to show her concern, Jo is too self-protective to accept her concern.

The play ends as Helen, thrown over by Peter, returns to the flat; she kicks out Geoff and moves in herself, ostensibly to help Jo give birth, but more realistically, to take over her daughter's life.

Our students have always loved reading *A Taste of Honey* aloud in class, taking turns reading the various parts, and acting out some of the scenes. The entire play (only eighty-seven pages) can be read aloud in class over a period of two weeks. Below we describe some of the issues from the play which lead well into discussions, role-plays, and writing assignments.

Sharing: Helping or Hurting

Reading the sections where Helen and Jo tell each other about their marriage plans (pp. 26–29, 39–45), we look at ways a mother and daughter can block communication with one another. We compare Geoff's supportive relationship with Jo to Helen's. We explore ways mothers and daughters can communicate with one another. (See mother/daughter role-plays, p. 71.) **What makes some conversations supportive? What makes other conversations negative or hurtful? What are positive and negative ways a mother can be a protector or** counselor? What are positive and negative ways a mother can be a friend?

Pressures on a Mother

We look at Helen's life and explore all the pressures we imagine she feels. What are the pains and joys in her life? What would she wish to be different? What problems are beyond her control? What problems does she bring on herself? How do the pressures affect how she treats her daughter?

Mothers without Fathers

We discuss the pressures Helen feels in raising Jo without a father. What is it like for a mother to bring up her children alone? What are the difficulties? What are the benefits? Reading the section where Jo asks Helen about her father (pp. 42–45), we discuss what it's like for a girl to grow up without a father. What role might a father play in her life? How does her relationship with her mother change? When we taught this section, we explored Jo's interest in her own birth; we talked about the way every child wonders about her parents' love for one another or about the events that led to her own birth.

Cooperation or Competition

By examining the competition between Helen and Jo over Helen's boyfriend (pp. 29–35), we try to understand what might be behind competition between a mother and a daughter. We look at other potential areas of competition between a mother and a daughter (appearance, personal happiness, level of education, etc.). We discuss the alternatives to competition. What are ways that a mother and a daughter who compete might work through the competition to a more supportive relationship?

Support or Control

In discussing the final scene, raising the question of "What's going to happen next?" or "Why has Helen returned to Jo's flat?" (pp. 76–87) can lead to valuable debate about the responsibilities of mothers and daughters to one another. When should a mother "support" her daughter? When, if ever, should she "control" her daughter? Are there situations when the mother of an adolescent girl should lay down the law? What is the line between "support" and "control?"

Writing Assignments

Writing assignments we have given while reading *A Taste of Honey* include:

1. Write a letter from Jo to Helen in which Jo describes what she has really wanted from Helen as she has been growing up.
2. Write a letter from Helen to Jo in which she describes what she wishes she could have provided for Jo, and where she tells Jo what she really wants from Jo as her daughter.
3. Write a follow-up scene for the play, which takes place between Jo and Helen after Jo's baby is born.
4. Write a poem about or addressed to a mother, your own if you want.

When we gave this assignment, a number of our students had trouble getting their thoughts down in class time, but in the coming weeks they brought in poems that they wrote at home. "I couldn't sleep, so I stayed up all night writing this." "A number of the poems were tender; a few were angry. Here is one from each end of the spectrum:

M — more
O — of
T — the
H — hope
E — enters
R — rapidly
[Donna Sullivan]

To My Mother
You are like a bear when
I don't like what you say.
You are like loud rock music when
you say go to bed.
You are like a horn when,
you screech all day.
You are like a little black rat when
I say shut up.
You are like a tank trying
to run me down.
You make me feel like a savage lion,
ready to bite your head off.
You make me feel like a big
tornado wanting to blow you away.
You make me feel like killing you
on a bright sunny day.
[Robbin Luzaitis]

14: Father/Daughter Readings and Questionnaire

Relevant Readings from the Books

Anne Frank: The Diary of a Young Girl: Anne writes often of her love for her father. In describing their conflicts she is forgiving of his blind spots (pp. 39–42). As she comes into womanhood, and spends time with her first boyfriend, her father is protective. She writes him a letter insisting on her independence (pp. 202–205). She continues to yearn for closeness, but recognizes the ways in which each fails to understand the other (pp. 234–236).

Daddy Was a Number Runner: As a young girl, Francie adores her "laughter-loving," "prideful" father (pp. 20–21, 61–67). As the book progresses, she sees him as more real, and less ideal, as he fights to keep his pride while getting busted (pp. 67–73), deals with a humiliating social worker (pp. 77–79, 90–91) and moves out on the family to live with another woman (pp. 162–166, 182–183).

I Know Why the Caged Bird Sings: Maya's contacts with her father are infrequent. As a child, when she first meets him, she is impressed by and uncomfortable with his pretentiousness (pp. 44–49). Years later, when she spends a summer with him and his girlfriend, she learns more about his lifestyle ("medical dietician" turns out to mean kitchen worker in a naval hospital). Once, she sees him relax into himself when she goes with him on a jaunt to a Mexican bar (pp. 191–213).

A Tree Grows in Brooklyn: Francie loves to spend time with her charming, singing-waiter father (pp. 30–37, 146–147). As time goes by, she experiences his alcoholism (pp. 213–218) and she comes to see his dreamy nature as impractical (pp. 193–200). At the end of his life, when he is thrown out of the Waiters Union, she sees him disheartened (pp. 241–247). His death is a sad and sobering experience for the family (pp. 247–263).

"I'm not sure how it is for them. Fathers down my way aren't at home a lot. They're out working, or looking for work—or they're just out. I can't say how a man feels; it's just different," one of our students commented. For daughters, the lives of fathers are often mysterious, more mysterious than the lives of mothers, who are women like themselves, around more, running the household and raising the kids. Some daugh-

ters may never have had a father in the home.

In this activity, the relationships of fathers and daughters are explored. Readings from the books provide the daughter's perspective, while we build in the father's perspective through discussions and a panel.

As children, the daughters in all four of the books admire and idolize their fathers; as they grow up, they come to see their fathers more fully as people. For example, in her early diary entries Anne Frank writes:

> I adore Daddy. He is the one I look up to. I don't love anyone in the world but him. He doesn't notice that he treats Margot differently from me. Now Margot is just the prettiest, sweetest, most beautiful girl in the world. But all the same I feel I have some right to be taken seriously too . . .
>
>   I'm not jealous of Margot, never have been. I don't envy her good looks or her beauty. It is only that I long for Daddy's real love: not only as his child, but for me, Anne, myself. [P. 40]

In later entries, Anne writes her father a letter defending her right to kiss her first boyfriend, who lives upstairs, and asserting her independence (p. 202). When he is hurt and disappointed, she blames herself. ("Oh, I have failed miserably; this is certainly the worst thing I have ever done in my life.") Finally, at the very end of the book, she is ready to make a more realistic assessment of what is positive and what is negative in their relationship:

> For that matter, I can't confide in anyone, unless they tell me a lot about themselves, and as I know very little about Pim [Anne's name for her father], I don't feel that I can tread upon more intimate ground with him. Pim always takes up the older, fatherly attitude, tells me that he too has had similar passing tendencies. But still he's not able to feel with me like a friend, however hard he tries. [p. 235]

These passages are particularly rich for discussion and writing assignments because Anne writes with so much insight into her feelings. Having read and discussed Anne's perceptions about herself and her father, some students might be open to exploring their own relationships with their fathers. Anne's letter to her father—"I believe, Daddy, that you expect a

declaration from me, so I will give it to you . . ."
(p. 202)—provides a usable format for a writing
assignment.

> Write a letter of a daughter to her father in which
> you (as the daughter) try to communicate to him
> about the parts of you he doesn't know or under-
> stand. You might want to assume you have just had
> a disagreement, perhaps over a boyfriend, or the
> hours you keep, or some other issue.

This is a difficult assignment, especially for
those who are fatherless, and should be combined with some other, less personal, writing
choices (see "Techniques." p. 18). Students who
do choose to write a letter could benefit from
reading the rest of Anne's statement to her
father.

In the other books, the changes in the father/
daughter relationships are described, but not
really explored in such detail. All the books,
however, lend themselves to an exercise in
which students answer a set of questions, early
on in their reading, and again upon finishing the
book(s).

1. What are the daughter's feelings toward her
   father?
2. What specific incidents or interactions have
   affected her feelings?

The questions help students think about the kind
of situations that reveal other sides of a person
whom they think they know very well. In the
discussion, it is useful to try to separate out the
daughter's changing feelings and perceptions as
she matures, from the actual changes taking
place in the father.

For the most part, the readings give the
daughter's point of view. It is also important for
students to focus on the father's point of view. A
good beginning question to consider is: "What's
it like to be a father?" Our students have commented: "A father's got the power, you know,
the last word." "He can go out and have a good
time." "He has to support the family." "He has to
discipline the kids when they get out of line."
Have the class try to imagine what it might be
like to live with these expectations, or restrictions. What if you didn't like disciplining the
kids, or you wanted to take care of the baby?

(See "Adult Sex Roles," p. 119.) What if you
couldn't find a job? How would it feel if you
didn't want to, or couldn't, meet the traditional
expectations?

Next, we explore what it's like to be a father
to a daughter, as opposed to a son. Are there
responsibilities a father has to his daughter?
What might a father want for his daughter? One
student summed up her understanding, "A
father feels it's his thing to take care of his
daughter and make sure she stays out of
trouble." Why is a father often protective of his
daughter? How does a protective upbringing affect a daughter's view of herself? What are steps
that a father and daughter could each take to
grow beyond their roles as "protector" and
"protected"? A role-play might be useful here:

> You are John, the father of a fourteen-year-old
> daughter, Judy. You love your daughter and are
> concerned about her welfare. You've noticed that
> she's been staying out really late with her friends
> lately. Now she comes to you and asks to go away
> for the weekend. You don't know if you can trust
> her and her friends to stay out of trouble.

> You are Judy, age fourteen. Your friends have ask-
> ed you to hitchhike with them up to New Hamp-
> shire to go camping this weekend. You come to
> your father to tell him your plans and to get permis-
> sion. You want to convince him.

After the role-play, each of the participants
should be asked to explain what was motivating
their character. What was behind the father's
concern (and perhaps refusal)? What was behind
the daughter's insistent urging? If the first role-
play ends in an unresolvable conflict, ask the
participants (or other students) to play it through
again, this time really working to come out with
a compromise (see "Techniques." p. 71).

If it is possible to arrange, a panel discussion
of fathers give the students a way to test out their
conjectures. The men invited to be on the panel
need not be fathers of the students in the class.
Try to invite two or three men who have
daughters, at least one of whom is the father of a
teen-age daughter. They should be willing to
answer questions about their feelings as fathers.
(It might be necessary to hold a special class session in the evening to make this possible.)

The students are very curious (and a little apprehensive) about what the panel members will say. They should prepare for the panel in the class period preceding the visit. Our students have been especially interested in the following:

1. How did you feel when you had a daughter instead of a son?
2. What do you want for your daughters?
3. When do you think a sixteen-year-old daughter should be home at night?

4. Do you worry about your daughter more than about your sons?
5. Do you spend time with your daughter? Doing what?

The students might be very shy about asking these or other questions. To facilitate the process, you should type out the questions ahead of time, giving the fathers some sense of what interests the class.

FRIENDS

INTRODUCTION

> I walk up behind you
> thinking you don't know
> I'm there
> Suddenly
> you turn around
> looking me straight in the eye
> I lift my head
> slowly looking at you
> straight in the face
> you laugh, i laugh
>
> The laughter is over
> silence all around us.
>
> [Robbin Luzaitis]

Relationships with friends go through dramatic transformations during adolescence. It is a time when young people need someone to talk with, but often have trouble giving or accepting support. Friendships with males are complicated by sex; friendships with females are complicated by competition. In this section of the unit, we discuss these complications, in order to help students move beyond them.

The first two activities explore the general questions: "What is a friend?" and "Whom do you talk to?" Students then focus on the topic of boyfriends, comparing a situation where a young woman says "yes" to a situation where she says "no." The next two activities serve to recreate familiar situations in which young women

compete with or exclude each other when they could be giving mutual support. Students participate in a series of role-plays in which a young woman has to choose between a man and her loyalty to another woman; and they do a group role-play on getting accepted by a "crowd." The section ends with students reading "O Yes," a short story by Tillie Olsen, that deals with societal pressures to "stick to your own kind."

ACTIVITIES
15: What Is a Friend?

Relevant Readings from the Books

Anne Frank: The Diary of a Young Girl: Confined to their attic hiding place, Anne can only remember her old girlfriend (p. 107) and yearn for a new girlfriend (p. 119). The only other person her age is Peter, who eventually becomes her boyfriend.

Daddy was a Number Runner: Francie has one close girlfriend, Sukie. They hang out together, get into mischief together (pp.42–44), and, more often, have fights (pp. 16, 39). There are hints that the relationship has depth and complexity (pp. 28–29), but their feelings toward each other are not really portrayed.

I Know Why the Caged Bird Sings: Maya has a childhood friend (pp. 118–120). But in her adolescent years, her closest peer relationship seems to be with her brother, Bailey.

A Tree Grows In Brooklyn: Francie is also very involved with her family. She distrusts women (p. 209) and never develops a close female friendship.

The theme of friendship is not fully explored in any of the four suggested books. Therefore, in addition to discussing the readings, we explore what it is to be a friend, or to have a friend, through a discussion and a writing assignment.

At the risk of getting some corny responses, along with the more substantive (which can be thorny), ask each student to make a list of all the things that a friend is to her. Encourage students to think of their own friends, what they do, how they act, what they say, etc. Once everyone has gotten some ideas down, the class shares lists. In our classes, concepts of what a friend is have ranged from "someone to hang around with" and "someone who'll go down the river with you to get high," to "someone you can talk to about yourself" or "someone who you don't have to talk to, but they know what's going on." Other responses have been more negative: "I don't know if I ever really had one."

To get at the more subtle aspects of friendship, ask the class to consider whether a friend has any special responsibilities. "Are there things you feel you should do for a friend, even if you don't like doing them?" "Are there things you might have to hear that you don't like hearing?" "Is it your responsibility to be honest with a friend? To show your anger if you feel it? To let them know when they have hurt you? To conceal certain things from them, in order to protect them?" We also discuss friendships and responsibilities with brothers and sisters. "Can a brother or sister be a friend? What's special about a friendship with a sibling?"

This discussion is a difficult one for most students. They are not used to talking in these terms. Friends and friendship are taken for granted, seldom analyzed. In every group, however, there will probably be a few students who respond to these questions—and the whole group will benefit from being asked to think critically.

We follow this discussion with a writing assignment on friendship:

Writing Topics: Friendship

1. Write a short story about two young women who go through an adventure together and become friends.
2. Write a dialogue or short play in which a brother or sister stands up for or helps out a sister. (Pick an incident from your own life or make one up.)
3. Write a memory of a time you asked a friend to do you a favor that was a difficult thing for the friend to do, or a time a friend asked you to do a favor that was difficult for you.
4. Write a poem about what it is to be a friend.
5. Write a poem to one of your friends or to your own sister or brother.

What Is a Friend?

Is a friend someone who
Never notices you when you have
Something to say?
Or is a friend someone who
Always tells you what is wrong with you
And gets mad at you if you say
Something to them?
Or is a friend someone that will
Stab you in the back if you ask them?
If that is so,
I have no enemies.
Are you my friend?

[Billy Igo]

"Do you care about me?"
"Yes."
"Do you love me?"
"In some ways."
"Would you hold out your hand in
  My need to slap it?"
"The possibilities are endless."

[Lisa Allison Weinberg]

16: Whom Do You Talk To?

"With my girlfriends I can really be myself, but with guys I worry about how I look and what they think of me." "I hate girls; I hang around with guys. I can do whatever I feel like when I'm with guys, and not feel stupid." "I've never just been friends with a guy." Through discussing a questionnaire, "Whom do you talk to?" and doing follow-up role-plays, this activity explores who the students turn to for support, and examines some of the sources of trust and distrust among friends.

Students often have different feelings about their friendships with females and their friendships with males. They also make important distinctions between males who are friends, and males who are boyfriends. To start this activity, the teacher can try to draw out the range of opinion in the class about male/female friends: Are female friends different from male friends? Are male friends different from boyfriends? Are there some things you do or share with each, which you don't do or share with the other? The following questionnaire helps to focus the discussion on specifics. Ask all the students to fill it out, while assuring them that they are not expected to hand it in. It is a private worksheet, to help them see their own patterns.

Whom Do You Talk To?

Answer the following questions by choosing one or more people from this list, or choosing "no one" if you don't talk to anyone.

best female friend
best male friend
boyfriend
mother or father
sisters or brothers
teacher, youth worker, or other adult
no one

1. If you broke up with a boyfriend, who would be the first person you'd tell about it?
2. When something you feel proud or happy about happens to you, whom do you tell first?
3. Whom would you talk to about sex?
4. If you don't like a class at school, or if you're excited about a project you're doing at school, whom will you talk to?
5. If you are angry about something going on at home, whom will you talk to?
6. If you did something illegal, whom would you talk to about it?
7. If there is something about your appearance you're not satisfied with, with whom are you most likely to discuss it?
8. Whom would you talk to about what you like or dislike about your boyfriend?
9. Whom will you talk to about not feeling well physically?
10. Whom will you cry with?
11. Who knows you best?
12. With whom do you act most like yourself?

Most students enjoy going over the results of the questionnaire, but they shouldn't be pushed to share; they learn about themselves simply by filling it out. We've found that it's impossible to have a satisfactory discussion on all the questions in one class period. It makes sense either to spread the discussion out over two classes, or to get the group to select the questions which interested them the most and then to stick to those in the discussion.

We find that most of our students seek the support of their best female friends when they have problems with their boyfriends or with their families. Their distrust of other females seems to arise specifically in competitive situations involving males. Further, it is usually a girlfriend, a brother, or a sister who knows them best. There are some subjects which many of our students don't discuss with anyone. "If I'm down I just watch TV or go out and get wrecked." "I write about stuff in my poems. I don't have to talk about it."

In the discussion, try to explore what it is that allows students to talk with one friend, yet blocks them from turning to another. Why might someone want to talk about an experience or a feeling? What might you get out of a good talk? What does it feel like to keep most things to yourself? The discussion could move to the advantages and disadvantages of keeping things to yourself.

During the discussion of the questionnaire, we have experimented with role-plays which get at the differences in talking about the same issues with different people. Once we did a role-play where a young woman talked to her sister, and then to a male friend, about having broken up with her boyfriend. She and her sister had a give-and-take discussion, where her sister drew on her own similar experiences. In the conversation with the male friend, the young woman was clearly asking for help; the friend wanted to take care of her, hinting that he might be interested in picking up where the boyfriend left off. After the two role-plays, we compared the conversations. "Did the young woman talk differently to each?" "How were the two conversations supportive?" "Was either conversation unhelpful in any way?" "Which made her feel better?" "Which was more helpful in the long run?"

This activity encourages students to learn about their own patterns of sharing or keeping things to themselves. Often they are surprised to learn how much they turn to their girlfriends for support. Perhaps, by listening to each other and looking into themselves, they are now more prepared to find new ways to share with and support their friends.

17: Boyfriends—Saying "Yes" versus Saying "No"

Relevant Readings from the Books

Anne Frank: The Diary of a Young Girl: Anne Frank describes her budding romance with Peter, the son of the family in hiding with the Franks. She follows her feelings from her beginning crush (pp. 148–149) through the first kiss (pp. 189–192) to her experience of passion (pp. 195–197).

Daddy Was a Number Runner: Francie is not too interested in boys. She gets very scared when the son of family friends catches her behind the stairs and tries to kiss her (pp. 91–93). She has a crush on a boy from out of town, but shyness prevents her from approaching him (pp. 158–162).

I Know Why the Caged Bird Sings: Maya is confused and insecure about her body and her sexuality. Beyond her close relationship with her brother, her interactions with males are very limited. As she gets older, to prove to herself that she is a normal, healthy young woman, she propositions the best-looking young man in the neighborhood (pp. 232–241).

A Tree Grows in Brooklyn: Francie's two-day encounter with a soldier is romantic and painful (pp. 393–409). This is balanced by a slowly building and serious friendship with a young man she meets at college (pp. 378–385, 417–420).

A Taste of Honey: Jo has a short romantic interlude with a sailor, and she becomes pregnant. He proposes to her (pp. 22–26) and propositions her (pp. 36–39). She has a close friendship with a homosexual art student (pp. 46–59, 69–76).

Boyfriends is a hot subject; discussing feelings about having a boyfriend (or not having one), about first experiences with sex, or about the reality of "being" with a man versus the fantasy, requires trust. We don't explore these issues with a group until they have worked with us and with one another for at least a month. As with other highly charged issues, we try to make use of the sections in the books dealing with boyfriends and sex. (See Unit V, "Sexuality," for a fuller discussion of our approach.)

In this activity, we explore the considerations that go into the decision to make love, the tensions between "saying yes" and "saying no," through comparing two readings. The first is an excerpt from *A Tree Grows in Brooklyn* in which Francie says "no" to her soldier boyfriend; the second is an excerpt from an unpublished novel by Marge Piercy, in which Maude says "yes" to her steady boyfriend, in the back seat of a car. If both excerpts are read aloud in full, you will probably need two class periods to read, discuss, and compare. If students read the selections at home, you should have them read key passages aloud in class, asking them to listen for both the sources and the consequences of Francie's and Maude's decisions.

In the reading from *A Tree Grows in Brooklyn,* Francie has a two-day romance with a soldier, Lee. Although he is engaged to someone back home, he asks Francie, "Would you mind if I sort of made believe that you were my best girl—just for this evening?" (p. 395). In acting out the charade, Francie falls genuinely in love. On the night before Lee leaves town, he asks her to "stay" with him; he tells her he won't marry his girl back home. Although Francie is tempted, she turns him down.

> "I . . . couldn't."
> "Don't you want to?"
> "Yes," she answered honestly.
> "Then why . . . ."
> "I'm only sixteen," she confessed bravely.
> "I've never been with anybody. I wouldn't know how."
> "That makes no difference."
> "And I've never been away from home overnight. My mother would worry."
> "You could think of some excuse . . . tomorrow."

"I wouldn't need to think of an excuse. I'd tell the truth."

"You would?" he asked in astonishment.

"I love you. I wouldn't be ashamed . . . afterwards if I stayed with you. I'd be proud and happy and I wouldn't want to lie about it." [P.403]

The Marge Piercy story (available in *Bold New Women*, edited by Barbara Alson Wasserman) begins with Maude going through the ceremony of preparing herself for an important date with her steady boyfriend, Mike. Alone together in Mike's mother's car, Maude and Mike are nervous; this, it is revealed, is the night they have planned to make love for the first time. When they first leave Maude's parents' house, they both are tense.

"Why don't you say it? Or don't you?"

"Say what?"

"What would I want? Except that you love me. If you do. ' I stare at him in his hostile slouch over the wheel.

"Of course I love you."

Beside the loading ramp of a dark building he pulls over. "Why didn't you say it?"

"When? You never gave me a chance."

"You climb in the car and sit as far away as you can . . . ."

"But you . . . Lets begin again. Good evening Mike."

"God I've missed you these three days. From the time I get up in the morning, and it's not your voice waking me over the telephone . . . ." [P. 27]

Both are virgins; they are unsure of what to do. When they try to make love, Maude worries that there may be something wrong with her.

"Does it hurt you?"

"A little."

"Look, am I in the right spot?"

"The right spot?" Sudden terror that he is forcing the wrong opening. "I don't know. Can't you tell?"

"Maybe you should guide me in."

"But Mike, I don't know where it is."

"You don't! Jesus"

How can he speak so harshly! "Why expect me to tell you? You're the one who's supposed to know how."

"Mike, am I different from other women physically?"

"How do I know?"

"Haven't you—"

"I've had just as much experience as you've had." He turns his head away.

"Please look at me. I'm glad. Because we're even then." [Pp. 28–29]

After making love awkwardly, they settle back into their friendship.

"Well, at least we got through, old friend." He grips my shoulder. "You're a good soldier. Want to call it quits for tonight? I'm for a hot pastrami sandwich." [P. 30]

Francie said "no." Maude said "yes." A good way to compare the two is through a role-play: Maude and Francie become friends and discuss the different alternatives each of them chose. The doubts and confusions typical of either decision can emerge, providing the starting point for a group discussion.

In the follow-up discussion, the class begins by identifying the reasons for each decision. What are the similarities and differences in the two relationships? One relationship was long-term and the other was a two-day romance, but both young women felt that they were in love, both were frightened by the novelty of a sexual encounter. Further, the class could imagine what "making love" might mean to each of the young women. Our students have identified with Francie. "She was scared shit." "She knew he was taking off on her." They have also identified with Maude. Comments have ranged from romantic to cynical. "She really liked the guy." "Maybe she liked going out in the car."

When we debated the consequences, most students agreed that Francie protected herself from hurt. ("He just wanted to use her.") But some insisted that she "blew it." There was also disagreement about Maude. A few students felt that she may have regretted her decision, while others were sure she felt good about it. "They loved each other. They would of gotten around to it soon." "She knew he'd be comin' round more often now." Looking at the consequences provides an opportunity to discuss birth control.

Students discuss the awkwardness of the first experiences of using birth control (see Unit V, "Sexuality," p. 140.

Discussing Francie and Maude allows you to examine important decisions for a young woman as she begins to go out with men. It allows a class to explore what it means to have a good relationship, what is involved in making the decision to make love. As teachers, we hope to get across the message that there are no clear-cut answers. Both saying "yes" and saying "no" can bring problems as well as satisfactions. What is important is that we make those difficult decisions ourselves and don't let our boyfriends or a sense of what we think is expected of us dictate our decisions for us.

18: Girlfriend and/or Boyfriend—Working Through Competition

In these role-plays, the students have an opportunity to weigh their commitments to their girlfriends against their commitments to their boyfriends, to examine the reasons for the kinds of choices they make, and to consider the consequences.

In the first role-play, the issue is clearly raised; a young woman chooses between her loyalty to a close friend and her interest in a male (For help in facilitating role-playing, see "Techniques," p. 27.)

Mary: You are sixteen years old. In the group you hang around with, you have two girlfriends you're pretty close to, but no particular boyfriend right now. One of your close girlfriends, Kathie, has been telling you for weeks about a crush she has on Donny, the cousin of one of the people you hang out with. You think Donny is pretty cute, too, but haven't made a play for him because of Kathie.

Donny: You are seventeen years old. Your cousin introduced you to a group of young women he hangs out with. Some of them are really "fine." You've decided to call one of them, Mary, to see about getting together with her sometime. You want a chance to get to know her a little better, away from all the others. One evening, you call her on the phone.

When we did this role-play, the student who played Mary began the phone call with a firm mind; she would not "back stab," but would remember to keep her friend's feelings in mind. As the conversation progressed, she softened, and by the end, she agreed to see Donny that very night. "He's so sweet. I just couldn't turn him down," she kept reiterating. "I wish I knew a guy as sweet as him; I know I'd fall for him." In discussing the consequences, our students agreed that she might hurt her close girlfriend. Nonetheless, they couldn't fault her. If she really liked Donny, they couldn't blame her for going out with him.

The second role-play grows naturally out of the first. If, in the shared ethic of many students, having a boyfriend often takes precedence over allegiance to a girlfriend, how do two close girlfriends deal with competition over a male? How do they work it through, while keeping their friendship?

Joanie: You are fifteen years old. For the past year you haven't had a boyfriend. You've spent a lot of time with your best girlfriend, Sarah. Sometimes you go out and do things with Sarah and her boyfriend, Jack. About a month ago Jack started paying a lot of attention to you. Last week he came by your house by himself. He let you know that he liked you a lot and was interested in going out with you. You agreed to go out with him. You like Sarah a lot and you feel guilty about your decision. You don't want to lose the friendship.

Sarah: You are sixteen years old. You have been going with Jack for a year. Your other close relationship is with your best girlfriend, Joanie. Often, you and Jack spend time with Joanie. The three of you go out together, since Joanie doesn't have a boyfriend. This morning at school you heard from another friend that Jack and Joanie were going out. You are hurt and angry. Furthermore, you have a lot of pride about not showing how upset you are. Youj want to save your friendship with Joanie, but you are mad at her. You confront her about what's going on between her and Jack.

When we suggested this role-play, many important and unresolved questions were raised for our students. At first, they weren't sure that the two women should talk at all. "What good will it do?" "They'll only fight; it's better if they don't get into it." We pointed out that the tension between them might get in the way of their friendship. We asked, "Can you think of ways they might help each other?" "Are there ways they can strengthen their friendship by being straight with one another?"After some discussion, our students agreed to try the role-play. Each assumed her role with strong feelings and some nervousness. Awkwardly, they got out their feelings and tried to understand one another. In the class discussion that followed, the other students agreed that even though it had been a hard talk, it seemed worth having.

Doing these role-plays can give students an opportunity to reflect on the choices which are bound to come up in their own friendships. Further, it can introduce them to some untried ways to sustain those friendships which are shaken by competitive incidents or feelings. A good follow-up activity is listening to, and reading aloud, Holly Near's song, "It's More Important to Me."

19: Getting Accepted—Group Role-Play

How do you get accepted by a group? Do you change yourself to conform to a certain set of attitudes or a group style? Do you "do your own thing" and fight to be recognized as different, but legitimate? The previous activities have focused on individual friendships. Here, through a group role-play, students explore ways that high-school-age young women "get accepted" by a crowd. They look at what they may gain, and what they may have to give up, by becoming part of a crowd.

To introduce the concept of "getting accepted" we suggest a short excerpt from A Tree Grows in Brooklyn (pp.318–323). On her first day at a new job, Francie is ignored and ridiculed until she conforms to the group by laughing at their usual scapegoat.

Francie stared at him, astonished. Then she couldn't help it—it had sounded so funny—she burst out laughing. Mark gulped, turned and disappeared down the hall. Everything changed then. A murmur ran around the table.
"She laughed."
"Hey! The new girl laughed!"
"Laughed!"

A young Italian girl linked her arm in Francie's and said, "Come on, new girl. I'll show you the terlet." [P. 321]

The teacher asks: "How did Francie get accepted?" "Why do you think it made a difference to the group whether or not Francie joined them in laughing at the boy?"

By participating in a group role-play, the class explores different ways a new person might break into a group (see "Techniques," p. 27). The "new girl" role-play is set up like a game. Members of the class sit in a closed circle. One student volunteers to be the new person; she leaves the room to give the rest of the group time to decide on a "passport," something that she must say or do in order to be "accepted." The group then chooses a "ringleader," who leads them in their chosen style of behavior. When the "new girl" returns to the circle, she tries to figure out what to say or do by paying careful attention to the behavior of the group. She locates the "ringleader," and pays particular attention to her. Once the "new girl"acts out the "passport" to the leader's acceptance, someone else volunteers, and the game begins again.

When we have done "new girl" role-plays, we have encouraged the students to pick "passports" which are both simple to figure out and fairly true to life. One time the "new girl" had to swear in order to be accepted; another time she had to flatter the ringleader; a third time she had to let the group know that she had a boyfriend.

It's always fun to play the game, to make up "passports," to act out the roles, to discover how to break into the group; it's harder for the students to relate the game back to their own lives. When we asked the students how "new girls" are let into their friendship groups, some students resisted making the comparison; they claimed that their friends are different; others, intrigued, began to connect examples from the role-play to their own lives.

"The kids I hang around with don't like girls who get dressed up; we dress real casual—like, you know—overalls and stuff." It's much easier to think about crowds from other neighborhoods than to analyze your own. "Kids from down there don't like us 'cause we don't dress right for them. They all wear platforms and skirts."

After sharing some anecdotes, the class discusses what you gain and what you lose in winning the acceptance of a group. The gains are obvious: "You've got your own people to hang out with." "When you get in trouble there's people to back you up." The losses are less obvious. After giving it some thought, our students began to talk about self-respect. "If you're not true to yourself, you can't respect yourself. And if you don't respect yourself, who will?"

At the end of the discussion, ask the students to think of times when they had differences with the attitudes or activities of a group. "Did you stick with your own ways or did you go with the crowd?" "What did you gain?" "What did you lose?" Whenever we do this exercise our students remind us that some young people learn early to express their independence. As one powerful young woman put it, "I always do what I think is right, and I've got plenty of friends. I don't care what anyone else thinks, anyway."

20: "O Yes"—Friendship against Society's Pressures

It is a long baptism into the seas of humankind, my daughter. Better immersion than to live untouched . . . . Yet how will you sustain? [From "O Yes" by Tillie Olsen]

During junior high school, young people often become increasingly aware of society's divisions. There is a "sorting" out among different groups. Through reading Tillie Olsen's story, "O Yes," we explore the pressures against friendships which cross racial, ethnic, or class lines. We discuss what it's like to lose a friend because of these pressures, what it's like to sustain a friendship despite the pressures.

"O Yes" is a story about the painful dissolution of a friendship between Carol, who is white, and Parry, who is Black. In the first part of the story, the action is centered in a Black church, where Carol and her mother are the only white people in attendance. Carol's mother, Helen, and Parry's mother, Alva, have been close friends and neighbors for many years; their children have been best friends. To revive the friendship between their daughters, which is beginning to

wane, Helen and Alva bring Carol to Parry's baptism.

The service is very emotional; people sway to the rhythm of the sermon, shout out and clap, "O Yes." People thrash in the aisles. Carol, terrified, faints and is carried out of the church before her friend, Parry, is baptized. Outside, Carol is comforted by her mother, Alva, and Parry. When Alva tries to explain, Carol, overwhelmed, can't listen.

The second part of the story follows Carol and Parry's friendship in the months after the baptism, as they spend less and less time together. At school they are "sorting," as Carol's older sister, Jeannie, calls it.

And it's all where you're going. Yes and Parry's colored and Carrie's white. And you have to watch everything, what you. wear and how you wear it and who you eat lunch with and how much homework you do and how you act to the teacher and what you laugh at . . . . And run with your crowd. [P. 54]

After school, while Carol is going to a club, the library, or her friend Melanie's house, Parry has to babysit, because Alva works in the afternoons. Carol has the time and space for homework, but Parry doesn't.

When Carol has the mumps, Helen asks Parry to bring home Carol's books. Parry drops by with the books, masking her discomfort with a cheerfully cynical stream of talk, and is gone. "Next mumps is your buddybud Melanie's turn to tote your stuff. I'm getting the hoovus goovus . . . . Any little thing I can get, cause I gotta blow . . . . Joe . . ." (p.59).

Parry doesn't tell Carol about the humiliation she experienced at school when she requested Carol's books from the Dean.

Does your mother work for Carol's mother? Oh, you're neighbors! Very well, I'll send along a monitor to open Carol's locker but you're only to take these things I'm writing down, nothing else . . . . [P. 57]

Later, after Parry leaves, Carol weeps in her mother's arms. For the first time, she gets out her feelings about the baptism. "Mother, why did they sing and scream like that?"

Emotion, Helen thought of explaining, *a characteristic* of the religion of all oppressed peoples, yes
your very own grandparents. [P.60]

Helen soothes and holds her daughter, but
doesn't share her thoughts.

> "Mother, a lot of the teachers and kids don't like
> Parry when they don't even know what she's like.
> Just because. . . . And I'm not really her friend any-
> more. [P. 61]

The story ends with Helen holding Carol in her
arms, "sheltering her daughter close, mourning
the illusion of the embrace" (p. 62).

Like other stories by Tillie Olsen, "O Yes" is
understood most fully by our students when they
read it aloud in class, discussing it as they go. To
facilitate understanding, we've changed the
story into a modified "story-play," including a
descriptive list of the characters. To change the
story into a play, we write the names of the
characters who are thinking or speaking on the
left. Here's a sample from our modified version:

> *Everyone:* Any day now I'll reach that land of
> freedom
> Yes, oh yes
> Any day now, know that promised land
> *(The youth choir claps and taps to accent the swing
> of it. Beginning to tap, Carol stiffens.)*
> *Carol:* "Parry, look. Somebody from school."
> *Parry:* "Once more once," says Parialee, in a new
> way she likes to talk now.
> *Carol:* "Eddie Carlin's up there. He's in my math."
> *Parry:* "Couple cats from Franklin Jr. chirps in the
> choir. No harm or alarm." [P. 40]

Students take parts, and read aloud from their
own xeroxed copies of the "story-play," while
the teacher reads the narrative.

The descriptive list of characters explains
briefly who the characters are in relation to one
another and to the action of the story. Here is a
sample from our list:

Characters

Helen. Mother of Carol and Jeannie; she's a white
working-class woman.
Len. Helen's husband, father of Carol and Jeannie.
Alva. Helen's friend and neighbor, mother of
Parry, Lucy and Bubbie; she's a Black working-
class woman.

We use this list to introduce the characters

before we begin reading the "story-play" aloud,
as well as for reference while we are reading.

You will probably need one full class period
to read and discuss each part of the story. The
first part of the story lends itself to discussion of
the cultural differences between various ethnic
and racial groups and the differences between
various religions. "What is the difference between Parry's and Carol's churches?" "What did
Alva mean by 'church is home, maybe the only
place they can feel how they feel, and maybe let
it come out?' " In one of our discussions, a Black
student who had participated minimally in
earlier classes, lit up and explained the story to
the rest of the class. "I know what this story's
about. I know what it's like in some of them
churches. It can get pretty wild. I know about
that. I can see how a white girl might freak out in
there. Yes I could."

Next, you can look at some of the potentially
threatening differences among cultures. Are
there parts of the Italian way of life which might
"freak out" the Irish, or vice versa? Are there
aspects of the Puerto Rican way of life that might
"freak out" the Blacks? Why are people "freaked out" by these differences? Are the differences
themselves frightening? You might point out that
people are taught to be afraid of the differences.

The second part of the story is about the
pressures against Carol and Parry's friendship,
and how it must feel for them to become increasingly distant from one another. "Do you think
Carol and Parry's friendship can survive?" "Is
Helen doing right by Carol in encouraging her to
hold to the friendship?" "What is the role of the
school in separating the two friends?" "What are
other forces which separate them?"

These questions have stimulated our students
to talk about themselves and their friendships.
"This same thing happened to me. Me and a
Black girl was real tight in grammar school, then
by junior high we stopped hanging around
together." A Black student in the class discussed
her friendship with one of the white students,
"Me and you has always known each other.
That's 'cause of my aunt and your mother being
tight. When we was kids I always went over your
house to eat or you was at mine. But it's not
always like that. Lots of folks don't stick."

SCHOOL

INTRODUCTION

I really thought I was cool, being a freshman, knowing I could hang out with the sophomores and juniors. I was cutting classes. I didn't know anything about credits and didn't bother asking about them, and when the end of the year came, I found out that I had no credits! [Cheryl Greene]

Outside of the family, school is the main institution affecting a person's growing up. By the time adolescents reach sixteen, they have spent from eleven to thirteen years in school. Although often critical of school, students tend to accept the institutional judgment of their abilities and projections about their futures. It is important for them to learn that there may be larger patterns that encompass and explain some of their isolated experiences.

In this section, we try to help students develop more perspective on their school histories and become more aware of the ways school serves to reinforce and perpetuate class, sex, and race distinctions. In the first activity, the whole class participates in a role-play that exaggerates the way people get labeled in school. This is followed by readings from *A Tree Grows in Brooklyn* that explore how class biases affect both the self-images and the learning of the students. In the next activity, students reflect on their own experiences by writing their school autobiographies.

ACTIVITIES

21: School Daze—Group Role-Play

It can be difficult to begin a discussion about schooling experiences while in a classroom. "We're here every day; who needs to talk about it." For this reason, we usually begin with a role-play that exaggerates some of the elements of school. This sparks everybody's reactions and memories.

We find that this role-play works best when students are not forewarned (see "Techniques,"

p. 27). As they enter the room for class, students find the seats set up in neat rows, with a different role-label card on each seat. Role labels include: troublemaker, sleeper, good looker, brain, teacher's pet, cheerleader, bullshit artist, class clown, all-around good guy or girl, average student, anonymous student. The students are simply told to find their seats and get into them. With a little prodding, most students will choose a role and a seat and settle into the part suggested by the label. We insist that they wear their labels so that we can "take proper attendance with seating chart." The teacher then calls the class to order, starting a lesson on any subject. We usually try a lesson on democracy, because so many students have experienced just such a lesson in the past.

In conducting the class, the teacher reinforces all the labels, always calling on the teacher's pet, suspecting the troublemaker of trouble, reminding the good looker that "looks aren't everything; you've got to have a brain, too." Five to ten minutes of this is generally enough—for you and the students. By then the teacher is usually having serious "control" problems, and the students are running out of things to do in their roles.

The discussion centers around the way the students have been affected by labeling in their own schooling. We begin by talking about the role-play. "How did people feel playing these roles?" "Are these the right roles for schools you've been to?" "Are some roles more often male or more often female?" "Were the roles played realistically?" "Was the teacher realistic?" Then we ask everyone to say which one(s) of these labels comes closest to describing the role or roles they have actually played in their schooling.

"I was definitely the troublemaker; you wouldn't have believed what I was like then." "In fourth grade I was the teacher's pet. She loved me." "Nobody even noticed when I was absent, I was so quiet." This exercise usually leads to interesting anecdotes about schooling experiences. Although told humorously, many of these stories contain painful memories or end on a note of self-criticism. "I never was too smart.""I never was much at school anyway."

We encourage students to share these memories—funny, sad, embarrassing, or painful. When it seems appropriate, we point out to students the disparity between the labels they have carried previously and their behavior in the women's course, where they have had an opportunity to be themselves. We ask students to think about whether they would have done better in school if more had been expected of them, if more attention had been paid to them. We ask students whether they think their sex, or class background, or race has had anything to do with their experiences in school.

These are complex questions that obviously cannot be wholly answered in a class discussion. The point is to encourage students to reevaluate their schooling experiences, and the self-images that developed out of those experiences. Having a successful schooling experience in this course itself can be an important step in this reevaluation process.

If you wish to pursue further issues of class or race discrimination in schooling, there are several readings we would recommend. Discussions of class privilege can be introduced by a number of sections in *A Tree Grows in Brooklyn.* If you are not reading the whole book, the following sections can easily be excerpted: pp. 133–141, 142–144, 146–154. (An additional resource is Tillie Olsen's story, "O Yes," which hints at the pervasiveness of racial tracking. See p. 85 of this unit for a fuller description of the story.)

This first excerpt from *A Tree Grows in Brooklyn* raises the issue of class discrimination.

> She had been in school but half a day when she knew that she would never be a teacher's pet. That privilege was reserved for a small group of girls . . . girls with freshly curled hair, crisp clean pinafores and new silk hairbows. They were the children of the prosperous storekeepers of the neighborhood . . . Francie, huddled with other children of her kind, learned more that first day than she realized. She learned of the class system of a great Democ-

racy. . . . Obviously, the teacher hated her and others like her for no other reason than that they were what they were. [P. 133]

When students read this, there is often a shock of recognition. "The rich kids were always in the A.T. [Academically Talented] classes. "We were all put in the achievement classes, you know, for the dummies." "We were always put in the back of the room. The girls who dressed better were put in front." Some students maintain that "Money has nothing to do with it. It's how smart you are."

Another selection from the same book portrays an alternative to a class-biased teacher. This teacher is tuned into the whole group and excited by his subject (p. 143). After reading both short selections, we ask: "What difference does it make to have a teacher like the second one who tries to interest all the students?" "Have you had teachers who treat all students as people?" Some students can't remember any teachers who cared about them. Their stories are bitter. Others can remember two or three teachers who were "different." "I had this one young teacher; she was cool. She always had the class occupied."

After sharing anecdotes, students discuss the difference it might have made in their self-images and in their learning, if all the teachers, and the schools themselves, had reflected egalitarian values.

22: Writing a Schooling Autobiography

To examine their own schooling in the light of our role-play, readings, and discussions, we suggest that our students write schooling autobiographies. Here is the assignment we've given:

> First, make a list of all the schools you've been to and then think of one or two experiences you had in each of these schools that gets across a sense of what it was like for you. You might want to think of one good and one bad experience.
>
> Then, write a paper that tells the story of your life in schools.

Students who had trouble writing more than a paragraph or two on other assignments, wrote two and three page papers on this one.

I was going to the Roberts School for six years, but my first four years were not bad, except for when I was kept back in the fourth grade. I was sick in the hospital for a long period of time . . . Miss McCann was my fourth grade teacher. She sent me to the special class . . . I stayed in that class for one year, then I was sent to a vocational school. All this going from one special class to another was hardly necessary!

In the fall I finally made it to my freshman year. Then I really thought I was cool, being a freshman, knowing I could hang out with the sophomores and juniors. I was cutting classes. I didn't know any-

thing about credits and didn't bother asking about them, and when the end of the year came I found out that I had no credits. [Cheryl Greene]

Most students adopted a similar tone—a kind of ironic humor about their younger selves and their own naïveté. Through writing the schooling autobiographies, students come to appreciate the progress they have made in understanding themselves and the system. (For more suggestions on writing an autobiography, see Autobiography—Growing Up Female, p. 92.)

SELF

INTRODUCTION

I am water

Something that can absorb the
hardest substance and not be
harmed. Something that is at once
both weak and strong. Which can
yield but never be conquered.
I can adapt to any shape
poured into a cup.
I appear to be ineffective
but in time I can wear down
the sturdiest rocks
by my constant dripping. My
form is constantly changing but
my spirit and essence are unchanged.

[John Sullivan]

An important part of growing up is defining an identity and learning to accept that identity. Family, friends, and institutions, all play a role in that process. Another important part of the struggle goes on internally, in the young person's relationship with herself. In this section we ask students to be self-reflective, to try to integrate some of what they have learned about themselves.

The section begins with the question: "Is there a woman inside whom no one else knows?" Through reading an entry in *Anne Frank: The Diary of a Young Girl*, learning new vocabulary,

reading a poem by Marge Piercy, and doing a writing assignment, students try to answer this question for themselves. In the next activity, students focus on their "external selves," their bodies. They read "A Poem in Which My Legs Are Accepted," discuss how they feel when they look in the mirror, and share their own poems. In the final activity, students write autobiographies that tie together many of their thoughts and feelings about growing up female.

ACTIVITIES

23: Self Alone—The Woman Inside

Relevant Readings from the Books

Anne Frank: The Diary of a Young Girl: An actual diary, this entire book is about "the woman inside" of Anne Frank. With great sensitivity, she records the inner process of her coming into womanhood.

Daddy Was a Number Runner: Throughout her childhood and early adolescence, Francie has a recurring secret fantasy of escape from her current life and identity. Ken Maynard, her favorite movie cowboy, comes thundering down Fifth Avenue on his white horse, swoops Francie up in his arms and rides off with her into the sunset (p.84). As she gets older, the image dims, until finally, one day, sitting alone looking out the front window, she realizes she can accept and love herself and her life (pp. 183–184).

I Know Why The Caged Bird Sings: Throughout much of the book Maya feels like a very awkward adolescent. She is insecure and, at times, self-pitying. Her feeling about herself changes when she lives for a month in a car junkyard with a gang of homeless children who accept her completely (p.216), and when she gives birth to a beautiful child, who trusts and needs her (pp. 244–246).

A Tree Grows in Brooklyn: As a young girl, Francie likes to be alone, reading and fantasizing (pp. 7–8, 25). Years later, while dressing for a date with her boyfriend, she looks in the mirror and reflects on the self of her childhood (p. 429).

Are you different when you're alone with yourself? Is there a woman inside whom no one else knows? In this activity we address these questions about a young woman's relationship with herself.

The last entry in Anne Frank's *Diary* centers on Anne's perceptions of her "dual" self: one self that she shows to the world, and another, deeper self, that she never shares with others.

> I'm awfully scared that everyone who knows me as I always am will discover that I have another side, a finer and better side. I'm afraid they'll laugh at me, think I'm ridiculous and sentimental, not take me seriously. I'm used to not being taken seriously but it's only the "light-hearted" Anne that's used to it and can bear it; the "deeper" Anne is too frail for it. . . . Therefore, the nice Anne is never present in company, has not appeared one single time so far, but almost always predominates when we're alone. I know exactly how I'd like to be, how I am too . . . inside. But, alas, I'm only like that for myself . . . I am guided by the pure Anne within, but outside I'm nothing but a frolicsome little goat who's broken loose . . . I . . . keep on trying to find a way of becoming what I would like to be, and what I could be if . . . there weren't any other people living in the world. [Pp. 240-241]

This excerpt has resonated for many of our students. Most of the young women feel that there are aspects of themselves which no one else sees. "No one really knows me." "I don't let on what I'm really thinking to nobody." "I travel 'incog.' It's the only way." To deepen discussion,

we ask, "What holds a person back from showing the self inside?" "What do you imagine would happen if you showed people who you really are?" "Are there particular masks that women often feel they must assume to hide their inside selves which are different from typical masks that men assume?" "What are some masks that men assume?" "Anne Frank describes her mask as a 'frolicsome little goat' or a 'giddy clown'; how would you describe yours?"

To accompany the reading, we teach the following vocabulary from the text: contradiction, dual, exuberant, superficial, deep, sentimental, indifferent. We've added related words to our list, which aren't found in the text, but may be used to elucidate its meaning: self-reflective, perceptive, self-conscious, self-assured, vulnerable. All of these words may be used as tools by our students in thinking about their relationships with themselves.

The excerpt from Anne Frank's *Diary* can also serve as an introduction for a discussion of what it's like to be alone with oneself. We ask our students: "Like Anne, are you different when you're alone with yourself?" "Do you enjoy being alone?" "How do you feel?" "What do you think about?" "Are there things you can learn when alone with yourself?" "How could you make better use of that time?" Many of our students have said that they don't like being alone: "I keep thinking about the past and I get really sad." "I get freaky thoughts; sometimes I'm so scared." There are a few who treasure that time: "That's my best time, when I read or write poems or do photography." "You can never be alone at my house. That's why I stay up so late, until everyone else is asleep." "When I'm alone outside at night, I feel free."

24: The Woman Inside— Writing Assignment

Sometimes when I look in the mirror
I don't see me. I see an image of me.
Certain things about me are there when I look.
A few good points, but mostly bad.
Every now and then it's a stranger I see,

Telling me not to look anymore
And that scares me.
[Annie Bithoney]

Talking about one's innermost self is difficult for many people. Students feel less exposed in a **writing assignment. Marge Piercy's poem "The woman in the ordinary"** (from the collection, *To Be of Use*) helps students to get into a mood conducive to the assignment.

The woman in the ordinary

The woman in the ordinary pudgy downcast girl
is crouching with eyes and muscles clenched.
. . . .

inside the girl who imitates
a Christmas card virgin with glued hands,
who fishes for herself in others' eyes,
who stoops and creeps to make herself smaller.
In her bottled up is a woman peppery as curry,
a yam of a woman of butter and brass,
compounded of acid and sweet like a pineapple,
like a handgrenade set to explode,
like goldenrod ready to bloom.
[P. 32]

Writing choices might include:

1. Using "The woman in the ordinary" as your model, write you own poem about yourself entitled, "The Woman Inside."
2. Write a poem, description, or short story about yourself when you are alone.
3. Take time each day to be alone with yourself and to write your thoughts in a diary. (This is for you; you don't need to hand it in.)
4. Write a story or poem which begins: "If there weren't any other people living in the world…"

25: Accepting Your Body

Kathleen Fraser has written a poem, "Legs," that inspires lively discussions (from *No More Masks*, edited by Florence Howe and Ellen Bass). Here are some excerpts:

Legs!
How we have suffered each other,
never meeting the standards of magazines
or official measurements.
Here you are—solid, fleshy and

white as when I first noticed you,
    sitting on the toilet,
    spread softly over the wooden seat,
having been with me only twelve years,
    yet
as obvious as the legs of my thirty-year-old
    gym teacher.
Legs!
O that was the year we did acrobatic
    in the the annual gym show
How you split for me!
. . . .

I hated you and still you have never
    given out on me.
. . . .

You are the endless scenery
behind the sinewy elegance of his two dark legs,
You welcome him joyfully
and dance.
And you will be the locks in a new canal between
    the continents.
    The ship of life will push out of you
    and rejoice…
        in the whiteness,
            in the first floating and rising of water

[P. 253]

Students identify with the poet's initial shame: "I always hated my legs." "Joe says I got the biggest ass at Washington Elms." "Nobody ever sees me in a bathing suit. Not with my shape. I wear cut-offs when I go swimming." We ask: "Where do you get these pictures of yourselves?" "What makes you think one kind of figure is better than another?" "Do you think men worry about their 'figures?'" Often the students are surprised to hear one another's self-images. "I never thought you were fat!" "You think you have it bad; I don't have any chest at all." Their feedback is almost always reassuring, and it's a relief to learn that people who look good to you have insecurities, too.

The second part of the poem, where the poet "accepts her legs," is less accessible to our students. First, we figure out what she's talking about in plain language, then ask whether anyone has had a similar experience. Occasionally, a student will concur, "I like my body, even if it's not perfect. It's mine, isn't it?"

Writing assignments we've done to follow up this activity include:

1. Write a poem which begins: "When I look in the mirror I feel . . ."
2. Write a poem addressed to some part of your body, in which you remember your history together.
3. Write a poem in which you become some part of your body. Write about what you feel and what you do.
4. Write a poem to your body, in which you address each line to a different part.

Here is one poem we received:

Hands

i am warm
most especially
and soft
my work
easy
but I sweat
hard los
i detect congestion
untangle knots
smoothe and soothe
i can roll powerfully
entering a defensive
fist
i can move
with purple lightning
speed
i may hold
the weight
of your heavy, resting
head
I can heat your buns
toasty warm.
[Julie Scanlan]

Students love to write poems to or about a part of the body. Some of our best have included: knee, mind, hands, legs, face, and navel.

26: Autobiography—Growing Up Female

To give the students an opportunity to reflect on and integrate their thoughts and feelings about their own lives, growing up female, we suggest that they write autobiographies.

The teacher prepares a list of questions to help the students focus on key issues in their current lives, histories, and thoughts about the future. Here's a sample list:

Growing Up Female

History:

1. What do you remember most about your childhood?
2. Was being a child easier or harder than being a young woman? Why?
3. What memory stands out when you think about your change from being a child to being a young woman?
4. What are the main ways you have changed in the past five years?

Present:

1. What are some of the best things about your life as a young woman?
2. What are some of the most difficult things about your life as a young woman?
3. How do you spend time on an average day? (How is your time divided up: i.e., school, work, friends, family?)
4. How do you feel about school? If you work, how do you feel about your job? What's it like?
5. Who are the most important people in your life? (family, friends?)
6. What are some of the positive things you get out of your friendships? (with males? with females?)
7. What are some of the difficulties you experience in your friendships? (with males? with females?)
8. What is the most interesting thing that has happened to you lately?
9. What do you do or think about when you're alone?
10. In what ways are you presently changing?

Future:

1. In what ways do you expect to change in the future?
2. What are your future plans?

Each student makes notes on these questions for her own use. The questions are not intended to provide an outline for the autobiography, but, rather, to give students a sense of the kind of issues and experiences that could be included in their papers. Once they have made notes on the questions, they divide into small groups to briefly discuss their notes. Reading the questions together and sharing some of their responses will prepare them for writing (see "Techniques," p. 18). Sharing time should be strictly limited. There's a danger of talking it out and not any longer feeling a need to write about it.

When the students begin to write, we encourage them to draw on the notes which most interest and excite them in trying to give a real sense of their current lives and life stories. We suggest that they read through their past writing assignments to see whether they can find descriptions of people, incidents, or feelings which they might want to incorporate into their autobiographies.

Once all the autobiographies are written, we like to type them up as a collection, to make a group biography of the class. It's exciting for students to read through the finished product. They feel a particular pride in having written thoughtful papers about their entire lives. Every time we've assigned autobiographies, someone has exclaimed with wonder: "I can't believe I did this. I've never put anything like this together before."

COMPARISONS—SELF AND OTHERS

INTRODUCTION

Growing up poor I got a bad education. The teachers often figured, if your parents didn't teach you, why should they? But the parents of poor kids can't teach them because they only had a tenth-grade education themselves. Rich parents have gone to college and have books around the house and talk very highly educated so that the kids pick It right up. Also the poor kid's father might work as a dishwasher and a rich kid's father does a professional job like a doctor or a lawyer. [Deborah Stewart Hedges]

This section helps to broaden the students' perspective beyond the experiences of young working-class women like themselves. Growing up as a low-income American female is compared to growing up as a male, or growing up middle class, or growing up in another, totally different culture. The activities of this section can be taught sequentially, as they are presented here, or they can be distributed into other sections of the "Growing Up Female" unit, to broaden the scope of those explorations. The advantage of doing the comparisons here is that students may be able to use what they have learned about themselves in their investigations of people with different kinds of experiences.

The activities start with the most accessible, yet different, population, and move further and further afield. In the first activity, students interview young men in the school about their experiences in growing up. Then they take a trip to a middle-class suburban high school to meet students who are growing up in more privileged surroundings. In the third activity, they read excerpts from Margaret Mead and write a monograph about the "American girl," from the viewpoint of an anthropologist from another society. As a final activity, they integrate their insights by making a Super-8 film together.

ACTIVITIES

27: Interviews with Young Men

"We talk, you know, but not about that kind of stuff." Regardless of how much time young women and young men spend together—in a crowd, dating, or going to school—they probably have not shared much about their experiences growing up or about their concerns as adolescents. The structure of this exercise helps them talk with each other about these topics.

Recognizing the assignment as a chance to learn more about their male contemporaries, students usually are enthusiastic about making up questions. They tend to be most interested in finding out about current attitudes and behavior, they have to be reminded to include issues of growing up. Our students have developed the following questions:

1. What toys or games did you play with when you were little?
2. Have you always been treated the same as other kids in your family? If you have sisters, are the rules the same? the chores the same?
3. Did you feel closer to your male relatives or female relatives when you were growing up?
4. When did you first get interested in girls? What did you think of girls when you were five?, ten?, fifteen?
5. What were you most afraid of when you were little?
6. What are you most afraid of now?
7. What do you like in a female?
8. What do you think of girls that wear a lot of make-up?
9. Do you like girls for their personality or looks?
10. Do you think about the way you dress and look?
11. Who can you talk better to, a girl or guy?
12. Did you ever hit a girl, or would you?

The class can decide among several procedures for selecting interviewees. One procedure is for the teacher to locate a class or a school club with a number of males that roughly equals the females in the women's course. Their teacher or leader then introduces the interviewing project to them, and, as a group, they design their own interview questions for the young women. When the groups get together, female/male interviewing teams are matched through a lottery-draw system. Another possible procedure is for each student to find her own young man to interview outside of class. He can be anyone—a friend, a boyfriend, a brother, a classmate (see "Techniques," p. 28).

We have preferred to use the first method, because students can learn from the experience of doing an interview and from being interviewed. When we did this assignment with a male

class, its members presented questions that interested and surprised our students:

1. What do you like in a boy?
2. Have you ever found a boy with those qualities?
3. What do you admire in a girl?
4. What do you think of women's lib?
5. What do you think about getting pushed around by men?
6. About supporting them? About equality between men and women?
7. What are you afraid of—being raped? ripped off? arrested? beat up? anything else?
8. Do you like to fight?

Another advantage in getting together with a male class is that the interviews are more likely to be done systematically and seriously in the classroom setting. Furthermore, if there is time, the whole group—including both females and males—can get together at the end of the interviewing session and share some of the similarities and differences they found. If the interviews are done outside of class, only the young women will be in class for the exploration of patterns (see "Techniques," p. 30).

In a mixed class, female and male students within the class could, of course, interview each other. It might make sense in this situation to do the interviews earlier on in the unit, in order to name some areas of similarities and differences that could be explored through the readings and discussion of the unit.

Talking about these issues with young men is, in itself, an important learning experience for the students. Thus, in sharing the results of the interviews, it is very important to allow a good deal of space for stories about the interviews. "He was really embarrassed about that question." "I didn't know whether to be really honest with him or not." The students should be encouraged to talk about themselves as well as about the interviewees. "How did you feel asking him these questions?" "Were any especially hard to ask? Why?" "Can you imagine asking them outside of an interviewing situation?"

In compiling results, the goal is to identify female/male similarities and differences, both in their experiences in growing up and in their concerns as adolescents. To provide everyone with the "raw data," you could list the questions on the chalkboard or on a large sheet of paper, and then ask each student to insert a shortened version of her interviewee's answers to each of the questions. Then everyone can look over the information and search for patterns. "Were there any questions most of the males answered the same way?" "Were there any questions which reveal big differences among the males?" "Did any answers surprise you?" "Comparing these results to previous discussions in the unit, what seem to be major differences between growing up male and growing up female?" If the class compiles the results with a male class still present, the discussion could focus first on finding areas of agreement and disagreement among the females and among the males, then on looking for similarities and differences between males and females.

A writing assignment provides a way for the students to continue thinking about what they learned from their interviews (see "Techniques," p. 18). Two possible writing choices are:

1. Compare growing up male in Cambridge to growing up female in Cambridge. Include at least three ways it is similar and three ways it is different.
2. Describe what you would imagine as a typical day for a sixteen-year-old male in Cambridge. Begin with what he is thinking about as he wakes up, and how he goes about choosing what he is going to wear that day.

28: Trip to a Suburban High School

Most students have mythical ideas about what it's like to live in the suburbs, to "have bucks," to go to one of "those fancy modern-type schools." But few have actually had the chance to learn about suburban middle-class life at firsthand. In this activity, they take a trip to a nearby suburban high school and interview students there. Although only a brief exposure to suburban life, the trip does give the students some sense of what it's like to grow up in such a community. And, in the process, they also bring to the surface and gain insight into their am-

bivalence toward their own lifestyles and experiences.

If possible, you should try to locate a fairly prosperous, nearby suburban community where someone you know is a teacher. (See p. 33 for more detailed suggestions about arranging trips.) The best situation would be to visit another women's class. This gives the two groups some common experiences and concerns to draw upon. If you cannot make this arrangement, it is still important to talk to the teacher ahead of time, explaining to her the composition of your group and the purposes of your visit. She can then inform and prepare her own class.

Students prepare for this trip as they do for any interviewing situation—by compiling a list of questions. Because a number of students will have preconceptions or stereotypes about the suburban young women they will meet, it might be a good idea to begin by surfacing these expectations. "They'll probably all be snobs." "They'll think they're better than us." Students can then try to develop questions that will match their preconceptions against reality.

To encourage fairly specific questions, we suggest five separate categories: 1) Home Life; 2) School Life; 3) Friends and Street Life; 4) Problems or Trouble; 5) Hopes, Dreams, and Future Possibilities. Students choose the category that interests them most and meet in a small group to develop questions. (This should only be done with a class that has done interviewing before; for techniques to use with beginners, see p. 29.) We end with an extensive interview sheet, including the following questions:

1. What do you do on a typical evening? on a weekend?
2. Where do you hang out? Do you ever hang out on corners? Does your mother let you hang around with whom you want?
3. Do you ever get into fights? If so, what kinds?
4. Do you get high? smoke dope? drink? If yes, what age did you start?
5. Do you have a car? a bike?
6. What are some of your favorite songs? What radio station do you listen to?
7. Do you like to travel? If so, where have you gone?

8. Do you have chores to do at home? If so, what? If you don't, who does them?
9. Do you get an allowance? How much?
10. Do you fight much with your parents? If so, what do you get hassled about?
11. What do you think of school? What's the best and worst thing about it?
12. What would your mother do if you got arrested?
13. Do you steal? If so, what kinds of stuff? Why?
14. What would your mother do if you got pregnant by your boyfriend?
15. Do you ever walk around alone at night?
16. What are you most scared of?
17. If you had one wish, what would it be?
18. What are your goals for the future?
19. How much of what you hope for do you think will happen?
20. How do you plan to reach your goals?
21. Who influences your plans?
22. Would you like to be richer than you are now?
23. Do you think you should work if you get married?
24. Does your mother work? How does (or would) your father feel about it?
25. Have you ever had a job? If so, doing what?
26. What do you do in the summer?

Supplied with copies of these questionnaires for every student, we set off to visit Newton High School—a brand-new multimillion-dollar edifice in a nearby suburb of Cambridge. "Is this the day we're going to Newton?" had been asked by one student or another for the four days previous to the trip. When the day finally did arrive, everyone was there on time, excited about the trip and noticeably dressed up for the occasion. By the time we arrived, however, the excitement had taken on a more cynical edge; the predominant emotions were closer to hostility and insecurity. "Oh, isn't that sweet, a parking lot for all their Camaros." "They probably think we're freaks. Everybody's staring at us."

Even more than during most trips, the teacher's presence and comments are crucial to helping students through these first bad moments. You can say things like, "Some students here

probably do have cars. It's pretty hard to go anywhere in the suburbs without them." Or, "People are looking at us because we're new faces and we look lost, but we really don't look too different from anybody else here." Once in the classroom with the suburban students, people will feel more comfortable. It is probably a good idea to form the interviewing teams (of two or three students) fairly quickly, giving the students a chance to start talking and sharing. The teachers can use this opportunity to float from group to group, listening, perhaps helping people over difficult moments. Much of what you hear will be useful material for later discussion. For instance, in Newton, we overheard this interaction:

> *Cambridge student:* "Do you like to travel?"
> *Newton student:* "Yes, but I haven't really been anywhere."
> *Cambridge student:* "Yeah, me either."
> *Newton student:* "I mean, I've just been around the United States—Oregon, California, you know."

In a later discussion with our students, back at The Group School, this interaction became a starting point for a discussion of the differing expectations of the two groups.

After about thirty or forty minutes, the teachers should pull the teams together for some quick processing of the interviews. "What are some of the similarities you found in interviewing each other?" "Where are there differences?" "What surprised you the most?" If there is time, each interviewing team is asked to comment on these questions. It is valuable for students to review the results of their interviews and interpret some of their data while it's still fresh in their minds. This is a time for summing up and sharing. Later on, back at their own school, the students will have a chance to analyze their feelings.

When our students interviewed Newton students, almost all of the teams reported finding similarities in their responses to questions dealing with relationships with parents or relationships with friends (especially boyfriends). More differences emerged in comparisons of how people spend their free time and of their plans for the future. Our students were amazed that the Newton women did not "hang out" and the Newton students were equally amazed at how much time the Cambridge women seemed to spend in that activity. The difference in the two groups' future plans was summed up by one of our students who said: "Sure, we're all going to college—only they really will!"

At the next class session after the trip, the students review the whole experience of going to a suburban school and meeting its students. This time, they are asked to share more of their own feelings and thoughts: "What did you learn from the trip?" "Did anything surprise you? Disturb you?" "How did you feel about the person you interviewed? Did any of her responses stay in your mind?" "From what you saw, would you want to live in Newton? Why or why not?" "Did the trip affect or change any of your feelings about growing up in Cambridge?"

Any one of the questions will probably elicit responses from a number of students. One of our students could hardly wait to share her interviewee's "one wish." "Do you know what she said? She said, 'to be unselfish.' That was her wish! It made me feel weird. She has it and wants to give it away. I don't have it and want to get it." This anecdote, like many others the students will share after the trip, opens the door to a consideration of the effects of background and social class. Although these are extremely difficult issues to explore, we recommend that you use this opportunity to do so. The trip highlights the systematic inequalities of social class divisions, without leaving the students feeling like passive victims. Students come back from the trip very aware of (and sometimes jealous of) the privileges enjoyed by the suburban young women because of their families' incomes; but they also come back with renewed pride in their own resilience and strength. "I wouldn't want to grow up there. They never even go out at night. They're scared of more things than us; they haven't, you know, seen what we have about life."

The trip helps students get in touch with positive feelings about their own growing up. They begin to see ways in which the very

privileges of suburban, upper-middle-class life deprive people of certain experiences and opportunities to grow. At the same time, the differences between them and the suburban students in regard to future hopes and plans serve as painful reminder of the many obstacles that lie ahead.

Because so many feelings and issues are raised by the discussion, a writing assignment might be a good immediate follow-up. Two possible writing choices are:

1. Compare what it is like growing up in Newton with what it is like growing up in Cambridge. Include at least two specific ways it is similar and at least two specific ways it is different. If you want, share your feelings about which you would prefer.
2. Describe what you would imagine as a typical day for a sixteen-year-old female in Newton. Begin with where, when, and how she wakes up in the morning.

29: Cross-Cultural Comparisons

Through even a brief exposure to anthropology, students can gain perspective on some of the more painful and ecstatic moments of adolescence. A young woman staring at her figure in the mirror before going out, or letting a boyfriend touch her body for the first time, or arguing with her parents about what time to be in, is going through a very personal moment. But she is also experiencing a particular manifestation of age-old rituals, ceremonies, and taboos that have to do with the onset of puberty and the rites of passage into adulthood. Realizing this can be very helpful—and exciting— to young women.

Margaret Mead has written many books that include anthropological material on adolescence. Two chapters we have found useful in *Growing Up in New Guinea* are "The Adolescent Girl" and "The Adolescent Boy." Also very interesting is Chapter VI in *Sex and Temperament*. By reading short selections aloud in class (no more than twenty minutes at a time) and defining new words and anthropological terminology as you go along, you can make good use of this material (see "Techniques," p. 13). Students are amused by some puberty ceremonies—like the one during which a female runs the length of the house pursued by her grandmother, who is waving a burning torch over her and reciting an incantation; they are horrified by others—like the one which requires a young woman who has just attained puberty to sit perfectly still for five days in a cubbyhole made of mats near the center of her house. Their interest in these different customs, and your help with unfamiliar words, will carry them through the most difficult parts of the reading.

The first few pages of "The Adolescent Girl," in *Growing Up in New Guinea,* provide the class with a good beginning list of anthropological terms: puberty, ceremony, incantations, taboo. Although a very specialized kind of vocabulary, these words are worth learning, because they describe and throw new light on events and moments in the students' lives. We taught this vocabulary list by having students look at each word in the context of the sentence in the reading and then brainstorm specific examples from their own lives of the phenomena described by these terms. Students had a good time deciding what events in their culture constituted "ceremonies," especially "puberty ceremonies"; what could be called "taboos"; what could be labeled as "incantations."

The students' high interest in this discussion gave us the idea for a writing assignment that we strongly recommend. Ask the students to write about the "adolescent American girl" from the viewpoint of an anthropologist from another, very different society—like Manus, for instance. "How would the Manusian anthropologist see the American young woman?" "What would seem to her to be the significant rituals or ceremonies?" "What would be labeled 'taboo'?" This assignment works best as a group writing project. First, the whole class decides on four or five different customs, ceremonies, or themes to study in the life of the adolescent American female. Our class, for example, chose "appearance," "hanging out," "making out," "rock concerts," and "home life." Still together, the class writes a brief introduction to their study:

We belong to a team of anthropologists who have been doing research on the adolescent American female in the United States. We have been in the United States for two months, and although we have not yet mastered the language, we have done some close observation of American teen-agers.

Generally, the American teen-ager leads a very unnatural life. She is not allowed to be herself. She is overprotected by her parents. She seems to be happy because she is always showing her teeth, but we have not yet understood how she can be because of all the customs and taboos pulling on her.

Before puberty, the overclothed American female seems to resemble the American male. Girls and boys play the same games: hide-and-seek (one person is "it" and has to find all the others) and cops-and-robbers (boys chase girls with sticks), and many games where they throw around what looks like a rubber coconut.

At puberty, the parents seem to protect their daughters; often the son is regarded with great respect and is pushed and expected to become head of the family ["Women and Society" class, 1972]

Having agreed upon a general introduction, students divide up into small groups, with each group taking one custom or ceremony as its writing project. Before the groups start to work, the teacher should make sure that each group has some good ideas of how and where to begin. For instance, if the group working on the ceremony of "hanging out" is having trouble getting started, you might want to give them some questions to focus their thinking: Where does the American young woman spend her evenings? Does she spend time with other females? With males? Are there any taboos connected with "hanging out?" Encourage the members in each group to talk together before they actually start to write. Writing collectively can be difficult, but it will probably result in a more imaginative document.

When the groups have completed their work, everyone comes back together to hear the results. Sharing the groups' essays should lead to some lively discussion, since everyone has some expertise on the subject of this "anthropological research." When we did this assignment, our students were so pleased with what the groups had composed that they decided to publish the final manuscript for the rest of the school.

30: Making a Film about Growing Up Female

> My favorite part of the course was seeing the results of our film. I guess I have to admit it was beautiful. Completing the film was the biggest thrill of my school life. [From a student evaluation]

Making a film is an excellent way to draw together some of the themes and explorations of this unit. Having talked and read about the issues and problems of growing up female, having compared themselves to other people—both real and fictional—the class has the preparation for making its own film statement about adolescence.

Two very different kinds of statements grow naturally out of the themes of this unit. The students could either make an "anthropological" film about the "adolescent American girl," based on the manuscript they've written, or they could make a more autobiographical film about their own lives, based on what they feel they have learned and can articulate about themselves. It is important to offer the students this choice; either film will express a great deal about their experiences and ideas—but the first is much less directly personal than the second.

If the class chooses the anthropological approach, students should start with the already written manuscript and figure out how to translate it into film. What will be the major scenes of the movie? What will happen in each scene? What people or props are needed? What should be taped as a sound track? How much of the manuscript itself should be read on the tape? What songs might be appropriate? Many students may never have seen a Super-8 movie, especially one with a separate taped sound track. To give them a sense of the range of possibilities, it would be good to show them one.

If students decide they want to make the more personal film statement, the script should be drawn from their autobiographical essays. The

task here is to integrate the individual essays into a group autobiography that can be filmed. The first step in this process is for students to read their essays aloud. It is important for everyone to hear all of the material on which the film could be based. This sharing also gives the students another opportunity to learn about each other's lives. After each reading, there should be time for questions and comments about parts of the essay that seem especially vivid or especially unclear. Actual decisions about which parts of each person's autobiography to use should be left to small groups. After all the essays have been read, the class should be divided into groups of three or four students. Together, the members of each small group will select one or two scenes from each person's life to film and will decide which parts of the essays to use as script. They should also figure out where they need to film, who will be in each scene, what props are needed, and what would be an appropriate sound track.

A film project draws on everybody's ingenuity and talents. The structure of the work encourages people to depend on each other for help and support and to work together closely. There are many important interdependent aspects to the work: scriptwriting, directing, set designing, lighting, acting, filming, taping, and editing. Students who have found it hard to participate in discussions all term may find that they like taping the sound or filming a scene. Students who have enjoyed role-playing all term may want to perfect their talents as screen actors. The variety of tasks is such that everyone can make an active contribution. In mastering a camera, or a tape recorder, or an editing machine, students gain a new sense of competence and self-worth. They cannot believe they can make these machines work; and, in fact, they often do not believe it until they see the rushes and realize they were responsible for all of those images and sounds. The rewards of doing a film project are great, for the individual students and for the group as a whole.

Accomplishing that final result also takes a lot of hard work, from both the students and the teacher. Even before the project can get underway, the teacher faces several major organizational problems. First, there is the problem of locating decent equipment. At least one Super-8 camera, a cassette tape recorder, lights, and an editing machine, are all essential. And, if you do not know how to run this equipment yourself, you must also find someone who can come in regularly to train the students and to oversee the film, sound, and editing crews. Then there is the problem of the expense. A ten or fifteen-minute color film can cost from $70 to $100. Although these problems are considerable, we found all of them to be solvable, once we had overcome our own fears about engaging in such a project with little help from "experts." Many schools do have most of the required equipment; many also have film budgets or special curriculum project budgets. There is almost certain to be someone on the faculty, or a volunteer from the community, who takes home movies and can teach the students to use the equipment.

Clearing the first set of hurdles makes the project conceivable. Students can begin work on the scripts and can begin learning to use the equipment. The next step is to set up a realistic production schedule. Depending on your situation, you might want to work on the film in a concentrated way for about three weeks or in a less concentrated way over a period of ten to twelve weeks. If you want to do it in the shorter period, you will need to have the script ready before you start. You will also have to devote daily time and energy to keeping an overview of what should be filmed next and who and what is required for that filming. If you are spending one, and sometimes two times a week, over a longer period of time, there will be more lead time for making arrangements, making changes in the script, etc. The other advantage to the longer time-span is that film can take four or five days to process. If you are filming once a week, you can see your most recent results before each new filming. On the other hand, the results might be better if you do the project within a shorter, more focused period. Either way, you and the students who have been most involved in the filming and editing will almost certainly have to spend time outside of the regular class periods to complete the project. There will be certain shots to film, certain interviews to tape, last minute editing to do.

Once there is a detailed list of scenes and a production schedule, the group is ready to begin filming. A division of roles and responsibilities now becomes essential. Each student has to decide where she wants to focus her energy: acting, directing, managing props, filming, taking sound, editing. A student could, of course, be involved in more than one aspect of the work, but it is a good idea for each student to have one main area of focus. Obviously, in a large class it is hard to involve every student at the same time. The situation is much relieved if there is another adult helping you (preferably one with experience in filmmaking) who can take part of the class out filming, while you work with the rest of the class, viewing their previous footage, getting their next scenes ready, etc. If you make the autobiographical film, each small group can constitute its own film crew, perhaps drawing on other students occasionally as actors. But, again, this assumes that another adult is involved.

The finished film is not only a creative restatement of some of the themes of the unit, but it is also a mechanism for reaching out to other people. The class should decide what audiences they would like to have view their film. Depending on factors like time and mobility, you might want to test out responses to the film among wide and diverse audiences. When we made an anthropological film, we showed it to the whole Group School and then took it to classrooms in the local public high school, to suburban classrooms, and to local youth projects. After each showing, the students lead discussions, drawing out peoples' responses to the content of the film. The experience of talking with groups of strangers and of receiving positive feedback for their accomplishments was enormously valuable for the students who participated. The group of students who made the autobiographical film felt more protective of their product. They preferred to limit their showings to the Group School community.

NOTES TO THE TEACHER

Combining Skills and Content

This unit, more than any other in the curriculum, centers around readings. In exploring the issues of growing up, students are asked to read novels, autobiographies, plays, short stories, and poems. Often, readings are followed by discussions that draw both on the written material and on similar events or experiences from the students' own lives. Frequently, discussions lead up to writing assignments where they are asked either to summarize their feelings about the characters and situations in the readings or to write their own poems, stories, or autobiographical essays. While giving strength and coherence to the unit, this emphasis on reading and writing raises problems for some students and creates some new tensions for the teacher.

There may be students who have never read a book and feel blocked about reading. There may be others who feel they cannot write—either because they can't think of anything to say or because they fear their handwriting or grammar or spelling will be atrocious. Becoming aware of who is having these particular difficulties takes time. If a student refuses to do an assignment or simply avoids it, she could be displacing some anxiety about the content or she might feel inadequate and frustrated by her lack of skills. The teacher has to try to interpret which is the problem.

One of our students withdrew more and more during the first four weeks of the term. When we brought in the second book, she finally exploded: "How do you expect me to read that book when I haven't even finished the first one?" She helped us realize that we needed to give attention to her reading. Another student balked at all the writing assignments. "I hate this class. The minute anyone starts talking, all you say is 'Write it down. Write it down.' All we ever do in this class is writing." We were able to provide the first student with a reading tutor to help her

get through the second book. As a result, she began to participate more in discussions and other activities. In the case of the student who was blocked on writing, one of us took the time to work with her individually. We tape recorded some of her ideas, transcribed the tape, and let her work from that draft. After a few taping sessions, she was less intimidated by writing, although she still ended the course feeling, "The class was good; but there was too much writing."

When there are more than a few students in the class whose participation suffers because they are ashamed or handicapped by lack of skills, you have a number of options. You can decide to devote some part of class time every week to individualized work on skills. This requires preparing punctuation, spelling, and reading exercises that correspond to each student's needs. If you have access to tutors, you can set up tutorials for students who need individual help. This approach lessens the load on the teacher and has the added advantage of leaving class time for explorations of the course content. Your other choice is to circumvent the problem by emphasizing content rather than skills. Most of the subjects can be explored with a minimum of reading and writing. However, unless there are other places in school where the students are working directly on their skills, it is a loss to choose this option. Because students are interested in the subject matter, they may be more motivated than usual to work on their skills. This also may be the class where they are most comfortable in admitting their lack of skills.

Combining skills work with thematic explorations, however, also poses problems for the teacher. In this unit, students begin to share some personal concerns. For this sharing to be comfortable and fruitful, the atmosphere must be one of openness and trust. The teacher has to find a balance between being supportive and accepting, while at the same time being able to motivate students to work on their skills and stretch themselves academically. When a student pours her heart out in an essay, how can you comment on the grammar? When you become aware of the many problems in a student's life, how can you turn in a grade for her? These are very real tensions which you will have to work out.

When we look over a student's writing, we focus a great deal of attention on the content, commenting on where her ideas seem clearest and most interesting, where her descriptions are most vivid, where more explanation is needed. We also encourage students to read their material aloud to each other, giving this kind of criticism. Only after discussing the writing in this way do we look for grammar and spelling problems. Even then, we only focus on one problem in any given paper (see "Techniques," p. 21).

Grading can be problematic in this kind of course. In our school there are no grades, only complete/incomplete. The class works out a contract around the quantity and quality of participation that is expected. In more traditional situations, we recommend working out a system with the students that seems fair to them. The important thing is that they not feel that the grade is based on how much a teacher likes a student or finds her experiences in growing up interesting in themselves.

Classroom Dynamics

Many of the activities in this unit are designed to help students overcome isolation and see that their personal experiences and feelings are shared by others. Sometimes, however, sharing leads to comparing, which becomes competitive.

Activities that touch upon personal appearance, dating, or sex are particularly likely to exacerbate competitive feelings. As young women, the students have been socialized to assess their own value by comparing themselves to one another. "My ass is much bigger than yours." "You've got a nice complexion; my face is covered with zits." One student's problem becomes another's secret victory. If one gets thrown over by her steady boyfriend, another who doesn't

have a boyfriend is relieved. In courses where there is little interaction among students, these conflicts would probably remain dormant. But in discussing issues of growing up female, students may be afraid that other people will laugh at them or feel no empathy for their problems.

Differences among the group tend to become antagonistic when students are feeling most insecure and competitive. What better release for these feelings than long-standing neighborhood or racial rivalries? "I'm not saying anything with *them* here," is a comment we often hear near the beginning of a term with a new women's class. One year when we taught "Growing Up Female," the class was made up of two cliques of young women from different neighborhoods. As the material became more immediate and personal, tension between the two groups mounted. In any discussion that concerned appearance or boyfriends, the two groups would withdraw into hostile silence. Outside of class one student commented: "I'm not talking with them. They wear platforms and tight shirts and think they're so cool, but the guys like us better, anyway, for being more natural." In reflecting on the situation, we realized that, in fact, the two groups did dress differently—one "dressing up" and the other "dressing down." When the topic turned to dress or dating, this difference became a competitve one.

The way the teacher handles these situations is crucial to the success of the course. Especially during the first few weeks of the unit, it is important not to move too far in the direction of personal sharing. Students' lives are an important part of the curriculum, but not the whole curriculum. In every discussion, role-play, or writing assignment, there should be the choice to talk about the characters in the books, or generally, about "people." There are new concepts, ideas, and skills to learn that are less threatening to the group and that can be helpful to students in understanding their own experiences.

If competition does arise, there are several approaches to try. First, you can try to speak to the insecurity and shame that underlie the competition. You could, for instance, make the point that there are many acceptable ways to look and act. It's okay not to be slender, big-breasted, or "hooked up with a guy." It's okay to wear make-up or to choose to go without it. Further, you have to be careful to give rival groups and individuals equal time and attention. When students doubt themselves, they become needy and demand attention as a measure of approval. "I know you don't really like me. You never help me out with my papers. You're always too busy helping one of them." In this competitive framework, when one student gets attention, the others count it as their loss. It's not helpful to anyone for a teacher to "choose sides." Both "sides" require support to overcome their needs to compete.

Activities from the curriculum can be utilized to alleviate competitive tensions. For example, an interviewing exercise can be structured to match up pairs from antagonistic neighborhoods. Other activities can break down competition through cooperative projects that bring students together, overlooking their differences. In making a movie, or putting on a play, students depend on one another to create a good production; afterward, they share a common pride in their joint effort.

Sometimes it's useful to define conflict when the source is clear to you. In the unspoken battle between neighborhood cliques described earlier, we finally spoke directly about the competition in a class discussion. We said that we had noticed that girls in the class chose different ways of dressing for school. We made it clear that their competition around dress made us feel uncomfortable, that we did not want either group to feel that it had to change its way of dressing, but that we wanted both groups to be open to the differences. Once the tension was acknowledged openly, the entire group was able to relax a little. One of the girls even suggested they pick a day to "switch," trying each other's mode of dressing. Although this idea never caught on, the sharp differences in the way the two groups dressed did break down to some extent during the next few weeks.

In defining tensions in the group, it is not necessary (or desirable) to turn the situation into an encounter. "Carol, how do you feel about Marcia coming in dressed up for class?" "Joan, how do you feel when you hear Susan say that?" Rather, the teacher can define the problem in a more general way and enlist the class in finding ways to overcome it.

The Teacher As Counselor

In most courses of study, the students' lives are not an important part of the curriculum. Rarely are they called upon to expose their own thoughts or feelings to the teacher or the class. Students may find such courses boring, but they become accustomed to the built-in safety of the situation. Expectations are clear; they are to do the assignments, hand in the work, participate in the class. Interaction with the teacher or other students is limited. Students can always hide what they are really thinking or feeling.

In this unit, the themes and issues have been selected to resonate with the students' own personal concerns. The methodology encourages students to draw connections between themselves and the material. For example, in discussing or writing about the novels and autobiographies, they are asked to think of similar experiences or moments in their own lives. In follow-up activities, they role-play characters in situations drawn both from the readings and from their own experiences.

Because of the unusual content and structure of this course, the relationship between teacher and students takes on new dimensions. Most students encounter few adults they can talk to openly. Having shared some personal experiences and feelings with you in class, students may begin to seek out your help, advice, or friendship outside of class. Some students just want a chance to talk informally, to expand on conversations begun in class. Others may need help with difficult situations in their lives. Students have come to us with questions about birth control, fears of pregnancy, problems with boyfriends or parents, sadness about the death of a relative or friend, to name just a few. In our setting of a small, alternative school, we find it possible and desirable to put a great deal of energy into personal interactions with students.

Often we choose to counsel students one-to-one.

When a teacher confers one-to-one with her student, a first conversation often sets up the expectation or need for further contact—going to the doctor together, making a call together to a lawyer, or simply meeting in a few days to talk again. These contacts are often as important as the initial conversations. Without such contacts, a student may be left hanging with a practical or emotional need. She may be waiting for assistance in finding an abortion clinic, waiting for the teacher to write a letter to her employer, or waiting for further adult assurance or insight concerning a private experience or feeling which she has shared for the first time.

Before working individually with her students, a teacher needs to consider her own commitments: the constraints on her own energy or time and her ability to follow through. We have found that even with the best intentions in the world, we cannot give students sustained help or support if we are over-extending ourselves. Eventually, pushing yourself too hard can lead to feelings of exhaustion, resentment, and finally, the desire to withdraw. It's important not to promise more than you can deliver. It is better to be clear from the beginning about your level of involvement.

Spending time with students outside of class is not an essential part of teaching this unit. Students can learn a great deal about themselves and each other, and receive valuable support from the teacher within the confines of the classroom. Teachers working with more than 120 students, teaching five classes a day, may not be able to make the choice to take individual time with students. If, however, you want to be able to provide some personal support to students and know you do not have the time, a possible solution might be to team teach this unit. One teacher who tested this material teamed up with a guidance counselor from her school who wanted a chance to work with students one-to-one. Another teacher received permission to team teach with a city-funded youth service outreach worker. Her job gave her the flexibility and resources to follow up on individual students' concerns.

Even if you develop this kind of arrangement, or have the time for counseling, as we do, you may feel overwhelmed by the number or magnitude of a student's problems. Young women from low-income backgrounds have many needs, and few resources or services are available to them. No individual teacher (or alternative school, for that matter) can make up for that disparity. It is important to exercise caution in responding to requests for personal attention, and to avoid a "savior" mentality. When students first began to come to us for help, our immediate tendency was to try to "solve" all their problems, to leap to solutions. Often, this is not very helpful to the student, who, in fact, needs time to explore her feelings about the probblem and work out her own solutions. The best help you can give her is a chance to talk.

Sometimes a student is clear about what she needs and wants, but does not know how to go about getting it. In those cases, the teacher can play the role of advocate, finding a resource person or agency that might be able to respond to the student's needs and then helping the student obtain the necessary services from that agency. We have found that students obtain much better services from certain institutions if there is an articulate adult helping with their cases.

To increase your effectiveness as an advocate, it is important to become familiar with the resources that are available in your community. In some areas, there are resource guides available, such as *The Woman's Yellow Pages,* produced by the Boston Women's Collective. A guide provides you with starting points, but there is still work to be done in evaluating these services through phone calls and personal visits. Over the past five years, we have found a number of services that we feel comfortable recommending to students: health clinics where doctors or nurse practitioners take the time to describe different methods of birth control and to explain gynecological procedures; mental health facilities that can provide psychiatric services free to low-income clients; drug and alcohol groups specifically for teen-agers.

Before making referrals, you may have to consider whether you want to discuss the referral you are recommending with the parents of the student. In our experience, the students often do not want their parents to be involved at all and sometimes refuse help if parental permission is a prerequisite. Depending on the situation—the age of the student, the nature of the problem—we make a decision about whether parents have to be informed.

There are many difficult matters of judgement involved when you are trying to help or counsel students. "Am I the right person to be helping this student or does she need a different kind of help? Should I be pushing this student to confront and act on her problems quickly, or does she need time to reflect on her own? Am I risking too great an involvement in a difficult family situation?" If you are doing much of this work, you will have many questions such as these and will probably need regular supervision and support. Supervision can be invaluable in helping you determine how to respond to a student's request for help. We have been very fortunate in having weekly supervision available to us from the psychiatry department of the city hospital. The service is granted to us as part of their community service program. Public schools sometimes employ psychologists or have an arrangement with a local guidance or mental health center to which referrals are made. Through following up connections such as these, it may be possible to arrange for regular supervison. Even if there is no one trained in supervision who is available to you, probably you have someone in your school with counseling training who could talk with you regularly. If the guidance counselor cannot team teach the course with you, she might be able to meet with you every week, listen to you describe your individual contacts with students, and offer you advice on how to proceed.

IV: ADULT SEX ROLES

OVERVIEW

Who Am I
I am the mother of your child.
I am the shoulder you lean on.
I am the one who cleans your house.
I am the one who does your laundry.
I am the one who is always there.
I am the one who cooks your meals.
I am the one who mends your clothes.
I am the one who waits for you at night.
I am the one who loves and adores you.
I am the one who stays home all day and night.
I am the one who you keep at home and never let out.
Who Am I? I am the woman of the past.
[Janet Ferreira]

This unit examines the roles assigned to and chosen by women and men in American society and compares them with sex roles in different times and cultures. Through interviews, case studies, and speakers, students are exposed to both traditional and alternative adult sex roles. Reading about a Victorian marriage, a divorce in China, childraising among the Arapesh of New Guinea, students examine a wide range of roles and relationships. Although distant from their immediate experiences, this material can help students define their own values and weigh their own options. The goal of this unit is to help prepare them for a future as adult women with expanded options, able to self-consciously accept, reject, or modify the roles society hands them.

The opening activities involve defining sex roles and looking for examples of them in students' current lives and experiences. Students give their associations with such terms as "wife," "single woman," "bachelor," "father," and list typical female/male roles. They do a vocabulary exercise on words commonly used to describe female/male personality traits. Two more personal activities consist of keeping a journal of observations about sex-role distinctions in their own lives and discussing choices of lifestyle which appeal to them.

The next group of activities compares current American sex roles with those of other times and cultures. Students read and discuss Ibsen's play, *A Doll's House,* and an article by Felix Greene, "A Divorce Trial in China." They relate this material back to their own culture by writing poetry about what they want or don't want in a husband, by hearing from a counselor who works with families and then reading case studies of difficult relationships, and by learning about both the process and aftermath of divorce in the United States.

The unit ends with a group of activities on parenthood. The first exercise encourages students to think about motherhood as a conscious choice, rather than an inevitability. Afterwards they write a poem to their future daughters or to the daughters they do not intend to have. They next read a section from Margaret Mead's *Sex and Temperament in Three Primitive Societies,* which shows the way fathers in another culture participate in childbearing. This is followed by an alternative from their own culture—a male speaker who has switched roles in his family and is primarily responsible for the children. The last activity is one in which students examine their own ideas and interview parents about the best ways to raise children.

There is clearly much more to be said and read about adulthood and sex roles. Because the issues are future rather than current ones for our students, this unit is somewhat less comprehensive than "Growing Up Female: Childhood to Adolescence." We have chosen to touch on a number of important issues, rather than to explore them fully.

"Adult Sex Roles" could be used in either an English or social studies course, as analytic and reading/writing skills are equally stressed. Although it is written assuming an all-female class, it could be used successfully, with some modification, in a coeducational class. You might, for instance, want to find a play or novel with sympathetic male as well as female characters to use instead of *The Doll's House*. The activities, however, all include looking at men's as well as women's roles. Like Unit I, "Messages from Society," this unit deals with societal norms and raises basic questions about those norms. A major difference between these two units, however, is that the material used in "Adult Sex Roles" is more difficult and better suited to older students.

ACTIVITIES

1: Defining Sex Roles

The concept of "sex roles" may be difficult for students to grasp. In this opening activity, they learn the meaning of the concept by doing some simple word association and listing exercises.

We find it best to begin with a brief discussion of what a role is. Most students know that in a play a role is the part assigned to an actor. You can point out that off-stage, a role is still a part you play, sometimes by choice and sometimes not. A sex role is thus a role you get put into because of your sex. Because you are a woman, you are expected to act, and dress, and even think in certain given ways

Next, we introduce sex-role stereotypes by asking students to write down the first thing that comes to mind when they hear the following words: "wife," "bachelor," "father," "single woman," "mother," "husband," "divorcee." It is best to give one word at a time and allow no more than a minute for students to free associate. Afterward, students share their responses. The teacher's job is to point out those that reflect sex-role stereotypes, to raise questions about the accuracy of those stereotypes.

We follow this by asking students to list activities that are, in fact, expected of women because they are women, and of men, because they are men. Taking care of the children and doing the housework will invariably be mentioned as expected of women. The teacher should ask, "Why is it that way?" In our classes, there is usually at least one student who'll answer, "Because women are better at taking care of kids." However, the majority will respond with variations of "that's the way it's always been done." The students don't necessarily see any logic in the role division, and that's an important point for the teacher to underline. There are a number of ways to do this: by observing that there's no real reason why it has to be that way; by asking students whether they know of situations where the men take care of children or do the housework; by explaining that in some societies, like the Arapesh of New Guinea, which the students will be reading about later, the men and women are equally involved in raising the children.

2: Keeping a Sex-Roles Journal

Having defined sex roles generally, students are now ready to look for examples of sex-role distinctions in their own lives. Students are given observation sheets that tell them what sorts of things to look for. The sheet might suggest students try to observe: differences in what women and men/girls and boys *do*; differences in the ways women and men/girls and boys *are treated*; differences in the ways women and men/girls and boys *act*.

With these categories as a guide, students choose one area in their lives—family, school, work, girlfriends/boyfriends—to observe for a week. The assignment is to keep a journal in which they make daily entries on anything they notice or think about pertaining to sex-role distinctions. At the end of the week, students share their journals with the class. This exercise calls upon observation and writing skills. It provides a structure that encourages students who are not verbal, or who are shy, to share their ideas with the class.

In our class, some students wrote daily entries as instructed, while a number of them made somewhat more general observations about the ways sex-role distinctions have manifested themselves in specific areas of their lives. There was enough material to provoke lively discussions. For instance, one student who chose schools as her area wrote:

> In most schools, like for instance the Fitzgerald in North Cambridge, everything is done according to your sex, except for maybe the music class where they play the instruments. But all the other classes are done like society wants it to be done. For instance, when the teacher wants the blackboards washed, he always asks the girls to do it. (I said he because most of the teachers used to be males.) Or when they have a lot of books that need to be transferred to another part of the building, you know who gets asked. The males of course. The females are supposedly too weak to carry a few books. This happens in all classes, from kindergarten up to the eighth grade. [Donna Gillespie]

When this excerpt was read to the class, several who had gone to the same school added other differences: "The teacher's pet was always a girl." "Boys got sent down to the office more often."

In the discussion about school that followed, divisions other than those based on sex also emerged. We learned that the class distinctions had been as prevalent—and more painful. Someone began with the comment: "The girls with the nice little dresses always sat in front, while we kids from the projects were always put in the back of the room." There seemed to be immediate recognition of this as a truth, with another student saying, "The teacher always helped the rich kids, never us. I just sat there all day."

Another journal entry which sparked discussion was one on girlfriends/boyfriends:

> Boy meets girl and thinks he owns her. This is what usually happens when they get together. It doesn't start from the beginning, usually after a while like a couple of days, or maybe a week, but don't worry, it will happen eventually. He starts off being very nice and then it happens. He pushes you around like you're shit. Always hits you and smacks and punches you and figures now that he has you he won't lose you. (You can tell he don't know too much!) He orders you around like you're his slave. I really don't know if this is true for every couple, but for most of the guys I know who have chicks, this is how it goes. [Donna Gillespie]

There seemed to be some agreement on the accuracy of these observations, but a number of students said indignantly, "Well, I wouldn't put up with that shit; nobody owns me." In the ensuing discussion, there was general agreement that women should not allow men to mistreat them—a discussion that perhaps strengthened the resolve and self-respect of the participants.

3: Vocabulary—Personality Traits

This vocabulary exercise gives students useful words to describe different aspects of their own and other people's personalities. The broader purpose of the activity is to help students recognize and move beyond common societal stereotypes of female/male personality traits.

Students are given a list of vocabulary words which are arranged in pairs and include: intellectual/emotional, aggressive/passive, independent/dependent, serene/hysterical, competent/incompetent, callous/vulnerable, paternal/maternal. The teacher should alter the list depending on the words already in the students' vocabularies. Given the dual purpose of this exercise, the words should be new ones to the students.

After students are familiar with what the words mean and have used some of them in sentences or games (see "Techniques," p. 23), they are asked to go through the list and write down one specific person they know who fits each word. Assure them that the actual name of the person can be kept confidential. The teacher then reads aloud each vocabulary word and asks how many people named a male, how many people a female. Some patterns reflecting societal stereotypes will almost certainly emerge in this initial listing. Mainly women will be named as emotional, dependent, hysterical, passive, and maternal; men as aggressive, independent, competent, and callous.

The next task is for students to go back to their words and think of a person of the opposite sex from the person they originally named who also fits the word. For a number of words, this may be hard to do. In the discussion that follows, you should ask students which words they were able to apply fairly easily to both sexes, which words gave them trouble. It is important to acknowledge together that there are, in fact, men and women who are emotional, or who are competent, or who are dependent.

If there are cases where none of the students in the class can think of both a man and a woman who fit a given adjective, the teacher might try to suggest someone. In our class, none of the students could think of a maternal man. We suggested that one of the male teachers at school who had brought his infant son with him to work for most of the year, changing his diapers and feeding him, could be called maternal. The students agreed, and in the discussion that followed, moved to the point of defining "maternal" as a kind of behavior possible to either sex.

4: Class Discussion—Choices of Lifestyle

Many students are familiar only with adults who choose to get married and have children. Before students begin to examine these specific choices in succeeding activities, we ask them to envision their futures. We introduce them to alternatives to the nuclear family such as living on your own or living in a group. By listening to our students think aloud about their futures, we get information which helps us in planning activities. By discussing with them options other than marriage and motherhood, we broaden their sense of the ways in which adults can choose to live.

The questions we have used to shape this discussion include:

1. How do you define adult?
2. Do you consider yourself an adult?
3. How do you see yourself living in three years?
4. How do you see yourself living in ten years?
5. Do you know anyone who lives in a group or a commune? Can you describe what that's like?
6. Would you want to live alone? Do you know anyone who does?
7. What would be the advantages or disadvantages of living with a roommate?

A common definition of adult seems to emerge: "being able to handle hard situations" or "knowing everything you need to know about life." Beyond that, it is hard to generalize about the points of view students express, as different groups of students (and the same students at different times) react differently to the questions. In one group, most of the students saw themselves as adults; in another, although the age range was similar, very few did. In one group, all the students saw themselves in ten years as married, with children; in another, several saw themselves without husbands and without children, but didn't know how they would be living. Few have been interested in living alone, although the idea of a roommate is sometimes seen as an appealing alternative to living as a couple. Some always respond with curiosity to the idea of group living; others dismiss it as "what hippies do."

Whatever their responses, our students have consistently expressed interest in how and why their teacher(s) live the way they do. We've found it fruitful to share our experiences with them, especially when the choices we've made about lifestyle aren't traditional ones. One year, we held the discussion at night, in the apartment of one of the teachers of the class who lived by herself. The situation itself provoked comment. "You know, I've never seen anybody who lived alone." You can do just what you want here, can't you?" Another time, because students had been interested in the idea of group living, but didn't know anyone who lived that way, we arranged a Saturday trip to visit one of the teachers of the class who lived in a cooperative group. It is not necessary to go outside the classroom, however. The teacher can broaden students' experiences simply by describing the kinds of living situations she has been in since she became adult and by being honest about the pros and cons of each.

If students express interest in further exploring any one of the alternatives to nuclear families that have been mentioned, the teacher might try to find suitable reading or speaker for the class.

5: Roles in Marriage—A Doll's House

Many adult women find themselves in the role of "wife." It is a role around which there is an increasing amount of controversy. Should a wife be at home most of the time? Is her main concern to please her husband? Can she demand anything of him? What about choosing not to be a wife at all? These and other questions can be discussed through reading *A Doll's House*. This portrait of an upper-middle class Victorian marriage gives students the opportunity to compare their own observations and ideas about marriage to an ultra-traditional model. The struggle which wife/hero Nora goes through, and her eventual decision to leave her husband to become an independent adult woman, raises a number of relevant and current issues. Despite the different period and class differences, students can relate personally to Nora. *A Doll's House* thus serves to broaden the scope of their experience without being too foreign. There are clear parallels with themselves or people they know.

Reading the Play

The length and difficult language of the play is both a disadvantage and an advantage. The language may confuse students and prevent their understanding important interactions between characters. On the other hand, the play will challenge them to build new reading skills. We try to ease length and language problems by focusing primarily on the first and third acts, and by doing most of the reading together in class. This helps students through to the last scene of the play, which invariably engages their sympathies. This method also allows you to discuss difficult passages as they occur. Nevertheless, the teacher should be sensitive to the fact that some students will have a hard time reading the play, and thus, will have difficulty getting into it. The more sophisticated the reader, the more likely she is to enjoy it. As our classes always include students with different reading levels, we suggest that anyone who is interested read the second act on her own, at home; but we summarize what happens in that act for everyone, so that the class can move on together (see "Techniques," p. 15).

If they've never studied any women's history, students need a framework to help them understand Nora's situation. A good way to introduce the play is to look at some pictures of Victorian women in the book, *The Revolt of the American Woman*, by Oliver Jensen. The pictures convey a great deal about the situation of women in the 1800s; we provide other information in a running commentary.

We usually start by mentioning that women were considered inferior; were often treated like children; weren't allowed to vote, to speak in public, or to go to college. We include what happened when a woman got married: her property and her children were legally her husband's; the husband could legally beat or imprison his wife. We end by pointing out class distinctions: the only occupations open to poor women were factory, domestic, or sewing work—all poorly paid. Rich women, like Nora, weren't allowed to work at all. They were supposed to be pure and innocent, to lead an incredibly sheltered life in the home. The history surprises students. "I wouldn't like to have lived then," is a common reaction.

This background increases the students' grasp of the play's implications. When Nora's husband comes in and says, "Is that my little squirrel bustling about?" students recall that women were generally treated like children. Knowing how few rights women had, they see the significance of Nora's central action: they understand that borrowing money behind her husband's back, forging his name in the process, was against the moral as well as the legal codes.

Using a Comparative Approach

A comparative approach, in which discussions, exercises, and role-plays move students back and forth between Nora's life and their own, helps students better understand relationships in the play and in their own lives. For instance, the outrage students always express at the beginning of the play about the way Helmer refers to Nora as "my little lark," "my sweet little spendthrift," etc., can lead to sharing ways in which the students feel patronized or belittled by males they know. "Are you given nicknames you don't like?" "Are you teased in ways you don't like?" To deepen the discussion, the teacher can bring up the way Nora uses her child/doll role to get what she wants. Again, questions can direct students to look at their own lives. "How do you get your boyfriend to do what you want?" Students had no trouble coming up with three common methods—"crying," "hanging up on the phone," and "acting nice."

Emphasizing Possibilities for Change

In all of these discussions, it is important to focus on the options that are open to women, the changes they can make in their lives, as well as on the ways they may feel oppressed. Although she lives within the restrictions of Victorian standards, Nora does change and become stronger. This is a central message of the play. A comparison of Nora at the beginning and at the end of the play helps students focus on the possibilities of change. We suggest using the following questionnaire after the class has read Act I and again after they have finished reading the play.

1. What things would make Nora happy?
2. What things would make Helmer (Nora's husband) happy?
3. What things would Nora be afraid of?
4. What things would Helmer be afraid of?
5. In what ways is Nora like you?
6. In what ways is Nora different from you?

The first time the students fill out the questionnaire, they share their responses and try to come up with a good composite picture of the two main characters. The teacher then collects the questionnaire and holds it. After finishing the play, students answer the same questions once more. The teacher then gives back their original questionnaire, so that they can compare the two sets of answers.

Students' opinions of Nora may undergo dramatic changes. One student's response about what would make Nora happy changed from "money, games, candy" to "to have a man treat her with respect and as an equal, who would talk, really talk with her, not to her." Even students who have had trouble reading the play understand the change in Nora and usually respect her for it.

Looking at the questionnaires sometimes shows students the ways in which their attitudes about themselves, as well as about Nora, have changed over the course of discussing the play.

For instance, in answer to the question, "In what ways is Nora like you?" one student originally wrote, "She helps him, but don't let him know. So he feels like a man." Her response to the same question at the end of the play was, "She's like me, thinking she could be better off doing things more for herself." Asking students to reflect on the differences in their two sets of responses, you may be able to help them come to terms with their own struggles to be stronger and more independent in their relationships.

Choosing Issues

In the course of reading A Doll's House, numerous issues emerge having to do with women's roles. These can be discussed on a variety of levels. An important job for the teacher is to choose a couple of these issues to focus on, based on what will be particularly relevant or eye opening for students. Possibilities include: who you can talk to and confide in, the advantages and disadvantages of marriage, the advantages and disadvantages of living on your own, the possibilities for changing role patterns in relationships. Around these issues, the teacher can plan a discussion, a role-play, a listing, or a writing assignment.

With one group, we chose the issue of women being financially dependent on men, because several students had expressed the view that a good boyfriend is one who "takes you out lots of nice places." Similarly, someone else had defined the ideal husband as one who would "buy me lots of clothes and have a job to support me forever." Given the lack of money in their families, this attitude is perfectly understandable. Nevertheless, we thought it would be important to raise the notion that being supported could be a mixed blessing. Our way of doing this, without seeming too critical of the students, was to start with Nora, listing together the problems she had as a result of being financially dependent on her husband. The list students generated included having to act like an idiot to please him, having to beg him for money all the time, having to pretend a lot. We then asked them whether they knew anybody who had similar kinds of problems, with either husbands or boyfriends. One student said she had a friend who "hated her husband's guts," but didn't leave because of the children. "I'd get rid of him though," she added. "Welfare is better than that slob." Another, talking more personally, said that she felt weird asking her boyfriend for money, even though she did it sometimes. Because the issue touched so closely on what our students want for themselves, we deliberately didn't push them too hard.

Follow-up

There are many ways to follow up a reading of *A Doll's House*. If one of the several movie versions is in the vicinity, or on TV, the class could see it together. Students can compare Nora and Helmer's relationship with the relationship between the parents in the books they read in Unit III, "Growing Up Female." A possible writing assignment is to have students tell what they would have done in Nora's place. Another is to have students imagine what happens to Nora after she leaves her family. A role-play in which Nora gives advice to a young woman of today airs students' thoughts about marriage. A companion reading we have sometimes used is "Gold Flower's Story," from Jack Belden's book, *China Shakes the World*, the story of a young peasant woman struggling against the marriage codes in China before the revolution. Like *A Doll's House*, "Gold Flower's Story" presents a rather bleak portrait of a marriage. However, the hero's growing realization that with the help of other women in her village she can escape her husband's tyranny, is exceedingly positive.

6: Writing a Poem on Husbands

In this exercise, students are asked to think personally about having a husband. As they write poems about what they want in a husband, or why they don't want a husband, their own values become clearer to them.

To get students started, we use Diane Wakowski's poem, "What I Want in a Husband Besides a Mustache," available in her book, *The Motorcycle Betrayal Poems*.

The poem is simply written, intentionally composed in the style of a list of qualifications for a job:

I want a man to be steady
To plan to be married to me
at least 50 or
60 years
with no sabbaticals. . . .
I want a man who is mechanical,
physical,
likes to build,
works with his hands.
[P. 36]

Given class, age, and educational differences, Wakowski's ideal husband is quite different from the husband our students want. The point in reading the poem is not to examine her values, but rather to provoke students' ideas.

The class starts by reading the poem together in class. Some of the more explicitly sexual lines can be cut without weakening the purpose for which the poem is being used. (We've used the poem uncut, but the girls giggle, refuse to read certain words, and sometimes skip whole lines.) Easy to read, the poem requires little, if any, explanation. The teacher should avoid placing any value judgment on any of the poet's "wants," just as no value judgment will be placed on anything the students write.

A brief discussion follows the reading, to allow students to generate their own ideas by thinking together.The simple questions, "Do you want a husband?" "How would you like him to be?" are enough to get the discussion going. Several of our students wanted someone who was nice to them, but not too nice. They were nervous or suspicious of someone who treated them too well. They wanted husbands who would "like your friends" and "go where I want to go." One was adamant about not wanting a husband at all.

We usually allow the discussion to continue until the majority of students have begun to contribute ideas. They are then asked to write their own poems, called "What I Want in a Husband," or "Why I Don't Want a Husband." Although most will choose the former, it is important to include the alternate assignment. Without it, the implicit assumption is that they all plan to get married.

Initial fear of writing a poem can be overcome by suggesting that students think of it as a list, with each item becoming a line in the poem (see "Techniques," p. 20).

One of the poems that resulted when we did this exercise shows, among other things, the way in which Wakowski's poem had suggested a model without influencing the content:

**What I Want in a Husband
Besides Long Hair Is . . .**

no smelly feet
no bad breath in the morning
someone who is not a slob
someone who will tickle my back
just as much as I will tickle theirs

Someone who has patience
Someone who will accept my good
and bad points
Someone who respects his mother

Someone who is kind, understanding,
gentle.
Someone who wants a million kids
Someone who has a job to support
our million kids
Someone who french kisses
Someone who makes love good
Someone who can take my nagging.

7: The Complexities of Being in a Couple

In this activity we move the focus from husbands to relationships. We begin by asking students what kind of relationship with men they would like to have, if any. The answers may overlap with the poetry writing assignment, but here students should be encouraged to think realistically about the interactions involved in a strong marriage or a long-term relationship.

Having expressed their dreams or desires, students, in the rest of this activity, are asked to concern themselves with some of the problems and dilemmas to be faced in achieving these goals. Why are marriages or long-term relationships sometimes difficult? How can couples work out their problems? When is separation or divorce the only real solution? Questions like these are addressed, to give students handles on what can be done when a relationship is in trouble.

To provide an overview, the activity opens with a speaker who does family or marriage counseling. It is important that the counselor work with working-class couples and families; thus, the talk will deal with the kinds of relationships students are familiar with. Community multi-service centers, which usually employ family counselors, are a possible resource. Public hospitals often employ psychiatric nurses or psychiatric social workers who do community mental health work. Because ministers frequently counsel couples who are having problems, another possible resource is a local church. We ask the speaker to talk from her or his experience about the kinds of problems couples have and the ways those problems are resolved (see "Techniques," p. 31).

The woman who came to our class was a psychiatric nurse from the local city hospital. She described the strains on marriages she knew about, stressing financial problems, alcoholism, and resentment on the part of women towards husbands who were seldom around to help. She talked about how she helped clients evaluate whether the situation would change and how change might come about. Our students didn't ask many questions. For some, the subject was too removed; for others, it probably touched too closely on their own families. But they were attentive.

To integrate their own ideas with what the speaker has said, students read and discuss the following case studies. Because we designed them for an all-woman class, they are written from the point of view of the woman:

Denise has been married to Jack for twelve years. Their three children are ten, eight, and four. Denise works part-time as a secretary in the school her kids attend. Jack was just laid off from his job and is looking for another one, but without much success. Denise doesn't feel he's trying hard enough; he claims there's nothing out there.

Their last few years together haven't been so good. Their sex life lacks excitement and she thinks he sees other women occasionally, although he isn't seriously involved with anyone else. They never talk about it though. In fact, they don't talk about very much, except about things regarding the children. They both find it easier to talk to other friends. Denise remembers how much fun they used to have doing things together. Now, in an evening, they just watch TV or sometimes play cards with the couple who live in the apartment next to them. Recently she's been feeling very depressed, although she's not sure why.

Janet and Michael are both twenty. They have been going out with each other since they were fifteen. This past year, they have been living together in an apartment with Michael's sister. Recently there have been a lot of tensions between them. Janet is in her first year at U. Mass/Boston, while Michael is working. She is trying hard to make a few friends to eat lunch with and do things with between classes. Michael is very possessive, particularly about her life at school. He gets mad at the thought of her having lunch with men and is always asking her accusingly about "who she met up with today." Michael also assumes Janet will cook dinner for him and do his laundry, the way his mother always did. Although Janet sort of feels that's her job, she also sometimes needs the time to study.

The other night, Janet was going to go out to a club with some other women. Michael got mad, insisting she was going to meet men. They had a big fight. Janet ended up going to her mother's for the next two days. Michael called her and apologized and told her he wanted her to come back to the apartment. She did, but things weren't resolved. Inside, Janet feels angry at Michael, and at herself, a lot of the time, but she doesn't know what to do about it.

Julie's husband Henry is drinking more and more. When they first got married six years ago, he drank, but only on weekends. Now he is having trouble keeping a job and has been fired from three jobs in the last year. Julie isn't sure what to do. When Henry is sober, they get along fine, but that's rare these days. When he's been drinking, it's like having another kid in the house, only worse. He's demanding, often irritable, and requires constant attention. Julie is working herself, but no longer feels she can leave their two children in Henry's charge. So she has been taking them to a babysitter. But she can't really afford it. She keeps telling Henry that he has to stop drinking, but it doesn't do any good. He denies that there is any problem and calls her an old worrier. He's right, she does worry all the time now—about Henry, about money, about the kids. She has considered kicking him out, but hasn't been able to bring herself to do it, as she still remembers and is in love with the old Henry.

After reading each case, students discuss what they think the woman should do. In our

discussion, there was little consensus. Reactions about Denise and Jack ranged from, "If he's having an affair, she should, too," to "They ought to go out together more." Referring to Henry's drinking, someone suggested she should make him go to Alcoholics Anonymous (AA); another student, who had an alcoholic parent herself, said she should kick him out until he stopped drinking, because otherwise he'd just keep at it. Because it was closest to their own relationships, students got most involved in discussing the case of Janet and Michael. As one said, "I get angry, too, because Arthur never takes me anywhere and doesn't want me to go out myself. I never know what to say either." In the course of the discussion, we noted that it was the students with the more possessive boyfriends who advocated Janet's standing up for herself and breaking up with Michael.

The teacher's role in these discussions is to push students to follow their suggestions through to the consequences for both members of the couple. "But what would happen to Julie if Henry left?" "What do you think Michael would do if Janet tried to break up?" The point is that relationships aren't simple and that there are no easy solutions.

Occasionally, students will bring up the question of gay women, either here or in the previous activity on husbands. When interest is expressed in finding out more about gay women, we try to arrange to have a speaker come in to the class. Many cities now have gay educational groups which provide speakers just for this purpose. We don't, however, initiate discussions on homosexuality in this unit. The topic is one adolescents are extremely uncomfortable with, and we feel it is better dealt with in the context of a discussion group in which the members have developed a greater sense of trust with one another than is likely to develop in a classroom context (see Unit V, "Sexuality."

8: Cross-Cultural Comparison— Divorce in China and the United States

A society's laws and traditions regarding divorce say much about societal attitudes toward women and toward marriage. In this activity, students see what happens in two very different societies when marriages aren't working out.

The activity starts with students reading together in class "A Divorce Trial in China," by Felix Greene. This short chapter from Greene's book, *Awakened China,* is also available as an inexpensive pamphlet. It is written as a transcript of an actual trial; in reading it, different members of the group can take different parts. Since the reading takes no more than twenty minutes, the first part of the activity can be done in one class period.

Although the students will probably know next to nothing about China, the marital situation presented in the trial is one familiar to them: the woman wants a divorce because her husband beats her, looks down on her, and neglects the children. The court session itself, however, is very different from any American trial. As one student said, "This is more like marriage counseling than a trial."

> *Judge:* How long did you love him before getting married?
> *Woman:* For a year. But I didn't get to know him very well. He talked very well and pretended to be a good man. He often asked me to go to the park with him or to some movies and kept asking me to marry him.
> *Judge:* How about your feelings after you got married?
> *Woman:* Not very good. He began to be rude and my state of mind became clearer and clearer. Since 1958 I have helped him with his work, so that though the feeling wasn't very good between us, it was still possible. But his temper got worse and worse and he often beat me. [P. 198]

The twenty-three-year-old judge obviously views his task as one of teaching the husband to look upon his wife as an equal:

> *Judge:* (bearing down on him) Don't you know there's a law which says that couples should help each other? If you thought her cultural level was low you should have helped her to improve it. You think you are her cultural superior—is that a right way of thinking? [P. 201]

And there is real concern expressed for the people involved:

> *Judge:* While we reprimand you, we want you to know that we understand how difficult it is to shed old attitudes. Our whole country is in the process of changing from one set of values to another. That is a very difficult task. Change of attitude can only come when we consciously become aware of the

old values which have to be eradicated. We understand the difficulties and ask you to do your best. [P. 206]

A good way to start discussing the reading is to ask: "Do you think the woman made the right decision in giving her husband another chance?" Opinion will be divided, and the debate helps to draw in students. The discussion then moves to the more abstract level of what students have learned about divorce and marriage in China. A question like, "Does everybody have to go through a trial like this?" helps students review the fact that it is only contested divorces which are taken to a people's court. If both marriage partners agree to the divorce, and provisions are made for the children, the divorce is granted automatically. When asked what marriages are supposed to be like in China, students' first responses will be general—husbands are supposed to treat their wives well, but they don't. Having students look back over the article to pick out specific quotations which refer to how the man is supposed to act will sharpen their responses. They'll find statements like, "The law says it is a shared duty to look after the children." The marriage norms that emerge stress equality; men and women are supposed to help each other, to respect each other, to share in the housework and raising of the children, to allow each other a social life.

We as teachers shouldn't expect students to be interested in dwelling long on China, or any other distant society. We may be very interested in the changing status of women in China, or in Chinese socialism, but students don't necessarily share our interests. At The Group School, we've learned to choose short, provocative articles like this one, or "Gold Flower's Story" (Activity 4, p. 113), which relate to what we are studying, but at the same time give students some sense of a changing China.

The comparison between divorce in China and in the United States can be made in several ways. One is to visit probate court and spend a few hours watching divorce trials. Another is to invite a woman who has recently gone through a divorce to come and talk about it. The advantage of the trip is that students get to see different types of divorces, while gaining a sense of how the court operates. The problem is that often it's hard to hear very much. A speaker, on the other hand, can include how she felt in her description of the trial, and also describe what happened after the divorce.

In either case, it's good to prepare students by having them share with each other what they already know about divorce procedures. Then the teacher can fill in any gaps. We particularly want our students to realize that until this year, in Massachusetts, there was no such thing as "no fault" divorce. Even when both members of a couple wanted a divorce, it couldn't be had on grounds of simple incompatibility. The law said that there had to be some other reason; the two most commonly used in Massachusetts courts were "cruel and abusive treatment" or "adultery." At present, if the divorce is uncontested, neither husband nor wife has to claim the other was at fault. But they do have to wait eighteen months before the divorce is legal, which is hard on people if they are anxious to remarry. We point out that the system is designed so that you have to have a lawyer, which even for an uncontested divorce will cost about $500. We discuss whether or not students feel it is fair that women almost always get custody of the children. As many of the students have parents who are either divorced or separated, the teacher should be aware that the topic may be a painful one for them. Make sure to leave space in any discussion about divorce for feelings, as well as information, to surface.

After the initial discussion, we've usually chosen the trip, because we like to utilize resources outside of the classroom, and trips are fairly easy to arrange at The Group School. We've learned that you need to take a lawyer along, to explain things when you can't hear what the judge or the lawyers are saying (see "Techniques," p. 33). In an hour or two, students get to see a number of divorces. Uncontested divorces are quick and done by rote, with different lawyers asking identical questions and getting identical answers. In contested divorces, it becomes clear that property is often the main concern. The lack of concern for the people involved and the impersonality of the court stand out in sharp contrast to the Chinese divorce proceedings students have just read about.

The activity ends with a discussion about what happens to a woman after a divorce or separation. We write a few questions on the board: "What is her living situation?" "Is she better off than before?" "What are some of the problems she encounters?" Each student then thinks of a woman she knows well who is divorced or separated and, in describing her to the group, tries to answer these questions.

9: Considering Motherhood

Most women become mothers. The goal of this activity is to suggest to our students that becoming a mother is nevertheless not inevitable—that positive decisions can be made about whether to have a child, when to have a child, and how many children to have.

The activity opens with a discussion framed by selected quotations from *Our Bodies, Ourselves,* by the Boston Women's Health Book Collective. We use the chapter, "Considering Parenthood: Shall I Become a Mother?" (pp. 239–247), to begin asking a few general questions, like "Do you think all women want to have children?" "Is it good to be able to choose whether you want to be a mother?" "Are there disadvantages in having such a choice?"

From the section, "Shall I Become a Mother—I Do Not Know," we choose the following quotation for students to consider:

> Many of us want to do things in the near future that we could not do if we had children. We want to have children in our late twenties or early thirties, after we have had a chance to be on our own and have a variety of experiences with work, relationships and travel. Some of us want to understand ourselves better emotionally before we become parents. [P. 244]

Questions to raise in the ensuing discussion include: "Why might some women want to wait until they're older to have children?" "When do you think someone is ready to have a child?"

To hear from someone who has decided not to have children, we use the following excerpt from the section, "Shall I Become a Mother—No":

> I like kids and like my friends to have kids . . . but not me. My mother gave up a career to have us, and acted like she was in prison the whole time. Now that we're grown up, she's back to work and finally enjoys her

marriage. I know a lot of women have kids and interesting work, but it's hard. My work demands most of my time and hardly pays at all—but I love it. My boyfriend is in the same situation. We just wouldn't risk it all to have a kid. [P. 244]

After reviewing this woman's reasons for not having children, we ask students to think of other reasons a woman might decide not to have children. It is important to point out that not having children doesn't preclude having a relationship with them. A woman without children of her own might spend a lot of time with her nieces and nephews, or she might live in a household with children, or she might choose to work with children in some capacity.

We end this opening discussion on motherhood by looking at the positive aspects. The Carol King song, "Child of Mine," quoted in the section, "Shall I Become a Mother—Yes," conveys many of the joyous feelings a mother has:

Child of mine, child of mine
Oh yes, sweet darling, so glad you are a child of mine.

Although you see the world different than me
Sometimes I can touch upon the wonders that you see
And all the new colors and pictures you've designed
Oh yes, sweet darling, so glad you are a child of mine.

Nobody's going to kill your dreams
Or tell you how to live your life
There'll always be people who make it hard for a while
But you'll change their heads when they see you smile.

The times you were born in may not have been the best
But you can make the times to come better than the rest
You know you will be honest if you can't always be kind
Oh yes, sweet darling, so glad you are a child of mine.
[P. 246]

To gather other women's thoughts on motherhood, students interview young mothers, middle-aged mothers, and women without children. Each student thinks of someone in one of these three categories whom she would like to inter-

view. Students with interviewees in the same category work together to develop questions.

Our students came up with similar questions to ask the young and middle-aged mothers:

1. Why did you decide to have children?
2. Do you ever regret the decision?
3. How many children do you have?
4. Do you think that's a good number?
5. How old were you when you had your first child?
6. Were you ready to have children then?
7. Did having children change your life?
8. What's the best thing about being a mother?
9. What's hardest about being a mother?

The questions our students generated to ask women without children were very direct:

1. Why don't you have any children?
2. Do you plan to have children in the future?
3. Do you work? At what?
4. Are you glad not to be tied down?
5. Do you regret not having children?

In doing this assignment, we urge students to interview women they know well, because they will probably get more out of the interviews. We tell them to make sure to write down the answers, then give them a week to complete the assignment (see "Techniques," p. 29).

The most effective way we've found to discuss the interviews is to ask for the responses of each group in turn. The students who interviewed young mothers report on their responses; then we move to those who interviewed older mothers; and so on. In this way, comparisons and contrasts emerge without doing a formal tabulation.

After students have had plenty of time to compare and discuss the results, we ask them to think about whether any of their own ideas have changed as a result of the interviews. Our students have had some interesting responses. "That woman who said she missed out on everything. I can see that." "I never thought about it changing my life much. I mean, it's really different to be a mother."

A good way to end this activity is to read and discuss the Tillie Olsen story, "I Stand Here Ironing." The story may be used to explore the question of when to have a child, an issue we feel is particularly important for our students to consider at this point in their lives. ("I Stand Here Ironing" is also used in an activity on mothers and daughters in Unit III, "Growing Up Female." For a description of the story and a suggested way to read it aloud together, see p. 70.) If students have recently read the story, you can just refer to a few passages which evoke the mother's feelings that she was too young when she had her first daughter. The class then moves right into a discussion of when it is the "right time" in your life to have a baby, if ever.

10: Writing Poems—Mother to Daughter

Here we give students a chance to reflect on and integrate their thoughts and feelings about becoming mothers, or not becoming mothers, themselves. When we first did this exercise, we simply asked students to write poems addressed to their future daughters. When one student handed in a poem entitled "To My Never to Be Born Child," we realized our mistake. We learned from her not to assume our students intend to have children. Since then, we have been careful to phrase the assignment differently. We now ask students to write poems to their own future daughters, or to the daughters they do not plan to have.

We introduce the writing activity by handing out a poem written by Ellen Gray, a high school student, entitled, "For the Daughter I May Someday Have." (Anthologized in *Daughters in High School*, edited by Frieda Singer.)

> Walk tall daughter.
> You are young and your choices
> Are as open as your brothers.
> . . . .
> We will have succeeded only if
> From our bittersweet choices
> You are born with what we fought to attain.
> Daughter, I give you pride.
> [P. 179]

Often, in a group of low-income high school students, there will be at least one who is already a mother. We've found that these women, as young—and usually unmarried—mothers, have

been blocked by shame or embarassment from sharing their own experiences. These classes on motherhood have provided an important framework for them to explore their own thoughts and feelings about being mothers, without necessarily making direct reference to themselves.

Once when we gave this assignment, one of our students who is the mother of a three-year-old was able to write a poem expressing the ambivalent feelings she had been reticent to share in conversations. For weeks after writing it, she carried the poem around with her, reading it aloud to teachers, friends, and family.

Someday, I Would Be a Mother

Someday I knew that I would have a baby. I didn't know that, that someday would be now.

I am not very glad and very sad that, that someday is now. I am kind of early in life for that responsibility.

I just know that someday Coochie you will be strong and smart in all ways. I hope you will go to The Group School like Mommy did.

Someday Coochie, we will live in a big, brown house, with a yard, and a room for you full of toys.

[Jane Reale]

11: Cross-Cultural Reading— The Father's Role in Childraising

American fathers have traditionally had a minimal role in the day-to-day raising of their children. Reading about the Arapesh of New Guinea, a society in which men share equally in childcare from the day the baby is born, counteracts notions about the inevitability of the American way.

This activity is based on reading the third chapter in Margaret Mead's *Sex and Temperament in Three Primitive Societies*. In describing the birth of an Arapesh child, the chapter focuses on the role of the father, who is as crucially involved as the mother at every stage of the process. Immediately after the baby is born, the father lies down with the mother and the newborn infant, and the three remain in bed for several days. The father is now, as the Arapesh say, "In bed having a baby." Childbearing and childrearing are believed to be as heavy a drain upon the man as upon the woman. If one comments about a middle-aged man as good looking, an Arapesh will answer, "Good looking? Yes . . . well, but you should have seen him before he had all those children." We use this reading not only because it demonstrates alternative roles for fathers, but also because it stretches students' reading abilities and introduces them to a society even more different from the United States than China.

Students need some introduction to the Arapesh before plunging into the chapter. The teacher should read the first two chapters of *Sex and Temperament*, picking out general points about the Arapesh to use in an initial, brief presentation. We usually stress the ways in which Arapesh society contrasts most sharply with American society, pointing out the egalitarian, cooperative nature of the culture and the fact that neither Arapesh men nor women like to assume positions of leadership and authority. We've avoided having students read the first two chapters of the book on their own, because Mead's writing style is turgid, and the material is presented in such detail that students are likely to lose interest fast. For one class, we took the liberty of rewriting the third chapter, to make it more readable.

The reading can either be done in class or at home, as the third chapter is only eight pages long. We base our decision on the reading ability of the students in the class. For weaker readers, it's always easier to read relatively difficult non-fiction together in class. On the other hand, if the reading is done at home, there will be more time for the discussion. In either case, to help in pulling out important details, students make a list as they are reading of all the things an Arapesh father has to do in connection with the baby, both before and after it is born. Pausing after each paragraph, in order to add to the list, provides a good way of summarizing the reading as you go along.

We use the list of the father's tasks in several ways. To underline the Arapesh belief that the baby's health will be endangered if the father doesn't take this participatory role, we look at each item and ask: "What do the Arapesh think will happen if the father doesn't do this?" For comparison, students make a list of what

American fathers do before, during, and after the birth of their children. Invariably this second list is shorter. It becomes clear to students that the American father's role is not thought to be as crucial—unlike the Arapesh, an American baby can survive without a father.

The follow-up discussion focuses on the question: "Who works harder to have a baby, American or Arapesh fathers?" There's liable to be disagreement about the first part because, as one student pointed out, you have to remember that the American father "is out working to make money to support the baby." Students tend to agree, though, that Arapesh fathers probably feel closer to their babies as a result of participating so fully in the birth process.

A good way to conclude and to lead into the next activity is to ask whether it's possible for an American father to have a greater role in raising a baby and to look at whether that would be advantageous for the mother, for the father, and for the baby. In raising these questions, however, the teacher should be sensitive to the fact that in the students' experience, fathers are often not only uninvolved, but totally absent. As a teacher, you should be especially careful to frame questions in an open-ended way and to make sure that both sides of any issue are explored. If, for example, most of the students feel that it's better for the baby to have an involved father, you can point out mildly that it depends on the father. You don't want students, as a result of the discussion, to feel bad about a situation over which they have little control.

12: Speaker—Alternative Father

An interesting way to follow an activity on family roles in another culture is to present students with an alternative from within their own culture. We do this by finding a male speaker who has participated in the birth of his children and who is either equally or primarily responsible for the raising of his children. (See "Techniques," p. 31, for methods of selecting and preparing speakers.)

In preparing questions beforehand, our students expressed interest in such things as how the father felt watching the baby being born;

why he was staying home; whether he ever felt weird about it; whether he liked housework. Thus, when he arrived, we asked him to start by describing the process of natural childbirth, to talk about how and why he and his wife made the decision that he would stay home, and to talk about his feelings about being the "mother" in the family.

During the class, the teacher can be a participant, asking questions that she is interested in or that she knows a given student would like to ask if she weren't too shy. Afterward, the teacher should encourage and make opportunities for students' reactions. We've found that it's better to wait until the next meeting for this, however, as students are often reluctant to talk about films or speakers immediately after the event. A few simple questions will help get the class to get started: "Did you like the speaker, or not? Why?" "Is he different from men you know?" It isn't necessary to have a long discussion. The point is just to have students think a little more about what they have heard, while sharing their impressions.

The teacher should carefully watch student reaction during discussion of the Margaret Mead reading on fatherhood. If fathers seem to be too painful a topic, it might be better to skip this activity. Another possibility for a speaker who can present an alternative role is a woman who has decided not to have any children.

13: What's Best for Children?

Our students have had considerable experience with children. Most come from large families and have friends with children; some have children of their own. A good way to end this unit on adult sex roles is to have students air their own ideas about how children should be raised and to gather information on how parenting actually occurs.

We begin the activity by pointing out to students their own expertise in matters regarding children. We add that we hope the unit has given them more ideas about childcare. "Is there a best way to raise a child?" we ask, to open the discussion. Some of the responses: "You have to want it, that's what's important." "You gotta love it."

"It's best to have a father there too." "I like the way the Arapesh did it."

When students have warmed up to the subject, we hand out a questionnaire which focuses their attention on options for childcare and on sex-role stereotyping in children. The questionnaire reads:

Children are taken care of in different ways:
Child is at home with mother while father works.
Child is at home with father while mother works.
Child is taken care of by relatives or is in day care, while both parents work.
Child is taken care of by both mother and father while both parents work part-time.
Child is taken care of by mother who collects welfare; father isn't around.

From a child's point of view, are any of the above ways best? Why?
Are any best from the parents' point of view? Why?
How should boys be dressed?
How should girls be dressed?
What toys are best for girls?
What toys are best for boys?
Are there any rules you think a parent should make for boys as they get older?
Are there any rules you think a parent should make for girls as they get older?
What kinds of things should daughters be encouraged to do or not to do?
What kinds of things should sons be encouraged to do or not to do?

Give students plenty of time to complete this questionnaire. Then have them go around in a circle, sharing their answers for each question. In one class, the process of reviewing the first two questions gave rise to an argument about whether fathers could care for children as well as mothers. Over half the group felt that they couldn't. As one student put it, "That guy [referring to the father who had spoken to the class] was different. Most men aren't good with kids like that." The same group, however, took a strong feminist approach to the socialization questions. For instance, they tended to feel that parents should treat daughters and sons in similar ways.

A good way to supplement the questionnaire is to read together the section, "Sharing Parenthood," from *Our Bodies, Ourselves* (p. 242). This section discusses the problems women and men face in trying to balance parenting and working. It advocates such changes as decent pay for part-time jobs, which, if achieved, would benefit parents and support parenting.

If students enjoy interviewing mothers in Activity 9 (p. 117), the teacher can suggest that they now do another interview, this time asking parents questions similar to the ones they have just answered themselves. The goal is to gather data on how children are taken care of in practice. Students can decide whom to interview and whether they are going to do one or two interviews. We would urge, however, that fathers as well as mothers be interviewed.

With a few revisions, the questionnaire students have filled out becomes a good interview form. For example, the question "Are there any rules you think a parent should make for girls as they get older?" can be changed to "What rules do you have for your daughter?" Students

should, however, be encouraged to add new questions and eliminate any they don't think are important (See "Techniques," p. 29).

As students have already gone around the room once, discussing their own answers to the questionnaire, we suggest a different format to share the results of the interviews—a written summary and critique of the interview. Writing this summary will help students work on their skills and will help them look once more at their own ideas in the light of what they've learned from others. Students can be given the option of summarizing each answer and their own reaction to it or summarizing the entire interview and then writing a couple of critical paragraphs.

When the summary/critiques are done, they should be shared with the entire class. Because students often put a lot of work into writing papers, we suggest typing them up on dittoes, running them off, and distributing them to all students in the group.

NOTES TO THE TEACHER

In teaching a unit on adult sex roles, it is very difficult to avoid reflecting the middle-class bias of the women's movement, with its emphasis on careers for women and on women being aggressive about demanding both help and independence from their husbands. Due to the limits of class mobility in the United States, our students are not likely to enter professions or to marry men with sufficient flexibility in their jobs to allow them to share equally in childcare. We have to try to think about what options are realistic for our students and to present those in a nonthreatening way.

Avoiding Middle-Class Bias

Because "Adult Sex Roles" dwells on roles in the family, it may touch off strong feelings in students about their own families. If they hear you express a special respect for women who have

jobs as well as families, they may feel that you're implying that mothers who stay at home are not worthy of respect. Some may feel defensive, either about their parents or their own future plans. "My mother never wanted to get a job. We were enough of a job for her." "My father was too tired to help around the house." "Hey, if some guy wants to support me, I'm willing." Others may feel ashamed of the typical role divisions in their family and worried about repeating these patterns themselves. Still others may feel proud of their mothers, or fathers, for resisting typical roles.

While we want to help students realize that sex-role patterns can be challenged, it is important not to come on too strong with the way things "should be" in a family. Drawing on different time periods and different cultures, the material itself presents a variety of lifestyles and patterns. We try to frame open-ended questions, like, "Who do you think works harder for his baby, an American or an Arapesh father?" Judgments made by the class are about people in a reading ("Did Nora make the right choice in leaving her husband?"), not about students or their families. We also point out the possible effects of social class on family sex-role patterns. Rather than setting up certain women as models of independence, we try to talk about how hard it is for a family to arrange for childcare when there is very little money; we ask students if they know of good day-care centers in their neighborhoods.

Thinking about Change and the Future

While keeping a journal, or reading *A Doll's House*, or deciding "what I want in a husband," a student may start re-examining the sex-role patterns in her own life. She may realize that she does not want to marry the same kind of man her mother did, nor want the same roles her mother has resigned herself to. Or, she may become more aware of problems with her boyfriend. Afraid that there are no real alternatives to her mother's life, not yet ready to break up with her boyfriend, she may feel threatened by these thoughts and want to forget about them.

Making any change in your life is a difficult process. We as teachers have to try to be as supportive as possible. A comment like, "It's very scary to think about breaking up with Gary, isn't it?" shows that we recognize a student's feelings and are sympathetic. If students express their fears, we should be careful not to dismiss them or disagree with them. We should avoid pointing out differences between what a student says about women in general and how she herself acts. The student is probably already painfully aware of these contradictions. If we try to push students when they feel threatened, they will often adopt an even more traditional stance. So we try to be sympathetic and not to expect that the students will become feminists overnight.

It's easier for students to think about the future if the teacher is careful not to make value judgments about the various roles women may wish to choose. What we try to emphasize is the importance of making conscious choices, rather than automatically accepting the role you find yourself in. It helps to have students look at the advantages *and* disadvantages of getting married, or working, or having children. We also try to make the environment supportive and open, so that students can think about what they want for themselves, without fear that their aspirations will be disapproved.

V: SEXUALITY

OVERVIEW

I love
the feeling
of our lips' touch
slipping each
other's tongues
into our mouths
as you squirm
your hands
all over
my sensitive body
[Robbin Luzaitis]

As they become adolescents, young women experience an exciting rush of new sexual feelings. Their bodies look different and feel different to the touch. Often they begin to experiment with sex. Unfortunately, the environment in which they make beginning choices about their sex lives is one of limiting and some times contradictory messages. From the media, schools, churches, friends, or families, young women often absorb a double standard—one that allows males to experiment with sex but labels females who do so as "no good"—or they learn, more simply, that sex is "dirty." At the same time, there are counter-messages from the current revolution in sexual values, which tell them to "know what's coming down," to "get liberated," to "get with it" at younger and younger ages. Whatever their choices, they will have chosen "wrong" from the standpoint of one set of values. Often confusion over conflicting values is internalized as shame, guilt, fear, or insecurity.

We try to provide an alternative to both sets of messages. Our point of view is that a woman's sexuality is at the center of her self. Her body can be a key source of pride, pleasure, and expression. In expressing herself sexually to another, she should be *true* to herself, reaching

out and exploring as much, or as deeply, as she feels ready to do.

Without a framework to discuss conflicting values or their feelings about sex, young women question privately whether it's normal to feel as they do. "I wonder sometimes if I'm a freak, if my body works right, if other girls have the same kind of feelings as me?" Clearly, women's courses can communicate strong positive attitudes toward female sexuality while giving students an opportunity to learn about the feelings, fears, or fantasies they have in common. Because sexual issues are personal, rarely discussed in depth, and highly charged, we've found it makes sense to set up a separate Women's Discussion Group with special groundrules and expectations.

For the past six years, we have run a sex-education-focused Women's Discussion Group with a goal of creating a comfortable, safe environment where students can 1) support each other in talking about issues in their sexual lives, and 2) gain information relevant to their bodies and sex lives. Through the support they get from one another and the women teachers, they learn to value themselves more fully as sexual beings. Through the course content, they become better equipped to make informed, deliberate decisions, thus gaining more positive control over their own personal lives.

For the teacher, a crucial commitment in leading a sex-education-focused Women's Discussion Group must be to listen for the students' attitudes, feelings, experiences, and questions about their changing bodies and about sex. Unless discussions and activities begin with the students' own concerns, there is no way a teacher can communicate new, positive attitudes toward sexuality or teach the young women to share with and support one another.

Each group of students is different, depending on mix of ethnic background, race, class, age, neighborhoods, and the individual experiences of the members. Ours are somewhat different each year. Yours will be different from ours. Nonetheless, we would like to share some of the patterns we have observed in the sexual lives and attitudes of our own students, as it is through working with these students, and making these observations, that we make our recommendations about approach and content in this unit.

It's important for the teacher to be aware of the messages regarding sexuality that come from the home. The parents of our students provide a variety of models through their own relationships. Some parents have solidly monogamous marriages which serve as models to their children of people who continue to enjoy one another personally and sexually. Others "are still married, but it's hard to believe they ever had sex." One-half to two-thirds of our students come from families in which the mother has raised her children alone. In some families where the parents have split up, the mothers, or fathers, go out with, or live with, new lovers; some are remarried. Within the home, some of our students have suffered the sexual attentions of stepfathers or of their mother's boyfriends.

Some mothers monitor or support their daughter's sex lives; others are quite clear that their daughter's sex lives are their own, to live as they wish. Some mothers throw out their daughter's pills if they find them in a dresser drawer or in her purse. A few suggest that their daughters take birth control pills when they realize that their daughters are having sexual relations. Some mothers are opposed to abortions for their daughters; others insist on abortions if their daughters become pregnant.

Unconscious attitudes toward sex can be expressed subtly or indirectly through innuendo or omission. Often the indirect messages about sex at home are negative, like those in the society at large. In many homes sex is not discussed, except in jokes; the underlying feeling is that sex is exciting, but dirty. For our Irish, Italian, and French Canadian families, these messages may be compounded by the guilt-inducing teachings of the Catholic Church.

Education about sex occurs in a limited way in many homes. Some students remember that their mothers explained "the facts of life" to them when they were nine or ten or when they first menstruated. Others pick up some information from brothers and sisters; most learn bits and fragments of information on the street. Most of the students have learned myths about sex. These are either dispelled as they grow older or continue to haunt or confuse their adult lives. "My sister told me that when a boy stuck his tongue in my mouth it would make me have a baby. So the first time a guy kissed me that way I went around for weeks thinking I was pregnant." "I heard from a friend that if you use Tampax you lose your 'thing.' She said that guys can tell." Clearly, some information, albeit inaccurate, is shared among friends. Sexual sensations, on the other hand, are a taboo subject, especially among girls.

At thirteen, fourteen, and fifteen, most of our students hang around with a group of friends from their neighborhood. In the evenings, they often congregate on a certain street corner or on a courtyard or doorway of one of the neighborhood housing projects. Unlike middle-class young women, who can spend their time in their dens or in their own bedrooms with their friends, our students share their bedrooms with a brother or sister, and there usually isn't enough room in the parlor for a group of teen-agers. Most of the students experience a series of crushes on young men within their friendship groups; they have intermittent relationships with boyfriends, lasting from a few days to a couple of months. Some have sexual relations with these short-term boyfriends, almost always without birth control. Other students, perhaps held back by fear of their intense new sexuality, do not form attachments to males at this age. Still others launch relationships at fourteen which take up most of their time and seem to last for a number of years. These young women usually have sex with their boyfriends, most often without birth control. Occasionally, one of these relationships leads to an early pregnancy.

As they get older, the young women hang around less. Some gather at the apartments of young couples living together or at the apartments of friends. Others go to dancing and drinking clubs, sometimes with a date, sometimes with a girlfriend to meet males. More of the relationships with boyfriends are serious and long-term. The older students tend to begin taking more responsibility for their sexual lives by using the pill; a few who get into long-term relationships remain virgins. "I want to save it 'til I'm married." Some of the older students do not have close relationships with males; many who are still virgins insist, "I wouldn't stay that way if I met the right guy."

For the younger women, sex beyond kissing is often quick and unsatisfying. It is sometimes more like coping with an attack than a mutual process. Too often they are used by males, who may punish them afterward by not talking to them or calling them "pigs."

The older students have learned about equal sexual relationships through hearsay, but they have difficulty making use of what they have learned in their own relationships. They've heard of orgasm, but most of them aren't quite sure what it is. They've heard that there are different ways to make love, and they may have tried some out, but often these seem disgusting to them. The concerns they raise center more on how to cope with sex than on their own pleasure or self-expression.

The younger women, with their sporadic sexual encounters, rarely use any means of birth control—almost never with a partner who is new, often not even in an accustomed relationship. These young women seem unwilling to admit to full and conscious participation in the sex act; while complying, they nevertheless do not act on their own initiative, nor do they plan ahead for sexual encounters. Their thinking translates best as, "If I'm not using birth control, I'm not really sleeping with a guy."

The older students usually take more responsibility for their sexual relationships. Often they "go on" the pill, which they are able to get through a neighborhood health clinic—although they often "go off" in mid-month when they run into problems such as gaining weight or spotting. Few, if any, of the males take responsibility for contraception—although some, when they are going out steadily with a girlfriend, may ask her daily, "Did you take your pill?" Everyone has heard of "rubbers," but few have used them. An occasional student will use a diaphragm; but in general, the planning required by a diaphragm is not characteristic of high-school-age women.

When they have found themselves pregnant, our students have handled it in a number of ways. Sometimes they have their babies and bring them up at home with the help of their mothers. Financial neccessity dictates that many young unmarried mothers raise their children in their mothers' homes. While these young women are subjected to some criticism from neighbors, they seem to experience somewhat less social stigma than their middle-class counterparts. Mothers seem willing to help raise their daughter's children, although with some mixed feelings. "She should be grateful. I bring up her kid. I know plenty of mothers would have kicked her out in the street. Don't get me wrong, I love the kid; he's my dream, you know." Occasionally young women marry the fathers of their babies; but these marriages rarely last.

Having a child can be a way out of a role a young woman doesn't like—at home, at school, or in relations with a boyfriend. It can be a way to give life new meaning; it can be an avenue to independence, through a small income from welfare. When young women feel inadequate in school and discouraged about the prospects of getting meaningful work, having a child can give them a real sense of being needed, providing an area in which to exercise competency. The young women who begin to raise children at fourteen, fifteen, or sixteen, early acquire many survival skills: childcare skills, how to deal with hospitals and schools, how to insure that money comes in (through encounters with the welfare bureaucracy). They learn what it means to have responsibility for another human life.

Students who decide not to keep their babies usually get abortions rather than carrying their babies to term and putting them up for adoption. Those who get abortions against their own instincts, through the coercion of a mother, boy-friend, or counselor, are likely to get pregnant again and again, until they have a baby. On the other hand, those who consider abortion seri-ously, weigh their options, and make their own decisions (whichever way), often gain maturity in the process.

In the following unit, we will describe both an approach and suggested topics for a sex-educa-tion-focused women's group. Because we are writing about a discussion group, as differen-tiated from a regular class, our terminology will be different; we will refer to the teacher as "the leader," and the students as "the members" of the group.

The format of this unit will also be different. The unit is divided into two sections. In the first section, Approach, we describe ten method-ological concerns in leading a Women's Discus-sion Group. Because the issues are personal, and charged, we make sure that the group setting is particularly safe and comfortable for sharing; hence, the genesis of our approach.

In the second section, Topics, we briefly describe some of the content we teach in the Women's Discussion Group. In both sections, we draw on our experiences—our ideas about how to lead such a group have progressed in the past six years. We're growing, and the attitudes of our students have changed. Bear this in mind as you use our recommendations; listen to the variations in your own experience and, most of all, learn from your students as they grow and change.

APPROACH

1: What Makes a Discussion Group Special

By its very nature, a discussion group pro-vides members with an opportunity to learn to listen to, and support, one another. A discussion group revolves around the interaction and con-cerns of the participants. When one member raises a question, a feeling, or an idea, it

becomes an issue for the group as a whole. Discussions are organized by the order of con-cerns as they emerge, as opposed to a logical order. This might mean, for instance, that a discussion of birth control would precede in-struction on anatomy, even though logically an understanding of anatomy can provide a foun-dation for understanding birth control. Behind this organizational principle is the belief that members can gain deeper understanding and grasp information more fully when they are com-pelled by interest, curiosity, or a quest to know or share.

Through the structure of a discussion group, sex education information can be introduced in a way that allows young women to absorb and retain it. There is always a balance between teaching information and sharing related feel-ings. We have found that when a lot of informa-tion is taught without enough room to explore feelings, the members of the group simply won't retain it. On the other hand, when the informa-tion is linked to feelings, the members can often make positive use of what they learn in their own lives.

For instance, we link information about the pill, diaphragm, or condoms to feelings about us-ing or not using birth control. Often the young women are blocked from using birth control by feelings or fantasies which they have never discussed, or even examined privately. Explor-ing a personal fear or a myth can dispel its force, allowing someone to make the gynecological ap-pointment that she has been avoiding.

While we believe that it's crucial to maintain a balance between feelings and information, we also believe that each group leader should deter-mine the balance which is most comfortable for her. In leading your group, you will need to make decisions about how much information to teach, how much to explore feelings, how much to focus on the interaction among the members themselves. If you have a background in counseling, you may want to allow more room for feelings; if you know biology well, you may want to spend more time teaching the physiology of reproduction.

Beyond a sense of your own strengths, your decisions about the balance between feelings and information must be informed by your goals. Your goals will make the difference in how you lead your group, how often you intervene in interactions among members, how many resource books you bring in, how much time is planned, how much time is open to the members to structure themselves.

2: Ground Rules

To establish a setting for supportive sharing, it is important that a Women's Discussion Group begin by agreeing on basic ground rules; through these ground rules, expectations are clarified, and members feel that the group is a safe place.

There are certain issues around which ground rules are often needed. These include: number of group members, admissions requirements, the closing and opening schedule, confidentiality, talking about other members of the school or community, bringing guests, attending with altered consciousness caused by drugs or alcohol. Some ground rules are set by the leader, and are non-negotiable, while others are set by the consensus of the group in the first meeting.

A crucial first decision for the leader(s) is to determine which ground rules are non-negotiable and which should be opened to the group. There are no formulas for this decision; what makes sense for one group, may not make sense for another. There are, however, certain key considerations which should inform your decision. Keep in mind the goals of the group; the basic characteristics of the membership (mix of age, ethnic background, racial background, etc.); and the goals, structure, or expectations of the outer institution or community (school, teen center, drug program, etc.) where the group is offered. Finally, in determining what ground rules to open up to the group, remember your own needs. Clearly, you don't open up an issue for group consensus when a potential outcome would be intolerable for you as a leader. Your own needs are important and should be respected. For example, as a leader you may not be willing to work with a group of students who are stoned or who have been drinking. This, then, becomes a non-negotiable ground rule.

In our sex education groups at The Group School, we have experimented with a variety of combinations of negotiable and non-negotiable ground rules. Some combinations have caused real problems in the dynamics of the group and the school at large. We have now arrived at a comfortable balance, which facilitates our goals while protecting us from incurring predictable problems.

Examples of Non-Negotiable Ground Rules

We've found that within our small community it is important to put the leaders of the group fully and clearly in charge of "gatekeeping"; i.e., determining the number of members, admissions requirements, and the schedule for opening and closing the group. These gatekeeping decisions are non-negotiable.

In the first year of the Women's Program, we completed a wonderful first term with a close seven-member group. The members were elated by the experience. "I don't feel like a freak no more." "I never thought I could've talked like this." Within a small school, word spreads quickly from friend to friend; everyone is connected through a complexity of interlocking friendships. When time came to sign up for second term classes, every young woman in the school wanted to join the group. In this first-year experiment, all of our ground rules were negotiated by the entire group. We, as leaders, asked the group to decide whether or not they were willing to open to new members. We didn't share our own biases, but made sure all points of view were heard and weighed. In deliberating over the decision, the members suffered pressures from friends both inside and outside the group. The decision couldn't remain impersonal; personal friendships and feelings were at stake. In working toward consensus, conflicts emerged within the group. Finally, after a series of painful meetings, the members made an uneasy decision to keep the group closed—"because we won't be able to talk good if there's too many. . . " "We've all got something together now and we'd have to start all over again with new kids."

During the second term, the decision continued to haunt the group, and it was discussed throughout the small-school community, where many feelings had been hurt. Continued harassment from outside, coupled with guilt the members felt inside, made the group members increasingly uneasy with one another. At the end of the year when the group terminated, the members expressed a backlog of anger toward the leaders "for making us close the group." "After that it wasn't the same." "That ruined it." No one could articulate exactly how she felt the group had changed, but the underlying message was clear: the leaders had put the members in an untenable position. The members were asked to either include or exclude their friends from a class which was precious to them personally; the choice was loaded. In opening the group, each of them potentially had a lot to give up, while in closing the group, each jeopardized important friendships.

The key we discovered was to give members the opportunity to share in making agreements about how they wished to work together, without burdening them with decisions that would thrust them in destructive conflicts over inclusion and exclusion, putting their loyalties to their friends and the group to an unnecessary test.

As gatekeepers, the leaders decide the numbers limit; we've made twelve the absolute outer limit, although we find eight or ten preferable. Further, the leaders determine admissions requirements; our only admissions rule is that there be no sisters in the group together. Two years in a row, in our group, tensions between pairs of sisters prevented them from sharing their feelings and experiences; the situation exacerbated conflicts among group members, who were drawn into taking sides. Finally, the leaders determine when admissions is open and when it is closed. Even when membership hasn't reached the numbers limit, we've found that there are times when the addition of new members interferes with the dynamics of the group and its progress in learning mutual sup-

port. At other times, a group may need new young women to bring spirit to listless discussions, to help the members move beyond an impasse in working together. When decisions about opening and closing the group are in the leader's jurisdiction, she can take group needs into consideration.

Examples of Negotiable Ground Rules

Just as a discussion group can become a stronger framework for sharing when the leader establishes clear non-negotiable ground rules, a discussion group can be strengthened when the members discuss and agree upon certain ground rules together. In our groups, we've had valuable debates and made valuable agreements arising out of questions about confidentiality, talking about other students or teachers in the school, and bringing guests.

The discussions about confidentiality always help the members to relax with one another. Like other basic ground rules, it's useful to make a decision about confidentiality in the first class; until the confidentiality rule is set, group members will be uncomfortable about sharing. In our groups the agreement has been the same each year: "Nobody's going to say nothing outside this room." And, they never have, at least not anything that has come back as an issue to the group.

In some groups we've found it imperative to make a ground rule that deals with the problem of talking about other students or other teachers in the school. This need has arisen particularly in years when the members of the discussion group are a friendship group outside of class. If so, they tend to view the group less formally; they fall into using the time to gossip about individuals or about neighborhood friendship groups with whom they're in conflict. "I hate that bitch; she's such a flirt and then she comes down on me for having sex!" "That's one teacher I'll never take a class with again. She's too strict." "Those girls come over the projects all dressed up to score our guys. The guys can't stand 'em either." When the discussion degenerates into a complaint session about someone who isn't present, the leaders point out that the discussion is not only unfair to the people being discussed, but often lacks value for the members of the group. "Let's not concern ourselves with them in this group. There's a lot more we can learn by focusing on ourselves."

Setting a ground rule about bringing guests raises key issues about the expected level of intimacy of the discussions. If a group insists that "it's cool to bring a friend if you want," the leader directs attention to the possible consequences. We ask, "Will you talk about personal issues when a guest is present? " "Do you want to talk about your personal concerns in this group?" In most of our groups, the members have decided to preserve a framework where they can "really talk." They have decided to allow a guest only when she is seriously considering joining the group. "She can come once to find out if it's what she wants, and then she can join, but she can't just hang on trying to make up her mind."

3: Safety

It's difficult to talk about sex, birth control, feelings about our bodies and our personal relationships. Often these are topics which group members have never discussed with anyone before, and which they may not even have explored very much in their own minds. Sharing thoughts about these issues, even listening to discussions of them, can make the young women feel particularly vulnerable.

Not Letting Members Hurt Each Other

Part of the leader's role is to make sure that the members feel safe in sharing. Establishing ground rules is a first step. Beyond the ground rules, the group members depend on the leader's overview and interventions to ensure safety. The members need to feel that the leader is aware of the dynamics of the group, that she will intervene if one member says or does something which is hurtful to another.

Members of a group can hurt one another through direct arguments, or more insidiously, through indirect behavior or statements. In our groups, the members rarely attack one another

openly; they defer on the surface to an ethic of tolerance or support. They hurt each other indirectly, sometimes by intention, and, at other times, by indirection; there's no outward conflict, no outward response, except, perhaps, a withdrawal from the discussion by the hurt member, a sullen expression, or a hunched back.

Indirect attacks tend to be formulated as general statements with an implied target. "I hate girls who do it with a lot of guys." "It makes me sick to see a girl make a fool of herself for a guy, and the guys can't stand it neither." Unintentional hurtful statements can also feel like attacks. Without knowing that her classmate has had an abortion, a member may say, "To me anyone who has an abortion is killing her baby."

Whether the attack is intentional or unintentional, the leader's task is to legitimate differences, not to let one statement stand as a value judgment. She tries to elicit other views from the group and communicates that there are many different points of view. When it's clear that the hurt was intended, she may try to draw out the direct criticism, so that it can be discussed openly. She can request of the member who made the general slur, "Could you say more about what you mean? Try to be specific." The leader's task then becomes to help the two members hear one another, so that they can move toward resolution or toward acceptance of their differences.

Not Letting Members Hurt Themselves

A member of a discussion group can hurt herself by sharing feelings or experiences which the group is not ready to hear or which she is not really ready to expose. In addition to protecting members from one another, a leader ensures safety to a discussion group by protecting members from themselves.

Sometimes a young woman will enter a group at a moment in her life when she feels a tremendous need to talk about a highly charged personal issue. She will open up to the group prematurely, upset the other members, and expose herself inappropriately. One year, a young woman came into the third meeting of the group and announced that after a fight with her boyfriend, she had tried to commit suicide by lying down on the tracks of an oncoming train. The group was rendered speechless. They had clearly not yet built a group relationship which would allow them to give support to a would-be suicide; in fact, even later in the year, the group might not be an ideal place to deal with such a charged issue.

The leader's role was to move the discussion away from this focus, without leaving the young woman feeling totally unsupported and unlistened-to. "I don't think this is the best place to talk about that experience; we all don't know each other well enough to help on things like that. It sounds very heavy and painful; maybe you and I can talk more about it after class." Although the intervention was awkward, both the other members and the young woman, herself, were relieved. An appropriate level of sharing was reestablished in the group.

4: Environment—Place, Time, Comfort

In a course where discussions take more direction from the interaction of the participants than from a lesson plan, the quality of the environment has an increased significance. Environmental choices—a comfortable space, a special time of day, the availability of food and beverage—are important in creating an open atmosphere.

To help the members feel that the group belongs to them, you can offer it at a special time of day and in a special place, somehow set apart from other classes and activities. Because the group is based on personal sharing, privacy is an important consideration in determining both space and time. "We don't want nobody around listening to our business."

A setting influences discussions—the size of the room; its shape, colors, arrangement of tables, chairs. We've found that a relatively small cozy room helps the group to feel more relaxed and open; we like to meet around a round table or to sit in a circle on comfortable chairs or pillows. (Of course, it's important to have room to breathe; a cramped, unventilated space feels like a pressure cooker during "heavy" discussions.)

Time of day also influences discussions. We found that late afternoon and evening allow for privacy and seem "special." Further, the members are more relaxed when the discussion group is their last class. In the morning, they have to go on from the group to another class or to work. In the afternoon or evening, members are not pressured by other commitments; if a discussion needs more time than the allotted hour, it can easily continue.

Food and drink help make the members comfortable. We always provide some combination of cookies, fruit, milk, juice, coffee, tea, or hot chocolate; in the winter, hot drinks help to warm up the discussions. Discussions about feelings, particularly sexual feelings, can make everyone feel anxious; food helps us to keep on talking. Further, food provides a small added incentive to come to the group. On a day when a member is anxious about continuing a particular discussion, or feeling lazy, an offering of cookies and milk can encourage her to come to class. We prefer intrinsic incentives—but we'll rely on the cookies in a crunch!

5: Leader's Role—How Much Should the Leader Share?

The most fundamental personal attitudes toward being a woman are uncovered in a women's discussion group. The leader, as well as the members, brings to the group her own sexual identity. The strength of the group is derived partially from the depth and richness of the leader's understanding of the issues in her own life; in leading the group, she draws on her own life experiences and personal values.

At the same time, the strength of the group depends on the leader's sensitivity to, and awareness of, values which are not her own. In this respect, she must be certain that her own experiences and values don't get in the way of establishing a framework that will be supportive for the members. The leader needs to set limits to sharing her personal experience, in order to maintain clarity and control in the best interests of the group.

A leader must deal with this tension in her role, finding the right balance between sharing and holding back. How explicitly should she share her own viewpoint? How fully should she share her experiences and feelings? In the Notes to the Teacher in Unit I (pp. 43–45), we introduce some of the issues a teacher of a women's course must address. It would be valuable for a leader of a sex education group to review that Note. In the following pages, we will discuss the particular ways these issues arise when the subject is sexuality and when the format is a discussion group, as opposed to a regular class.

The Leader's Point of View

In leading a discussion group, we are motivated by strong beliefs, combined with a commitment to communication and support among women. We have goals that include teaching the young women to take a positive attitude towards their own sexuality, to take positive control over their personal lives, to be understanding and supportive of other women.

Often members of a discussion group have grown up with a basic distrust of other women and a negative, guilt-ridden attitude toward their own sexuality. Their points of view on abortion, sexual relationships, masturbation, homosexuality, birth control, all spring from these negative, distrustful attitudes. Clearly, as leaders, we want to turn around these attitudes. The problem becomes to find the best way.

Why not simply share our point of view? When a group member voices a strong point of view against abortion ("You won't ever catch me doing it. I think it's murder . . ."), why not counter it by presenting an alternative understanding? First (and we need to teach ourselves this lesson over and over again), the members can learn more fully and deeply through the process of challenge and debate with one another than they can from hearing the leader's point of view. There are usually group members present who represent the proabortion point of view; both proabortion and antiabortion members benefit

from articulating their own viewpoints and exploring their reasons. Second, when a leader challenges the deeply ingrained values of group members, she risks breaking trust; she may cut herself off from the very members she is trying most to reach.

There are situations, however, when it is worthwhile for a leader to risk sharing her point of view. Perhaps no members, or only one member, represent a point of view the leader holds dear. If she has established enough trust to defend an unpopular idea and to be heard, the results can be positive. There have been several occasions when we, as group leaders, have directly debated with group members such issues as abortion, birth control, and a woman's right to independence; we have found that members were able to grow through that direct sharing and debate.

The Leader's Personal Feelings and Experiences

"I don't like that '69'. Would you ever do that?" Every discussion leader has found herself at that tense moment when a group member asks her a direct question about her personal experiences or feelings. Here, as in making the decision about whether or not to share ideas, there are no absolute rules. There are simply some useful considerations.

A number of important factors argue against personal sharing on the part of the leader. The leader's foremost role is to facilitate the learning and sharing of the group members. When a leader speaks about herself, she risks blocking or discouraging the members. While intending to back up a point by drawing an analogy from your own life ("When I was thirteen I was really afraid of being alone with a guy, too . . ."), you may inadvertently cut off a group member. A group member might feel that you don't want to hear about her life or that you are more interested in talking about your own life. A member may well wonder, if the leader is going to bring her feelings and life problems to the discussions, then who is going to keep the group on track as a whole? "Who is going to protect me from saying the wrong thing or protect me from these people to whom I have made myself so vulnerable?"

The leader's role puts her in a position of power in relation to the members. Members turn to her for sanction, to place limits on their behavior or on the content of what they share in meetings, as well as for judgments of approval or disapproval of their experiences and feelings. Because of her power, when a leader shares from her life, her anecdotes and feelings carry particular weight. Group members may assume that the experiences and feelings of the leader represent the "correct" way to be and feel. If a group leader says, "I first went to bed with a guy when I was seventeen," the group members may compare themselves to the leader as a model; they may well feel both inadequate and judged if they began to experiment with sex at thirteen or if they are still virgins at seventeen.

In our judgment, even when the members of a group ask about your personal experiences, they do not really want to hear much about them. In the spring of the first year of our women's discussion group, the members came in one day and demanded to know more about the personal lives and relationships of the leaders. "We come in here every week and talk about everything in our lives, and we don't know nothin' about you. It isn't fair!" they pleaded. First, the leaders suggested that the members talk about what they imagined the leaders' lives to be like. When the members continued to demand the "real story," the leaders decided to tell something about themselves. One was in the process of separating from her husband; the other was living on her own. When the leaders began to talk, the members cut them off and changed the subject. The message was clear: they wanted the opportunity to protest against our privacy, but they didn't want to hear about our personal struggles.

At the same time, there are persuasive reasons for a leader to share something of her personal life. Often a leader can build a warm and trusting relationship with members by reaching out to them in this way. An overly impersonal leader can seem like a judge—and discourage sharing on the part of the members. Further, there are times when a leader can make a crucial intervention in the discussion by sharing from her own life, if she is selective and sensitive to what the group can handle.

One year, we had a group that emphatically disapproved of the expression of feelings. The stated ethic was to "keep your shit to yourself." There were especially strong feelings that males should not show emotions. Everyone agreed, "Guys should stay cool." "I think it's screwed up when guys cry. When I saw my boyfriend cry I freaked out. I never wanted to have nothin' to do with him again." In response, one of the leaders talked about several men in her life who had learned to cry; she described their discovery that to cry was a strong expression, like other full expressions of feelings, such as shouting in anger or leaping for joy. In this instance, the leader's story provided the members a new, thought-provoking experience.

In most cases, however, in paying attention to the needs of the group, the leader will keep her experiences to herself. When asked for the third time, "Well, do you like that '69' or what?" she replies "What difference does it make if I say yes or no?" She enriches the discussion by turning it back to the group.

6: Making Sure Everyone Has Entry

One of the most difficult and most important tasks of the group leader is to make sure that all the members have entry into discussions. No matter how selective you may be in your admissions, your group will be made up of a diversity of young women with a range of experience, attitudes, openness, and facility to share with others. In fact, the members learn most in a group where there is diversity, and they teach each other through their differences.

Within a group, there will probably be members who are virgins, others who have a fair amount of sexual experience, and still others who fall somewhere in between. Some will be comfortable in discussing sex, while others will feel awkward, afraid, guilty, embarrassed. The task for the leader is to establish the legitimacy of a range in experience. A group works toward an acceptance of differences which leaves room for a virgin to talk about her inexperience, her fears, or her hopes; for a young woman in a serious sexual relationship to discuss her use of birth control or an unwanted pregnancy.

It is not easy for a group to arrive at a norm of acceptance. At the beginning, you can expect each member to be uneasy about her own experiences; usually she's worried that her own experience is either "too much" or "too little." She is threatened by the differences in the group and probably won't want to reveal too much about herself. The leader counters this shared fear by telling the members again and again, "It's okay to be in different places."

Beyond differences in sexual experience, group members usually express a variety of attitudes toward sexuality and what it means to be a woman; these attitudes range from the most "traditional" to the more "liberated," influenced by the women's movement. Opposing attitudes often come into conflict in a group. Sometimes the conflicts are expressed. ("The minute he snaps his fingers, she'll do anything he says. How can she let him ruin her life like that? I won't let nobody tell me what to do.") At other times, the conflicts create tension beneath the surface. Group members with opposing attitudes refuse to share when both sides are present and may withdraw from loaded discussions. The leader's role, once again, is to reaffirm the legitimacy of differences in attitudes, to support the members in articulating their opposing values, so that they can learn from one another.

In every group, there will be some members who tend to be quiet and some who talk a lot. One member may talk so much that she prevents others from talking. The leader needs to help silent members enter the discussion, to make sure that some members don't dominate at the expense of others. Before intervening, however, a leader should try to understand what lies behind the imbalance. It may be caused by tensions about "experience," or "lack of experience," or by a clash of values. It may also be caused by differences in verbal abilities, or by the relative comfort of individual members in the group situation. There are also, of course, differences in personality—some members may be big "talkers," while others may be withdrawn or quiet.

By observing their reactions to a topic in their facial expressions or body movements, the leader can sometimes help silent members to

speech. "You seem to have a strong reaction to this." It looks like what she's saying makes you angry." "You seem to agree with what she's saying. Have you had similar experiences?" Comments of this kind sometimes succeed in drawing a silent member into a discussion.

When one member talks incessantly, it is up to the leader to raise the issue of "full participation" for the group; she reminds the members that the strength of the group depends upon the participation of everyone. "Since we're all teaching each other, it's important that everyone have an opportunity to share." If the "talker" persists in dominating the discussions, we've found it can be helpful to approach her privately after class; we let her know that we value her contributions, but that we've noticed that when she contributes so often, it cuts off others. This intervention, while awkward, is sometimes necessary.

7: Sharing among the Members, Not Just with the Leader

When a group is just getting underway, the members tend to address their remarks to the leader, to ask the leader direct questions about her point of view, and to make eye contact with her, ignoring the rest of the group. "Adria, just guess what happened to me when I started taking the pill?" "Tell me what you'd do if a guy kept insulting *you*, Barbara, and then started laughing and asking you why you always got so upset?" "Susan, where can I go get a good doctor for cheap?"

When the members address the leader, excluding the other members, the leader can communicate indirectly that her relationship is with the whole group, not with individuals. One approach is to turn the concerns or questions back to the group. "What do other people think about that?" "Have others had the same experience, or are your experiences different from hers?" Another approach is for the leader to keep her attention focused on the group as a whole, while an individual is talking. Instead of making eye contact only with the person talking, she makes eye contact throughout the group, registering responses, so that the members can perceive her interest in them as well as in the person talking.

In addition to using these indirect techniques to encourage sharing, the leader can structure exercises with the explicitly stated goal of teaching the members to listen to and support one another. We sometimes use pairing exercises (see "Growing Up Female," p. 64); we go around the circle, inviting responses on a given topic; we break the discussion into small groups.

8: Negative Feelings about Sex

Negative feelings about sexuality sometimes surface in discussions. "It makes me sick to see guys in those bikini bathing suits. You can see everything!" "I don't let anyone know when I've got my 'friend.' It makes me embarrassed."

Negative attitudes about sex are often expressed as a feeling of being "dirty." "I feel nasty when I'm not clean. I shower at least once or twice a day." Society's Puritan judgments upon female sexuality are sometimes internalized by young women as feelings of shame, and even disgust, toward their own bodies. In one class, we examined an assortment of birth control and female hygiene paraphernalia (foam, condoms, pills, a douche, and a diaphragm). We discovered that almost every young woman was convinced she needed to douche regularly "after my 'friend' or after sex." Our task as leaders was to inform our members of the facts and help them explore the origins of these habits. In addition, we wanted to get across a sense that sex is healthy, not "sick" or "dirty."

We explained to the members that the body cleans itself naturally inside, and that if they wash their genitals when they shower or take a bath, it will certainly be sufficient. Many young women were surprised, and somewhat disbelieving, when we shared this information; some simply resisted its relevance to them. "I don't care. I want to make sure I'm really clean. You can do what you want." In the ensuing discussion, we explored the myths behind their habits—and the underlying feelings. "Where did you get these points of view about douching? Did

someone tell you these things?" "How does douching make you feel?" "How would you feel if you didn't douche. Why?"

In discussing feelings that sexual organs are dirty, as in discussing other negative feelings about sex, we do not argue against the attitudes of the members. We try to dispell myths and we point out that sexuality is a "healthy" part of life. We work hard at leading discussions where the members can learn from each other, gradually letting go of their own negative attitudes. Through getting out their disgust or anger and exploring their hidden assumptions about sex, members are able to get in touch with the more positive and joyous feelings which have been blocked off.

9: Support for the Leader

"I've had it. I can't get them to really *listen* to each other. Maybe they should just run their own group." Often a leader will reach a confusing or discouraging impasse in her own work. Viewing herself in the support role, she forgets that she, too, needs and deserves support. Coleading a group or meeting regularly with a consultant can provide the essential support a discussion leader needs to keep going.

Coleading a Group

In coleading a group, a leader can share the burden: someone else is keeping in mind the goals of the group and is aware of the dynamics; someone else is working both to deepen and to set limits on the discussions; someone else adds her perspective in evaluation and planning. Sometimes a second leader can also add an area of expertise. In the first years of our group, a teacher from the school was coleader with a psychiatric nurse, who had experience in leading groups as well as a working knowledge of birth control methods and the reproductive system.

The members also benefit from being in a group which is co-led. Two leaders, of course, provide members with alternative adults. Some members feel safer, more supported, more inspired by one leader, some by another. Having two leaders may stimulate more members to enter into group discussions. Further, two leaders can provide a positive model for the members through their own interaction. Through observation of two leaders working well together, members can broaden their concept of the potential in a relationship between two women. "You're really good friends, huh? Sometimes it's weird the way you know what each other are thinking."

There are a number of guidelines we follow in coleading groups. First, the leaders need to work at maintaining contact with one another throughout a discussion. Sitting across the table from one another, or on the opposite sides of a circle, makes it possible to maintain eye contact. With a glance or a gesture you can signal, "Let's not discuss that," or "Yes, that's a good direction to push the discussion." For example, one year the group members launched on a graphic discussion of the possible problems that can occur during pregnancy. Unbeknownst to the rest of the group, one of the leaders had recently supported one member through an upsetting miscarriage; she intuited that the member was upset by the level of discussion. With a glance, she indicated to the other leader the need to shift the topic.

The way you talk to one another is important. Remember that you can disagree. For instance, in discussing alternative methods of birth control, we have sometimes presented different views. One group leader recommended the IUD for women who had already had children. The other disagreed on the grounds that too many women risk infection or perforation of the uterus. The members had to weigh the arguments and decide for themselves.

Just as you can disagree about the content of a discussion, you can also disagree on the form or direction. If you disagree, you can let the other leader know openly: "I don't think we need to get into that here today." It's valuable for members to be introduced to different viewpoints and to learn that people can respect each other and disagree.

Finally, in working together, leaders must work at a genuine sharing of leadership. Sometimes one leader is more aggressive, or simply a bigger talker; she tends to take over. One leader may be shy or fearful; sometimes both are vying for dominance. These imbalances or tensions need attention. In some classes, it will make sense for one leader to take the major responsibility for a given discussion. This division of work is fine, as long as there is agreement between the two leaders, so that one leader doesn't suddenly feel that her position has been usurped.

Evaluating and planning together can be mutually supportive. The leaders should take time for an evaluation immediately after a group meeting, if possible. With the meeting still fresh in mind, you can ask, "Which questions evoked good discussion?" "Which comments were helpful?" "What issues were raised that we might pursue in the future?" "Could we have worked better with one another?" This can be a time when one leader tells the other, "I felt you didn't listen enough to the group members. You talked too much yourself." Or, "When you asked the group, 'Who can you cry with?' the discussion really deepened!" Both leaders can also reflect on their own work and ask for help from each other. "I've got to be careful not to let my own experience with marriage get in the way of an open discussion. Maybe you should take leadership when marriage comes up, for the time being."

Meeting with a Consultant or Supervisor

Often when a member of the group raises a complex issue, or the dynamic between two group members begins to baffle us, we look to a more distanced perspective. In leading a discussion group, particularly in the beginning years, it can be crucial to meet with a consultant or supervisor. During the first two years of our group, we met weekly with a supervisor through the Community Mental Health Division of Cambridge City Hospital. Once we had established basic ground rules to suit our needs, we began to meet biweekly; we expect to continue to do so in the future.

One year we began the discussion group without supervision. Because the enrollment was fairly small and the group was composed mainly of members from one neighborhood friendship group, we decided we could handle it ourselves. By the end of the first term, we realized our mistake. With a close-knit group, and without supervision, we had become "stuck" at a certain level of discussion and were unable to push ourselves or the group beyond this. The discussion consisted mainly of participants telling stories from their immediate experiences. One session with our supervisor helped put us back in touch with our goals and gave us renewed energy to expand the group—both in membership and discussion topics. Our discussions were deepened through explorations of the feelings and common issues behind the stories.

A supervisor can help to clarify your goals or to rebuild your enthusiasm. Further, she can forewarn you of possible pitfalls and can help you to extricate a group from problem dynamics that may arise within it. The most valuable assistance she can give is to help you to observe carefully and to follow your own instincts. In our six years of supervision, the most important benefit has been to learn gradually to trust ourselves.

10: Resources

Discussions about sex are enriched by good resources. We always keep reference materials in the classroom and give at least one reference book or pamphlet to each group member for her own personal use. In the following note, we will describe three sample resources we have found particularly useful. We will not provide an exhaustive list of materials, but we hope to give you a sense of the range.

Our Bodies, Ourselves

Our Bodies, Ourselves, written by the Boston Women's Health Book Collective, is the most comprehensive book on women's health and sexuality. It covers a wide range of topics, from reproduction to rape to women and health care. The entire book is a powerful statement of self-respect; it is a call to women to find full, positive expression of their bodies, their sexuality, them-

selves. Each chapter of the book includes a technical explanation, an exploration of values or of issues raised by the topic, and selected quotations from a variety of women, exploring their feelings or viewpoints.

We buy copies of *Our Bodies, Ourselves* for all our members who request it and keep a copy available for group discussions. Unfortunately, the text is not directed towards young working-class women. The book is long and much of the text is difficult to read (full of long words and complex sentences). Further, several of the chapters discuss female sexuality in ways which tend to be threatening for our members. Chapters on masturbation, homosexuality, and the self-exam, while useful in opening up the attitudes of middle-class women, often shock and close off working-class young women. We work around this by reading selectively from the text during the meeting and by being sensitive to the responses of the group (putting the book away when the tension level gets too high).

For our purposes, the most useful passages of *Our Bodies, Ourselves* are the direct quotations, which provide a variety of points of view on each topic. Often we take turns reading aloud a series of quotations in class; the alternative viewpoints give impetus to our discussions. Unlike the text, which is sometimes hard to read for group members, the quotations are lively and readable. Here are examples from the chapter on venereal disease:

> I slept with this guy one night and a few days later thought I might have gotten gonorrhea. I was a little frightened about what to do. It was awfully hard for me to believe I had vd even though I had symptoms. My old fears came up about being a bad girl if I wanted to have sex and being punished with vd or pregnancy. [P. 167]

> vd is just like the chicken pox or German measles. It should be dealt with like a disease and not as a moral thing. [P. 168]

We also use the table of contents of *Our Bodies, Ourselves* to uncover members' interests at the beginning of a new discussion group, often identifying topics which members might otherwise neglect to think of, or which they are embarrassed to mention. Commenting on the table of contents is a non-threatening way of sharing concerns.

Conception, Birth and Contraception, a Visual Presentation

The best illustrations we've found are in *Conception, Birth and Contraception, a Visual Presentation*, by Robert J. Demarest and John J. Sciarra. Although this book is expensive, we recommend that you buy one copy as a classroom resource. Through beautiful drawings and a text which continues to direct the reader back to the illustrations, it covers male and female anatomy, the reproductive cycle, the development of the fetus, birth, contraception, pregnancy, and menopause.

The illustrations are very accurate; because they are drawings, not photographs, our members are able to sustain looking at them without getting offended. Too often the photographs in other books we have provided threaten the young women. "I can't look at that." When we look at illustrations in *Conception, Birth and Contraception*, group members crowd around, fascinated, either silently attentive or bursting with questions.

The print is large; the text is clear in style. The information is fairly technical, but presented in a way that is understandable through reference to the illustrations. Here's a sample:

> Illustration 23 shows how the erect penis distends the vagina. The path that the spermatozoa follow from the testes through the vas deferens and through the urethra of the genitourinary system is also shown. When ejaculation occurs during sexual intercourse, the semen containing the sperm is deposited at the upper end of the vagina at the cervix of the uterus. From this point, the sperm must travel through the cervical mucus, across the uterus, and up into the fallopian tube where they meet the egg and fertilize it. [P. 42]

We keep *Conception, Birth and Contraception* on hand in all our classes. Sometimes we look up an illustration to help us visualize something that comes up in a discussion. At other times we build a class around illustrations and reading from the book.

"How to Take the Worry Out of Being Close, An Egg and Sperm Handbook"

The most accessible pamphlet we've found on birth control is "How to Take the Worry Out of Being Close, an Egg and Sperm Handbook," by Marian and Roger Gray. This is short and highly readable. The style is humorous and unfortunately a little "cutesy." (Probably the style will offend the leader but not the group member.)

The booklet covers the basic methods of birth control. "The basic idea in birth control is to keep egg and sperm from getting together. Various chemical, mechanical, and 'natural' means can be used to accomplish this . . ." (p. 3). The section on each method of birth control includes a description of the method, the effectiveness, the advantages, and the disadvantages. There are usually a couple of words of advice as well:

> Even if you usually use another method, condoms are good to have around in case a pill is forgotten or the diaphragm is home and you aren't. [P. 13]

When we've used the "Egg and Sperm Handbook," we've taken a class or two and read it aloud, stopping along the way for feelings and ideas. In our most successful use of the booklet, we asked members to examine the classroom birth control paraphernalia as we read. Afterward, members took home their copies of the pamphlet and several items from the birth control kit as well!

TOPICS

1: Anatomy and Physiology of Reproductive Organs

By teaching the anatomy and physiology of the reproductive system, we hope to help the group feel more fully connected to their own bodies. Sex becomes less mysterious; a foundation is laid for understanding the dfferences in the various methods of birth control. Both the pictures and text of *Conception, Birth and Contraception* (pp. 3–31) are excellent resources for this topic. (There is particularly good coverage of the anatomy and physiology of the male, which is missing from some of the other texts.) The chapter in *Our Bodies, Ourselves* (pp. 24–27) is also a good resource, although we find that the anatomy section (which focuses on a self-exam) can be threatening to young women.

In teaching anatomy and physiology, it's always important to remember to go over only a little information at a time, and then leave room for discussion of feelings. "Did you ever know anything about those parts of your body?" "How do you feel about having all of that going on inside you?" The personal quotations from *Our Bodies, Ourselves* can be useful in sparking discussion around these questions. The following sample sets off a good discussion about the unity of a person's mental and physical self:

> Recently, as I became more aware of my body, I realized I had pretended some parts didn't exist, while others now seemed made of smaller parts. I also discovered mental and physical processes working together. I realized that when my chest pulled down and felt collapsed I felt unhappy or depressed. When I felt sad my chest would start to tighten. When I became aware of the connections, I could start to change. Gradually, I felt a new kind of unity, wholeness in me, as my mental and physical selves became one self. [P. 25]

2: The Reproductive Cycle (Menarche through Menopause)

In teaching the reproductive cycle, we center on the experiences of the young women; again, we give as much information as we think they can absorb. Both *Conception, Birth and Contraception* (pp. 32–41) and *Our bodies, Ourselves* (pp. 31–37) have clear sections on this topic. (The description in *Our Bodies, Ourselves* is more technical and includes some good quotations on feelings.)

We've found that discussions about the onset of menstruation (menarche) are a good avenue to discussion of the menstrual cycle in general. We will often begin the topic by asking, "What was it like when you first got your period?" Novels and first-hand accounts can enrich a discussion of menarche. (See "Growing Up Female," p. 64,

for a pairing exercise on Becoming a Woman, and an activity on menstruation based on an excerpt from *Anne Frank: The Diary of a Young Girl.*

Although many adolescent women aren't personally concerned about menopause, some have experienced menopause second-hand through their aunts, mothers, or neighbors. It's important to raise the topic, explain some of the facts, and allow the group members to share some of their stories, or concerns, about the women they know. There's a chapter on menopause in *Our Bodies, Ourselves* (pp. 327–336) that you can read together if a particular interest surfaces in your group.

3: Birth Control and Abortion

"The pill makes you fat." Many young women don't use birth control, or their use is irregular. We've found that the reasons have more to do with embarrassment, shame, or guilt, than a lack of adequate information or resources.

We accompany all teaching of birth control information with many discussions and role-plays about how it feels to use or not to use birth control. Role-plays are particularly good tools for revealing some of the hidden blocks against birth control. We've set up role-plays between a young woman and her mother or older sister (in which the young woman asks about birth control or has her pills discovered); between a young woman and her boyfriend (in which he suggests she use the pill, or she suggests he use condoms); between two girlfriends (one uses birth control and the other doesn't); and, finally, between a young woman and the man at the local pharmacy (where she buys her birth control device).

For information on birth control, *Our Bodies, Ourselves* (pp. 181–215) and "How to Take the Worry Out of Being Close" both present clear descriptions, including the effectiveness, advantages, and disadvantages of each method. "How to Take the Worry Out of Being Close" is more accessible, but *Our Bodies, Ourselves* is more up to date and detailed.

We've had some of our best classes on birth control when we've brought in a birth control kit to examine as we discuss the different methods. You can probably get a kit at a local Planned Parenthood office; you can put one together yourself by collecting a variety of pills, a diaphragm, condoms, sample IUD's (from a local clinic), etc. One year, our group had a surprisingly joyous time, handling all of the paraphernalia, asking questions and reading aloud from the books. One young woman suggested we patent the "Bicentennial Diaphragm," imprinted with a picture of the American flag. They left the classroom in disarray, with a trail of foam on the discussion table. The next day, one of the group members informed us, "Me and Johnny tried out one of those rubbers last night. He didn't know how to use it right." Here, as throughout these discussions, we made the point that both members of a couple share equally in taking responsibility for contraception.

In discussions of abortion, strong feelings are raised. The chapter in *Our Bodies, Ourselves* (pp. 216–238) is thorough, but dense for members of our groups. On this topic, in particular, they have a lot they want to express, themselves. Further, they are wary of the tendency of the leaders to defend abortion. We've found it can be useful to invite in a counselor from a local abortion clinic to present the facts. She can advocate abortion much more comfortably than the group leaders. If she offends some of the members, they can debunk her afterward, when the visit is discussed. In some classes, we've focused on abortion legislation. While many of our group members say they wouldn't get an abortion, most will defend the right of each woman to decide for herself. (See Unit IX, "Women's News," p. 221, for reading and writing about abortion legislation.)

4: Pregnancy and Birth

The groups have shown particular interst in learning about pregnancy and birth through hearing from mothers or fathers about their experiences. They want to hear the stories of a classmate who gave birth under medication, or a speaker who gave birth "naturally," even when they are unable to focus on a reading describing the same process.

We recommend teaching about pregnancy and birth through the combination of a speaker and film. Most maternity hospitals can supply you with a film of a birth. Group members find films on natural chidbirth particularly interesting; some may wish to consider natural childbirth as one option: "Maybe with all those classes on breathing it wouldn't be so bad." *Our Bodies, Ourselves* has three chapters on pregnancy and birth (pp. 248–316) and *Conception, Birth and Contraception* has good illustrations, particularly on the stage of growth of the fetus (pp. 57–88).

It's important for young women to think about pregnancy and birth in the context of whether or not, or when, they want to have children; to consider parenthood in the context of their personal relationships, schooling, and working life. Further, it's crucial for them to consider the role of the father in the birth process and in raising the child. (Activities focusing on these issues can be found in Unit IV, "Adult Sex Roles," pp. 117–121.)

5: Going to Doctors—The Gynecological Examination

We want young women to learn to respect and care for their own bodies. This means, in part, that they should demand good medical care. Along with yearly physicals, they need to get yearly Pap smears, as well as yearly gynecological examinations for those who are sexually active or who have reached age eighteen. (See *Our Bodies, Ourselves*, pp. 121–122.) In addition, they need to pay close attention to the messages from their own bodies, to check themselves for lumps in their breasts or other irregularities. Unfortunately, many young women are afraid of exploring their own bodies, and afraid of doctors. ("I won't go to doctors. I faint if I even walk in the door of a hospital.") In our groups, we work to help members to deal with these fears.

Usually there are some members in a group who have gone for gynecological examinations. With the aid of a reading from *Our Bodies, Ourselves* (pp. 121–122), they can explain to others what happens in the examination. Usually, the apprehensions of the women who have never been examined far outdistance the actual terrors of the examination. They are relieved to hear the accounts of their classmates. "It's nothing. You just lie on the table and put your feet in those things. I had a woman doctor and she explained everything as she went."

While the accounts of some members are positive, others are not. "This doctor didn't say anything about what he was going to do, then he hurt me when he put that metal thing in. When I started to cry he told me I was too much of a big girl to act like a baby." We encourage these members to tell their stories, too, and we give them concrete support; for example, we ask them if they would like the name of a doctor who is known to treat women considerately.

Many of our members have asked the group leaders to accompany them to a clinic for their first gynecological examination. We've found that going with a young woman to her first examination can be an important contribution to her welfare. We can give her sympathy and encouragement through the interminable wait in the reception room, then discuss the examination with her afterward. Often, group members we've taken to their first examination have come back to us for help—when they've forgotten to take a pill, when they've had vaginal infections or venereal disease. Building trust with the group through discussions or first visits to the doctor, allows them to come to us in times of personal crisis when they can greatly benefit from the counseling of an adult woman.

If the members are particularly interested in health care, there's a good chapter to read in *Our Bodies, Ourselves* (pp. 337–370). A class trip to a community health center can be informative and enjoyable. Like the discussions of the examination, a trip to a clinic alleviates some fears. (See Unit VIII, "Women Organizing Themselves," p. 210.)

6: VD and Vaginal Infections

Our first goal is to counter the myth that VD is a punishment for having sex. Although not stated explicitly, this is often the underlying message from high school health classes, religious teachers, parents, and even doctors. Further, we want to inform young women that there presently is an epidemic of venereal disease; that the consequences of the disease are serious; and that there are cures.

The chapter on these topics in *Our Bodies, Ourselves* (pp. 167–180) is a valuable resource; it is worth reading aloud in the group. The beginning of the chapter focuses on the awkwardness of talking openly about the problem of venereal disease. This is a good starting point for a group discussion. The latter part of the chapter deals with symptoms and treatment; this is information eveyone should have. There is also a section in *Our Bodies, Ourselves* on other vaginal problems (pp. 136–151), which is a good reference.

7: Taking Care of Your Body— Exercise, Nutrition, Self Defense

We work to make the group members aware of ways they can take good care of their bodies through exercise, improved nutrition, and self-defense. It adds a new dimension to a discussion group, to try "doing" some of these things.

To encourage members to exercise, we follow the meeting of the discussion group every other week with a trip to a pool and sauna. Through exercising and relaxing together, the young women begin new habits which they carry with them into their own personal lives. In the discussion group, we explore some of the feelings members experience when we go to the pool, like embarrassment at wearing a bathing suit, self-consciousness in swimming, or excitement about turning around some of these old resistances.

To raise the consciousness of the group about nutrition, we read some basic information and guidelines in *Our Bodies, Ourselves* (pp. 99–110). We follow this by making a chart of what all the members of the group have eaten for the past several days. Many are amazed to get an overview of their own inadequate eating habits. One year, we followed up our short study on nutrition by sponsoring a highly nutritious dinner for the whole school. We decorated the walls with posters on the various vitamins, proteins, carbohydrates, etc.; no one was allowed to smoke while we were eating.

Learning self-defense is another way of taking care of your own body. If the members in a group are interested, you may want to invite a woman who knows karate or judo to give a demonstration in your class. This can be followed by discussing circumstances in which it might be useful to have learned self-defense skills.

8: Relationships with Family, Friends, Boyfriends, Yourself

We encourage the participants in a discussion group to talk about their sexuality in the context of their relationships with their family, their friends, and themselves. Often discussions about relationships arise naturally in the group as they connect to a given topic (birth control, going to the doctor, abortion, etc.). At other times, we use activities to deepen the discussions. Many activities on personal relationships can be taken from Unit III, "Growing Up Female." Role-plays and discussion questions from the section on Family (pp. 67–78), Friends (pp. 78–86), and Self (pp. 89–93) can be used in a discussion group with only slight modifications.

9: Sexuality—Feelings and Fantasies, Masturbation, Homosexuality, Making Love

Feelings and Fantasies

Our goal is for group members to learn to accept, explore, and rejoice in their sexual feelings. The process of learning about sexual feelings is life-long; a women's discussion group can strengthen the members in that process.

We wait until the members of a group have developed comfort and trust with one another before we raise "sexual feelings" as a discussion topic. Even after a group has worked together for some time, discussions about sexual feelings

usually don't flow easily. We've found that reading personal quotations from *Our Bodies, Ourselves* can move us toward discussion.

> When I'm feeling turned on, either alone or with someone I'm attracted to, my heart beats faster, my face gets red, my eyes feel bright. The lips of my vagina feel wet, and my whole genital area feels full. My breasts hum. If I'm standing up I feel a rush of weakness in my thighs. If I'm lying down I may feel like a big stretch, arching my back, feeling the sensations go out to my fingers and toes. These are special feelings whether I do anything to act on them or not. [P. 39]

Too often young women think of sexual feelings, particularly when they are not directly connected with "being with a guy," as "sick" or "weird." In discussing this quotation, we hope to communicate that it's normal to feel sexual—alone, with a friend, reading, seeing a movie, or with a lover. We also let the group member know that it's all right to have sexual fantasies, that fantasies can be a creative exploration of feelings and the world. On the whole, the members seldom recount their fantasies to the group, but they seem to find it liberating to hear that fantasies are "okay." Occasionally, a group member will venture a reference to her own fantasies: "Before I go to sleep I think about all kinds of stuff. Don't you? It kinda helps me go to sleep."

Masturbation

We want to free young women to explore their own bodies without guilt. In learning to masturbate, they can learn about their own body rhythms and responses; this can both give them pleasure and help them expand their love-making creatively with others.

Masturbation is a taboo subject for many young women. To explore their bodies itself is taboo, and to discuss it is certainly unheard-of. Women in our groups have rarely raised the subject of masturbation for discussion. Nevertheless, when a comfortable opportunity arises, the leaders raise the subject. We point out that masturbation is normal, healthy, and can enrich people's sexual lives. If the members don't pick up on the discussion, we let it drop. It's enough to air the issue occassionally and communicate a relaxed, positive attitude.

Homosexuality

Our goal is to get across the idea that it's normal and healthy for everyone to experience some homosexual feelings. It's important that young women learn to accept these feelings in themselves and learn to be tolerant of people who choose to express their feelings in their relationships.

Our group members are particularly threatened by the possibility of being labeled homosexual. Every time we've started a new group, one of the members will look around the circle, made up entirely of women; and raise the specter of homosexuality: "The last thing I'd ever want to be is a lessie." When a group begins, we usually choose not to engage in an extended discussion of homosexuality. We point out simply that "there are many different homosexuals with different kinds of lives, just as there are heterosexuals with different kinds of lives. Some are happy; some aren't. Some are people you probably would get along with; others aren't."

As a group progresses, the members become more comfortable talking about homosexuals. With greater ease, they usually become more tolerant. Sometimes they tell stories about people they know. Often their experiences are limited. Their concept of homosexual men is of effeminate gays who dress, move, and speak with affectation. They picture lesbians as tough, "like hard guys." Some members are surprised to learn that many homosexuals live their lives very much as they do.

Talking about homosexual feelings remains difficult even after a group has been going for a while. It's important that the leader reiterate that everyone has some homosexual feelings and that those feelings are perfectly normal. Reading the following quotation from *Our Bodies, Ourselves* can help members talk about their own experiences:

When I was about seven or eight I had this best friend Susan. We loved each other and walked around with our arms around each other. Her older sister told us not to do that anymore because we looked like lesbians. So we held hands instead. [P. 44]

After reading this aloud in class one young women commented, "Me and my girlfriend used to sleep in the same bed when we were little." Another responded, "I stil like to sleep in the bed with my girlfriends if they stay over. Do you think that's wrong?"

Making Love

We hope members of the group will learn to see sex as a part of their lives that they will continue to explore creatively as they grow older. Through our discussions they discover that there is a lot that they can learn from one another, and that there are good resources available. The chapter on sexuality in *Our Bodies, Ourselves* (pp. 38–60) is an extremely valuable resource for both the members and the leader.

When we discuss love-making, it is also crucial that we discuss virginity. In a given group some members are usually virgins, while others have had various amounts of experience with sex. All of them feel conflicting pressures—pressures from boyfriends or friends to have sex, pressures from family or religion to resist. The leader should reaffirm that "it's okay for people to be in different places." A young woman should only make love when she feels ready; this may be when she's fourteen or when she's twenty-two; it may be only after a long relationship; it may be in a short-term one; it may be when she's married.

We want young women to learn to strive for communication with their lovers about sex. Talking about their sex together, two people can find better ways to communicate with their bodies. This quotation from *Our Bodies, Ourselves* can facilitate a discussion.

I enjoy sex with Mike more than I have with anyone. When we get turned on we make the most beautiful music together! Still sex often feels difficult for me. When I feel good about myself and close to him and when the pressures of our children and my work and my friends are not demanding a lot of my energy, our sex is very fluid and strong. When I feel angry or sad or depressed or very childlike or needy, or any combination, or busy with other people in my life, I have a hard time being sexually open with Mike. We've talked about this, and he experiences a lot of the same ups and downs and distractions as I do. [P. 48]

After reading this we ask, "Can you talk about sex with your boyfriends?" "What are some of the things that get in the way?" *Our Bodies, Ourselves* has a good list of some of the barriers to communication (p. 50). After making our own list, we read and discuss the list in the book. At the close of one such discussion, a member leaned over and whispered to one of the leaders, "I really don't like it that much with David. It gets weird. Do you really think I could say anything to him?"

We let the group know that all of them have the capacity for orgasm, but it may take time, creativity, and patience before they discover what gives them the most pleasure and how to let themselves let go. Many young women don't realize the importance of the clitoris to their sexual stimulation. We find it useful to read aloud the section on the clitoris from *Our Bodies, Ourselves* (p. 45). For some young women, orgasm is a mysterious word. A few have never heard of it, others aren't quite sure what it means. A group tends to get very still and quiet when the subject first comes up. Sometimes, someone will ask, "How do you know if you've had an orgasm, anyway?" Again, we read from *Our Bodies, Ourselves* (pp. 46–47) about the different stages in female orgasm. Further, we point out that males naturally reach orgasm more quickly than females; a couple needs to explore ways for the male to take more time, and for the female to reach a high level of arousal, before the male enters her.

Discussions on subjects of virginity, the clitoris, orgasm, are charged. As leaders we must be sensitive to the level of tension in a group. We raise the topics, do a little reading, ask a few questions, but we do not push. We leave plenty of room for the group members to change the subject and breathe a little. We need to remember that a short discussion can resonate for a long time.

VI: MEAN STREETS

OVERVIEW

Late at night, as I walk the streets
I hear screaming and yelling,
The noises, the breaking of bottles,
kids scattered around the streets,
drunk, on dope, and not caring
about life and getting really messed
up, the craziness and killings still
go on,
while there are others who live the
straight life, and don't care,
cops are around, giving beatings, and
making busts, and they protect no one
but their fellow friends, the landlords,
the force, and the high class pigs who
think they're too good for us,
There is no one around who really cares,
so why should we?
[Colleen Long]

For young women growing up in the city, "mean streets" is an all-too-accurate description of the way they experience their environment. When we offered a woman's course with this title, every young woman in the school signed up for it. Their fascination with the term reflects both their feelings of pride in their ability to take care of themselves in any situation and their feelings of fear or shame about living on those streets and becoming toughened or, perhaps, trapped by them.

Collectively, the students know a great deal about what occurs on these "mean streets," although this is generally not information they are used to sharing in a school setting. In most of their schooling experiences, they have probably been required to ignore or denigrate this information, to give up their street identities, and to deny their neighborhood ties. The approach we outline in this unit attempts to turn that process around: the information is important; it is a legitimate part of the curriculum.

By facing head-on the difficulties and temptations of their environments, and by exploring the types of help that are available in overcoming them, students can gain an increased sense of control over their lives. In this unit, neither the problems nor the services are presented as inevitable. The emphasis is on elements of choice and discrimination.

The unit develops a case-studies approach. After an initial listing activity, in which students brainstorm about the kinds of problems young women might have, or the kinds of trouble they might get into, the class reads ten case studies about young women with just such difficulties. The discussion focuses on how and why these young women have fallen into a downward spiral of self-hate and despair, and then on how they might begin to make some small, but positive, changes. To give more flesh to the case studies, students interview friends who have had similar problems and read newspaper articles about young women "in trouble." Writing and vocabulary assignments follow, in which students think specifically about one of the young women presented in the case studies and write about her.

The next few activities explore what happens to young women when their problems bring them into the criminal justice system. After an exercise called, "Who is the criminal?" students take a trip to court and hear from a court-related speaker. They then read and write about women whose journey through the criminal justice system leads them to prison.

The final set of activities focuses on the individuals, agencies, and organizations that attempt to help people deal with the "mean streets." Students develop criteria by which to examine and evaluate services that are available to young women in trouble. They take trips, listen to speakers, and interview people in an attempt to survey and evaluate existing services. Their ability to make evaluative judgments in this final part of the unit is partially dependent on the success of the first set of activities. The more students feel like experts on the problems, the more they will feel they have the right to choose among services, the more they will demand that these agencies serve their needs.

"Mean Streets" could be integrated most easily into a sociology or current problems course. If you wanted to include males, you could add male case studies and investigate agencies that service males as well as females. In our experience, this subject matter is equally appealing to both sexes. When we taught the unit to a coeducational class, we had the students make up their own male case studies, after having read the female ones. Students wrote interesting and moving case studies that greatly added to the unit. Another possibility would be to combine this unit with "Growing Up Female: Childhood to Adolescence." Both focus mainly on young women, but deal with different aspects of their lives and experiences. A number of the books suggested in "Growing Up Female" are very relevant to the explorations in "Mean Streets" and, in fact, could be used to enrich the discussions, trips, and investigations of this unit, even if it is taught by itself.

ACTIVITIES

1: Brainstorming about "Trouble"

This activity starts with a few simple, direct questions: "What are all the kinds of trouble young women in Cambridge (or whatever city yours is) tend to get into?" "What kinds of problems cause young women to need or seek out services?" The teacher can provide additional structure by suggesting that students think in

terms of three categories: 1) types of things young women get brought to court for; 2) crimes in which they are the victims; and 3) problems that are nonlegal (such as unwanted pregnancy). If students have been reading one or two of the books suggested in the "Growing Up Female" unit, they could also be asked to list all of the problems facing the main female characters in those novels. All of the resulting lists are written on the board.

In brainstorming about these questions, students are encouraged to draw freely on their own experiences, on the experiences of their friends, on stories they have heard from other people. The point of this activity is to get students to share what they know about girls or women in trouble and to legitimize their sources of information. It is best if every student in the class is asked to contribute to this initial list.

Students' lists generally reflect experiences with drugs, shoplifting, getting pregnant, getting raped, running away from home, truancy, getting arrested for drinking in public, etc. We find it useful at this point to relate their lists to some of the larger trends and patterns. We mention to the students that new studies show that males tend to get into crimes that cause damage to people or to property—assaults, breaking and entering, vandalism, carrying a weapon—while females tend to get into self-destructive crimes, such as drugs, prostitution, or petty larceny. Even more interesting is the fact that males tend to be arrested and arraigned mainly for offenses that are considered criminal in adults as well as in juveniles, such as burglary or car theft, whereas females tend to be arrested for such offenses as running away, truancy, incorrigibility, or sexual delinquency, which are not regarded as crimes in an adult. We ask the students if this has been true in their experience and, if so, whether they can think of any explanations.

Two articles we have found especially useful are: "The Myth of Sexual Delinquency" in *Women: A Journal of Liberation* and "Juvenile Delinquency: The Sexualization of Female Crime" by Meda Chesney-Lind in *Psychology Today*. Both make the argument that defiant behavior on the part of young women tends to be immediately interpreted as sexual acting out, and that the courts operate under two sets of juvenile delinquency laws, one for males and one for females.

2: Case Studies

Based on our students' answers to the previous listing activity and, more generally, on our experience in working with low-income young women, we have developed a series of ten case studies, presented below. All portray young women with serious problems. The problems range from legal to nonlegal, from situations in which the young woman is the victim to those in which she seems to be responsible for her own predicament. We have tried to create problem situations that will not only seem real and familiar to the students, but will also raise the issues of individual responsibility and lead to explorations of possible sources of support and help. Depending on the problems that arise on the listing activity, the teacher should feel free to add new portraits or to delete or modify those below. It is also possible to present the cases to the class, allowing students to modify them to follow their own experiences more closely.

Laura: Unwanted Pregnancy

Laura has had boyfriends before, but never one she's cared for as much as Sam. She and Sam have been seeing each other practically every night for the past six months now. On her seventeenth birthday, they began sleeping together. Sometimes they fight, and sometimes they find it difficult to communicate, but they really care about each other.

Now Laura is very upset with both herself and Sam, because she has found out that she is pregnant. She has told Sam, but was unable to have a good conversation with him about what to do. It is clear they are not ready to get married. But Laura still has other serious questions: Should she get an abortion? Should she keep the baby? Should she have the baby and give it up for adoption? What does Sam really feel? Laura just keeps asking herself these questions, over and over; she can't think about anything else. And she has to act quickly, one way or the other.

—Why do you think Laura and Sam didn't use birth control?
—Where can Laura go now for help? (Specifically, for a pregnancy test, to get advice about having the baby versus an abortion, to get an abortion if she decides on that, to find help and support if she decides to have the baby?)

Linda: Runaway

Linda has never gotten along with her stepmother. They have been fighting ever since her stepmother married her father two years ago. Now things are worse than ever. Linda is fifteen; her father works two jobs and is hardly ever around. Linda likes to go out a lot to hang out with her friends, but her stepmother won't let her. She says she doesn't want Linda hanging around with that "rough crowd," or getting into trouble, but Linda thinks she just wants her around to clean the house, cook the dinner for the young children, and babysit, while her stepmother goes out with her friends.

One day last week, things really blew apart. Linda didn't come home until 11:00 P.M., when she was supposed to be home at 5:30. Her stepmother was so mad that she slapped Linda and called her a whore. That was it for Linda. She packed a small bag and ran away to Cambridge, where she sort of knew a few people. For several days now she has slept in a hallway. She is getting more tired, hungry, and lonely every day. And she's sure one of the neighbors will report her to the police soon.

—What do you think will happen to Linda?
—Where might she go for help? (First, for temporary shelter; and next, for help if she decides that she doesn't want to return home to live.)

Maureen: School Truant

At sixteen, Maureen has really begun to hate school. She promised her mother she would graduate high school, but that was before she realized how boring it would be. The way she sees it, the teachers are only there because they're too old to do anything else, or because they enjoy torturing students.

About two months ago, Maureen and her friend Karen figured out a system of cutting, while fooling their mothers into thinking they were at school every day. But yesterday the school called her mother to tell her Maureen was suspended for cutting until she and her family came to see the principal. "You're going back to that school even if I have to drag you down there myself," was her mother's only comment.

—What should Maureen do? What are her alternatives?

Pat: Drinking and Drug Problem

At sixteen, Pat drinks a six-pack every night. Whenever she is going to a party or really wants to "have a good time," she adds a couple of downs (or whatever else she can get) to her regular six-pack. When she is wrecked, she gets rowdy and ends up in fights. The next day she can't remember what happened the night before. Her friends are beginning to get disgusted with her.

Yesterday, after one of her particularly violent drunken evenings, she woke up with a black eye and a broken tooth. She looked at herself in the mirror and felt sick. The only thing that made her feel better was remembering that she had some downs left from last night. They would help her through the day.

—What would it take to make Pat want to stop?
—Where could she go for help?

Jill: Rape

Jill is sixteen years old. She is a senior in high school and working at a nursing home from 4:00 to 7:00 in the evening. One night Jill was coming home from work. When she got off the bus, a man also got off and followed her down the block. No one else was around. When she rounded the corner onto her street, he grabbed for her, pulled out a knife, and forced her into an alleyway. He raped her and then ran off, leaving her there.

Jill has been so upset that for a few days she hasn't dared to tell anyone about what happened. She keeps asking herself, "Was there anything I could have done?" "What if I had kicked him really hard?" She is physically injured and in a state of emotional shock.

—Whom could Jill talk to?
—Where could Jill go for help?

Janet: Hassles with Welfare

Janet is seventeen years old and has a two-and-one-half year-old child. Since her baby was born, she has been living with her mother; but she is very anxious to move out and live on her own. Her mother's apartment is really crowded, and she is always hassling Janet and treating her like a child, even though Janet has her own child.

She needs to find a place, to arrange for welfare money to pay for it, to get money for furniture, to arrange some kind of day-care for her child, so that she can stay in school and graduate. Her social worker isn't much help. She wants Janet to stay put at least until she finishes school. She says it's "easier that way." But Janet doesn't think so.

—What steps can Janet take to deal with her situation?

Sarah: Depression

Sarah comes from a family where everybody is always fighting. It seems as if there is never a quiet moment. It has always bothered Sarah, but lately it's been driving her crazy. The louder her mother and sisters fight, the quieter and more withdrawn she becomes. She was always pretty quiet, and kept to herself, but lately she has gotten to a point where she won't even come out of her house. She has stopped going to school altogether. But unlike last year, when she used to go shopping with a friend or just sit around by the river, now she just stays in the house, usually in the bedroom. Sarah seems really depressed all the time, and she won't talk to anybody about what's bugging her. She just says, "I don't feel like doing anything."

Her mother is mad at her and thinks she's being lazy. She's threatening to kick her out if she doesn't go back to school or go out and get a job. Sarah just listens to her mother yell and doesn't do anything. Lately, Sarah has begun to think she needs some help. She is afraid she might hurt herself, or do something crazy.

—What can Sarah do?
—Where can she go for counseling?

Marlene: Ex-prisoner

Marlene has just been released from Framingham—finally—after two-and-one-half years. She was sent up on a charge of passing bad checks; in addition, she had a string of earlier arrests for shoplifting. Her lawyer told her she'd get a suspended sentence for sure—especially since she had a six-month-old baby. Well, he was wrong. The judge didn't seem to care about the baby. They put her child in a foster home and threw her in jail.

Marlene spent two-and-one-half years sewing stripes on American flags, reading, and trying to get her head together. She feels like she understands a lot of things now that she never did before: about how and why her life was so hard, about what it meant to have an alcoholic father, about growing up as a woman in this society. She knows things are going to be tough now, but she wants a fresh start.

—Where can Marlene get help? (Specifically, in getting her child back? in finding friends and support? in finding a job? in finding an apartment?)

Carole: Shoplifting

Carole has become more interested in clothes lately. Maybe because she's more interested in men. Since she never has any money, she's gotten into the habit of ripping things off from stores. At first, she couldn't believe how easy it was. Snatch, and it's yours. Lately, she's been getting careless.

Last week, she was surprised by a Security Guard at Martins' Sportswear, who grabbed her arm and started pulling her toward the office. When she asked him to let go, he made a nasty remark about "street scum" and pushed her against a wall. Carole let her temper get the best of her and bit his hand. Now she's charged with shoplifting and assault and battery on an officer.

—Where can Carole go for legal advice and help?
—What might happen to her?

Mary: Tenant/Landlord Problems

Mary is fed up. She and her mother and her five younger brothers and sisters live in a five-room apartment. Since they moved into the apartment four years ago, they've had trouble with leaks and plumbing, fuses blowing all the time, etc. Her mother has tried not to complain too much because their rent has been relatively low for Cambridge ($125 monthly) and it's hard to find a place, with six kids and two dogs.

But this winter everything has gone wrong. First, the heat didn't work at all; they finally were able to get some heat coming up, but not enough—especially with no storm windows. (The landlord has told them to put plastic over the windows.) Then the plumbing in the bathroom got stopped up, which caused water to drip into the kitchen. The ceiling in the kitchen started to come down. Each time Mary or her mother has complained to the landlord about these things, he has said how destructive the younger children and dogs are, and how they should be trained to respect property more. He's also muttered under his breath about eviction. Mary hates the apartment and the landlord. She knows her mother is reluctant to do anything about the situation.

—What can Mary do?
—To whom can she turn for help?

Case studies have the advantage of being impersonal, yet personal at the same time. While most students are reluctant to talk in front of peers about their own problems, or those of close friends, they respond enthusiastically to talking about an imagined person with the same needs and experiences. "This is definitely me." "This sounds just like my sister, you wouldn't believe her." "That bastard, I'd kill him." We suggest reading these case studies aloud together, allowing time for reactions and discussion during, and after, each reading. As they are reading, students will often spontaneously tell stories about themselves or other people; they will offer advice; they will cast blame. While this is going on, the teacher's role is to encourage students to be anecdotal and, at the same time, help them to listen to each other.

The questions after each case study help structure a fuller discussion that explores possible solutions as well as the dimensions of the problems. This is a difficult transition for the students. Their defeatism quickly surfaces and leaves some of them silent. Others become angry. "She could have avoided it; she didn't have to go sleep with the guy." "Her stepmother is a real bitch." "I hate that clinic; they ask you all these questions about your sex life, like you were a whore or something." Sometimes the anger is directed at the young woman being described; sometimes at the other people around her; sometimes at the agencies that are supposed to help. To the extent that the case studies remind people of situations they have been involved in, they will have strong feelings and opinions.

It is important to allow for these assessments of blame or fault and to get the full range of opinions about each case study. But it is also important to move students beyond these debates toward some positive suggestions. Students should be encouraged to think of any small steps that the young woman could take to begin to make a change. Asked in this very limited way, a few people might have some ideas: Laura could overcome her shame enough to tell one of her friends about her pregnancy predicament; Maureen could try to find an alternative school; Pat could admit to herself that she has a drinking problem. These actions would not result in immediate, dramatic changes in these young women's lives. But they might relieve some of the tension and get people started toward some changes. You could suggest that the students think of times in their own lives when they were in bad predicaments. Was there anything they, themselves, or friends did that helped them out?

Sometimes, the best way for a person to help herself is to seek out services provided by other people. After each of the case studies, there is a question about where the young woman could go for help and support. This is a chance for students to share both positive and negative assessments of various agencies they or their friends have utilized. An annotated list of agencies should be started on a large piece of posterboard. As students investigate agencies in later activities, they can add to the list. The point here is to establish the question of where to go for help and to get people thinking of themselves as

legitimate evaluators of services.

The case studies activity makes the point that experiences students have are shared by many other people. An additional small exercise further develops that idea. The discussion of the case studies can take three or four days. During that time, students can be asked to check the newspapers for any articles about girls or women in trouble. Since "trouble" is often what is news, almost every week there is something interesting to be found. A sample of items our students brought in included: an article from the local town paper on rape; an article, "Delinquent Girls Increasing" from one of the area daily papers; an article from an area weekly on Joan Little's trial; and a column from the other daily declaring that women's liberation has "gone too far," because women are now committing more violent crimes than in the past. Even if only one or two items are found, it is a valuable exercise and broadens the perspective. Once they start looking for such articles, students are more likely to notice them on a day-to-day basis. If you set up a bulletin board, students may well continue to bring clippings in.

3: Interviews with Young Women in Trouble

Having discussed the case studies at some length, the students do some of their own investigative work. An interesting project is for each student to find one person to interview who has been in a kind of trouble similar to that described in one of the case studies. The goal is twofold: to learn more about what it is like to be in this kind of trouble, to learn more about where you can go for help (see "Techniques," p. 28).

With some reflection, almost everyone can come up with one person to interview. Students should be assured that these interviews can be kept anonymous. Our students' friends are often surprised that a class is studying a problem they have experienced, but ultimately they are flattered and glad to share. Once they have their interviewee in mind, students prepare by taking part of a class period to write out some questions. In previous units, they have developed questionnaires as a group; this is a chance for them to apply this skill. Some guidance from the teacher is helpful. You might suggest some categories of questions: 1) background information on the person; 2) experiencing the problem; 3) sources of advice and help, good and bad. Under each category, students write specific questions to ask their particular interviewee. The teacher should circulate around the room to help students put their questions into final form.

Even though the answers may be very brief, they generally add valuable new dimensions to the students' understanding of the problems and valuable new information about possible sources of help. For instance, this is a typical interview submitted by one of our students:

Q: When did you get raped?
A: Two months ago
Q: When you got raped, was it at night?
A: Yes
Q: Where did you get raped?
A: In North Cambridge
Q: Did you know who you were raped by?
A: No
Q: Did you tell the police?
A: No
Q: Why?
A: Because if I didn't know the guy, they wouldn't.
Q: Did you go any place for help?
A: Yes
Q: Where?
A: A rape crisis center
Q: Did they help?
A: No
Q: Why?
A: Because I needed mental help, not physical help. I still felt the same way I did before I went in there.
Q: Did you go any other place?
A: No
Q: Why?
A: I felt after that, that the only one that was gonna help me was me!
Q: When you got raped did you fight?

A: Yes
Q: Did it help?
A: No
Q: Why?
A: Because all I did was get tired and beaten up.
Q: How did this affect you?
A: It messed up my head for a while, but I'm getting everything together now, so it really doesn't bother me that much any more.
Q: How about other guys. Do you trust them?
A: Yes, I'm not going to judge all men by just one sick bastard. From now on I'll be more careful. [Diane Tomaino Arsenault]

Brief as it is, this interview is powerful. It makes the experience seem very real. If there is time and interest, you could have the whole class go over each interview together and attempt to come to some conclusions about the kind of trouble being discussed. Another possibility is to have each student write a summary paragraph on what she learned about the problem from the interview, including how it affected the person she interviewed, what kinds of help might be useful to others with that problem. The student who conducted the rape interview wrote these observations:

> To me I don't think there is really any kind of help for a girl that has been raped, because no matter who talks to them or tries to help them, even though they might have been raped themselves, it's going to remain inside their head for the rest of their lives.
>
> I have talked to a lot of girls who have been raped. Some feel guilty because of it and some feel they should have done a lot more than what they did.

In writing paragraphs such as these, students build their skills in interpretation and summary. When read aloud in class, these summaries help to reinforce the point that much can be learned from the experiences of people within the students' own friendship circles.

4: Writing—A Day in the Life . . .

Two writing assignments are suggested here; both enrich the descriptions in the case studies. The first requires students to "get inside" one of the young women, in order to write about a day in her life. The second involves helping one of the young women to find ways to deal with her problem. These assignments can be spaced a number of days apart, or you can choose to use only one assignment. If there is only time for one, we suggest the second, because of its positive emphasis on movement and change (see "Techniques," p. 18).

Assignment One

Describe a day in the life of one of the young women in our case studies. Choose one of the following: 1) Getting into trouble—the day it all began; 2) Hitting bottom—the worst day in her life; 3) A good day—when she doesn't let anything get to her.

Students can choose to write in either the first or third person, depending upon which is more comfortable. Several of these topics lend themselves well to a play or dialogue form. Students who have trouble writing essays might want to try their hand at a short play.

Karen: Therese! Block me or I'm going to get caught.
Therese: No, you're not. Just be cool.
Karen: Therese, if we get away with all this I'll be happy. I took the tags off the clothes.
Therese: I hope you did. I am stuffing the clothes in the bags fast Karen, so I hope you're looking out for me.
Karen: Let's walk all the way around to the other department. No one is watching; Therese, we have made it now.
Therese: I hope we do all right.
(So they walk to the door, and the lady in regular clothes says. . .)
Policewoman: Hey young ladies, wait a minute. Come upstairs to my office for a minute.
(So the girls walk up the stairs with the clothes and the lady says. . .)
Policewoman: You have been caught shoplifting.
Therese and Karen (speaking at the same time): Sorry, Miss, but these are our fucking clothes! [Teresé T. Gray]

This student was able to use her familiarity with the situation, and her comfort with

dialogue, to create a good play. It was the first writing assignment she felt good about. Everyone in the class enjoyed reading it aloud together and encouraged her to submit it to the Yearbook.

Assignment Two

Choose one of the following letters to write:

1. Imagine you are a close friend of one of the young women in the case studies. Write her a letter in which you try to give her some helpful advice about her problem.
2. Write a letter to someone you care about who has a serious problem she needs to deal with.

Students enjoy writing about getting into trouble. But they also do very well at writing about getting out of trouble. When encouraged to take on the role of helper, they are amazingly creative in their suggestions and mature in their tone.

Dear Sue,

I am so sorry to hear about your problems. But if you would really like my opinion, I honestly believe you should have an abortion. I know it will be hard on you at first, but later on in life you'll be grateful. You have to think of the baby. I mean just because you're having a baby doesn't mean you're a woman. You'll be taking a lot of responsibilities, more than you can handle. Think of what you have to offer it. Do you want your baby to grow up in a project? You're not married, so the baby would be considered illegitimate. Would you like to live on welfare? Do you want to depend on a check every other week, which only gives you $60–$70 for rent, food, and clothing? That's just enough for the baby. What will you live on?

Now think of yourself. You're only sixteen. You have your whole life in front of you yet. Don't you want to finish school and be something? With a baby, your chances are going down the drain. And wouldn't you like to live in your own home? With a husband? Travel around the world and see different people? Have a diamond ring on your finger to show off?

Later on in life you can have as many children as you like. Right now think of yourself and what the poor innocent baby is going to have to go through. I can't make you have an abortion and nobody else can either. But believe me, whatever you decide, I'll always be your friend.

Love,
Debby

A number of young women in the class chose to write letters to fictional friends with problems similar to ones they themselves had faced recently. It gave them a chance to articulate thoughts and feelings they had about their own situation. Several other students wrote letters to actual friends. They felt good enough about their advice to want to mail those letters.

5: Vocabulary—Labels with Negative Connotations

Often students have heard themselves or their friends described with labels they do not understand. In this activity, we teach words that are commonly used to describe or label young women in trouble: incorrigible, promiscuous, deviant, paranoid, defiant, introverted, extroverted, defensive.

Having taught the words and their meanings through various short exercises (see "Techniques," p. 23), the teacher can point out to the class what all these words have in common and ask which of these words the students consider especially condescending (you might use this opportunity to teach the meaning of this last word, too—an easy definition is: "like a put-down"). There are two follow-up exercises that help students to see that the behavior these words describe can also be looked at in other, less negative ways.

First, ask students to try to match up the vocabulary list with another list of somewhat less loaded words and phrases; i.e.:

incorrigible	free
deviant	shy
promiscuous	protective of herself
paranoid	stubborn, unchanging
defiant	outgoing
introverted	different
extroverted	highly sensitive
defensive	standing up for herself

Lines should be drawn between the two terms that might be used to describe the same person. Next, each student writes two descriptions of the same person. The first description, using words from the right-hand list, should be written as if by the young woman's best friend, or as her own lawyer might describe her in court. The second description, using words from the left-hand list, should be written as the prosecution, or a police officer, might describe her in court. This exercise helps students to see how the choice of words determines the overall effect of a description or presentation.

6: The Criminal Justice System

Some of the trouble young women get into has legal ramifications. What women get arrested for and how they are treated in court is an interesting topic in its own right. A look at women and the criminal justice system is a good transitional activity between focusing on the troubles and problems of women and focusing on the sources of help. The court, after all, is a major agency handling girls and women in trouble.

An exercise we call "Who is the real criminal?" serves as an interesting introduction to an exploration of the criminal justice system. In this exercise, six or seven students are given cards, each of which describes a specific individual:

You are a woman, twenty-two. You make your living by selling your body to men. In other words, you are a streetwalker.

You are a man, forty-three. You travel a lot for your job. Sometimes you get lonely in a strange city and look for a prostitute you can be with for a few hours.

You are a young woman, fifteen. Your stepfather sometimes picks on you and occasionally hits you. Your mother doesn't say anything. so you have run away from home.

You are a young man, fifteen. Your stepfather sometimes picks on you and occasionally hits you. Your mother doesn't say anything. So you have split for California.

You are a young woman, seventeen. You never have money for clothes, so whenever you really want something, like Christmas presents or new spring clothes, you lift it.

You are a young woman, seventeen. You are from a rich family and can have anything you want. Sometimes, while you are shopping, you get bored waiting for a salesperson and just walk out of the store with the item you were going to buy.

You are a young woman, nineteen. One night you were attacked and raped by a man you vaguely knew. You got a gun and then went looking for him at a bar you thought he frequented. When you saw him you shot and killed him.

You are a young woman, fifteen. You were arrested for drinking in public. The police officer who arrested you grabbed your arm so tightly that he really hurt you. So you bit his hand.

Each person with a card has to decide whether she has or has not committed a crime. The "criminals" go to the left-hand side of the room; noncriminals to the right. Each person with a role then speaks and explains why she has or has not committed a crime. After each speech, one other member of the class becomes either the speaker's prosecutor or her defense (whichever is opposite to the speaker's definition of herself). Thus, each one who says that she is a criminal has a defense; and each one who says that she is innocent must hear an argument alleging her guilt. The whole class then votes on each person for a final decision.

This exercise raises many issues: How do we define crime? Is it defined by what there are laws against? Do the laws apply equally to everyone—rich and poor, male and female, white and Black? Is crime defined by what the courts do? If the court never prosecutes the man in a prostitution case, does that mean he has not committed a crime? If the store doesn't bring charges against the rich young woman, is she innocent? If a mother brings her daughter to court for running away, is the girl more criminal than a boy who runs away and is let go?

Trip to Court

Students almost always enjoy a trip to court, and it is one of the easier trips to arrange. If you are bringing a small group, you can arrive in the morning when criminal court opens and sit through as many hours of the proceedings as you like. A larger group may have to be arranged in advance (see "Techniques," p. 33). It is best to visit the nearest big city court, where there is likely to be a variety of cases.

The class's assignment is to look at all the ways women are involved in the proceedings—

as defendants, plaintiffs, victims, or lawyers. What kinds of crime does it seem women are arrested for? When are they the victims? How are women treated by the judge? Are they treated differently from men? Are there differences in the way the judge treats women defendants, victims, and lawyers? So much is usually going on in court that it is good to have a clear focus and know what to look for. It is, of course, unpredictable what the class will see on any given day. In a big city court, most days the first defendants will be drunks (men) and prostitutes (women), who were picked up the night before. Beyond that, the cases might be anything from robberies, to frauds, to assaults on police officers. Some judges, conscious of their audience, speak up loudly; others mumble and can't be heard. But no matter what the conditions, the chances are good that students will come away with a beginning sense of women's position in the criminal justice system.

Speaker from Court

Since the class is not able to see the proceedings of juvenile court, which are private, we invite a probation officer or lawyer very familiar with the legal problems of young women and the workings of juvenile court to come to class. The speaker can be a substitute for, or an addition to, the trip.

The class prepares for the visitor by pooling all their questions. Particularly in the case of a juvenile probation officer, they will probably have more than enough ideas of what to ask. They might also have suggestions as to whom you could invite. The speaker must be one who has information about the acts that females (young and old) are arrested for, how they are treated once arrested, what they tend to be incarcerated for, how they are treated during incarceration, and what happens to them afterward. If the speaker can do so, it would be useful to have these answers compared to those for males.

Most probation officers will stress the services available through the court, and they will explain that the whole probation process is intended to be helpful to females with serious problems. Many of the younger officers will say that they know the young woman is not always at fault for difficulties at home, but that at least the court can intervene and perhaps help out in a bad situation. A good question to raise in the class meeting that follows the visit is whether the courts can act effectively as a "helping" agency. Have students ever known this to happen? In what situations might the court intervene effectively? If not, why not? In this discussion, students may tend to be cynical and express a basic distrust of the courts. As one student said, "Watch out for people watching out for you." This distrust may well come from painful personal experiences, but it may also, at times, stand in the way of a young person's recognizing and receiving real help when it is needed. At this point, it is enough simply to get an expression of the students' feelings. The whole issue of what makes a good helping agency will be dealt with in more detail in the next activity.

Either in connection with the trip or stimulated by the classroom visitor, the issue of a double standard of justice will arise. Although it is a difficult, somewhat abstract question, the class will be in a position to think about whether the court is operating on different assumptions about why females and males commit crimes and, hence, how they should be treated.

Sometimes students have had direct experiences that speak to these issues. One student brought before a juvenile judge as a runaway and stubborn child was asked: "Why do you dress like a boy?" and lectured on how things would be fine at home if she were more ladylike. Then she was sent to the court psychologist. Obviously, nothing comparable would be said to a male: in fact, it is highly unlikely that a male would be brought in for stubborn child or runaway offenses. Hearing it said that these offenses are not really criminal may be very helpful to some students who have been in these situations. The discussion may cause these students to express tremendous bitterness at parents who brought them to court. When that happens, the students generally get sympathy and support from their classmates.

7: Women in Prison

If students are very interested in the topic of women and the criminal justice system, you might follow up with materials on women in prison. An entire issue of *Women: A Journal of Liberation* is devoted to "Women Locked Up." Two interviews with young women in prison are especially good. One of these is "A Prison Interview with Lydia." Lydia, 19, is in jail for prostitution and robbery. She talks about drugs—which represent "the desire to escape reality," particularly the reality of loneliness—and about the role drugs play in landing her in prison. Another powerful interview is "Life in Prison."

> I was six months pregnant when I was arrested. I got absolutely no medical attention for the next three months. I never saw a doctor at all. It was my first baby so I didn't know anything about it. My water burst at 3:00 A.M.. I told the matron but she told me I'd be all right. They wouldn't take me over specially. The regular bus for the hospital left the prison at eight in the morning so I went on that. I think it was the loneliest I've ever been in my life.

The young woman goes on to speak about the absence of exercise facilities for women, which, combined with the starchy prison diet, results in the female prisoners' getting fat. This woman also offers an analysis of the system:

> You see men's and women's prisons are founded on very different principles. Men's prisons are supposed to protect society from the hardened criminals. But in women's prisons they try to lead you back to the fold. They try to teach you how to be a housewife and how to depend on men. In other words, they see you as having been led astray. You have no mind of your own.

The class could profitably spend several days reading over these articles together and discussing the experiences of women in prison. These sessions lead to writing assignments:

1. Write a letter to the prison authorities from a woman prisoner whose child has been taken away from her and put up for adoption.
2. Write a letter from a mother who is in prison to her child; and/or write a letter from the child to the woman.

3. Write all the thoughts of a woman who is sitting in prison awaiting trial for killing a man who attacked her.
4. Write a woman's thoughts as she is making the American flag as part of her work assignment in prison.

Some students identify very strongly with the women they have been reading about—perhaps because they, themselves, feel loneliness and shame, perhaps because they feel they might someday be locked up. The depth of their involvement with these women is illustrated by the following excerpt from one student's paper:

> All I think of is when the guy came at me, there was nothing I could do but to kill him. If I hadn't he would have killed me and probably more.
>
> Here is the guard now. I am walking down the corridor. There are doors and gates with all kinds of locks. I am so scared. What's going to happen to my baby? I hope nothing happens to my sister when she is out working, trying to support my daughter. Here I am crying because of these so-called men. I was out paying my taxes and Nixon did this to me. Oh my god, I am just sitting here saying my prayers. "Please don't let it happen. Where is my lawyer? She knows I am innocent." [Deborah Stewart Hedges]

8: How to Evaluate Counseling Services

This activity prepares students to investigate services for women. Before plunging into this activity and the next, students may need a chance to discuss the rationale for such an investigation. Some students may have had unpleasant experiences with traditional agencies and, therefore, be resistant to studying them. "What do you want to talk to *those* people for?" "My mother said she'll *never* go back to that place." "They treat you like you're mental or something."

One way to encourage student interest is to let them know that new and alternative services have been developing, and that the class will have a chance to visit and evaluate some of these innovative ventures together. You might also want to suggest the possibility of the class's compiling a list of agencies, with descriptions of the quality of their services, that could be distributed to other young women.

The first step in looking at services is to think about criteria for evaluation. What makes a place seem helpful? What makes an experience terrible? Each student fills out the following form:

What are the specific things you would want to know about a place before you'd send a friend there or go there yourself?

1. List two or three things that would encourage you to trust and use a place.
2. List two or three things that would make you not want to go to this place.

You may want to move around the room and help individuals with this assignment. While most students have no trouble reporting their personal reactions to agencies they've visited, they may need your help to translate these reactions into general criteria for evaluating other agencies.

The class shares and pools the lists. Generally, they like places with: "young people there, who dress casual"; "comfortable chairs"; "people you can talk to"; "no waiting." They don't like: "people who make you feel cheap"; "if they tell your mother"; "too nosey".

The compiling of the list is followed by role-playing in which people have a chance to play out both "good" and "bad" situations and get into a fuller discussion of the crucial differences. We use three situations, two of which include counselors who behave in ways the students have identified as "bad" in their lists. One involves a counselor closer to their ideal.

> You are Joanne, a pregnancy counselor. Your counseling style is to be very, very warm and understanding (especially when young women come to you with a pregnancy problem) and a bit overbearing. You ask many questions and don't really leave much space.

> You are Rachel, a new alcohol and drugs counselor. You, yourself, have just gained a lot of information on alcohol and drugs and their effects. You feel it is very important for young people to have that information so they can make informed choices. Your tendency as a counselor is to give a lot of information about drugs and alcohol; you do not tune in very much to the feelings or emotional level of your client. Actually, you are a little afraid of getting in over your head.

> You are Carol, a counselor who does a lot of work with adolescents. Your style is to be warm and under-

standing and also to leave lots of space for your client. You think it's important in a first interview to try to find the level of the problem and to give the young person a sense she can get help if she wants it, that it's good to seek help when you need it, and there's no need to feel bad about it.

The client roles are found in the case studies. The first is Laura, with the unwanted pregnancy; the second is Pat, with a drinking and drug problem; the third is Sarah, who is very depressed.

It is probably best for the teacher to play the counselors, since the roles require a familiarity with several counseling techniques. Students will be familiar with the clients' problems, as these are drawn from the case studies they have read. Students should not be told ahead of time what the counselors will be like. They are asked to watch the role-plays carefully and to write down things they like and don't like about the counselor's style. At the end of the role-plays, the clients tell how they felt and whether they got the help they needed. Following this, students read aloud the lists made while the role playing was in progress (see "Techniques," p. 27).

The discussion of the role-plays helps students to clarify what they value in a counselor. They criticize Counselor Number One for being "too gushy." All I wanted was help getting an abortion, not all that 'how are you feeling?' stuff." Counselor Number Two is seen as having different faults: "She was ignorant, always looking in her books." "She didn't care about me at all." Counselor Number Three is usually better liked. Once, when a student played that role, everyone agreed that "she was really nice and really helpful."

Interesting issues are also raised by the way students play the client roles. Often they don't know how to make clear what they want or need; when they start to get "turned off," they withdraw or become negative. Sometimes they come into the mock counseling session with hostility. One time a student role-played a situation she, herself, had been in—pregnant and confused about what to do. She was very resistant to the counselor's attempts to discuss feelings. It was hard for us to know whether this came from her reluctance to remember the real experience or from the deliberately bad counseling we were affecting in the role-play. In the discussion, we avoid confronting individual students about their personal styles of asking for help. But we do ask students to consider the more general issue of whether there are particular styles of asking for help that are more, or less, likely to get results.

9: Investigating Services

This activity focuses on visiting agencies that are relatively new and alternative in the sense of taking a more client-centered approach. Many students have been to traditional agencies; in the previous two activities they have had a chance to share these experiences. At this point, it is important for them to see that there is—at least sometimes—a choice. This supports the main goal of the activity, which is to give students the sense that they have the skills to examine agencies and the right to choose one that will serve them best.

Careful preparation before a visit to an agency greatly increases the value of the trip (see "Techniques," p. 33). We ask each student to begin by making two lists:

1. What do you want to notice about the physical environment at the agency?
2. What do you want to notice about the person you are interviewing?

In writing these lists, students should be encouraged to draw on their criteria for evaluation from Activity 8, and on their observations of the counselor's style in the role-plays. The class then works together in teams to formulate questions they want the agency to answer. Each team is given a different category under which to list specific questions. Categories might include: services, goals, philosophy, staff, clients, confidentiality. The services team might then list:

What services do you offer?
Whom do you offer services to?
Who performs the services?
How many people can you serve?
Does it cost anything?

Finally, the teams share their questions to see whether there is any overlap and to explain their questions to each other. The questions that remain are then typed on a ditto-master, so that everyone has her own set. Each student chooses at least one question prepared by her team to ask during the visit.

Identifying agencies that are both interesting to visit and open to visitors may be difficult. We generally try to arrange at least two trips—one to a court-related facility, such as a halfway house, where the "clients" are themselves present; one to a community service directed at youth, such as a drop-in center or a youth consultation center. Other possibilities include a multiservice center, a community health project, and a specific crisis agency—such as a rape relief center or a community organizing group that provides such services as tenant or welfare advocacy. If you are not planning to do Unit VIII, "Women Organizing Themselves," you might want to arrange one trip to a service agency run specifically for and by women. (See p. 210 for a fuller description.)

The teacher will probably have to do some calling around to identify agencies which have good reputations and are likely to provide positive alternatives. It is best to establish a contact with a specific person who will know, in advance, what you are interested in finding out and who will be willing to guide you and your group through the agency.

We located a halfway house to which the courts refer young people with severe drug problems. The residents were expecting us and were very open to talking about their experiences at the house. Our students, who might have been tongue-tied with staff professionals, were able to learn much from talking with the residents. Students were surprised by what they found. Expecting a prison-like atmosphere and sullen inmates, they found young people who were, on the whole, feeling very positive about their program. The residents explained it to us carefully, telling us about the daily therapy groups and about the system of earning increased responsibility in the house. Our students were deeply im-

pressed by the strengths demonstrated by the residents and the program. Students who had been generally resistant to therapeutic approaches in the role-playing class saw the positive results in this setting and were challenged to reexamine their judgments.

At the agencies where we have visited with staff, rather than with clients, students have had more difficulty in getting answers to their questions. They are sometimes embarrassed to be asking so much and are unsure of whether the person has really spoken to their concerns. What seems to work best is visiting the type of facility they, themselves, have had experience with, such as a drop-in center. More comfortable in a setting that is familiar to them, they are able to be more observant.

The programs of some agencies lend themselves better to classroom presentation by a speaker than to on-site visits. For instance, there may be little to see at a pregnancy counseling center, except a waiting room. The only advantage of such a visit is that the students learn their way to the place. Although speakers generally do not provide as fruitful a learning experience as on-site visits, one or two speakers are a worthwhile substitute if visiting can't be arranged. The exercise of determining criteria and the role-playing of counseling situations are valuable in and of themselves. And the speakers can begin to open people's eyes to new possibilities for help.

We brought in two women who work with alcoholics and their families. Their alcohol unit is in a local hospital which is much hated by the students and, therefore, one which the students would not consider visiting. The speakers were able to cut through this hostility quickly by describing alcohol problems in their own families and then speaking eloquently about the effects of alcoholism on the people close to the alcoholic. Only then did they describe the work they try to do with the people who come to them.

Our students had incredibly strong reactions to this presentation. It was either their favorite or most-hated class of the whole term. This was a powerful reminder to us that our students cannot look at and evaluate services dispassionately. The services they are looking at may be dealing with problems they have or are close to. Some people take offense at having to think about these issues in school. "I get enough of it at home; I don't need to study it here." Others, however, are glad to have a chance to think about these problems systematically and to find out about services that are available.

When trips or speakers touch directly on issues in the lives of some of the students, the students may become suspicious that the hidden agenda of the unit is to help them deal with their problems. The teacher has to find ways to reassure students that the point of the investigations is to give them new information and to help them to look critically at services—not to label people in the class as being in need of drug help, or alcohol help, or pregnancy counseling. Referring back to the case studies helps to direct attention away from students themselves. The class can talk in terms of whether a service would be useful in Sarah's case, or in Laura's. Another way to give a sense of broader purpose to the investigation is for the class to have a final task in mind—such as compiling the information on services into a small pamphlet for other people

Entries like the following can be very helpful to students who did not take the course:

> Bridge over Troubled Waters is a counseling center in Boston where anyone can go for free counseling. Most of the people who go there are between the ages of fourteen and twenty-four, many of them runaways, on drugs, etc. Problems with parents seem to be common. If anyone wants to go, all they would have to do is call 227-7114, and make an appointment with a counselor. The people are really nice there and when you go in they always offer you coffee, sandwiches, cookies and apples. Bridge was a very warm atmosphere and the counseling I got there was sympathetic and helpful. [Beth McCombe]

In the class period after each trip or speaker, the group should go over the answers to their questions and concentrate on what seemed positive and what seemed negative about the service being investigated. Asking people to come to a consensus about whether or not they would recommend this service helps to focus the discussion. Whenever possible, they should be asked to compare the service to others they know about and rate it according to their original criteria. This activity reinforces the clients' or advocates' rights to evaluate and choose their services.

NOTES TO THE TEACHER

War Stories

This unit leaves many openings for "war stories"—student anecdotes about somebody getting into serious trouble, or barely eluding police, or picking a fight. Every case study may touch off a story like this from someone in the class. Our students' lives are full of this kind of drama (at times embellished in the telling by imagination and desire for excitement). They sometimes know young people who have died from overdoses, people who have been beaten

by police, wives who were beaten up by husbands, friends who got pregnant at thirteen, people who have shoplifted hundreds of dollars of merchandise and have not been caught. Sometimes they, themselves, have been in these situations.

Up to a certain point, this "mean streets" life is a source of pride to them. They enjoy telling an audience of their peers their latest exploits or the newest neighborhood scandal. They get pleasure from saying things that might shock or amaze the teacher, whose life is bound to be somewhat less "exciting." If we are not careful, a dynamic can get set up in the class, in which everyone is competing for the teacher's attention, each trying to outdo the others' stories. This is not a healthy atmosphere. Much of the behavior the students are describing is self-destructive, as well as destructive to others. To allow stories to be told is tacitly to sanction this behavior.

We used to think it was desirable for students to tell these stories—that it meant they trusted us; that it meant they wanted to deal with the realities of their lives. This is partly true. But we began to realize that in their recounting of events in the classroom, they were not really facing what went on, and why it went on, and how it could have been stopped or avoided. In the middle of telling an eager audience about how her brother just ripped off a brand new Fuji, a student is in no mood to discuss the ethics or consequences of stealing. Even if we raise these issues, we are not heard. These are issues that are better discussed at a quieter moment, alone, or in a small group. Told to a large group, these stories create a false sense of camaraderie, a mentality of "we're all in this together," when, in fact, the individuals end up suffering the consequences of their actions very much alone.

The teacher's task is to create an atmosphere that encourages the sharing of everyday experiences, without dwelling on "war stories." Students can be encouraged to make connections between the case studies and events in their own lives; they can be encouraged to use this unit to think about what they do on the street, what happens to them in the many hours they are not in school. But if the "war-stories" dynamic starts to spiral, the teacher should resist indulging it. Our emphasis has to be on moving forward, on change, on people helping themselves and others to overcome self-destructive patterns of behavior.

We have sometimes even said something as direct as: "I don't want to hear about that now." Even though this might seem an abrupt or cold reaction, we have found it has ultimately resulted in better relationships. In fact, part of the students' reasons for telling us these stories in the first place may be to get us to disapprove of their behavior, or ask them to stop. Because they are ambivalent about wanting these limits, they tell us at a time when we cannot respond and they cannot hear us. If we refuse to deal with them on their terms, and instead approach them at another time, it may be possible to cut through this confusion to a meaningful dialogue.

Blame and Responsibility

Often students use "war stories" to cover a deep ambivalence they feel about themselves and their lives. Just beneath the tones of bravado are feelings of shame and self-hate. Sometimes an incident occurs in their own lives which dramatically reveals these feelings. Last year, a young woman who was a cousin of one of our students was raped by four boys, whom several of the students had known for ten or more years. For days, none of our students told us about the rape, even though we had been discussing rape very recently in class. When we finally did find out about it, and spoke to one of the students most closely involved, her comment was very telling: "These are my friends. Now you see what kind of people I hang out with." This incident was too close to her feelings of shame to be shared in a group, or even alone with us. Until we spoke with her, we did not know why some of the students seemed depressed in class and anxious to avoid any personal discussions.

Although students may not directly express these difficult feelings, their self-hate can manifest itself in reactions to the activities in the unit and in interactions with each other and the teacher. When we first taught this unit and were looking for a book to read, we gave the class the beginning passage from a new novel, *A True Story of a Drunken Mother*, by Nancy Hall. In this passage, an alcoholic woman picks herself off the floor after a drunken slumber and decides to turn on the gas to kill herself and her children. Everyone was immediately involved in the story and the students asked for the whole book. The complete degradation of that scene was, in some ways, very attractive to them.

Excited to have found a book that they liked, we went out and purchased copies for the class. But by the time we were fifty pages into the book, more than half the class was resisting it. People were losing their copies, forgetting to read the assignments, skipping class when we were to discuss it. We had to face the fact that, although the main character's struggle with alcoholism was very relevant, the book was too discouraging to the students, and too close to painful experiences in their own lives. They responded to the first few pages of the book as they respond to the immediate drama of crises in their own lives—with excitement. The problem comes when the crisis gives way to a sobering, seemingly hopeless day-to-day reality. By the time they had read a few chapters, they were angry at the main character, angry at their own alcoholic parents, angry at themselves for their own uncontrolled "drunks." And we learned of this only indirectly—through their anger at us for assigning the book.

Shame and self-hate are paralyzing emotions. The more students blame themselves for their problems, the more discouraged they feel about the possibility of turning things around in their lives. Teachers confronted with such depths of self-hate and defeatism are tempted to try to convince students that their problems are, in fact, not their own fault. The blame should be placed elsewhere—on society, on the unresponsive institutions and oppressive conditions of their lives. Our first tendency was to disagree with any student who blamed a young women in the case studies for her own problems. We would argue that schools should offer birth-control training; that there should be more teen centers in working-class neighborhoods to alleviate the need for escape through drugs; that the courts should decriminalize running away.

But we can easily overindulge in emphasis upon the horrors, atrocities, and injustices that poor people, minorities, workers, sharecroppers, American Indians, migrants, and women have suffered in the USA. Students may already be so overwhelmed by these oppressive conditions that they are disillusioned and immobilized. Knowing how much is stacked against them makes them feel more defeated and powerless: how can an individual hope to change society—or even one major societal institution, like the courts? Sometimes seeing society as the villain makes students feel justified in acts of primitive rebellion—like ripping off a bicycle from a college neighborhood—because "I don't have a rich daddy who will buy one for me whenever I want." The underlying rationalization seems to be, "if you can't change the whole, at least take what's yours."

It is obviously not our intention to reinforce defeatism or to give justification to criminal activity. The goal is to reverse the downward spiral, to give students the sense that, in spite of what is stacked against them, they can exercise some control over their lives and work with other people toward some changes. To some extent, this means that we have to avoid portraying the individual as a passive victim of the system, and we have to acknowledge her own participation in the events of her life. It is, of course, also important to acknowledge the oppressive conditions and institutions, but the emphasis should be on the decisions that are in the young woman's control, the choices that are available, the gains that can be made through collective action.

VII: WOMEN AND WORK

OVERVIEW

One of the long-range goals in working with low-income young women is to give them tools that will enable them to take control of their future. A crucial tool is awareness of issues concerning work. Young women need a sense of the possibilities and limitations of the work world. It's important to give them the opportunity to explore different jobs and to explore their own and other women's attitudes toward work, before they have to start working full-time. As many won't go on to further schooling, and will have to look for full-time work upon graduation, this opportunity should be provided in high school.

Nine out of ten women in America work at some point in their lives. Despite recent legislation which prohibits discrimination against women in wages and hiring, an earning gap between men and women not only exists, but has been growing wider. In 1955, full-time women workers earned 63.9 percent of men's salaries, while in 1971, they earned only 59.5 percent as much. Even so, for working-class women, where the earning gap is widest, the pay is often the only attraction of working. The jobs available to them—in a typing pool, on an assembly line, a department store, or as a telephone operator—are tedious, routine, and dead end. Furthermore, blue-collar women workers are most vulnerable during times of depression. In August 1973, 7.1 percent of women in blue-collar jobs were unemployed, compared to 4 percent of men. One of the reasons for the vulnerability of blue-collar women workers is that only one out of seven belong to unions, although union women earn $1,500 a year more than their nonunion counterparts.[1]

That working-class women are exploited makes the topic of women and work a delicate one to raise with our students. On the one hand, we want them to understand the ways in which women, particularly poor women, are exploited, since without awareness, resistance to the exploitation is impossible. But given the students' lack of aggressiveness, self-confidence, and skills, all of which stem from growing up poor and female in the USA, they are likely to get only those jobs which are most exploitative of women. We don't want to be too discouraging, because many already feel that it's going to be impossible for them to get a job or to like their work.

Our unit on "Women and Work" is designed with this conflict in mind. Our approach is to explore the different kinds of work available to working-class women and to look at both the advantages and disadvantages of those jobs. To do this, we rely heavily on first-hand accounts of working conditions by women workers, including struggles to change conditions. Activities in which students gain personal insights are intermingled with ones in which they gain sociological political understandings. We do not condemn jobs our students aspire to, even if these are jobs like cocktail waitress, flight attendant, or secretary, in which a woman's sexuality is exploited. Instead, we try to help students see the differences between the "real work" in these jobs—like evacuating passengers, or organizing an office—and the exploitative aspects of these jobs—like having to be young, attractive, and single to be hired.

Because "Women and Work" is a long unit, involving twenty-four activities, we have divided it into five sections, primarily for teaching, but also for reading purposes. The first section introduces students to the issues and approach of this unit; the second deals with factory work and factory organizing in the nineteenth and twentieth centuries. The third section is an examination of jobs other than factory work, commonly done by women, such as housework and clerical work. In the fourth section, students explore unusual jobs that women are now doing. The last section is a very personal one, in which students focus on their own needs and expectations concerning work. We have begun each section with a brief introduction, consisting of the rationale for the section and a list of the activities in it.

"Women and Work" is long enough to be a four- or five-day-a-week, full semester course. We use it as a combined English/social studies course, but it could also be taught as a vocational course. If the teacher is teaching a shorter course, we strongly recommend picking some activities from each section, rather than skipping an entire section. Three units combined—"Adult Sex Roles," "Women and Work," and "Women Organizing Themselves"—would make a well-integrated, year-long course, preferably for older students or students in their second year of women's studies. If you are interested in teaching a women's history course, you could combine the section on factory work in this unit with the section on the suffrage in "Women Organizing Themselves." We caution, though, against teaching history in isolation, because it is hard to keep high school students interested and because it is important, always, to link historical and contemporary events.

ESTABLISHING A FRAMEWORK

INTRODUCTION

This introductory section is designed to help students discover patterns in relation to women and work, and thus give them a framework for the examination of specific kinds of work which follows in other sections. In the first activity, students list and compare jobs currently done by women and men. In the second, they look at the work the women in their families have done over time by making family work history charts. The two activities are also intended to introduce students to the approach used throughout the unit, in which the topic, "Women and Work," is looked at in both sociological and personal terms.

ACTIVITIES

1: Listing Jobs Done by Men and Women

When you compare the work that women and men do in our society, you find that the work women do has lower status, requires less training, and is poorly paid. When women and men, in fact, do identical work, their jobs are sometimes given different titles to allow employers to pay female employees less. The purpose of having students list and compare jobs normally done by women and men is to allow them to see some of these patterns.

In a first class, it's good for a group to work together on something. The structure of this exercise, thus, is to have students generate the list of jobs together. The teacher makes two columns on the board—women's jobs and men's jobs—and asks students to name all the jobs they can think of. Valuable debate will arise. One student will want to put "cab driver" in the men's column, while another will argue, "There are plenty of lady cab drivers in Cambridge!" The teacher should let the class decide what's going to go where. You can help by posing a question like, "Are most cab drivers men, or is it about equal?" In the process of arriving at some consensus, students realize two equally important facts about work: most jobs are done primarily by men, or primarily by women; however, at the same time, there are few jobs which are exclusively male or female.

When the list is finished, students look for the differences in the kinds of work women do versus the kinds of work men do. In one class, the distinctions that students zeroed in on were that men's work called for more physical strength and endurance, and that women's work called for more patience and gentleness. In both cases, there was some debate over whether these distinctions were inevitable or desirable. One student, who had worked "rehabbing" a house over the summer, said indignantly, "I can do any job a man can do." She admitted, however, that she had let the males in her crew do all the hard work. As evidence that men can do maternal work, another student said that her brother liked to babysit better than she did.

Other ways to help students see patterns from the list include looking at men and women's work within the same field and seeing whether appearance is an important part of any of the jobs. Asking students which, if any, of the women's jobs depend on a woman's appearance, introduces the notion of sexual exploitation which is developed in later activities. Model, prostitute, actor, flight attendant are sure to be picked out; sometimes students will mention secretary and waitress as well. In contrast, they are unlikely to find any men's jobs which depend so much on appearances. Draw lines between jobs within the same profession (nurse/doctor, elementary school teacher/college professor) and ask students to consider the disparities between men and women working in the same field. This enables them to see that men's jobs have more status and power, even when women and men are doing the same kind of work.

The listing exercise is followed by giving students copies of a chart to examine which shows, among other things, difference in pay scale for women and men doing similar work. We use it because it documents a crucial fact about women's work—inequity in pay—which students haven't been able to observe from the lists they've generated. Originally published in Ms.,

this particular chart is good because it's easy to read. As it may be difficult to get hold of, we've reprinted the part of it which includes data on working-class jobs (see p. 168). Students will respond indignantly to the chart, some being outraged by the different qualifications (the data column), others by the salary columns. Often they'll want to know how people get away with paying women less for equal work. That's a complicated question, and you will have to decide how much you want to get into it.

We point out that many employers are primarily concerned with profit and thus prefer to keep salaries low. They rationalize paying women less than men by assuming that women who work are not the primary supporters of the family, that the money they earn is extra spending money. Our students can see, just on the basis of their own families, that this is a false assumption, since their mothers' income is crucial to the family. We mention that, although the Equal Pay Act of 1963 makes it illegal to pay men more than women for the same work, employers get around this, as the chart shows, by calling a job "Administrative Assistant" if a man is doing it and "Executive Secretary" if a woman is doing it. We also draw on what students know from personal experience. If you really need a job, you'll take it regardless of the pay; you don't have much choice. Also, you may not realize you're being discriminated against. Unless there's a union, which sets and publicizes pay scales, you probably don't know what other workers around you are getting paid. One way to end the discussion is to ask any students who are working to try to find out what men working alongside them are earning, then to report back to the class.

If you are trying to build English skills, a good follow-up to this activity is a vocabulary lesson using words which describe qualities needed in the work men and women do. A list we have used included aggressive, cerebral, docile, lucrative, menial, meticulous, mundane, nurturing, pragmatic, rational. (See "Techniques," p. 23, for suggested ways to teach these words.) Discussion of the words will also serve to summarize

Inequality in the Workplace: A Comparison of Female and Male Salaries

Job Title	Employer	Data	Male Salary	Female Salary
First Level Management	Bell Systems	Average salary of employees in 30 districts	$14,169	$11,194
Executive Trainee	Retail chain store	1971 Wharton MBA	$14,000	$12,000
Staff Writer	American Medical Association	Male: 6 months experience Female: 5 years experience	$13,000	$13,000
Academic Librarian	University of California, Berkeley	20 years experience (median salary)	$12,570	$ 8,745
Male: County Agricultural Agent Female: County Home Economist	U. S. Dept. of Agriculture Extension Service	Salary: National average	$11,678	$ 9,743
Male: Head Grocery Clerk Female: Head Bakery Clerk	Giant Foods	Salaries	$196.72 per week	$142.60 per week
Male: "Administrative Assistant" Female: "Executive Secretary"	Eastman Kodak Co.	Starting salaries: High school graduates, 2 years technical schooling	$181 per week	$126 per week
Station Installer	Pacific Telephone & Telegraph Co., San Francisco	Male: Promoted after 72 months as Frameman (1971) Female: Promoted after 72 months as Operator (1971)	$156.50 per week	$124 per week
Male: Waiter, full-course meals Female: Waitress, full-course meals	Restaurants and hotels	1970 U. S. Average, includes salary and tips	$3.80 per hour	$2.85 per hour
Male: "Janitor" Female: "Maid" (similar duties except less vacuuming and more coffee-cup washing)	Lawyers Cooperative Publishing Co., Rochester, N. Y.	Starting salaries	$150 per week	$87.50 per week
Payroll Clerk	Offices	Average salary in all metropolitan areas (released February 1971)	$147.50 per week	$117 per week
Order Clerk	Offices	Average salary in all metropolitan areas (released February 1971)	$139.50 per week	$106 per week
Male: Stock Clerk I Female: Secretary I	City of South Bend, Ind.	Salaries	$ 6,439	$ 5,452
Male: University-wide Mail Clerk I Female: Library Assistant I	University of California, Berkeley	Male: High school graduate Female: College graduate	$ 6,360	$ 5,484
Retail Salesclerk	Loveman's, Montgomery, Ala.	Average salary for employees with more than 8 years experience (1971)	$2.57 per hour, 2% commission	$2 per hour, no commission
Messengers	Offices	Average salary in all metropolitan areas (released February 1971)	$94 per week	$87 per week
Male: Line Assigner Female: Plant Service Clerk	Pacific Telephone & Telegraph Co., San Francisco	Same duties according to U. S. court ruling, 1970	$90 to $156.50 per week	$78 to $109.50 per week

insights students have gained and to stimulate new insights about work.

2: Charting Your Family Work History

In the previous activity, students examined the economic and social position of contemporary women in the work world. Here they consider women's work in both personal and historical terms by charting their family work histories, starting with themselves and going back as many generations as they can.

The form we hand out looks like this:

Family Work History		
Generation	Women: Jobs Held	Men: Jobs Held
Great grandparents (great-great-aunts, great-great-uncles) great-grandparents)		
Grandparents (grandmothers, grandfathers, great-aunts, great-uncles)		
Parents (mother, father, aunts, uncles)		
Your generation (you, sisters, brothers, cousins)		

Although the activity focuses on the work women in their families have done, we include male relatives for comparative purposes and to enable students to get a fuller picture of their families. The chart we originally used listed specific relatives—grandmother, grandfather, mother, father, etc. We realized later that the chart had the potential of making a student who was missing a parent, or who couldn't find out anything about her grandmother, feel badly. In the revised family work form, therefore, the focus is on as many members as possible of a given generation.

In giving out and explaining the charts, the teacher should stress two things: 1) that the purpose of the activity is for students to try to find out as much as they can about the work their relatives have done; and 2) that being a housewife is a job and should be included in their list. Students are asked to start with their own generation and fill in as much as they can in class. The teacher can then help students figure out ways to get the rest of the information—sitting down with a grandmother, calling an uncle, talking to their parents, etc. We usually give them a week to try to complete the charts.

Not being able to finish the chart at one sitting has certain advantages. In the rest of the first class and maybe the next, students can compare notes about the jobs they or their friends have had. Our students have done such jobs as saleswork, clerical work, factory work, cleaning office buildings. But they often feel there's nothing to say about their jobs, beyond the fact that they're "boring." Often they won't talk about their jobs because they feel inadequate about their performance or ashamed of the job. Interestingly, in looking back over four years worth of students' writings, we were unable to find a single poem or story which mentioned work either directly or indirectly. When the teacher tries to draw them out, though, students will get more analytical about both the positive and negative aspects of their jobs. One student remarked, "The more I think about it [she was doing clerical work at the time], the more I realize how bad things are at work . . . my time is never my own. I am told exactly what to do, when and how, and if I don't, then that's it." Another student described the pressures of working on an assembly line, how fast you had to go all day long, and the fact that all day you only got two ten-minute breaks, plus a half-hour lunch. The positive feelings expressed stem from the benefits of having a job, rather than from the particular job itself. The fact that working makes them feel independent, adult and helps them meet new people emerges in such comments as. "I can't always be dependent on my father, I need money for my own stuff"; "I'm old enough now to have a job"; "I like it 'cause I get to meet lots of other kids there."

You may find that your particular group of students has had little work experience, either because they are younger or because in our depressed economy it is becoming increasingly hard for teen-agers to get jobs. They may know nothing about jobs their siblings or friends have had, beyond what they get paid. If this is the case, then part of the collecting of family work histories should include interviewing siblings or friends about their jobs, as students may pick up information that will be useful to them when they do start working. Rather than discussing jobs students have had, interim time can be used to talk about whether the students need or want to work, and what kinds of jobs they'd like to get.

Our students seldom know much about even their parents' work, and thus the process of filling in the chart can be an eye-opening experience for them. It's important when they've finished to allow time for them to share what they've found out, especially about what the women in their grandparents' and parents' generations have done. One student discovered that her grandmother had left Nova Scotia because it wasn't considered proper for a woman to work there. Another reported that her grandmother had emigrated from Italy and worked in the textile mills in Lawrence, Massachusetts. Another brought out the fact that her mother had held two jobs for the last fifteen years. "I never really knew what she did before," she confessed.

When personal anecdotes have run out, the class makes a huge group chart of the work done by the women in their families. The teacher should make out a chart beforehand, similar in format to the individual charts, and then students can work together, filling in the data, using different colored magic markers for different generations. When the larger chart is put on the wall, the class can try to see whether there are any patterns.

One important lesson we all learned is that the students' female relatives have always brought money into the family, be it through jobs, through welfare, or sometimes a combination of the two. Another thing the composite chart revealed is that there is little or no upward mobility in the families of our students. In many cases, grandmothers and mothers did the same kind of work our students do. This is in contrast to the men, who often reveal a pattern of downward mobility. Grandfathers were carpenters, longshoremen, fishermen, cooks. As those trades declined, fathers entered the job market as unskilled factory workers.

In discussing the work charts, we want students to feel pride in the work both the women and the men in their families have done. This often involves reiterating that housework and raising children is work, and hard work at that. One way to look at the welfare system is to see it as a recognition that women should be paid for raising their families. We stress that the jobs available to working-class people, and women in particular, have been and continue to be limited. It is necessary to point out that the causes of poverty lie more in powerful economic and social forces than in personal misfortune. For instance, in Cambridge, blue-collar jobs have been eliminated as manufacturing has given way to research and development firms.

This particular activity can give the teacher much information to be drawn upon in the activities that follow. When looking at specific jobs in more detail, the teacher can refer back to work students have done and their experiences in those jobs, or she can invite mothers or grandmothers to come talk to the class. The teacher, therefore, might want to hold on to the work charts for future reference.

FACTORY WORK AND ORGANIZING

INTRODUCTION

We devote a section in this unit to factory work because since the nineteenth century, factories have been a major source of both jobs and exploitation for working-class women. In the early 1800s, the only occupations open to women at all were factory work, sewing, teaching, or domestic work.[2] In those factories, women often worked fourteen to sixteen hours a day, for about $1.50 a week.[3] The hours have gotten shorter, but the exploitation of women continues. For the country as a whole, in 1971, there was a 41 percent gap between the earnings of male and female assembly line workers.[4] Women tend to do the most debilitating jobs and have little chance for promotion.[5] Gains have and are being made, however, through union organizing and, most recently, through new women's caucuses within unions. These promote concerns of special interest to women, such as equal pay, training opportunities, day care, maternity leaves.

Activities in this unit are intended to give students a sense of working conditions for women in nineteenth- and twentieth-century factories, as well as a sense of how women have struggled to change those conditions. Students start by reading first-hand accounts of factory work in the 1840s. They are introduced to basic labor concepts through a vocabulary exercise and then learn about nineteenth-century women organizers, unions, and strikes from biographical accounts. A comparison with the twentieth century is made by interviewing women who work in factories, by visiting a factory, and by talking to a woman currently involved in union organizing. The section ends with a role-play of a TV panel show which helps students summarize what they've learned.

The teacher may want to do some reading, herself, to teach the history part of this section, in order to answer questions about early factories and unions. Books it would be useful to look through include *Bread and Roses*, by Milton Meltzer, *We the People*, by Leo Huberman, and *Working Men*, by Sidney Lens. All are available in paperback.

ACTIVITIES

3: Reading about Factory Work in the Nineteenth Century

This activity involves reading and discussing two short passages about the lives of women who did factory work in the nineteenth century. The main reading is a chapter on "Women Who Work" (pp. 17–25) in *Bread and Roses*, by Milton Meltzer. We use it because it is short, geared toward high school students, and uses first-hand accounts like the following ones to document the appalling conditions that women worked under:

> The machines go like mad all day, because the faster you work, the more money you get. Sometimes in my haste I get my finger caught and the needle goes right through it. It goes so quick, though, that it does not hurt much. I bind my finger up with a piece of cotton and go on working. We all have accidents like that. . . . All the time we are working, the boss walks around examining the finished garments and making us do them again if they are not just right. So we have to be careful as well as swift. [P. 24]

> An ad in a Long Island paper called for a woman to sew on buttons. With glad heart I went, for what could I do better. . . .
>
> After making a satisfactory sample I was told that the price was two cents for a gross; no thread supplied. Bewildered, I made some mental multiplication, but I could not think of more than sixty cents for thirty gross of buttons. Of this I subtracted five cents for cotton and thirty cents for car fare, which left a total of twenty-five cents earnings.

However, I was elated at being of some help, and set to work as soon as I reached home. It took me one whole week to mount the 4,320 buttons, and when I delivered them, using my last five cents for car fare, I was told that only ten gross were mounted properly; that all I could get was thirty cents, and would I call next Saturday. [P. 23]

The companion reading is a one-page section from *The American Woman: Who Was She?*, edited by Anne Firor Scott, called "The Home Lives of Factory Women" (p. 19). It's a valuable supplement because it describes what happened to women when the long day in the mill was over: they began the cooking, cleaning, washing, and mending for their families. Their work went on past midnight, while the men were asleep after an evening spent in smoking, drinking, and talking union politics with cronies in barrooms.

It's good to begin the class with visuals, to help make the readings come alive. *The Revolt of the American Woman*, by Oliver Jenson, contains photographs of nineteenth-century factory workers and workplaces. Ideally, the teacher can have slides made of some of these pictures and project them, along with contrasting slides of middle-class or wealthy women, who weren't allowed to work at all. If you don't have access to facilities for making slides, you can just pass around the pictures for students to examine.

Students can read and discuss the material in one class. More time spent now will probably bore the group. The teacher should be prepared to answer questions, because students will be amazed and even disbelieving when they read about working conditions in 1860. "Why did women put up with it?" "Weren't there unions?" "What could you do, earning $1.56 a week," etc. You might also get students to draw parallels with today's conditions. Two things we point out, if they don't emerge in the discussion, are that women were paid less than men in the nineteenth century also (referring back to the chart students looked at in the opening activity), and that lots of women today also do two full-time jobs, one at work and one at home.

4: Labor Vocabulary

Understanding how working conditions changed involves understanding what a union is, what a strike is, etc. Unless your students have studied labor history, they may not understand such terms and will be confused if they go directly from reading about nineteenth-century working conditions to studying nineteenth-century organizing. We suggest using the following vocabulary list as a transition: union, collective bargaining, organizing/organizer, strike, boycott, picket, scab, wildcat strike, closed/open shop, arbitrator.

As it is the concepts, rather than specific definitions and usage which are important here, the teacher should focus on building a discussion on the words, rather than on devising worksheets. Before introducing the words, it's good to think about examples and anecdotes which students will be interested in, as well as about ways to connect the words to some of the reading which students will be doing in the next activity. We usually put the words up on the board and spend an entire class discussing them. We go over each word slowly, drawing on both our students' and our own experiences to explain and add to the concepts.

An excellent follow-up to this activity is to show the class the film, *The Inheritance*, made by the Amalgamated Clothing Workers to celebrate their fiftieth anniversary as a union. The film covers about seventy-five years of labor history—and manages to do so in an interesting fashion. Some of the documentary footage of early twentieth-century strikes is astounding.

5: Women Organizers of the Nineteenth Century

In this activity, the subject of how nineteenth-century working conditions changed is approached through examining the lives of women who struggled to bring about those changes. Students read and discuss an excerpt from the autobiography of Mary "Mother" Jones and then do individual reports, in the form of imaginative writing or role-plays, on other women organizers. We deliberately use the personal angle because it makes the same issues more interesting to students and because it provides them with positive female role models.

Mary "Mother" Jones was one of the most remarkable figures in American labor history. In 1880, she changed her life completely when she left her work as a seamstress to become a full-time union organizer. She was superb at dramatizing issues and planning effective strategies. For example, to protest child labor in the Pennsylvania textile mills in 1903, she organized a march of maimed, mutilated children of the mill, who went to Washington to visit President Roosevelt. The statement—picked up and publicized nationally—was that "Philadelphia mansions were built on the broken bones, the quivering breasts and the drooping heads of children." Shortly afterward, the Pennsylvania Legislature passed a law which kept all children under fourteen out of the factories.

A twenty-page excerpt from Mary "Mother" Jones' autobiography is available in *Growing Up Female in America: Ten Lives,* edited by Eve Merriam. Because the excerpt contains the highlights of her career as organizer, we use it in its entirety. To give the students a context in which to understand both this and the next reading, we often introduce the activity by giving them a brief history of unions, garnered from the books mentioned at the end of the introduction to this section. Although the Mary "Mother" Jones reading is too long to be done entirely in class, we suggest starting it together, aloud, to generate interest, and then having students finish it at home (see "Techniques," p. 15).

Our discussion in class centers around "Mother" Jones' organizing techniques and personality. Questions could also be asked to get at ways in which the companies tried to break strikes and prevent unions. We've found that even those students normally uninterested in history will enjoy the reading. As one student said, "'Mother' Jones, she's dynamite!"

If students want to learn more about the labor history and organizing they are being introduced to, a pamphlet called "Labor Heroines: Ten Women Who Led the Struggle" is useful. Written by Joyce Maupin, it contains simple, capsule biographies of colorful working-class women organizers.

To vary the reading/discussing pattern, we assign one of the two- or three-page biographical sketches to each student and then have them share "their women" with the class. One effective way to do this is to give each student a writing assignment to do after she reads the sketch which gets her to imagine herself as that woman in some dramatic moment. An example would be:

> Imagine that you are Clara Lemlich. Why did you decide to speak at the mass meeting at Cooper Union? Were you scared? How did you decide what to say? How did you feel when the crowd decided to follow your call to strike?

As students share their writing with the class, the teacher can ask them to fill in other details about their characters. An alternate way to pool the information is to have students role-play the women they've read about, and have other members of the class interview them about where they worked and what kind of organizing they did (see "Techniques," p. 26).

6: Interviewing Women Who Work in Factories

To compare factory work in the nineteenth century with factory work in the 1970s, students interview women currently working in factories and then visit a factory. The goal is to see in what ways working conditions have changed and to give students a basis broader than personal experience from which to consider the problems and benefits of factory work for women.

A good way to start is to have any student who has worked in a factory describe her experience to the class. This serves the double purpose of helping other students think about how they might like factory work and also suggesting topics to cover in the interviews.

We vividly remember a story told by one student. She was working in a factory in Cambridge where women were paid on a piecework basis, and where there were quotas on each type of machine. She'd get put on one machine, but as soon as she got good enough to reach the quota, she'd get transferred to another machine. The result was that she constantly felt inadequate and incompetent. What she didn't realize was that the employer didn't want her to get too good on a machine, because she'd start producing over the quota and they'd have to pay her more.

When students have worked out the interview form by generating questions together, they decide who they are going to interview. We usually have each student do one interview. The majority of them should be with women currently working in factories, but it will add to the subsequent discussion if a couple of the students can interview grandmothers or other older women who know about factory work in the early 1900s (See "Techniques," p. 29).

Our students found generally that women they talked with were indifferent about their jobs. They sometimes enjoyed the sociability of the work, but found it boring nevertheless. The overriding reason for working was for the money, often more than they could earn in other unskilled jobs. Of the ten women interviewed, eight didn't belong to unions and seven of the eight didn't care one way or the other. A few felt that the men in their factories got the pleasanter jobs, defined as ones that they could move around in.

Students were surprised about the pay. As one said, "I never realized I could make more money in a factory than at a register at Zayre's [a large department store]." They also noticed the lack of union participation. We pointed out that only one out of seven working women today are union members, whereas one out of four working men belong to unions. Although increasing numbers of women are joining unions, union leadership is still almost entirely male.[6]

While students are doing their interviews outside of class, we have used class time to visit a factory which has a large female workforce. This is particularly valuable if most of the students have never been inside a factory. The teacher should think about what kinds of factories in her area are likely to have mainly women workers (in the Boston area, garment and electronic parts factories) and call to see whether they give tours (see "Techniques," p. 33).

We visited a lingerie factory and were shown around by the foreman, who, typically, was male. The seventy-five women who worked there, whom the foreman repeatedly referred to as "the girls," were all involved in sewing underpants and thermal undershirts. Men did all the cutting and handled the shipping. The first question a student asked of the foreman was why only women were doing the sewing. "Because they're faster," he answered. The next question was why there were no Black women working there. "Black girls, they'd rather stay on welfare. They're lazy," was the response.

Through the blunt, tough questioning of the students, the discrimination against women became clear. The foreman explained that the women were paid on a minimum plus piecework basis, and usually made a total of $25 a day; he refused to say what that minimum was, or what they earned per piece. In the shipping department, which was noticeably quieter and more relaxed, a student asked one of the men how much he made. When he didn't answer, she persisted, asking whether he made more than the women. He just laughed, as though it were a ridiculous question. The foreman interjected, "If women did the heavy work, they'd get a man's salary, but no women could do it." A student came back with, "Well, if only women can do the sewing, why don't they get paid extra?"

If a trip can't be arranged, you might spend class time reading parts of an article called, "Two Jobs: Women Who Work in the Factories," written by Jean Tepperman and printed in the anthology *Sisterhood Is Powerful*. It describes the conditions and attitudes of women working in two factories in the Chicago area and raises for discussion some of the ways in which women are discriminated against in factories—no chance for promotion, more tedious jobs, less responsibility, and less pay.

7: Union Organizing Today

This activity exposes students to a woman currently involved in union organizing. The teacher can contact unions connected with major industries in the area to ask whether there is a woman union organizer who would be willing to talk to the class, and ideally, take the group on a tour of one of the union plants. If you're in the Boston area, you might try calling two of the more progressive unions in the area: United Electrical Workers and Amalgamated Meat Cutters, Packinghouse Division.

An alternative is to invite as a classroom speaker a woman who is involved in an organizing drive in her workplace. Based on information that emerges through the family work histories, or the interviews done with women working in factories, the teacher may already have identified possible speakers. If not, unions in the area might be able to suggest someone (see "Techniques," p. 31).

We invited a speaker, because the mother of one of the students in the class was working at Cambion, a factory in North Cambridge that was finally being organized after several unsuccessful attempts to get a union started. The mother wasn't herself one of the organizers, but had become involved and was supporting the union. As a couple of students in the school had already worked in this factory, and others might in the future, we thought it would be particularly appropriate to have the student's mother speak to us.

In class, she talked about conditions in the factory, how she felt about the union, and how the organizers had gone about organizing union elections. She also brought with her two letters which the company had been circulating among the workers to try to discourage them from joining the union. Among other things, the letters made use of red-baiting (associating unions with communism) and threatened that if the union came in, the company might be forced to move from the area. It was pointed out in discussion that this threat wasn't necessarily an empty one; many companies do in fact move to nonunion areas to save labor costs. Based on the number of questions students asked, we knew the class had been successful. One student reported back later that she had gone home and quizzed her mother about whether anybody was trying to get a union started where she worked.

8: TV Panel Show

Here we use a TV panel show to help students pull together what they've learned about factory work and factory organizing. It's an active, participatory way to review information, and it varies the pace of the course.

We explain to students that we're going to have a mock TV panel show, the participants being factory workers, organizers, and foremen from both the nineteenth and twentieth centuries. To insure a range of participants, we assign roles, making sure there is at least one factory worker, one foreman, and one organizer representing each century—and one moderator. We tell students that if they object to their roles, they are free to switch with another student (see "Techniques," p. 26).

To help students review material they've absorbed in the section, we have them fill in details about their roles themselves. All students are given index cards. Those representing workers and foremen are asked to fill in on their cards: who they are and how old, where they work and what they do, what working conditions are like, how they feel about their job. Those playing organizers are asked for slightly different details: who they are and how old, what they are trying to change, what they did and what happened. The student moderator is directed to write down questions to ask: she then confers with the teacher, who is the other moderator on the panel.

Students should be encouraged to use their imaginations about their roles. To help them fill in details, the teacher should have on hand material used in this section of the unit. Students with nineteenth-century roles can look through sections they read in *Bread and Roses*, in *Labor Heroines*, and in the excerpt on Mary "Mother"

Jones. Those with contemporary roles can be the women they inteviewed, looking back over their completed interviews. The organizers and the foremen of the 1970's should mentally review the speaker's visit and the trip.

The moderators start the TV show by having each of the women introduce themselves and describe very briefly where they work. This helps to get the actors in character. From here on, the directions the panel moves in will be determined by the particular group. The moderators can get at comparisons by alternating questions between the nineteenth-century and twentieth-century women. They should also encourage the women to respond to each other, not just to questions the moderators ask.

The exchange we remember had to do with industrial accidents. One student described how her hair kept getting caught in the Spinning Jenny and torn off. Another, getting enthusiastically into the role-play, held up for the camera her missing middle finger—lost on the assembly line. The student playing the foreman did a stunning imitation of the foreman in the lingerie factory, and managed, during the show, to put down every woman on the panel.

JOBS COMMONLY DONE BY WOMEN

INTRODUCTION

This section focuses on jobs other than factory work which are commonly done by working-class women. The goal is to help students think about the pros and cons of jobs they may want to do or may find themselves doing. The activities alternate between those in which students explore various kinds of work, as they did with factory work, and those in which they think more personally about work they could do, or would want to do, and how they would handle various job situations.

The section begins with suggestions to the teacher on how to choose and use selections from Studs Terkel's *Working*. Activities 10 through 12 are on housework, emphasized because it is already so much a part of our students' lives and will undoubtedly continue to be so. Students start by making a housework collage and discussing their feelings about housework. They then calculate the monetary value of all the work a housewife does and consider whether she should be paid a salary. The next activity involves reading a first-hand account by a household worker who has begun to organize other such workers. The assumptions underlying all three activities is that housework is real, hard work which is undervalued in the society.

Activities 13 through 15 expose students to the clerical field. In the general introduction, they learn a little of the history of clerical work and some statistics; they do a fantasy exercise. Through visiting both a large company and a small office, students see a range of clerical jobs they might be able to get. Some of the disadvantages of office work are then seen through a speaker who is involved in organizing office workers.

In the two activities that follow, issues of sexism are raised. In Activity 16, students read a series of case studies involving on-the-job sexism and discuss ways they might handle those situations. They then look at sexual harassment in their own lives and brainstorm about ways to change it. Activity 17 has students examining three "glamorous" jobs: modeling, prostitution, and being a flight attendant.

The section ends with a look at service work. A nurse, a day-care worker, and a social worker form a panel to talk to students about their jobs.

ACTIVITIES

9: How to Use Working by Studs Terkel

Studs Terkel's *Working* is a collection of interviews with more than one hundred people who talk about what they do all day and how they feel about it. It provides rich material for examining jobs done by women. The book is fascinating, informative, and provides an alternative to speakers. Because the book is now available in paperback, we suggest that the whole book be given to students to read, and that sections from it be used throughout the "Women and Work" unit.

Activity 17, Glamour Jobs, is the only activity in the unit based on the reading of specific selections from *Working*. At the end of several other activities, selections are recommended as valuable follow-ups, because they provide more material about the jobs being examined. Other excerpts which are not specifically mentioned are also worth reading, however. Our purpose here is to suggest ways to use the book and to recommend certain excerpts not mentioned elsewhere in the unit.

The *Working* interviews we choose for students to read are by working-class women, doing jobs our students might someday have or might fantasize about having. We try to select interviews that express either positive or politicized attitudes about work. One major goal in choosing excerpts is to help students see both the "real work" of jobs, which women have a right to be proud of—the typing done by a secretary, for example—and the exploitative aspects, like making coffee, which many women resent. Another goal is to help students look more closely at jobs which on the surface may seem either very ordinary or very glamorous.

Many of the interviews, while short enough to read in class, have sufficient interest to be assigned for reading at home. We usually read one or two together in class and assign an additional one for homework. The total number of interviews to use depends on time and interest, but whatever the total number, the teacher should intersperse readings with other kinds of activities (interviews, writing, etc.) so that students don't get bored (see "Techniques," p. 16).

When students have read a given account, we want them to think about how the person feels about her work and why, the pros and cons of the job, and how they think they would like the job. We may also get them to compare the job they've just read about with other kinds of work they've been introduced to in the unit. Almost all the interviews with women raise general women's work issues, such as exploitation or lack of prestige, which the teacher can cull for discussion. Although discussions, writing assignments, or role-plays can be used equally well to get students to think through these issues, we suggest alternating between them to vary the pace of the classes.

Certain techniques help to keep a discussion focused. The teacher should prepare questions beforehand. The group can list pros and cons as the woman worker sees them, and then as they see them. In a small class, you can go around the circle asking each student to talk about how she would like the job. If the discussion is an informal one, the teacher should summarize student reactions at its end.

Possible writing assignments are (see "Techniques," p. 18):

1. Imagine you're a flight attendant (receptionist, waitress, etc.). Describe a typical day in your life and your feelings as you go through the day.
2. Write a conversation between two friends, one who wants to be a bank teller (day-care worker, telephone operator, etc.) and the other who has strong feelings, either in favor of or against her decision.
3. If you could choose between being a housewife, a secretary, or a flight attendant (hooker, hospital aide, etc.), which would you choose and why? Include what the job is like and what the advantages or disadvantages would be for you personally.

Possible role-play situations include (see "Techniques," p. 26):

1. Two women arguing over whose job has more status (is more valuable, etc.).
2. Two women talking to each other, one who wants to get a particular job, the other who has that job and wants to quit.
3. Two women who have the same job, speaking to a class, one who likes her job, the other who doesn't. (See Activity 17, p. 184, for a role-play of this type.)

Interviews we suggest using include the waitress and the supermarket checker, both older women who love their jobs and take pride in the skills they've developed; the bank teller and the hotel switchboard operator who feel their jobs are important, but realize and resent the fact that they don't have any prestige; the young telephone operator who feels put down at times, but also enjoys the power of being able to tell people to put more money in, or cutting them off; and the ambivalent hospital aide, an eighteen-year-old who says bitterly that she can't stand the patients, feels guilty about her "rotten attitude," but who also obviously cares for her patients and who wants to be a nurse. These are good supplementary readings to give students a sense of jobs commonly done by women, but not fully explored in this section of the unit.

10: Housework Collage

An enjoyable way to begin to look at housework is to have students make a housework collage from pictures and ads in magazines. While they are clipping and pasting pictures, students have a chance to talk informally about their experiences with housework and their attitudes toward it.

This activity can easily be completed in one class period. The teacher brings in a pile of magazines and instructs students to look through them, clipping pictures or word slogans which have to do with any aspect of being a housewife or doing housework. If students are encouraged to think about what they want their finished collage to say about housework, it will often help them select pictures. After twenty minutes or so, students will have plenty of pictures and can be-

gin pasting them up. (For a more detailed description of collage-making, see Unit I, p. 39.)

As students are working on the collage, informal comments will go around the room about how they always have to do this at home, or how much they hate to do that. Or they'll react to the pictures they're cutting out—"Look at the way she's serving everyone!" "If we only had a dishwasher." The teacher should encourage anecdotes, and add her own, without trying to turn it into a formal discussion.

When the finished collage is up on the wall, it will speak for itself. Housework involves a number of different tasks: a woman's work is never done.

11: The Value of Housewives

"What do you do?" "Nothing, I'm just a housewife." The purpose of this activity is to examine that "just," which so many of us have internalized, and to build English and job skills. The activity will take at least two class periods.

Students start out by generating together a chart, modeled on one published by the Chase Manhattan Bank in 1972. The outline of the chart, which the teacher should put up on the board, is:

What's a Wife Worth?

Job	Hours per week	Rate per hour	Value per week
	Total hours:		Total value:

The bank's survey records the work of middle-class women. We ask students to fill in the chart themselves, with data reflecting their own family experience.

Before starting to fill in the columns, students should list all the tasks a housewife does—mending, taking care of children, etc. They can refer to the housework collage, if necessary, for suggestions. Students then give to each task on this list the job-title it would carry outside the home; for example, "mending" translates into "seamstress," etc. This preliminary list of housework tasks helps students fill in the "job" column of the chart. To calculate the "hours per week," each student should figure out how much time is spent a day doing that job in her family. After the class reaches some consensus, that figure is multiplied by seven. To fill in "rate per hour" the teacher should draw on whatever she and students happen to know, without worrying too much about accuracy. With a little math, which students can help to do, the "value per week" is arrived at, and the chart is finished.

The process of filling in the chart will take about an hour. Students will want to talk about the differences in their families which invariably emerge as they compare how many hours per week their mothers spend on housework. They'll start sharing their knowledge of the work world in trying to decide what the hourly wage is for the various jobs. When one of our students said that cooks got paid $7 an hour, another responded, "That's only if you're a male cook. No woman gets that much." A third remarked, "Even men who do cleaning get more than women do. I know, from that office building I used to clean in." The activity is intended to provoke just these kinds of discussions, so teachers shouldn't be in a hurry to complete the chart.

The students will be most interested in and shocked by the total hours per week a housewife works and what she would be paid for that work weekly outside the home. One student said, "I never realized how many different things my mother did." Her sister, also in the class, answered, "Well, you'll never catch me working 104 hours a week." Another noted that her mother received less from welfare per month than she was worth, according to the chart, per week. At some point the teacher might ask, "Why do women say, 'I'm *just* a housewife'?"

A good way to end this first half of the activity is to ask someone to volunteer to make a large, colorful copy of the chart, so that it can be put up alongside the housework collage for all to see.

To look further into attitudes about housework and to build English skills, the sec-

ond half of this activity involves reading the "Just a Housewife" section from *Working*, which consists of interviews with two women. The first woman likes being a housewife, but has internalized the society's negative view of her job:

> Somebody who goes out and works for a living is more important than somebody who doesn't. What they do is very important in the business world. What I do is only important to five people. I don't like putting a housewife down, but everybody has done it for so long. It's sort of the thing you do. Deep down, I feel what I'm doing is important. But you just hate to say it, because what are you? Just a housewife?
>
> I love being a housewife. Maybe that's why I feel so guilty. I shouldn't be happy doing what I'm doing. Maybe you're not supposed to be having fun. I never looked on it as a duty. [P. 398]

The second woman, a mother of five on welfare, sees her job as work, and hard work at that:

> Welfare makes you feel like you're nothing. Like you're lying back and not doing anything and it's falling in your lap. But you must understand, mothers, too, work. My house is clean. I've been scrubbing since this morning. You could check my clothes, all washed and ironed. I'm home and I'm working. I am a working mother. . . .
>
> Some men work eight hours a day. There are mothers that work twelve hours a day. We get up at night, a baby vomits, you have to be calling a doctor, you have to be changing the baby. When do you get a break, really? You don't. This is an all-around job, day and night. Why do they say it's charity? We're working for our money. We are giving some kind of home to these children. [P. 402]

We have students read the interviews at home and then discuss them in class, drawing particularly on the sections quoted above. (See Activity 9: How to Use *Working*.)

We end with a writing assignment which draws on both parts of the activity. The two choices we give are:

1. Write an essay on whether or not you think housewives should be paid a salary and why.
2. Compose a want ad for a housewife in which you list requirements, salary, fringe benefits, job security, etc.

Choosing the first topic, one of our students wrote:

> I think that it's a good idea for women to be paid a salary for housekeeping, but I don't think it should be taken out of their husband's salary, but it should be an addition. It would be nice to have like a housewives union and have housewives paid by the government depending on how much work they have to do and how many kids they have. [Judi Teeter]

12: Portrait of a Household Worker and Organizer

The situation of housewives, working without pay in their own homes, was explored in the previous activity. Here we suggest considering household workers who work for minimum pay in other women's homes. There are several reasons for this. Many poor women, especially Black women, do domestic work, either full-time or, like a number of our students' mothers, part-time, under the table, to supplement inadequate welfare payments. While a housewife's work is considered insignificant, the household worker's job is seen as degrading. Our students and their mothers have often internalized this viewpoint. The goal for this activity is to help students see that household work isn't intrinsically degrading; that it's the conditions women are forced to work under, not the work itself, which should be changed

This activity consists of reading and discussing a first-hand account of a household-worker-turned-organizer, published in Ms., February 1973: "Household Help Wanted, Female," by Josephine Hullatt. The opening sets the tone of the article:

> I'm going to make a very unfashionable statement: I've been a household worker for twenty years, and I've never been ashamed of it. When I tell people what I do, sometimes they're embarrassed. Or they think it's a joke and say, "You're kidding, Jo—you couldn't be doing that!" Sometimes I just smile and say, "Why not?" But "Why not?" isn't really enough any more. I'm organizing household workers to fight for their rights and dignity, and I have to explain why I feel the way I do.

Josephine Hullatt, a Black woman, goes on to describe the various families she has worked for and the conditions she had worked under. Some were better than others, but she was always dependent upon how generous her employers happened to be. We choose this article because it's personal, and in the end, very positive.

The article doesn't require extensive discussion, as it's extremely straightforward. You might start with students' personal reactions to Ms. Hullatt's story, and then move into a consideration of the ways in which household workers are exploited. As a way of summarizing, students might list all the things wrong with working conditions for household workers (no job security, no benefits, no protections under the Federal Minimum Wage Law, etc.). Our students were impressed by Ms. Hullatt, and in the course of talking about the piece, one student mentioned for the first time that her mother also did household work.

An alternative reading which serves much the same purpose is the description of organizing domestic workers in Black Women in White America, edited by Gerda Lerner (pp. 231–238).

13: Introduction to Clerical Work as a Field

The purpose of this activity, which uses a lecture/discussion format, is to introduce students to clerical work as a field and to prepare them for the trips and speakers in the next two activities.

We start by giving students a brief history of clerical work. An excellent article for the teacher to read and choose quotations from is Margery Davies' "Woman's Place Is at the Typewriter: The Feminization of the Clerical Labor Force," which appeared in the July-August 1974 edition of Radical America. Using the article as a source, and without going into too much detail, we explain that in the nineteenth century, most clerical workers—called "clerks"—were men. They did bookkeeping and office management, were seen more as management than as workers, and, in fact, the clerk job often was a stepping stone into managing the business. Women were allowed into the field starting in the late 1800s. Businesses were expanding and needed more labor. The typewriter had been invented; because typing was a new job that hadn't been identified as masculine, women who were employed as typists couldn't be accused of taking over men's work. From the start, however, they came in at lower pay, and as nonmanagement personnel. We use quotations from the Davies article to show the radical shift in ideology which took place: in 1900 it was being said that women were too frail to stand the competitive pace of the business world; by 1916, it was taken for granted that women worked in offices, and that certain feminine qualities made them particularly suited for the jobs. By 1960, 72 percent of all low-level clerical workers were women, and one-third of all women who worked were office workers.[7]

From Nine to Five, a Boston-based organization which supports the organizing of office workers, we got the following statistics about clerical work and workers in Boston, which we share with students:

In Boston, more than 200,000 women do clerical work.
Average earnings are $4430 a year ($85 a week).
Boston has the second highest cost of living of any city in the United States
Boston wages for clerical workers are third from the bottom because there are no unions and there's a surplus labor pool.

Next, we get students to list all the places where clerical workers work. One class came up with: insurance companies, banks, the government, businesses, law offices. We added Harvard and MIT, explaining that big universities usually employ large numbers of clerical workers.

To get students thinking about what clerical work is like in a more personal way, we end with a small fantasy exercise. (See Activity 22, p. 189, for suggestions of how to set up a fantasy.) The teacher tells students to close their eyes and imagine what it's like in an office. After a few seconds of silence, the teacher slowly and quiet-

ly asks a few leading questions to help students focus in their fantasies: "What do you like about your work? What don't you like about it?" "Are you alone? With other people?" "Do you move around during the day?" "Do you make decisions?"

The class ends with students sharing their fantasies. We tell them that the next thing we're going to do is to visit a large insurance company, to observe clerical work in action, and that they should hold on to their fantasies for comparative purposes.

14: Clerical Work in Large and Small Firms

In large companies, clerical work is increasingly being organized like factory work, with each clerical worker doing one operation—typing, keypunching, etc.—all day long. (The teacher might find it interesting to read the chapter on clerical workers in *Labor and Monopoly Capital*, by Harry Braverman, pp. 293–359. The chapter discusses the increasing degradation of clerical work.) The low pay and monotony of the job may be compensated for by extra benefits which the company gives its workers. In small, local businesses, you still find the more traditional secretary, who does a range of tasks and who has a certain amount of autonomy. In this activity, students tour a large company that recruits students out of high school; later, they talk to or visit a secretary in a small firm. One of our purposes is to show students the kinds of job options that are available to them in the clerical field. Because our students often view office work with the same feelings of inadequacy and anxiety that a college-educated, middle-class woman feels when she considers being an editor or a lawyer, another goal of this activity is to show students that office work is something they can do, if they want to.

To set up the first trip, the teacher should contact any of the large businesses, banks, or insurance companies in the area which hire a lot of clerical workers. If they recruit students straight out of high school, and if they are currently hiring, they are likely to have someone in personnel who regularly takes high school groups on tours and talks to them (see "Techniques," p. 33).

One year we visited the Prudential Life Insurance Company in Boston. Students saw a large typing pool, keypunch operators, secretaries with their own offices, women doing bookkeeping; they talked to a woman who was the head of personnel. Unfortunately, we weren't able to talk to any of the workers. The students' reactions were very interesting. They were all impressed by the benefits explained to them, especially the company-arranged, low-price tours to Europe, and the low-priced restaurant for employees right in the building. They remarked on the fact that many of the women working there looked about their own age and wore nice clothes.

The trip had a strong effect on one student in particular. When she saw the typing pool of fifteen women, she said, "I can do that!" Although she was taking typing in school, she had never really believed before that she could get a job with her skill. The idea of being able to get a job in which she would get dressed up, go downtown every day, go out for lunch, was very exciting to her. It gave her new confidence in herself.

The next year, with a different group of students, we visited the John Hancock Insurance Company, because the Prudential wasn't hiring and thus was reluctant to give tours. Although the working conditions were very similar, the students' reactions were quite different. They made comments like, "This isn't any different from factory work," and asked the man leading the tour whether women did anything but clerical work at John Hancock.

In setting up the second trip or speaker, try to find some woman or workplace that at least some of the students are familiar with. We talked to the mother of one of our students and then, afterward, made a brief visit to her office. She worked for the school department as a secretary in her neighborhood elementary school. Her job consisted of answering the phone, typing records, filing, and sometimes consoling unhappy kids.

Afterward, in reacting to her job, students naturally compared it with what they had seen on their tour of the larger company. "I wouldn't want her job. There's no one my age there." "It seems like she does more." The teacher should encourage such reactions, without agreeing or disagreeing, as they help students sort out what kinds of work situations appeal to them.

Especially if there are students in the group interested in becoming private secretaries, we suggest using the Executive Secretary section from *Working* as an accompaniment to the trips. We have students read this very short section, not because of what Anne Bogan says about her job, but because of the debatable attitudes she expresses:

> I feel like I'm sharing somewhat the business life of the men. So I'm much happier as the secretary of an executive than I would be in some woman's field where perhaps I could make more money. But it wouldn't be an extension of a successful executive. I'm perfectly happy in my status. . . .
>
> I feel the wife of an executive would be a better wife had she been a secretary first. As a secretary you learn to adjust to the boss's moods. Many marriages would be happier if the wife would do just that. [P. 91]

(See Activity 9, p. 177, for a general description of *Working* and how to use it.)

15: Speaker—Organizing Office Workers

If it can be arranged, we suggest ending this section on clerical work with a speaker who is involved in some facet of organizing clerical workers. In this way, some of the problems connected with office work, such as absence of job descriptions, lack of security, little hope for promotion, or no unions, can be raised in the context of women struggling to solve those problems.

This is not an easy activity to set up. The first problem is finding a speaker. You can try using the collective personal contacts of the group of students you are working with. If you are in the Boston area, you might call Nine to Five, a Boston-based organization which gives technical advice and support to people trying to organize office workers. If the organizer is doing organizing within her own workplace, a second problem is finding a time when she can talk to the class. If you have any flexibility in the time when your class meets, you might try using the woman's lunchtime, or perhaps you could hold an evening class at your home, making it simultaneously a social event for the students. One year, when neither of the above were feasible options, we, ourselves, talked at some length to a woman who was trying to organize clerical employees at MIT, then we reported back to the class. (For suggestions about ways to prepare the speaker and the class for each other, see "Techniques," p. 31. Basically, the speaker should be encouraged to share with students what she and other women in her office or company are doing, and why.)

Some time should be set aside afterward for students to reflect on the issues raised and to pull together their impressions of clerical work in general. You might start by having them compare some of the things the speaker said about clerical work with what they learned in the previous activity. Having students do a simple ranking exercise can help them figure out whether they would like clerical work, and in what kind of workplace. The ranking exercise we've used is as follows:

Rank the following in the order that is most important to you in a job:
____ working with people your own age
____ making as much money as possible
____ using your head
____ good benefits
____ freedom to make decisions
____ freedom to move around physically
____ status and prestige

In the following discussion, we've taken what students ranked first and second and looked at whether that exists in the kinds of clerical work they've been exposed to.

16: Sexist Behavior—How Would You Respond?

Here students explore possible responses to daily on-the-job sexism and the consequences of

those responses. They then move to discussing how sexist behavior affects them in their personal lives. The activity, which will probably take two class periods, ends with each student thinking positively and concretely about how to make changes in what happens around them.

Students start by reading case studies about on-the-job sexism. The situations presented are all real, coming directly from experiences students have had on their jobs. The teacher should feel free to add new cases and delete others, with an eye toward making the cases reflect the kind of work her students do.

Judy is applying for a job at an insurance company which involves typing and filing. The personnel manager interviewing her tells her, "We expect all our girls to look attractive. Naturally that means dressing properly. Pantsuits are acceptable, but jeans or slacks without matching tops aren't." He then adds, as an afterthought, "You should wear dresses though, to show off those nice legs of yours."

Debby is working nights at Kentucky Fried Chicken. Her job is to stand behind the counter and take orders from customers. Although there are other people in the kitchen, she is the only one visible to people as they come in. As a female, she feels very vulnerable; she is afraid a lot of the time.

Donna is working as a waitress at Brighams. Her supervisor is a man who is constantly either flirting with her or bossing her around. He'll do things like stand very close to her, breathing down her neck as she makes a sundae, on the pretext of making sure she's doing it correctly. Or one minute he'll be yelling at her to serve the customers faster and the next, he'll be calling her over, putting his arm around her, and asking her whether or not she has a boyfriend.

Marie is working at a fancy boutique in Harvard Square and had been going out with the manager. Now she's decided she doesn't really like him, and wants to break up with him, but she still wants the job. After she starts "being busy" whenever he asks her out, he starts making it hard for her to work there. He consistently gives her bad hours—both Friday and Saturday nights for instance—and either ignores her totally or makes nasty comments to her whenever they're both in the store at the same time.

The class first reads each case study together and brainstorms about possible responses. When different ways of handling the situation have been listed on the board, the teacher asks students to guess what the consequence might be for each of the responses listed. For instance, the consequences of always moving away from the manager at Brighams might be that he would yell at you even more. The consequences then also get put on the board, paired with the responses. Before moving on to the next case, the teacher tells students to make a note to themselves on paper about which response they would choose and why. At the end, students discuss their choices.

If your students have had little work experience, they may not have much to say in the discussion about responses and consequences, or they may only make the blanket response—"Well, I'd quit." If that is the case, the case studies should be read, just to give the students a sense of the kinds of situations they may run up against, and then the class should move on quickly to the second part of the activity, in which students focus on sexism in their personal lives.

Once they get going, students always seem to have plenty to say about sexist ways in which they are treated, so it isn't necessary to structure the discussion. Good questions to get things started are: "Does your boyfriend let you go out by yourself?" "Do your parents treat your brothers differently from you?" Although it may be hard to shift the talk from boyfriends and family, try to have students also think about sexism in their school and in their neighborhood.

We've sometimes had arguments erupt in class, when someone describes a situation and someone else responds by saying, in effect, "You're a fool to put up with it." Once a student said that her boyfriend wouldn't let her look at another guy and never let her go to clubs with her sister or her girlfriends. Another student answered, a little smugly, "Jesus, I can't believe it. Why do you go out with guys like that? My boyfriend lets me do what I want." The first student, needless to say, became very defensive; she began screaming at her classmate. Since this kind of exchange is not productive, the best thing for the teacher to do is to cut it off, bringing other students and their experiences into the conversation.

To end the activity with a focus on how to make changes, each student is asked to fill out the following form:

> There are ways that you can make some changes in what goes on around you. Below you will find several categories. Your task is to write down changes you think could actually happen to change sexist behavior in these areas:
>
> In My Family
> 1.
> 2.
> 3.
>
> At School
> 1.
> 2.
> 3.
>
> In My Job
> 1.
> 2.
> 3.
>
> In My Neighborhood
> 1.
> 2.
> 3.
>
> With My Boyfriend or Friends
> 1.
> 2.
> 3.

Although the teacher might want to circulate as students are filling out the form and respond to their ideas, this is a personal exercise and not intended to be discussed afterward as a group.

17: Glamour Jobs

Some of the ways women earn money may appear sexist and exploitative to the teacher. The students, on the other hand, may aspire to those jobs because they seem glamorous. In this activity, we examine three such jobs—"Hooker," "Model" and "Airline Stewardess"—based on those selections from *Working*. The goal of the activity is not to discourage students from wanting such jobs (except, perhaps, hooker), but to get them to look beneath the glamorous surface and get a more realistic sense of what the work involved actually is. (See p. 177 for a general description of *Working* and how to use it.)

We use these three selections from *Working* because all three women express ambivalent feelings about their jobs and the roles they're expected to play within them. The hooker describes a life of expensive clothes, clubs, and fancy restaurants, and sees her work as a game in which she has control: "As a bright, assertive woman I had no power. As a cold manipulative hustler, I had a lot." (p.103). On the other hand, she eventually went from being an elegant callgirl to being a streetwalker because of her drug habit, and acknowledges that the role she had to play involved numbing herself to the extent that "I couldn't turn myself back on when I finished working." The model likes her $50-an-hour rate, but says that "you feel like you're someone else's clothes hanger." The "airline stewardess" appreciates the fact that her job got her out of Nebraska and has allowed her to travel, but resents the way she is treated by the airline:

> They call us professional people, but they talk to us as very young, childishly. They check us all the time on appearance. They check our weight every month. Even though you've been flying for twenty years, they check you and say that's a no-no. . . .If you're a pound over, they can take you off flights until you get under. [P. 80]

It is important to point out to students that since the time that the interview with the "stewardess" was printed, organized pressure has forced the airlines to change hiring practices with regard to age, height, weight, sex, and appearance, with some resulting modification of the practices described above.

After students have read each selection, we use different types of follow-ups, for variety. Students have so much to say about the hooker that we hold an informal discussion, during which we have students review what happened to her, and why. After reading about the model, we do a writing assignment which makes

students think about what it's like to be a model: Imagine you're a model. Describe a typical day in you life and your feelings as you go through that day. (See "Techniques," p. 18.) We devise a role-play to get at the pros and cons of being an "airline stewardess."

The "stewardess" role-play we've used mimics many of the activities in the unit itself. Students play two "stewardesses" who have come to talk to the "Women and Work" class about their jobs. One is very enthusiastic about her job, the other isn't. The students who volunteer to play the "stewardesses" are given the following roles to help them:

> You are twenty-three, from Cambridge, and grew up in a housing project. You've been a "stewardess" for two years and you like your job. You had never been out of Massachusetts before and now you've traveled all over Europe, to Hawaii and California. You like the kind of people you meet on the job. You like how impressed everyone is when you tell them you are a "stewardess." You don't agree at all with the other "stewardess."

> You come from Cambridge and have been a "stewardess" for four years. You liked the job at first; you thought it was glamorous and exciting. Now you are tired of it. You feel as though you never get to see anything but the airports and hotels in the places you end up in after a flight. You're tired of being told exactly how to look and of having to constantly smile at passengers. You like the job when there are emergency situations, but the rest of the time you feel like a waitress. You think the other "stewardess" hasn't been doing the job long enough to know what it's really like.

The other students each write down at least one question to ask of their two speakers. Playing herself, the teacher then asks each of the "stewardesses" to describe their jobs and encourages students to ask questions (see "Techniques," p. 28).

18: Panel—Service Work

> Rank the following in the order most important to you in a job:
>
> <u>6</u> glamour
> <u>5</u> status, prestige
> <u>2</u> using my head

__4__ money

__3__ freedom to move around physically

__1__ having to make decisions

Rank the following in the order of your interest in them as jobs:

__6__ housewife

__3__ stewardess

__2__ nurse

__4__ clerk typist

__5__ factory worker

__1__ teacher

Finish the following sentence: "To me success is . . ." "having some influence on people, changing their lives." [From a student paper]

Nursing and teaching continue to be routes into jobs in which working-class women can gain a measure of independence and influence. Our female students often name such jobs as social worker, teen worker, nurse, teacher, when asked what they'd most like to do. They see these jobs as interesting, worthwhile, and worthy of respect. They are also undoubtedly reacting to the positive models presented by the women who work at The Group School and to the political attitude in the school, which stresses the need for improved quality in the services available to working-class and poor people. We try to encourage students in these aspirations and to aid them actively in getting the kind of training necessary. We feel that, in the long run, such jobs may well be satisfying to them; we think that working-class people should begin to be the providers of services directed to them in the past as clients.

This activity uses a panel/small group discussion format to expose students to a variety of social and health services jobs. The three or four women on the panel each talk briefly about their jobs. Students are then asked to choose which job they'd like to learn more about; and the class is divided into smaller groups, each lead by one of the panelists. The groups are intended to be a place for students to ask questions and to talk more informally and personally with the panelists.

The selection of both the jobs and the women doing those jobs is important. We pick jobs that students are interested in, and that are in dif-

ferent fields. Thus, we wouldn't have both a respiratory therapist and a nurse on the panel. We also consider the local job market and try to have at least two service fields represented in which there are jobs available in the area. Day care and medical specialties like X-ray technician would be two such fields in the Boston area. The combination of jobs we've settled on in the past has been nurse, day-care worker, and social worker. If interest is expressed in teaching, we use a teacher from The Group School who has had public school experience.

It's crucial that the panelists be working-class women, as the experience of middle-class and working-class women in preparing for those jobs, and their reactions to them, are likely to be quite different. We look for, and have usually been able to find, friends, relatives, or acquaintances of our students as speakers. We explain to them beforehand the structure of the activity, and ask them to focus in the introduction on both the training that was necessary to get the job and on the job itself. We explain that they will be leading the small groups (because the teacher will either be involved in one, herself, as panelist or will be circulating among the groups), and that they may have to draw the students out to get at their concerns. To accomplish this, we ask them to talk personally about their experience, to encourage but not count on questions, and to feel free to ask the students questions. (For a general discussion of choosing speakers and preparing both speakers and students for each other, see "Techniques," p. 31.)

We usually allow fifteen to twenty minutes for the panel part of the activity, five minutes for students to choose and get settled in their small groups, and another twenty or thirty minutes for the discussions. Before students choose their groups, the teacher should explain that choosing a group doesn't necessarily mean that someone wants that job, only that she wants to find out more about it or about the general field. Once the groups get going, it works best if the teacher can circulate among them, in case discussions bog down.

To vary the usual pattern of having the group discuss their reactions after the speaker or speakers have gone, we use a more individual follow-up to this activity. We give students a questionnaire to fill out at home which leads them to reflect on what they've learned:

1. Why did you choose the group you were in? Which group was it?
2. What do you think the best thing about the job is?
3. What do you think the worst thing about the job is?
4. Do you think you'd be good at the job? Why?

5. Would you like a job like that? Why?

The next day in class we have students share their reactions by exchanging their completed questionnaire with the questionnaire of the person nearest them who was in a different discussion group.

Other individual follow-ups include having students choose and read one of the service jobs selections from Terkel's *Working*, or, if a student was very interested in a particular job, trying to arrange for her to visit that panelist at work.

WOMEN IN UNUSUAL JOBS

INTRODUCTION

Women have begun to move into fields normally dominated by men. This section of the "Women and Work" unit introduces students to the more unusual kinds of work women are now doing. Again, the emphasis is on jobs realistically within the range of possibilities for students. The overall goal is to broaden their awareness of options for the future. In the first activity, students play "What's My Line?" with contestants representing unusual jobs done by women. Speakers are then brought in to talk about jobs students want to find out more about. The section ends with a writing assignment in which students imagine themselves as the first woman to break into a traditionally male field.

ACTIVITIES

19: "What's My Line?"

An enjoyable way to learn about unusual jobs women do is to play a modified version of the TV show, "What's My Line?" Three women, each of whom does a job students don't normally associate with women, come in to "be on the show." Students question them one by one, trying to get enough information from yes/no questions to be able to guess their jobs. Once they've guessed, they talk informally with each of the women about their work. The game provides a means of getting students to think about what a given job is like.

In lining up "contestants," we look for women who do a range of jobs which are unusual for women. Ordinarily, the jobs shouldn't be those requiring long, costly preparation, because part of the purpose of the game is to suggest possible job options for students. They also shouldn't be terribly obscure; the point isn't to stump the students. Jobs that fit our criteria include any one of the trades (carpentry, plumbing, printing), truck driver or cab driver, mail carrier, paper girl, housepainter, forewoman in a factory, store owner, or a woman who's set up her own business. A combination we used once consisted of a printer, a police officer, and a cab driver. We explain to "contestants" beforehand the rationale for the game, how it works, and that we'd like them to talk for a while about their jobs, after the guessing game.

To be able to play the game in one class period, students need some preparation. The teacher should explain in the preceding class what's going to happen. Usually several of the students are familiar with the TV show and can explain it to the others. We use the following rules: you can only ask yes/no questions; as long as someone gets a yes answer, she can go on asking questions; you can only make a guess when it's your turn. We also tell students that all the "contestants" will be women who do jobs women don't usually do.

In the class period before the game, students should prepare questions, as they often have a hard time thinking of yes/no questions on the spot. Generating questions is a valuable process in itself, because it makes students think about what distinguishes one job from another—wage versus salary, self-employed versus working for someone, etc. The questions our students listed included: "Do you work alone?" "Do you make a product?" "Do you provide a service?" "Are you self-employed?" "Are you paid by the hour?" The teacher can make copies of the questions and give them to students when they start playing the game.

During "What's My Line?" the teacher's main job is to watch the time. With three people, the minimum time you need is an hour. Ideally, the class should be one and one-half hours long—twenty minutes per contestant, and a half-hour at the end for general discussion. It's better if time limits are set on the guessing. If, after ten minutes, students haven't guessed the job by asking yes/no questions, we usually allow them another five in which they can ask any kind of question. After fifteen minutes, we usually stop and have the "contestant" say what she does, so that there are five minutes left for students to chat informally with her about her job.

We invite the "contestants," after their turn, to play the game with us. This adds a valuable adult dimension to the questioning and guessing, and it helps everyone feel more comfortable with each other. At the end of the hour, all three contestants are in the classroom together, and we have an informal discussion, in which students ask any questions they'd like. By the

time we reach this point, students are glad to move beyond the game format, and anxious to ask more specific or more personal questions, such as "How'd you get the job?" or "How much do you make?"

20: Speakers—Women in Unusual Jobs

Playing "What's My Line?" may whet students' appetites for finding out about women who do unusual work. If so, the teacher can ask students to think of some other jobs they'd like to find out about and arrange for additional guests to come and talk to the class about their work (see "Techniques," p. 31). If the list of jobs students want to find out about is long, and interest continues, we suggest alternating between speakers and selections from Working, to cover at least some of the jobs they're interested in. (See Activity 9, p. 177, for ways to use selections from Working.)

Our students generated the following list of speakers: nun, prostitute, lawyer, politician, entertainer, artist, model. Furthermore, they wanted us to arrange to have the nun and the prostitute come on the same day. That we weren't able to set up. We did, however, have a nun and a politician come in on successive weeks.

The politician, a Black woman from Cambridge, made an impression on all of us. She talked about her preference for thinking of herself as a Black politician, rather than a woman politician. Interestingly, however, she had become involved in politics when, as the mother of children in the Cambridge schools, she began attending school committee meetings. After she left, we talked with the students—who all happened to be white—about the fact that Blacks as a group, like women as a group, are discriminated against, and discussed the difficulty a Black woman might have in deciding which group to identify herself with.

21: Writing—The First Woman to Break into a Field

Most of the information on women in unusual jobs has come from outside sources. Here the students, asked to imagine themselves in a field colonized by men, provide the class material (see "Techniques," p. 18).

The assignment is:

1. First sit quietly and think about a job that now is very male-oriented and which normally you would not think about trying to get.
2. Write a composition about how you would break into this field.

In one class, jobs our students chose included being a priest, being a movie director, being Santa Claus, and being a professional athlete. One student's piece was called "The First Major League Woman Baseball Player."

> I would to to the person in charge and tell him I wanted to be in the major league. After he stopped laughing I'd have him watch me play and tell him I

was as good as any man. If he wouldn't let me, I'd fight it till the end and tell him off but good.

Sharing the compositions can lead to two different lines of discussion. One focuses on what women have to do to get jobs that are ordinarily done by men. Another raises the question of whether students feel that the jobs that have been written about will ever really be held by women. Two debates that we particularly remember were on whether women would ever be priests and whether women would ever be as good at sports as men.

As a follow-up project, each student watches the newspapers or magazines for a given period of time, looking for anything that relates to women in the field they've written about. The teacher can set up a bulletin board in class, on which the student compositions are posted, along with their clippings.

JOB NEEDS AND EXPECTATIONS

INTRODUCTION

Before you can start looking for a job, you should know what you want to get out of it. We end this unit on women and work by encouraging students to think personally about working. Three activities are designed to help them define their personal work goals, needs, and expectations. We start with a fantasy exercise, in which students imagine themselves in five years. Next is a self-evaluation exercise through which students realize that they do have job skills. Then they fill out a questionnaire on their job needs. At the end, they are in a better position to review specific jobs covered in the unit, to look through job catalogs, or to meet with a job counselor—all with the goal of finding specific jobs they might want to have.

ACTIVITIES

22: A Fantasy

The purpose of this exercise is to help students think about their futures by having them imagine what they'll be doing in five years. Because so many students feel that the only thing they can do is get married and have children, the fantasy is deliberately structured to encourage them to think of themselves as having jobs out of the home.

To be able to get into a fantasy, students have to be relaxed and the room has to be quiet. The teacher can help set an appropriate mood by waiting until everyone is settled and by speaking softly and slowly. You start by telling students to close their eyes, to relax, to let their minds wander. If a student can't stop giggling, you should gently ask her to leave, explaining that other students won't be able to concentrate. When the room has been quiet for a little while, you begin to read the fantasy, pausing after each line:

> You are going ahead in years to five years from now.
> You are waking up; what time is it?
> Who are you with? What is your room like?
> What is your apartment like? What is your neighborhood like?
> Picture yourself dressing for work; what do you wear?
> How do you get to work?
> What are your feelings as you go?
> What does your workplace look like? Picture it in your mind.
> Describe the other people you meet.
> What is your job? Picture yourself doing it.
> How do you feel doing it?
> Whom do you relate to during the day?
> Does the time pass slowly?
> Just imagine yourself doing your job for several minutes.
> Your day is ending and you are getting ready to leave. How do you feel?
> You leave for home. Picture yourself coming home. What are you experiencing?
> Slowly return to reality.

When the fantasy is finished, students go around the room, describing what they saw and felt. It helps to keep the fantasies vivid if the teacher asks questions in the present—"What's your job?" "How do you feel when you're working?" Don't expect answers to all parts of the fantasy, however. No one will have been able to visualize everything; moreover, the fantasy is intended merely to be suggestive.

23: Self-Evaluation

This activity focuses students' attention on skills they have, but have not recognized, or have not seen as related to jobs. the goal is to help build self-confidence and a sense of competency. The exercise also stimulates students to consider whether things they enjoy, or are good at, might lead to work.

We give students a three-page chart to fill out for this exercise, with accompanying written directions. Each page is identical:

Accomplishment:_____

Tasks Involved	Skills Necessary
1.	1.
2.	2.
3.	3.
4.	4.
5.	5.

1. Did you accomplish this alone or with other people?
2. Which task did you enjoy the most?

Directions:

Accomplishments: To choose an accomplishment for each page, think of something you did that you feel good about, like redecorating your room, building a chair, knitting a sweater, quieting a baby.

Tasks Involved: To fill in under tasks involved, think of all the different things you had to do to complete your accomplishment. For example, if you put "redecorating your room" at the top, the tasks involved might be: deciding on colors, buying paint, buying fabric, making curtains, painting, refinishing your dresser.

Skills Involved: To fill in the skills necessary column, think of the skills you needed to carry out each of the tasks. For example: imagination, persistence, math skills, being warm and gentle, comparing prices, patience.

We suggest starting the activity by having the class do a sample page from the questionnaire together, so that everyone understands the exercise. Once students start filling in their charts, the teacher should circulate, helping students think of tasks and skills, pointing out that the same skills appear in more than one list, being supportive or/and interested in their accomplishments, talking informally about different jobs.

When the self-evaluation has been completed, we try to encourage students to talk about skills they hadn't before realized they had. The teacher might want to go around in a circle, asking each student to name either the skills that appeared most often or the three tasks that she enjoyed the most. The group as a whole can then look at accomplishments individuals listed to see if they can come up with jobs which relate to those accomplishments. Students should consider whether any of the jobs appeal to them. Someone may realize for the first time that something she likes to do could actually become a job for her, or she could decide that although she likes to sew, for example, she wouldn't want to do it for a living.

24: Questionnaire—What Kind of Job Do I Want and Why?

Given the pressing need of students from low-income families to earn money, as well as the human need to find satisfying ways to fill one's life, it's never too early to think about future work. Thus, although this activity is most appropriate for older students, it can be valuable for all.

The structure of this activity is simple: students are given the following questionnaire to fill out and told to take as much time as they need to think about all the questions.

What Kind of Job Do I Want and Why?

Personal Needs
1. Do I want to do service work? (Helping people, waitressing, etc.)
2. Do I want to do physical work?
3. Do I want to do "head" work or office work?
4. Is it important that the job be satisfying or meaningful?
5. Is it important for me to enjoy my work?
6. Is it important to me what other people think of my work?

Mobility Needs
1. How long do I want a job for?
2. Do I want on-the-job training?
3. If training is available, will I accept less money?
4. Do I want the job to lead to something else?

Social Needs
1. Do I want to work with people or alone?

2. Do I want to work with people of my own age?
3. Do I want to work for a large company or a small company?

Financial Needs
1. How much money do I need? (approximately)
   rent:
   food:
   clothes:
   entertainment:
   schooling:
2. Do I need a job where I can earn a lot of money to save or to pay off debts?

Occasionally a student says that the questionnaire is irrelevant to her because she is getting married soon and won't need or want a job, or because she has a child and is living on welfare. The teacher should encourage her to answer the questions anyway. You can remind her of the family work tree, which demonstrated that the students' mothers and grandmothers had usually worked. Or you can review other parts of the unit which have shown women either needing or wanting to work outside the home at some point in their lives. Another approach is simply to ask whether she thinks she can count on being supported forever.

A follow-up to the questionnaire helps students think of specific jobs which meet the needs they have defined. A way to begin, which also serves the purpose of reviewing the unit, is to give students a list of all the jobs that have been discussed in the course of the unit and have them look at whether any of those jobs would meet their needs. Ideally, students could then use their questionnaire and that list as the basis for talking with a job counselor about specific jobs. This has been possible at The Group School because one of our two jobs counselors has usually taught the unit. If a jobs counselor isn't available, or if your students couldn't comfortably talk to the counselor, try gathering such resources as college or training school brochures; the "Occupational Handbook," a massive government publication describing jobs, available in most libraries; or a book called *Saturday's Child*, by Susanne Seed, for students to look through in the classroom.

NOTES TO THE TEACHER

Job Counseling Problems

A low self-image, the result of internalizing all the negative aspects of their lives (being poor, living off welfare, being told they're worthless) makes some students feel that they don't deserve and couldn't hold on to decent jobs. A student may get a job at McDonald's, hate it, but say to herself, "That's all I should expect," thereby ruling out other possibilities. Another student may have such a fear of authority (a result of years of feeling helpless at the hands of teachers, social workers, police) that she is afraid to make demands on her employer, or even to ask questions. She assumes that the employer is going to be against her, no matter how reasonable the request. The result is that the situation on the job quickly becomes overwhelming. If a student needs to get off work an hour early for a medical appointment, she may stay out the whole day, rather than ask to be let off early. When this happens two or three times, she's likely to be fired—which only makes her more afraid to ask for the hour off the next time.

Still other students feel inadequate about their abilities to get and hold any job. Students with learning disabilities, or low skills, are frightened by what may seem, to some, simple requirements. For example, because they are afraid they'll make mistakes with change, the job of cashier seems beyond them. Or they'll refuse to apply for an assembly line job, which doesn't involve math or English skills, because filling out an application intimidates them.

Low expectations, or feelings of inadequacy, whether they stem from lack of skills, fear of authorities, or a negative self-image, will emerge regardless of the level on which you're dealing with work issues. A student may refuse to get involved in the exploration of different jobs, by not asking questions or skipping classes, because it raises so many questions for her about her own abilities and future. Negative comments about the activities or speakers—"This is boring,"

"She's a fool to like that job"—may reflect a student's feelings that she wouldn't be capable of doing that job.

If a student is consistently negative, or hasn't come to class for a while, the teacher should try to help her pin down the reasons. Better done in a one-to-one conversation, you might ask whether anything in the course seems to relate to her own life, or lead her to talk about jobs she may have had. Expressing fears or doubts is always a first step toward handling them more positively.

"Women and Work" isn't designed to deal directly with those feelings, although activities like the trip to the company which hires clerical workers, or the case studies, increase the students' awareness of the possibilities. At The Group School, one-on-one jobs counseling, in which fears can be explored, and jobs skills courses, which build confidence by giving students practice in filling out applications, going to interviews, and talking to employers, specifically serve that purpose. The teacher using this unit shouldn't expect it to solve the problems discussed here. The most you can do is to be sensitive to the feelings the material may arouse in students. It helps to learn as much as possible about the students' own job experiences and to keep that information in the back of your mind as you're planning activities or discussions.

Avoiding Defeatism

As students start learning about ways in which women workers are exploited and the negative feelings women have about their work, they may become discouraged and feel hopeless. "Just my luck, I'll probably end up in a factory making $2.30 an hour." "If I tried to change anything, I'd just get fired." "Why should I work? If it's all that bad, I might as well let some guy support me." Comments like these express the disillusionment that may arise. When coupled with the low expectations and sense of inadequacy about work that students bring to the material, these feelings can immobilize them.

Although we try, through the choice of activities in the unit, to counteract feelings of defeatism, they're hard to avoid. We explore few professional jobs, so that students aren't presented with careers that may be inaccessible to most of them. On the other hand, women in professional jobs often have the most satisfying work experiences; thus, failing to touch upon them can be a missed opportunity to sound a positive note. Again, in the attempt to encourage positive attitudes, we often look at attempts being made to change exploitative working conditions; yet we are at the same time aware that while the attempts themselves may be positive, the organizers, in explaining the need for organization, may reinforce a sense of how unfairly women are treated.

We cannot and do not avoid pointing out objective facts about work, even when the facts are discouraging—such realities, for example, as the poor chances of women for promotion on assembly lines or the "first fired" pattern in most enterprises. But simultaneously, we try to shore up positive attitudes toward work. We show our interest in the jobs our students have, and we encourage them to think about the personal benefits they gain in working. We make an effort to find "What's My Line?" "contestants" and speakers who have positive feelings about their work, and see to it that those feelings emerge through our questions. We may choose the Waitress selection in *Working* simply because the waitress feels so positive about a job many women do, and despise. Where appropriate, we bring in information about training available for jobs. In these and other ways, we hope to present an honest appraisal of the injustices women suffer in the labor market, while cultivating in our students an appreciation for the real values to be found in work.

Notes

1. Nancy Seifer, *Absent from the Majority* (Middle America Pamphlet Series), pp. 28–33.

2. Claire and Leonard Ingraham, *An Album of Women in American History* (New York: Franklin Watts, Inc., 1973), p. 31.

3. Milton Meltzer, *Bread and Roses* (New York: Random House Vintage Books, 1967), p. 17.

4. Seifer, pp. 34–36.

5. Jean Tepperman, "Two Jobs: Women Who Work in Factories," in *Sisterhood is Powerful*, ed. Robin Morgan (New York: Random House Vintage Books, 1970), pp. 115–124.

6. Seifer, p. 33.

7. Margery Davies, "A Woman's Place Is at the Typewriter: The Feminization of the Clerical Labor Force," *Radical America*, July–August 1974, p. 7.

8. We would like to thank the Pilot School in Cambridge, Massachusetts for sending us this activity.

VIII: WOMEN ORGANIZING THEMSELVES

OVERVIEW

If the first woman God ever made was strong enough to turn the world upside down all alone, these women ought to be able to turn it back, and get it right side up again! And now they is asking to do it, the men better let them. [Sojourner Truth]

Women in the USA have been organizing and struggling for well over one hundred years against laws, institutions, and attitudes which have kept them from developing as full human beings. These economic, political, and social struggles, however, have been excluded from the American history we are taught in schools. This unit on women organizing themselves focuses on why and how American women have organized to fight for their rights. The goal is to show students that the current position of women in our society is based on a heritage of struggle *by* women, that power has never been granted *to* them without a fight, and that the need for women to organize themselves continues.

The approach we use to teach both the historical and the contemporary material in this unit is geared specifically to the skills and attitudes of working-class young women. Our students tend to find history boring, difficult, and irrelevant. We try to enliven it by using an autobiographical approach. We try to make it more accessible by teaching historical vocabulary and translating the language into modern forms. We make it more relevant by connecting it with current problems and struggles. Our students often view the modern women's movement with distrust and suspicion because their exposure to it has been limited to its polemics. Instead of asking our students to read the standard feminist literature, therefore, we ask students to look at the needs for, and results of, the movement as manifested in their community.

Introductory activities establish the fact that women have been ignored in the history we have been taught and explore the position of women in nineteenth-century America. Following this is a series of activities on the nineteenth-century women's movement and its leaders. These include examining the first women's rights convention in 1848, doing individual reports on feminists who should be famous, and writing a biographical children's book on these women. The suffrage movement is examined from the point of view of what it took to win; it is compared with the current struggle to get the Equal Rights Amendment passed. The struggle of Black women, fighting against their double oppression, is looked at through reading and writing about Harriet Tubman, Sojourner Truth, and Anne Moody, a young civil rights organizer in the South. An optional activity on labor organizing is included for those students who haven't studied labor struggles in the context of Unit VII, "Women and Work." The modern women's movement is examined through a combination of trips and speakers which focus on the needs women have and the groups, services, and businesses which women have organized recently to meet those needs. The unit ends with students themselves becoming organizers, by holding a women's day in their school, putting out a women's newspaper, or devising a strategy for changing sexist practices which affect them.

"Women Organizing Themselves" covers standard topics in women's history and thus can be used as an American history course. As part of a women's studies program, we would suggest using it with older students who have had other women's courses, because the material is more distant from students' immediate lives and problems. We might use it, for instance, to end a year which had included "Adult Sex Roles," "Women and Work," and Women's News."

ACTIVITIES

1: Were There Famous Women?

Why aren't women in the history books? In this activity, students consider this question and in the process begin to gain a sense of the position of women in the nineteenth century.

The activity starts with students listing on the board famous names that they can remember from American history. They then go back over the list, filling in the occupations of each of the people mentioned. Students will quickly notice that few, if any, women have been named, and that their occupations aren't as "important' as the men's. Martha Washington, Eleanor Roosevelt, Florence Nightingale, and Annie Oakley were the only famous women our students could remember, and the occupation of the first two was simply "wife of the President."

The teacher then puts on the board her own list of important women the students will be learning about in the unit. Our list, which included Susan B. Anthony, Elizabeth Cady Stanton, Harriet Tubman, Elizabeth Blackwell, Mary "Mother" Jones, drew a blank from students. "Who were they?" was the response. Because students will have a chance to study these women later in the unit, we only describe them briefly here, using any visuals we can find to make the women more real to the students. *The Revolt of the American Woman,* by Oliver Jenson, in paperback, has a number of pictures of Victorian women. The text of the book, however, is quite sexist and should not be used, except as an example of sexist history writing. *The Fight for Freedom for Women,* by Rose Tremain, has pictures of many of the women the class will be studying (we use some of the text in Activity 3).

Having briefly introduced these women, the teacher poses two connected questions: "Why aren't there many famous women in American history?" and "Why didn't you learn about them?" We allow students time to think of their own answers, before giving ours. Our students' answers

to the first question range from "They didn't do anything but take care of their kids," to "Maybe they weren't allowed to be famous." Answers to the second question included, "You could never learn anything good in regular schools" and "Maybe the teachers never heard of those women either."

One way to explain why there are so few famous women is to give students a sense of what it was like to be a woman in the nineteenth century. We explain that it was impossible to become a politician (like so many of the men the students listed) when you weren't allowed to speak in public or vote. It was impossible to become a scientist when you weren't allowed to go to college (because it was thought your brain couldn't stand the strain and you would get brain fever). Upper-class women were supposed to be pure and moral, which meant in practical terms never going anywhere but to church. Poorer women worked, but only as domestics or factory workers. The activities of the vast majority of women then, like so many today, were centered around their families. Women, thus, were doing a kind of work that has always been taken for granted and has never been recognized as making a contribution to society. Women, in fact, "weren't allowed to be famous."

To give students a better understanding of why they never learned about the women who were leaders, the teacher can ask whether they think it makes a difference that, until recently, men wrote the history books. We point out that even when women were prominently involved in a movement for social change, like the abolitionist movement, male abolitionists got much more attention in textbooks.

A good way to end this introductory activity is to give students a sense of what's to come, stressing that they are going to have a chance in the next activities to learn about and to teach each other the history that's been ignored.

2: Historical Vocabulary

Historical material is often uninteresting to students and hard for them to read. The purpose of this vocabulary lesson is to make the material students will be reading in the next three activities more accessible, while continuing to build their sense of the life of women in the nineteenth century.

A word list is drawn from the readings to come. Rather than give students the words and definitions, we give them the words in a sentence which makes the meaning fairly clear. They are asked to use the context to define the words, a procedure which builds valuable reading skills. The sentences themselves review or add to what students have learned about women in the nineteenth century, thus becoming a history lesson which students don't immediately label "history" and "boring." We give students a sheet that looks like this:

1. Feminism
Example: In this unit, we will be studying the history of *feminism,* the struggle of women to obtain equal rights with men.

2. Feminist
Example: Many American *feminists,* like Susan B. Anthony, thought it crucial that women be able to vote.

3. Autonomy
Example: Feminists in the 1800s believed in *autonomy* for women. In other words, they thought that women, not men, should decide what was "proper" for a woman to do.

4. Independence
Example: In the 1800s, it was hard for a married woman to have any *independence* from her husband because her property automatically became his when they got married.

5. Oppressed
Example: Before the Civil War, most Black women were slaves and thus were *oppressed* and put down both because they were Black and because they were women.

6. Abolition
Example: While fighting for the *abolition* of slavery, many American women came to realize that they had no rights, just as the slaves had no rights.

7. Status
Example: In the beginning of the nineteenth century, women were only allowed in low *status* jobs such as domestic work, factory work, or teaching children.

8. Sphere
Example: In the 1800s, a woman's *sphere* was very restricted. She wasn't allowed to speak in public, to go to school, or to hold most jobs. Only church and home were considered proper places for her.

9. Franchise
Example: Elective *franchise,* or the right to vote, was denied to women until 1919.

10. Suffragist
Example: Those who fought to win the franchise for women were called *suffragists.*

Once students have tried their hand at defining the words, the class goes over the definitions and examples together, with the teacher answering any content questions and expanding on the history. (For ways to have students use the words, thereby familiarizing themselves with the new vocabulary, see "Techniques," p. 23.) The teacher should try, however, to make any self-guided exercises reflect the historical content.

3: The First Women's Rights Convention

Don't let Chauvinists step on you
If you want Bread and Roses too.

The U.S. Constitution, along with the Declaration
Have failed to announce the triumph
Of Women's Liberation.

In July, 1848, Seneca Falls,
In New York State,
The hall was filled with radical women
Who didn't like the way they were livin'.

To be a housewife didn't take much knowledge
So they never had the privilege of going to
    college.
And so Elizabeth Cady Stanton had
The Declaration of Sentiments Written.

Now even the Quaker, Lucretia Mott,
Who first cooperated, protested the lot.

A few years later, Lizzie met Susan
Who didn't dig the idea of women losin'.
So joined Ms. Stanton, who again hit the lantern
And got the women back movin'.

In 1869, twenty-one years past
The Suffragettes knew the men couldn't last.
So in Washington D.C. held parades and marched
    again
Bringing a climax to their campaign.

[Kenny Stewart]

The first women's right convention, held in
Seneca Falls, New York, in 1848, represents the
public beginning of the women's movement in
the USA. It is, thus, an appropriate first example
of women organizing themselves for students to
examine. These next three activities are designed
to make the convention and its demands come
alive for students, while simultaneously building
skills in reading and deciphering historical material. In this first activity of the series, students
read and translate the Seneca Falls Declaration.

The class starts by reading aloud the brief
introduction about the convention in *Feminism,
The Essential Historical Writings,* edited by
Miriam Schneier (pp. 76–77). It contains the important background information, but it is a little
dry; thus, the teacher should try to make it come
alive by filling in details. We've used pictures
from *The Fight for Freedom for Women,* by Rose
Tremain as a source of information for this. We
usually elaborate on the story of how Elizabeth
Cady Stanton and Lucretia Mott were excluded
from the World Anti-Slavery Convention in Lon-
don, in 1840, even after they had been sent there
as official delegates. We get students to imagine
how they must have felt when, after their long
journey across the ocean, they were told they
could be observers only. We pause after the
description of Stanton's growing discontent with
family life; we get students to think about how
much more work it was then to be a housewife
and mother, as everything had to be done by
hand. We tell students that of the three hundred
people who came to Seneca Falls, some had

traveled as much as one hundred miles, by
horse, over dusty roads, to get there.

With this background, students launch into a
reading of the Declaration. The beginning of the
document is modeled on the Declaration of Independence: "We hold these truths to be self-
evident: that all men and women are created
equal. . . ." It then moves into a listing of the injuries man has perpetrated toward woman. For
example: "He has made her, if married, in the
eyes of the law, civilly dead." The ending is a
series of resolutions, the most controversial being the demand that women should be given the
vote. All of the demands were passed at the
convention.

Students read the first two parts of the Declaration (up to the resolutions) together. The content is not difficult, given what students already
know about the position of nineteenth-century
women, but the language is, and so the teacher
should be careful to explain unfamiliar vocabulary, to translate into modern language whatever
students don't understand.

When they get to the resolutions, the class
stops, the resolutions are numbered, and each
student is assigned one to "translate"; i.e., to
write down in her own words. As students are
doing this, the teacher should circulate among
them, to give any needed help.

One resolution read in the original:

Resolved:
That the women in this country ought to be en-
lightened in regard to the laws under which they
live, that they may no longer publish their degradation by declaring themselves satisfied with their
present position, nor their ignorance, by asserting
that they have all the rights they want.

It became in translation:

Resolved:
The women of this country should know the laws
so they're not satisfied with their position or say
they have all the rights they want.

When the resolutions have been rewritten,
they are read in order, with each student reading
the one she rewrote. The teacher can ask for a

volunteer to copy down the translated resolutions onto a poster which can go up on the wall.

In discussing the resolutions, we usually focus on the one which said that it was the duty of women of the United States to secure their right to vote. We select this one because it was the most controversial and because it launched a long suffrage campaign. We remind students that this was the only resolution which wasn't unanimously passed, and that there had been disagreement among the campaign organizers about whether they should include such a radical demand. Several complex issues are involved here, and it is important that students get at least a basic analysis of the situation. We want them to understand that it was precisely because getting the vote seemed so important that there was a great deal of opposition to it. Tremain provides a helpful analogy when she says that to "resolve to campaign for direct political power was, in the 1840s, the equivalent of a prisoner asking his jailor for the key to his cell" (p. 25). But we also want them to see that, in the long run, getting the vote didn't insure women full social, economic, or even political equality. For that, we turn to the current situation and look at the fact that although women can vote, they don't necessarily have the choice of voting for feminists. We also draw on examples of legislation like the Equal Pay Act, discussed in "Women and Work," (p. 166), to show the difference between having a law on the books and having that law enforced.

4: Role-Playing Reactions to the Convention

In the second of this series of activities, doing a role-play shows students the range of reactions to the women's rights convention of 1848. Students are first asked to imagine what the reactions to the convention might have been from men and women. "I bet the men hated it!" was one response we remember. They are then given roles representing different positions people held in regard to the convention and told to imagine

themselves a group of commentators reacting to the convention, as TV often shows a group of people reacting to, say, a presidential speech.

The roles we've used are:

You are a woman who went to the convention because you were curious about it. It had an enormous effect on you. It made you think for the first time how unfairly women are treated. It made you want to fight for women to get the vote, to be allowed in more jobs, and not to be a slave to their husbands.

You are a newspaper editor, male, who thinks women's rights is hogwash. Your wife is content to wait on you, let you make decisions, etc. You think the women's rights movement will never get off the ground because most women are content as they are. You are planning to write an editorial in your paper about how the women who came to the convention were a minority who don't represent the feelings of most women.

You are an abolitionist, male, who believes both Blacks and women should have equal rights with white men. You didn't go to the convention, but support all the resolutions and plan to help in whatever way you can to help women get the vote. One of your plans is to defend women whenever the topic comes up in conversation.

You're a woman who believes a woman's place is in the home. That's the way God intended it, and that's the way it should be. You think most women would have booed and walked out of the convention. Women don't want the vote, you believe, because they don't know enough to vote. It's better that men look after them and vote for them.

You're a Black woman, born a slave, but freed in 1827. You feel strongly about both the Blacks' rights and women's rights. You don't think the women's movement should forget Black women, because the Black women, most of whom are slaves, are in the worst position of all. You plan to go to the next women's rights convention and talk about your feelings.

You are a lawyer, male, who doesn't think women should be allowed to be lawyers. You don't think they are logical enough. They're too emotional. You also don't think they should be allowed to go to college because their brains aren't strong enough.

You are a feminist who spent three days traveling by horse to get to the convention. You supported all the resolutions, although you think that the country isn't ready for the idea of women voting and worry that that resolution may hurt the women's rights cause. It inspired you to start thinking of ways to organize opposition to the fact that when married, women have no property rights. You plan to organize a petition campaign in your city.

We tell students that in doing the role-play, they should convey the information and attitudes described in their role cards. The teacher, as moderator, starts the role-play by interviewing the different participants about who they are and what they thought about the convention. to keep the discussion going after these initial introductions, the moderator should set up interactions between particular participants, turning to one and then another with statements like, "I bet you don't agree with that comment," or "What do you think of what he just said?" To review at the end, the students read aloud the roles they were given, and the teacher points out that the roles represent the different types of reactions people had to the convention (see "Techniques," p. 27).

We end this activity by reading together *The Fight for Freedom for Women* (pp. 27–31), which gives a brief description of the continued organizing of women inspired by the Seneca Falls Convention.

5: Today's Declaration

The last activity in this group involves looking at the Declaration of Sentiments in the light of today. The goal is to show students the need for an ongoing women's movement.

The students go back over the list of injuries to women cited in the Declaration. Their task is to reach some consensus about which of these still exist today, then to list those on the board. This process can be extremely revealing for students, especially if they haven't taken many women's courses, and we always allow as much time as necessary for discussion and debate. To help them reach a consensus, you can remind

them of what they've learned previously about the situation of women, or you can provide specific information. You should avoid, however, saying point-blank whether or not you think a problem still exists.

The students we did this with had already taken other women's courses; with minimal information from us, they supplied the following list of injuries, based on the original list in the Declaration of Sentiments:

1. Because most politicians are men, women still have to submit to laws in which they have no voice.
2. Women are still expected to obey their husbands.
3. Women still get jobs which pay less and hardly get into high status positions.
4. Women still have a subordinate position in church.
5. There is still a different code of morals for men and women.
6. The society still works to destroy women's self-confidence and self-respect.

The most controversial were numbers 2 and 6. Several students felt that the notion of women obeying their husbands was "old fashioned," while another said she thought you still had to, and that was why she'd never get married. Someone else added, in agreement, "that's how my mother acts." We pointed out that the traditional marriage ceremony, still used in most cases, unless the bride and groom specifically ask to have it omitted, contains the phrase ". . . promise to love, cherish, and obey". The final consensus was that the idea that women had to obey their husbands was changing, but did still exist. The disagreement about number 6 stemmed from its abstract nature; students had a hard time finding examples. As many had taken the "Women and Work" course, we referred back to the discussions in that unit for evidence of ways that society destroys women's self-respect. Among these, students had talked about women growing up with the belief that being mothers and housewives was all they could or should do, and then finding that these roles are devalued by the society. Recalling that earlier discussion gave students a better grasp of the sixth declaration.

Of the injustices that no longer held true, students were most interested in how radically divorce practices had changed. At the time of the Declaration, the man always had guardianship of the children in a divorce. We talked about how divorce, now, can be unfair to the man, who almost never gets even joint custody of his children.

A good follow-up might be to have students write their own "Declaration of Sentiments," designed for a Teen-age Women's Rights Convention. It should be done as a group writing assignment, modeled loosely on the Seneca Falls Declaration. The teen-age declaration could be read and circulated at the Women's Day which the group organizes or put in the Women's Newspaper (see Activity 15, p. 211).

6: Writing Reports and a Children's Book on Nineteenth-Century Feminists

The thing I liked best was reading and writing about Elizabeth Cady Stanton. She was "bad." [Annie Bithoney]

Students have been introduced to the women's rights movement. They now have a chance to learn more about the women who led the movement, through reading about, writing about, and reporting on one woman each. When the reports are completed, the group makes them into a booklet for younger children.

To prepare for this activity, the teacher draws up a list of nineteenth-century feminists, with a one- or two-sentence description of each. The list we used had as many women on it as there were students in the class. With a larger class, however, you could have more than one student write about each woman. We chose Elizabeth Cady Stanton, Susan B. Anthony, Emmeline Pankhurst, Lucy Stone, Mary Wollstonecraft, Amelia Bloomer, and Victoria Woodhull. Students used the short descriptions we wrote to help them choose the woman they wanted to report on. For instance:

Victoria Woodhull: She ran for President in 1874. She was a stockbroker. She and her sister published a radical weekly newspaper in which, among other things, they advocated free love.

Unless you want this an exercise in doing a research paper, you should try to find one or two short essays or excerpts on each woman. These can be hard to gather. A few good sources we found are: selections from the autobiography of Elizabeth Cady Stanton in Growing Up Female: Ten Lives, edited by Eve Merriam, the biography Elizabeth Cady Stanton, by Mary Ann Oakley; and, for primary sources, Feminism, The Essential Historical Writings, used in the previous activity. For choices beyond these, you would probably do best to spend an hour or so in the women's section of a bookstore, looking for well-written, interesting biographical material. It's important to keep the sections short so that student's don't get bogged down in the first part of this activity.

Once students have chosen the women they want to read about and have material to read, they are given a list of questions to answer, to help them focus their reading. Our questions were:

1. What kind of background did your woman come from (parents, where she lived, etc.)?
2. What did she believe women's roles should be in: marriage, work, intellect, relationships with men, appearance?
3. What did she do in her lifetime which demonstrated her belief?
4. How do you think other people viewed her?
5. Compare her beliefs or lifestyle to your own: How are you alike? How are you different?

You can either ask students to answer the questions, or you can ask them to use the questions as an outline for writing a one- or two-page report. In either case, you should caution students that they may not have the information necessary to answer all parts of all questions, and that's all right. We chose the report because we wanted the students to have practice in writing the type of paper which involves putting information together. We would suggest using a combination of class and homework time for completing the assignment (see "Techniques," p. 18).

To share the information, students read their reports, or talk about what they found out, to the class. (If you don't do the children's book, suggested below, it would be good to type up and distribute the reports, as well.) A good way to help students listen to each other is to tell them to start their report by describing how their woman seemed similar or different from the last woman reported on.

A final project, which serves to summarize what students have learned in both this and previous activities, is to put together a booklet about these nineteenth-century feminists for younger children. (If students have done the unit on "Early Socialization," they'll remember writing stories for children with an alternative sex-role message, p. 51.) The project is introduced by referring back to the first activity, and the discussion of why students hadn't ever heard of these women. This time, we ask whether they ever read books or saw TV shows about historical figures when they were nine, ten, eleven years old. The only stories our students could remember were about men (Abe Lincoln, Paul Revere, Davy Crockett). If students have done any of the Messages from Society activities in the first two units, they'll see right away what effect this exclusion of women would have. If not, the teacher should spend a little more time on it, talking about what you might think as a child if the only famous people you ever heard about were men. The students are asked to imagine how they might have felt if they had read a story about Susan B. Anthony, for example, when they were younger. The reactions we got ranged from "I wouldn't have cared; it would have been boring," to "I think I would have felt proud."

After this introductory discussion, the group as a whole plans the book. What age should it be for? Who would read it? Should there be an introduction? Should the reports be used as written or should they be revised? Should there be illustrations? Our class decided to have a brief story about the women's rights convention and then to have a section on each woman. They agreed that the reports should be revised slightly to make them shorter, or clearer, or more interesting, and that they should be directed toward a nine- or ten-year-old audience. They were interested in photographs—which were not feasible —but were not interested in illustrations.

It's best to allow class time for writing the booklet. If several students have done reports on the same women, you can have them work together on a composite children's biography. If the whole group spends time editing the stories, students will probably get bored, as they have already heard all the reports once. Thus, we divide the class up into pairs, and then each pair exchanges papers for comments. Each student then has to test her biography on a nine- or ten-year-old. Once everyone is satisfied with what they have produced, the different sections are mimeographed and stapled together.

When the book is finished, it's important for the teacher to help the class to find ways of getting their work to a reading audience beyond the classroom. We decided to give each student in the school a copy, with firm instructions to give it to their younger sisters and brothers. An alternative—which is harder to arrange, but more satisfying for the writers—is to visit and read stories to a fourth- or fifth-grade class.

Our completed section on Elizabeth Cady Stanton read:

Elizabeth Cady Stanton was born in New York in 1815. She remembered how sorry she felt for her little sister when she was born because when everyone saw the baby they'd say "Too bad it's a girl!" That was the first time she thought about women being considered inferior.

Her only brother came home from college and died. She remembered when she walked in the parlor, her father sitting there, pale and silent. She climbed on his lap. Her father put his hand on her shoulder and said, "My daughter, I wish you were my son." She told him she would try and be like a son instead of a daughter. She learned to be courageous and run with the boys, leaping fences. She figured that if she was like a boy, her father would be more satisfied with her.

As she got older, she realized how unfairly women were treated in those days. They weren't allowed to speak in public, or to go to college, or to vote. She started fighting to change these customs. Many men didn't approve of what she was doing, but many women did.

In the winter of 1852, Elizabeth's cousin visited her in Seneca Falls, where she lived. She was wearing a bloomer dress, which was sort of like wearing baggy pants. In those days all women had to wear long dresses, which made it very hard for them to move around. Elizabeth approved of this new style. She felt that women shouldn't have to wear high heels, long skirts and heavy underclothes, and that they should have the right to dress comfortably, and be able to move without pain.

Elizabeth became very well known for being a controversial speaker as well as a writer for the cause of women's rights. She worked with her friend Susan B. Anthony and put out a women's newspaper, *The Revolution,* for two-and-one-half years. She traveled all over the country, by horse, to try and convince people that women should be allowed to vote.

She died in New York City at the end of her eighty-seventh birthday. Today we know what a great woman she was. [Annie Bithoney]

7: What It Takes to Win

The Struggle for Suffrage

No matter how limited the direct effects of the Nineteenth Amendment might have been, it did mean the removal of an institutional insult to women, a removal accomplished by women. It did mean that women banded together to struggle against the established forces of society. That shared effort, that defiance of entrenched male authority, that glimpse of possible triumph, could and should become part of the consciousness of all women. [*From Parlor to Prison*, p. 29]

The Nineteenth Amendment, which granted women the vote, was ratified in 1920, seventy-two years after the Seneca Falls Convention. In this activity, students follow the women's movement into the fight for suffrage, focusing on the organizing strategies they utilized.

We have been lucky enough to know a woman who took part in that struggle, who has come to talk to our students. Florence Luscomb's personal account of working to secure women the right to vote, with its combination of facts and anecdotes, has always been a highlight of the course. In the absence of such a speaker, you can utilize oral histories, such as the oral history of Elizabeth Ellsworth Seiler, in *From Parlor to Prison*, edited by Sherna Gluck.

The reading is introduced by giving students a general picture of the suffrage movement. *From Parlor to Prison* contains an introduction and a chronology which the teacher can use as resource material. Interspersed throughout the book are reprints of newspaper articles from the period, reporting on and reacting to suffrage activities. You can choose several of these for the class to read together. Particularly interesting are those describing a suffragist picket of the White House (pp. 237–239) and the women's subsequent stay in jail (pp. 241, 246).

Films are also useful for providing students with the necessary background. We've used "Women on the March," a sixty-minute documentary, available from the Boston Public Library. If you're not showing a film, try to show your students some photographs of suffrage demonstrations, as these will give them a sense of the courage and determination of the women involved. *Shoulder to Shoulder*, edited by Midge MacKenzie, even though about the English suffrage movement, has a number of exciting photographs which we've used.

As it is too long to read in class, students read the interview with Ms. Seiler at home. We use this particular interview because it describes most fully the various organizing tactics of the suffragists. Ms. Seiler worked for the Women's Political Union (WPU), the most militant of the women's suffrage groups and the first to seek the support of working women. One of her jobs was to go into towns in New York state to find supporters for the suffrage cause, then to organize them into local chapters of the WPU. A standard tactic for gathering supporters was street-corner speaking. Ms. Seiler always chose the corner outside the local bar, because that was where you would get the largest audience. She spoke on a number of topics relating to women:

> I remember once going to make a speech somewhere and on the way up there on the train an idea occurred to me and I used it. I picked up a copy of the evening paper and held it up in front of them and took one headline after another and showed how the things talked about in that headline applied to women. I went all the way across the front page and there wasn't a single thing in the news in which women didn't have a stake. That was the thing we tried to get over. [P. 208]

In discussing the reading, we focus on the tactics the suffragists used, and ask students to consider how they would have gone about changing people's minds on an issue like women's suffrage. A good way to conclude the discussion is to read and react to Ms. Seiler's statement about the modern women's movement:

> It's very hard to compare the modern women's movement to the original suffrage movement because today's movement is so much wider and deeper than suffrage. That was really a political job and it was handled like a political job, more or less. This movement now, I think, springs from much, much deeper grounds. It involves really women's estimates of themselves and what they feel they could contribute to the world.
>
> I think that whereas women felt it definitely unfair that they couldn't vote, I think women now conceive of the inequality as something a great deal more serious than a personal affront. They realize it has a lot to do with the kind of world we have and the mess we're in and that the only valid hope for the future lies in true equality. [P. 221]

Having read this, students can be asked to share what they know or have heard of the modern women's movement and say whether they think it is similar to or different from the suffrage movement.

The Equal Rights Amendment

Equality of rights under the law shall not be denied or abridged by the United States or by any state on account of sex. [The Equal Rights Amendment, Section I, passed by Congress March 22, 1972.]

If passed by the states, the ERA will become the twenty-seventh Amendment to the U.S. Constitution. The ongoing struggle to get both federal and state Equal Rights Amendments ratified provides a modern parallel to the fight for the vote which students have just studied. In this activity, we draw that parallel by having a speaker from NOW come in and describe the amendment, its significance, and the attempts to organize both for and against it.

NOW is suggested as a resource because the national organization has been active in the struggle to get the ERA passed and because there are local chapters in most cities. It's important that the speaker from NOW be prepared beforehand for the level and interests of the students. She should know, for instance, that students are not likely to be at all familiar with the ERA, nor with the intricacies of how you get an amendment passed (see "Techniques," p. 31). We asked our speaker to focus on the following questions: What would the ERA mean for women? What is its present status? What are the blocks to getting it passed? How have women organized both for and against it?

Our speaker devoted her time to describing the effects the ERA would have in the areas of education, in family and domestic law, in financial matters, in criminal law, and in employment. Our students were most interested in the fact that all federally funded training and manpower programs would have to admit women equally, and that criminal laws which apply to one sex only would be nullified. Thus, prostitution laws would probably have to be extended to cover male prostitutes or would be dropped from the books. The speaker mentioned the present status of the federal amendment—thirty-four states have ratified it, four more must do so by March 1979—and said that given the ease with which the Congress had passed it, no one had guessed how difficult it would be to win state ratification. In describing the organizing efforts of both its supporters and its opponents, it became clear that the ERA's opponents—a lot of them women and insurance companies—were the better organized. A few students had heard scare stories about the ERA, as, for example, that it would result in integrated public toilets. We ended with a discussion about why these stories had been persuasive, and whether students felt there would be an ERA.

8: The Bravery of Black Women

Sojourner Truth and Harriet Tubman

> Harriet Tubman had one hell of a life from the day she was born to the day she died. I don't think my life was anything like hers, but if it was, I don't think I would have been able to cope with it. Harriet Tubman had a choice between liberty and death and I think her choice was a good one. [Colleen Long]

> My beliefs were somewhat like Sojourner Truth's. I feel men shouldn't think they own women, or think women don't know what they're talking about. She wanted to let her feelings out, so do I. I was different though. I wasn't a slave and I don't have to beg people to speak. I don't care, if I have to say something, I say it. [Jane Reale]

Black women have had to organize to fight both racism and sexism. At times their struggle has been waged for all Black people, at others it has been more specifically in behalf of Black women. Although the examples studied in these next two activities don't technically fall under the rubric of women organizing themselves, the struggles are too important to ignore; and, as they involve women organizers, they seem appropriate for this unit.

The activity opens by reading Sojourner Truth's "Ain't I a Woman?" speech, reprinted in *Feminism, The Essential Writings*. We use it because implicit in her speech is the demand that Black women, slave and free, be included in the women's movement.

> That man over there says that women need to be helped into carriages and lifted over ditches, and to have the best place everywhere. Nobody ever helps me into carriages, or over mud-puddles, or gives me any best place! And ain't I a woman?

Look at me! Look at my arm! I have ploughed and planted, and gathered into barns, and no man could head me! And ain't I a woman? I could work as much and eat as much as a man—when I could get it—and bear the lash as well! And ain't I a woman? I have borne thirteen children, and seen them most all sold off to slavery, and when I cried out with my mother's grief, none but Jesus heard me! And ain't I a woman? [P. 94]

Because the speech was given at a women's convention in Ohio, three years after the Seneca Falls Convention, this first reading is set in a context students have already become familiar with. The introduction to the speech should be read by all, however, because it gives biographical material, raises the issue of the connection between the abolitionist movement and the feminist movement, and sets an evocative scene. As the editor relates, "Many women were far from happy at seeing Sojourner Truth walk in, and begged the chairman not to let her speak, for fear that 'every newspaper in the land will have our cause mixed with abolition.' " The chairperson, Frances Gage, not only let her speak, despite the hissing from both men and women, but recorded her speech and described the effect it had:

> The simple moving words of Sojourner Truth had an effect on the gathering which Gage described as "magical." Beforehand, the ministers seemed to be getting the better of the women, much to the delight of the "boys in the gallery" but the speaker had "taken us up in her strong arms and carried us safely over the slough of difficulty, turning the whole tide in our favor." [P. 94]

After reading the speech, which is very short, students discuss what Sojourner Truth meant by "And ain't I a woman?" They are then asked two questions: "Do you think it was good that she was allowed to speak at the convention?" and, "How do you think she must have felt as a Black woman, talking before an all-white audience?" In discussing the first question, the point is made that the women's movement has to include Black women. As white students consider the courage it must have taken for Sojourner Truth to stand up and speak, they develop new empathy for their Black classmates. For Black students, answering the question offers a chance to project, and thus to describe, the discomfort they may feel if they are in a minority in the class.

The second part of the activity involves reading and discussing "The Courage of Harriet Tubman," by Marcy Galen, an article in *Ms.*, August 1973. Although there are many other sources of material on Harriet Tubman, we've used this article because it is exciting and moving, because it mentions her involvement with the feminist, as well as the abolitionist cause, and because it's a good length (three pages).

The article covers the better known aspects of Tubman's life as a slave and then as a conductor on the underground railroad:

> She often disguised herself as a stooped old woman, shuffling down a Southern road singing hymns. Those hymns were actually prearranged signals to would-be runaways; Who would suspect that the lame old woman with the cracked voice was the fierce Moses? She was known to sally forth from a watched house on the Underground Railroad, garbed as an elegant and heavily veiled lady, to enter a carriage crammed with runaways.

The article tells of Tubman's speaking out at suffrage meetings—once taking time out between speaking engagements to liberate a fugitive slave from a courtroom. It tells about her career as spy, scout, and soldier for the Union, with details about a raid she led, with a handpicked detachment of soldiers, who burned plantations and liberated over eight hundred slaves. There are descriptions of Tubman after the war, when she retired, sick and poor, as the government had never paid her for her wartime service, and details of the eventual award to her—twenty-five years later—of a meager pension, only because she was the widow of a Union soldier.

The teacher should introduce the reading by finding out how much students know about the history of slavery in America, filling in the basic details they've forgotten, or never learned. Questions we pose afterward, once students have had some time to react informally to the reading, are: "What made her take the risks she did?" and "Why wasn't her work for the government

rewarded?" The former leads into a discussion of how individuals sometimes put a cause above their personal life; the latter helps students to see another example of the very racism and sexism which Tubman devoted her life to fighting against.

The Civil Rights Movement

In this activity, the struggle of Black women is brought up to date by examining the civil rights movement. The reading is an excerpt from *Coming of Age in Missssippi,* an autobiography by Anne Moody, which recounts the life and politicization of a young Black woman. Coming from a poor, rural family, she worked her way through Tougaloo College, becoming involved with, and eventually an organizer in, the civil rights movement. The section we pick for students to read is the description of Moody's participation in a sit-in at Woolworth's in Jackson, Mississippi, in the early sixties. Passages like the following give students an idea of the odds Blacks were up against:

> The boy lifted Joan from the counter by her waist and carried her out of the store. Simultaneously, I was snatched from my stool by two high school students. I was dragged about thirty feet toward the door by my hair when someone made them turn me loose. As I was getting up off the floor, I saw Joan coming back inside. We started back to the center of the counter to join Pearlena. Lois Chafee, a white Tougaloo faculty member, was now sitting next to her. So Joan and I just climbed across the rope at the front end of the counter and sat down. There were now four of us, two whites and two Negroes, all women. The mob started smearing us with ketchup, mustard, sugar, pies and everything on the counter. Soon Joan and I were joined by John Slater, but the moment he sat down he was hit on the jaw with what appeared to be brass knuckles. [P. 266]

Those of us who haven't started to label what happened in the sixties as history are surprised to find out that our students know little about the civil rights movement in the South. Introducing the selection from *Coming of Age* thus involves filling in students both about Anne Moody and about the segregation that sparked the civil rights movement. We were able to do the latter in a particularly interesting way, because one of the staff members in the school, a Black from the South, had himself been involved in those struggles. The class in which we were going to read the Moody selection began with his descriptions of prohibitions against Blacks, as well as of his remembrances of early sit-ins, boycotts, and pickets.

As in the previous activity, the follow-up discussion should draw on both personal and political aspects of the reading. A way of leading into both is to ask students why they think Moody and the others decided to participate in the sit-in, even though they knew they would get hurt, or at least arrested. Reminding students of the previous discussions about what it takes to win, we then add sit-ins, pickets, and boycotts to our list of tactics—and briefly discuss each one. Lively supplements include playing a record of freedom songs and doing a role-play of a sit-in or a picket.

When we did this activity, we decided to act out a picket. Three-quarters of the students became picketers of a restaurant which refused to serve Blacks; the rest were potential customers. The picketers were instructed to dissuade people from crossing the picket line without touching them. The customers were told to react the way they thought they would if really faced with the situation of planning to eat at a restaurant which they then find is being picketed. One student went on into the restaurant, one started to go in and then stopped when faced with a picketer who said, "Don't go in there"; two others just stood back. Afterward, we asked both sides how they felt. "I felt stupid, walking around like that." "I got mad at that ignorant slob who went in anyway." "I knew I could walk through, but it kind of kept me back." "It made me mad, their trying to stop me."

We conclude by coming back to the reading from *Coming of Age* and looking at the following passage:

> After the sit-in, all I could think of was how sick Mississippi whites are. They believed so much in the segregated way of life they would kill to preserve it. I sat there in the NAACP office and thought of how many times they had killed when

this way of life was threatened. I knew that the killing had just begun. "Many more will die before it is over with," I thought. Before the sit-in, I had always hated the whites in Mississippi. Now I knew it was impossible for me to hate sickness. The whites had a disease, an incurable disease in its final stage. What were our chances against such a disease? [P. 267]

Asking the question, "Why would people kill to preserve a segregated way of life?" got our class into a discussion of how hard it is for people to change; this in turn led to talking about why there was so much resistance, among whites in South Boston, to having their schools integrated. (If students don't bring it up themselves, the teacher might want to mention school desegregation in the North as a comparison.) One white student, showing a new-found empathy, even remarked that the Black students who went into South Boston every day were almost as brave as Anne Moody and Harriet Tubman.

9: I Like to Think of Harriet Tubman

To tie together the last two activities, students now do a writing assignment which allows them to draw on whichever of the readings inspired them the most. We introduce the assignment by reading "I Like to Think of Harriet Tubman," a poem by Susan Griffin published in the anthology, *No More Masks*, edited by Florence Howe and Ellen Bass.

The poem opens:

> I like to think of Harriet Tubman.
> Harriet Tubman who carried a revolver,
> who had a scar on her head from a rock thrown
> by a slave-master (because she
> talked back), and who
> had a ransom on her head
> of thousands of dollars and who
> was never caught, and who
> had no use for the law
> when the law was wrong,
> who defied the law. I like
> to think of her.
> I like to think of her especially

when I think of the problem of
feeding children.
[p. 307]

The poet then describes the ways in which men do not take women seriously. So inspired by the poem was one of our students, that she chose to read it as her presentation when she graduated from The Group School.

After briefly discussing "I Like to Think of Harriet Tubman," we give students the following choices:

1. Write a poem about Anne Moody, Sojourner Truth, or Harriet Tubman which begins with the line, "I like to think of . . . ."
2. Describe the thought going through Anne Moody's head as she sat at the Woolworth's counter.
3. Put yourself inside Sojourner Truth's head and describe the way she felt at the women's rights convention and why she decided to speak.
4. If Harriet Tubman or Sojourner Truth were speaking at a women's rights convention today, what do you think they would say? Write their speeches.
5. Was there ever a time when, like Harriet Tubman or Anne Moody, you chose your friends (or relatives or community) over your own safety? Describe the situation.

As a long-range follow-up, we've given students the choice of reading either the rest of *Coming of Age in Mississippi* or reading *The Autobiography of Miss Jane Pittman,* by Ernest Gaines. The latter, which was made into a movie for TV which students may have seen, is a simply written, first-person account of a Black woman, born a slave, who walked North as a child after the Emancipation Proclamation. It is shorter and easier to read than *Coming of Age.* As it begins during the Civil War and ends during a civil rights demonstration in the early sixties, it connects the short readings students have done in the last two activities. We assign the books for two reasons. We want our white, as well as our Black, students to understand more about the history of Black women in this country. Also, since there is very little reading in the rest of the

unit, we want to encourage students to read a book outside of class.

10: Labor Organizing, Then and Now

"Women and Work," Unit VII, contains activities on labor organizers and organizing. Activities 4 and 5 of that unit introduce students to labor vocabulary and to nineteenth-century women organizers. Activities 12 and 15 look at two examples of current organizing of women—domestic workers and office workers. These activities were included in "Women and Work," rather than in "Women Organizing Themselves," because we feel that the examination of different jobs should be linked with the study of struggles to change those jobs. The activities work best as we have placed them, for both philosophical and pedagogical reasons. On the other hand, struggles to organize working women are crucial; and if students haven't done and won't be doing the "Women and Work" unit, the teacher may want to include a section on labor organizing here, using all, or some combination of, the activities from "Women and Work."

If you decide to do this, there are several considerations to keep in mind. There is already a good deal of history in this unit. Students might have little tolerance for studying nineteenth-century women labor organizers. Thus, you may want to include only one of the readings suggested in Activity 5 of "Women and Work," or skip all of them. If you want to use the activities about organizing among domestic workers or clerical workers, you will have to introduce some information about the work itself, so that the organizing drive isn't out of context.

In addition to the current organizing drives described in "Women and Work," students might be interested in the recent struggles of female flight attendants around their work. This struggle has been particularly interesting because their demands have been directed as much toward the sexist nature of the job as toward issues of pay, leave, etc. An excellent article to use about flight attendants organizing is "Coffee, Tea or Fly Me," by Lindsy Van Gelder, in the January 1973 *Ms.*

11: The Day No Women Went to Work

The recent women's strike in Iceland—a day in which a large number of women refused to do whatever they normally did in order to demonstrate their importance—inspired the following activity in which students brainstorm and then write about what would happen if women didn't go to work.

The emphasis in this activity is to have fun with the idea of a general women's strike; the message that women count and contribute will come through even if the subject is treated in a light, humorous vein. We introduce the idea by getting students to brainstorm about what would happen if women who usually went out to work, didn't go, and if women who usually stayed home, went out. Each student is given three minutes to list all the things that wouldn't get done. At the end of that time, the lists are shared with the class. The lists will probably be fairly general. We then get students to visualize specific situations: imagine what would happen to the telephones; imagine what would happen in the schools; imagine what would happen in your family. We also ask students what would happen to the men, how they think men would feel, having to take their kids to work with them or having to answer their own telephones.

Once students have warmed to the subject, they spend the rest of the class time writing about what would happen "The Day No Women Went to Work." They can be as general or specific as they wish to be, focusing on the whole country, on Cambridge, or on a particular family. Some might want to write from the point of view of a man, showing how he's affected by the strike. At the end of the class, students will enjoy sharing what they've written (see "Techniques," p. 20).

12: Women's Bulletin Board

In this activity, the class designs a bulletin board about women and begins an ongoing process of adding material to it. The goal is to introduce students to the current issues of the women's movement.

To generate topic headings (abortion, women and work, etc.), the teacher can suggest a few categories which relate to women today, and then ask students to add their own. The headings that resulted in our class were: "Women and Work," "Mothers," "Day Care," "Abortion," "Women in Sports," "Women in Prison," "Welfare," and "Sexism." The teacher might want to point out that all these are different aspects of the term, "the women's movement," which students have heard so often. Students then transfer these headings onto strips of colored paper and arrange them on a large bulletin board or on one wall of their classroom. Our students wanted to devote a wall to the project; they named it "The Women's Wall."

Once the board is set up, we give students a week's accumulation of newspapers and a collection of magazines like *Time, Newsweek,* and *Ms.* to look through. Their task is to find and read one article to put up on the board. At the end of the class, we discuss some of the articles students have found and devise a system for continuing to add to the bulletin board. What our class decided was that each student would add something to the wall every week, and that once a week we would take part of a class to discuss the new material students had brought in.

13: Women Organizing Around You— Discussion Goups

Many women have gotten involved in the women's movement through participation in women's discussion groups. These groups, which usually result in a raising of feminist consciousness, or at least a feeling of solidarity, represent one of the ways in which women have begun to organize themselves. In this activity, a speaker is used to tell students what a women's group is all about. (See "Techniques," p. 31, for a general description of ways to find a speaker and prepare the speaker and the students.) For this activity, you should look for a speaker who feels she has changed through being in a women's group and who, ideally, has become involved in other kinds of women's projects, such as the ones to be examined in the next activity.

We prepare students by having them imagine what women might talk about in a women's group. One way to do this is to have the students go around in a circle, each one naming a topic she thinks would come up. If some of your students are in a discussion group, as are many of the Group School students, you could ask instead what kinds of things they talk about and how that might be the same or different from what older women would talk about. Then, referring to the topics mentioned, we ask how they think it might help women to have a chance to talk about these things with other women. Again, if students have been in a discussion group themselves, you could ask why they joined and what they got out of it. Another good question is, "Does it make any difference that the groups are only women?" At the end, the teacher adds whatever she can to the discussion, from her own experience with women's groups. We usually point out that women's groups have shown women that others share their feelings; such groups have given women the courage to try to change situations in their lives which keep them from being happy.

To help summarize after the speaker, you can raise the question of why the subject of women's groups should be included in a course on women organizing themselves. If you have the time to help your students get into discussion groups with other young women outside the school, or to help get a women's discussion group started in the school, a good way to end the activity is to ask students whether they'd be interested in being in a discussion group themselves. (See p. 125 for a description of how to set up a discussion group.)

14: Women Organizing in Your Community—Trips and Speakers

One of the positive effects of the modern women's movement has been the emergence of services and businesses directed to women. Women's clinics, restaurants, day-care centers, bookstores, rape crisis centers, and publishing companies, organized and staffed by women, have arisen in the last ten years in cities across the country. In this activity, students examine local examples of such institutions through a combination of trips and speakers.

The activity involves two to four trips or speakers, depending on time and on what's available in the community. The trips and speakers expose students to many of the issues being addressed by the modern women's movement. Students are given glimpses into the ways women have worked together to organize something they believed in, and the problems and successes they found. The activities provide students with models of women who are running their own institutions. And, finally, the trips or speakers acquaint students with services in their communities that they may want to use at some point in their lives.

If possible, the trips and speakers should represent different areas of concern. For instance, we probably wouldn't visit both a women's medical clinic and a counseling center for women, because they address themselves to a similar problem—the need for better health care for women. We have taken students to a day-care center, a women's health project, and a woman's bookstore. We have invited speakers from a rape crisis center and a women's prison rights group. If we feel that seeing the location of the project will have impact, we try to arrange to go there; if not, we invite a representative to come into the class to speak. In either case, we look for someone who was involved in initially organizing the service and ask her to describe how it got started, as well as how it currently operates.

We use the same approach for all the trips or speakers. We spend time beforehand looking at the need the service is filling and having students think of questions they want to ask. In the class afterward, students react to what they've seen and heard and compare the service with others they are familiar with. Especially if students have liked the place and think they might go there themselves, we might end by having the group write an article on it for the school newspaper or by having each student describe the service to some women they know in their neighborhood.

An example of the approach we use in studying women organizing in the community is contained in the following description of a trip we took to the Somerville Women's Health Project, a free medical clinic for the women of Somerville, Massachusetts.

The day before the trip, we talked with students about their experiences with doctors, particularly those consulted in gynecological matters. Although some students had doctors they liked, many seemed generally afraid of any medical procedure. "I faint whenever I get a shot." "I freak whenever I go near a hospital." To our surprise, a lot of the students had never gone for a gynecological examination or knew what a Pap test was. One student commented, "I don't like a man poking around in there." When another said that her doctor was a woman, someone else said, "I'd feel even funnier having a woman do it." However, when we asked them whether they'd see any advantage in a clinic for women only, one student said, "I can see that, you could be more comfortable," and others agreed. Students read excerpts we had selected from the "Women and Health Care" section of *Our Bodies, Ourselves*, by the Boston Women's Health Book Collective (pp. 337–374). After reading from the part on alternative forms of health care, we told students we were going to visit the Women's Health Project; we asked each one to think of one question that she wanted answered. Some of the questions were: "Do you need your parents' permission to get the pill?" "Is it really free?" "Are the doctors all women?" "What happens if a man comes into the clinic?"

A staff member from The Group School who volunteered at night at the Health Project as a lab technician came along on the trip with us. Before we met with the woman who was scheduled to talk with us, the staff member gave students a tour of the clinic and showed them how some standard laboratory tests were done. Students were surprised that their English teacher could do a blood and pregnancy test herself.

A working-class women who had been one of the original organizers of the clinic then spoke to us. She described how the clinic worked: it provided free medical care for the women and children of Somerville, with the focus on preventive care. Only women worked there, and all the nurses and doctors volunteered their time. Among other sevices provided, they had a weekly teen-age medical night, where teen-age women came for sex education, gynecological examinations and birth control. She also gave some of the history of the organizing of the clinic and described some of the recent problems between members of the staff. From the beginning, one of the major goals of the Health Project had been that it be run by working-class women from the community; this had caused some tensions.

In talking afterward, students said that they had been confused by the description of the staffing struggle within the clinic; we talked about the problem of who runs services for working-class people. We compared the situation to current struggles in The Group School around class and staffing issues. It was clear, however, that students had liked the atmosphere of the clinic. "It didn't seem like the doctor's at all!" "Everyone was so friendly." Seeing the way certain medical tests were done was a demystifying process. "Now I know what they're doing when they take your blood." Because our students aren't from Somerville, they couldn't use the Health Project themselves, but, as one student said, "I'm just glad I got to see a women's clinic. I didn't know they existed." Another added, "Why don't we have something like that in Cambridge?" We said that we thought that there was a women's clinic in Cambridge that had just opened, and the class ended with a plan to go together to visit this new clinic.

15: Students Organizing

Students have looked at a number of examples of women organizing themselves. Now it is important that they get a chance to become the organizers. This activity describes three projects which involve students in planning and organizing: a women's day in their school, a women's newspaper, and a strategy for changing discriminatory practices in their school or community.

Ideally, the group should develop either the women's day or the women's newspaper, depending on which interests them most and which seems most feasible, and then work on the strategy for changing something that affects their lives as women. The three projects, described below, it should be noted, were all generated from students' suggestions. In discussing them, if your students come up with an alternative, by all means adopt it. The goal of the activity is to give students a chance to organize something that they, as young women, feel is important.

Organizing a Women's Day in the School

Having a women's day gives students a chance to share their new women's consciousness with other young women and men in the school. It works best as a culmination of several units in the curriculum, because the day is most successful when students can draw on a variety of issues arising from being female. The process of organizing the day gives students experience with the following factors common to most organizing efforts: how to set up an event; how to raise other people's consciousness; how to get people to participate. Because the form the day takes will be determined in part by the nature of your school, preparation for a women's day in both a small and a large school is considered in the following description.

The process of preparing for the day is basically the same, regardless of the size of the school. The teacher should allow plenty of time for discussion and planning, first with the whole class, then with students in specific task groups. The teacher's role is to help students to be the planners.

It's good to start by talking about the purpose of having a women's day. "Showing the boys," "to get other girls to join the class," were some of the reasons our students gave. This usually leads into considering who the day is for. The first women's day we had at The Group School was very much directed at the young men. In planning the second one, two years later, a different group of students directed a number of activities toward their mothers and other mothers in the school.

Brainstorming about what could happen during the day is the next step. A good way to generate ideas is to get students to review what special events they liked best, and learned most from, in any of the women's courses they have taken. Particular films, speakers, trips, role-plays will be mentioned, and can be listed on the board. Before making any decisions, the group also lists what they've produced that they can share with other students. The teacher can point out that almost all the "products" can be used in one way or another. Posters, collages, and charts can be displayed as publicity for the day, as well as during it. The children's books, poems, and stories can be shared. The "Teen-Age Women's Declaration of Sentiments" (see p. 200) could open or close the day. Any film or video-tape students have made would certainly be a highlight. Once the two lists are made, the class can begin to decide which events they want included, drawing from the lists or from new ideas that have arisen. These decisions are only tentative, as students at this point don't know how long the day will be or what's available in terms of films, speakers, etc.

The group next considers the structure of the day. Where should it take place? How long should it be? Should there be classes going on at the same time or should they be canceled? Even though the structure will be largely influenced by what's possible in the school, it's good to let students figure out ideally what they would like. They can then work from there to fit the ideal into the reality of the school. Comments like "They'd never let us do that" lead into another major issue: how to get the day approved in the school. Even in a small school, students won't be sure who they have to get permission from, and the discussion becomes a valuable lesson in how decisions are made in the school.

When these general issues have been considered, it's time to break down into committees or work groups, with students choosing specific tasks. You could have a publicity committee, a permissions committee (which the teacher should be on), a schedule committee, and committes to plan, order, or arrange each of the events students want. Clearly, the committees will be interdependent: you need to know the schedule to arrange for a speaker; you need to know whether a given film is available, before you start making posters to publicize it. To facilitate the necessary sharing of information, the committees can meet during part of the class and then come back together at the end, to share their ideas, plans, or information.

Two basic models for a women's day in a small school can be seen in the two very different women's days we've had at The Group School. The first day drew almost entirely on student resources. The anthropological film students had made on growing up female in America (see Unit III, p. 99) was premiered. Volunteers acted out role-plays which the students had devised, all of them involving males playing females, and vice-versa. (To break the ice, the two drama teachers at the school had been coached to volunteer for the first role-play). Some of the role-plays involved groups. For instance:

Females play males: You are all in the gym in one corner and you are trying to impress each other with how "bad' you are, especially in relation to females. One male says he is into it, but he really isn't; another thinks he is real fine.

Males play females (gossip): You are all in a hallway getting high, talking about dating. One female isn't into it; two like the same male; one is easy with sex.

Others were paired role-plays:

Male plays female: You are playing a female who is pregnant and you have to go to your boyfriend and tell him. You've been going out with him for one-and-one-half years.

Female plays male: You have been going with your girlfriend for one-and-one-half years. You think you're in love with her, but you're not sure. She has just come to you with a problem.

After each of these role-plays, members of the audience of the sex being portrayed were asked to comment on the accuracy of the portrayal.

Other highlights of that first day included a lunch which the male students and teachers

cooked, and a Sadie Hawkins Day Dance, in which the females asked the males to dance. The original plan had been that during the dance, each young woman would ask one of the young men out on a date (they had drawn names from a hat), but as far as we remember, that didn't actually happen. All classes were canceled for the day; the activities took place one at a time in the central lounge; and most of the students and staff participated.

The second women's day, in contrast, drew primarily on outside resources, and most of the events were new to students in the class. What they had done was to gather into one day many of the people and films they had heard about during the term and wanted to see. Denise Levertov came and read poetry. Florence Luscomb (see p. 203), came in and gave her talk on how she participated in the struggle to get the vote for women. The films, *Growing Up Female: As Six Become One,* and *Men's Lives* were shown, as was a slide-show about women in prison. The day ended with a dinner and a concert from the Red Basement Singers, a Boston area, all-female group. The schedule of events and times was posted throughout the school, and students in the school were expected to come into the assembly room for things they were interested in. A number of mothers came along with their daughters and added greatly to both the events and the feeling of that day.

In retrospect, thinking about a women's day in a school such as ours, we feel that a day combining elements from both models would be most successful. A day that depends entirely on the participation of students suffers if few students are drawn to it. A day that depends entirely on speakers and films allows the participants to become too passive; after two or three of the events, many students drift off. If you call off all the classes, some students won't come into school at all. Thus, it seems better to have classes in the morning, but to leave the afternoon free. Other young women in the school are generally interested in the women's day and come readily. It takes a lot of energy, on the other hand, to get either the males or the mothers to participate. For either group, the more personal the invitation, the more likely they are to come.

Having a women's day in a large public high school becomes more complicated, although many of the suggestions made above are applicable. A suggested structure is to have events happening all day in one room, with, ideally, a separate room set aside for showing films continuously. Students can come see the events during their free periods; and teachers, if they choose, can bring their whole class to any of the events. Widespread publicity and cooperation from the teachers throughout the school are both necessary to make this structure work. Posters of schedules of events should be in evidence throughout the school. The planners should spent time beforehand talking to teachers from different departments, gathering suggestions for events, encouraging teachers to announce the women's day in their classes, and urging them to bring their classes to the various events. As students in the group will probably be too shy either to read their writings to to do role-plays, the day will probably rely mainly on outside resources. One suggestion is to make the events as varied as possible and include some active ones, like a women's karate demonstration.

If the all-day structure is not feasible, given the school or the energy level, a more modest offering is also worthwhile. The students might be able to plan and run one women's assembly. Or they might be able to get permission to use homeroom time for a day, or for a week, for events related to women.

In both small and large schools, some time should be set aside after the women's day for the students to react to, and reflect upon, their first organizing attempt. "Did you see the way Henry got into playing the pregnant girl?" "The film was dynamite!" "I thought more girls would have come." The teacher has to be sensitive to the fact that some students may feel that the day was a bust, or be disappointed that more students didn't come, or just feel let down now that it's over. It's important, therefore, to stress the positive occurrences of the day, and to focus on what the students themselves got out of organizing it.

Putting Out a Women's Newspaper

Like organizing a women's day, putting out a women's newspaper allows students to express their feelings and thoughts about what it means to be a young woman. Again, the project works best as a culmination of several units in the curriculum, because students will have material they have already written, to draw upon.

The process of producing the newspaper and getting feedback in order to evaluate the first issue is fully described in Unit IX, "Women's News," Activities 3 and 6. If the class decides to do this project, the teacher should refer to those two activities. If the newspaper is produced in the context of this unit, you will want to focus on its possibilities as a vehicle for raising consciousness. The teacher can remind students that Elizabeth Cady Stanton and Susan B. Anthony published a women's newspaper, called *The Revolution*, for two and one-half years. Copies of *Ms., The Spokeswoman, Women Today* and other current women's journals should be on hand for students to look through. Questions to pose in an initial discussion are: "Why do women want to put out women's newspapers?" "What good does it do?" As students begin planning the newspaper, they discuss each possible article in terms of what effect it might have on readers. The goal is to have students see their newspaper as a vehicle for expressing their ideas, thereby affecting other people.

Developing a Strategy for Change

This project involves several steps. Students identify institutions that are discriminatory or practices they want changed in their school and community; for example, lack of money for a women's sports program, a teen center with no programs for women. They next choose one problem situation and outline a strategy for changing it. If possible, they then proceed to carry out that strategy.

The purpose of this final project is to build student consciousness of conditions which adversely affect them as young women, allowing students to pull together what they've learned about organizing. The last phase of the project, which involves actually organizing, is optional. The advantages of carrying out the strategy that students outline are that it will teach them how to fight for change, and students' efforts may bring positive results for themselves and other young women. However, to organize, students will need ongoing support outside of class and you may find yourself in a difficult position with the administration of the school. It is better to decide beforehand what you want to do and to explain the project in those terms.

The project starts by having students list ways they believe their school either discriminates against them or fails to provide services from which they might benefit. Items which might arise include: lack of a women's program, a particular teacher who puts down female students, a restrictive dress code, being barred from certain vocational courses, insufficient numbers of or unsympathetic counselors.

Next, students make a similar list about their community. Things our students mentioned about their Cambridge neighborhoods were that there was no place they could go for birth control without parental permission; that there were no childcare facilities near them (resented because so many ended up having to care for younger children); and that there was no shelter or halfway house where teen-age women could take refuge if they had to get out of their own homes.

This first class ends with a general discussion of what it would take to change the conditions listed. The students' first responses will be pessimistic: "No way." "They don't care about us." "Why bother?" Specific questions can help them get beyond their negativism, giving them practice in analyzing how change can be brought about in policies or institutions. Questions to pose include: "How could you show people that the situation has to be changed?" "Is there a law which has to be changed first, or is the law on your side?" "Who could you put pressure on?" "How would you get support of other people?" "How many people do you need behind you to be effective?"

At the next meeting, students choose one issue that they want to work on. The choice can be made on the basis of which issue students feel most strongly about, or on the basis of which would be easiest to change. If the group is going to carry out its strategy, an issue within the school is probably most manageable.

When the issue has been picked, each student maps out a strategy for changing the situation. You can either ask them to list all the things they can think of which would help to bring about this change, or you can give them a more structured set of questions, similar to the ones posed as the group considered each problem initially listed. Allow ten or fifteen minutes for students to brainstorm by themselves, then compile all the answers on the board. The group as a whole next chooses what they think are the best ideas and decides on an order of implementation.

The following is a completed strategy for change which our students drew up around the demand that the school provide an office-skills training program:

1. Plan out an office-skills program, maybe with the help of Judy [the jobs counselor] or the academic committee.
2. Talk to all the girls in the school and get the names of all those interested.
3. Talk to Steve (head of Board of Directors and a staff member) about getting our proposal on Board agenda.
4. Get as many girls as possible to come to the Board meeting and present the proposal.
5. Get Board to agree to hire somebody to teach office skills or to find the money to hire somebody.
6. If the Board says no, call a community meeting to discuss it.

To carry out the strategy, different tasks can be assigned to small work groups. Class time should be taken on an ongoing basis to report on and discuss what's happening. If the group doesn't plan to do actual organizing, a good way to end the project is to write an article for either the school or community paper which explains the problem and then gives the plan for changing it.

NOTES TO THE TEACHER

Teaching History

Teaching the historical parts of this unit can be problematic. You may feel inadequate to teach women's history because, like so many of us, you never learned any yourself. Remember that you don't have to be an expert. In fact, your lack of background can be an asset in helping to set a tone of "learning this together"; and your own excitement, as you discover what women have done, can inspire students. On the other hand, it isn't easy to teach when you feel you don't know enough to answer questions or to elaborate on whatever students are reading. Doing some general reading before you start teaching the unit will help. A number of good texts are available, several of which are mentioned in the unit.

You may also become discouraged by students' lack of response. Even nontraditional history is somewhat abstract; and no matter how valiant an effort you make to enliven it with oral histories, role-plays, supplementary projects, etc., some students will remain uninterested. As long as you give students as much help as possible with the reading and provide a number of different entry points into the discussions, don't worry. You can't interest all students all of the time; different sections of the unit will inspire different students. It is also important for you to realize that some students may be learning a good deal, but not demonstrating or verbalizing that fact at the moment. Our experience is that if students are attending the class, then they are learning. We have seen many "passive" students demonstrate their mastery of some set of facts or skills months after we had concluded that they weren't interested in the class and weren't learning enough. One student, who sat quietly through the first two-thirds of "Women Organizing Themselves," ended up teaching an entire class on Harriet Tubman in an American history class she was taking the next semester.

Facilitating Students' Working Together

In the last section of this unit, students are asked to organize major projects, a process which involves both planning and working together. The teacher's role in this organizing process is a difficult one. It is easy to say that your role is to help students make and carry out their plans; in practice, it is hard to figure out when to push and when to sit back. If you make too many suggestions and do too much arranging, students won't get the chance to organize something themselves; and the women's day or the newspaper won't reflect their concerns. If you are determined to have students do everything, the project will probably never get off the ground. We try to strike a balance. When the class is brainstorming about possible events or articles, we make suggestions, too; but we do it after the students have had a chance to generate some ideas, so that our suggestions don't overshadow theirs. If students have decided, for instance, that they want to invite a certain speaker for the women's day, but balk at actually making the necessary phone call, we will do it for them, recognizing that shyness is holding them back. Above all, the teacher has to provide energy and enthusiasm when students get discouraged or bogged down. There is at least one low point in every project, when students want to give up. At that point we step in and do whatever we can to ease the difficulty and reinvolve students, even if it means that temporarily we are doing a lot of the work ourselves.

Certain problems invariably arise which keep students from working well together. The kind of intervention the teacher makes is crucial. For instance, students will want to divide into work groups on the basis of friendship. As they look around the room to see who else is raising her hand for a particular task, at least one student is likely to feel isolated. We always encourage students who aren't part of specific friendship groupings to join a committee that has on it one or more people who are generally friendly to everyone in the class. Beyond that, we don't make an issue of this tendency to want to work with one's friends. We focus on the different tasks that have to be done and let students group themselves.

The work groups may have trouble being serious and focused when the teacher isn't present. Especially if the committee is a group of close friends, a work session can easily degenerate into a gossip session. One of the ways around this is to circulate among different groups as they're meeting, offering encouragement and suggestions. Another way is to have the groups come back together at the end of each class to report to each other on what they have found out or decided.

As the groups do start working, anger may arise over the inevitable fact that students have different levels of commitment to the project. "Why should I do all this if they never come?" is a sentiment sometimes expressed and frequently felt. Another complaint may be, "Why don't you ask her to do it; she never does anything!" We encourage everyone to participate by giving small groups of students important tasks and, in some instances, by hand-tailoring jobs for specific students. We find ways to recognize both publicly and privately the hard work an individual student is doing. But we also legitimize different levels of commitment. After recognizing her work, one of the ways we might respond to a student is to say, "It's true, you're doing more than the others, but it's because you're more interested. You also get more out of it."

IX: WOMEN'S NEWS

OVERVIEW

Many young people find the media presentation of current issues inaccessible and uninteresting. They do not see how any of these distant events concern them. Young women, especially, have been socialized to confine themselves to very immediate personal or familial concerns. And they see these as private, of no interest to anyone else.

The goal of this unit is to develop a new and different conception of "news." Students work on producing their own women's newspaper or women's news show that bridges public and private concerns. They examine current issues in the news that are of direct relevance to women; they explore the ways these connect to their own lives. And, at the same time, they look at the ways issues, events, and experiences in their own lives could be of interest to other young people.

This unit is action- and outreach-oriented. many of the other units help students experience their world with new eyes and ears. Now they are asked to communicate that awareness to other young people in a way that will entertain, interest, and educate them. Producing a women's newspaper or news show will help students connect their learning inside of class to their world outside of class. It will help them see themselves as having ideas worth communicating, and see what they are learning as having a relevance and usefulness that goes beyond the classroom or the course.

Although this unit can be taught at any time in the curriculum, it is recommended as an especially good way to complete a term or a course focusing on women. If students have already explored other women's themes, they will be able to draw material for their articles from the surveys, questionnaires, trips, speakers, writing and reading assignments from other units. This unit will also give them a chance to review and utilize skills taught in earlier assignments. In reporting the news, they will utilize skills in observation, categorizing, summary, and interpretation. The unit can, however, stand by itself. In that case, the students draw their material from current events, experiences in their own lives, and new investigations and interviews; and they focus on learning new skills in journalistic writing and editing.

The first activity is a microcosm of what's to come. Students plunge right into creating a ten-minute women's newscast. Drawing material from newspapers, personal experiences, completed class projects, and writing assignments, each student contributes one brief item to the whole. In the next activity, everybody focuses on a major news event concerning women. The class examines newspaper articles about this event, both for the issues they raise and for the bias in the way the content is presented. The class then begins to make decisions about what content to include and what biases to reflect in their own news production. Individuals work on their articles or stories, with support from each other and the teacher. Class time is spent on exercises that stretch people's expository writing skills and on discussions of the content issues raised by different people's articles. Once the newspaper is distributed, or the news show presented, students interview members of their "audience" for feedback and criticism. Finally, they produce a second newspaper or news program.

Many of the activities in this unit could be integrated into current events courses or current events units of history courses. Usually, when current events lessons are done in the classroom, the focus is very much on men in the news. It would be an interesting addition to such courses to have students explore "women's news."

ACTIVITIES

1: Women's Newscast

This activity gets everyone started—both on thinking about the issue of what should be considered women's news and on producing something together. The task is to use one or two class periods to come up with a short, ten- or fifteen-minute women's newscast, comparable in format, but not in content, to the daily news programs on TV.

The familiar structure of a newscast provides many different entry points to students with varying interests and skills. Besides the featured news stories, the daily newscast generally includes a community report, an entertainment report, a sports report, and the weather. Sometimes there are special features, such as a fashion report, or a "news item of special local interest," or a human interest anecdote. and, of course, there are advertisements. Students can choose among any of these categories.

Some students might feel most comfortable leafing through a few current newspapers (brought in for this purpose by the teacher) to find interesting articles concerning women. They can rewrite one of these items in a shortened, newscast style. Others might want to look through folders of previous writing assignments to find those that they would like to contribute for their report. Another possibility is to pick up on survey or interview results from previous assignments and work these into a short newsworthy item. Or, students might want to report on something that happened to them recently, like

an incident with the police, or an event in their neighborhood.

Students need about ten minutes to choose their stories. During that time, the teacher moves around the room helping individuals to formulate ideas or select materials to use. A list is then put on the board of what the women's newscast will include. At this point, the class can choose an anchorwoman and decide on the order of items. Should Carole's poem come first? Or should the report on the abortion trial? When should the sports report be given? Alternatively, these decisions can be left to the anchorwoman's discretion.

After these decisions are made, everybody gets back to work for fifteen or twenty minutes to prepare their comments. If some students finish early, they can help others with more complicated stories, or help set up the room for the newscast, making props like signs saying "Newsroom" or "Eyewitness News."

When everyone is ready, the newscast can begin. If your school has equipment, it would be very good to audio- or video-tape the newscast. Since everyone is a participant, it will be hard for students to reflect on the content or presentation during production. Having a record of the newscast will be useful in the follow-up discussions and will give students something concrete to refer to as they reflect on what is appropriately included in women's news. The finished product will also help students feel proud of what they accomplished in so short a time. Our students have always been amazed at how good their newscast looks and sounds on video-tape (although most students claim to think they look hideous on the screen). Just seeing themselves on a television screen, announcing the news, gives an added legitimacy to the whole activity. An audio-tape, although less dramatic, serves the same basic function. If neither is available, you might want to invite in a few people as the viewing audience.

Our student newscasts have included items as diverse as a report (garnered from the newspaper) on an abortion trial; the results of a previous survey of articles found in women's magazines; a poem, written by one student and read by another, about street life in Cambridge; a review of the movie, "Alice Doesn't Live Here Anymore"; a weather report in which the weatherwoman put on increasing layers of outer garments as she moved from South to North on the map; and an advertisement for diet cola in which the participants all simulated "throwing up." Having completed the newscast, students are asked to review its content and compare it to a regular daily news show on TV or radio. "How was this newscast different?" "Which items would not have been included on the regular news? Why not?" "How do TV or radio commentators decide what to include?" "What type of audience would most appreciate the class's newscast?"

Students who are not particularly interested in TV or radio news, or in the daily newpaper, can use this time to get out their views: "The news is boring." "They never say anything I'm interested in." "Half the time I don't even understand what they're talking about." Having seen that they can create an interesting, entertaining newscast of their own, students feel less intimidated by traditional news presentations and more legitimate in their criticisms. They, too, have become "newsmakers."

2: Exploring a Current Issue

In this activity, students move from creating their own version of the news to looking at issues currently in the "official" news. The object is for students to explore a current issue in some depth, finding the ways this issue connects to their own interests and experiences, evaluating the ways the issue is presented by various news media.

We generally try to select major, ongoing controversial issues—such as abortion or rape—that are frequently treated in the newspapers. For instance, abortion has been very much in the news for the past several years, starting with articles on the liberalization of abortion laws which cul-

minated in the Supreme Court ruling of 1973; and, more recently, there have been articles chronicling the swing back to a more conservative, "right to life" position. In Boston there were numerous interesting articles, written from many points of view, about the trial of Dr. Kenneth Edelin, charged with manslaughter (and convicted) for performing an abortion on a woman three months pregnant. Rape has also been a current issue because of several major trials of women who killed men involved in raping them. The trial of Inez Garcia, who killed a man she alleged had just raped her, and the trial of Joan Little, who killed the jailor she alleged was raping her at gunpoint in her North Carolina cell, raise controversial questions about "justifiable homicide," as well as about rape.

The teacher's effort should be to select an issue that affects the students' lives. By checking through several newspapers for a week or two before this unit, the teacher can find a number of different articles about the issue, ranging from straight news reporting to features or editorial comments. The selected articles should be copied in sufficient numbers to hand out to the students.

The class begins its investigation of a current issue by reading over a descriptive news article together, Many students have difficulty reading a newspaper, because of the print size or because of difficulties with the vocabulary. It is probably best to stop at the end of each paragraph, go over the vocabulary, and summarize. By calling on students to help each other, and giving explanations or definitions when they cannot, you can help students through paragraphs that ordinarily would discourage them from reading the rest of an article. This exercise will both give students the necessary informational background about the issues and improve everyone's skills in deciphering journalistic style.

If it is necessary, the teacher can fill in additional information, not covered by the news story. With this background, the students can begin to form their own opinions about the issue under discussion. Should abortion be legalized, or not? Is it justifiable for a woman to kill some-one who has tried to rape her, or not? After a short debate on questions like these, it is good to hand out an article or two that present the differing viewpoints. These can be news articles or editorials. The debate in the paper can enrich and enlarge the debate in the class and lead to interesting writing assignments and further discussion.

Several years ago, when we studied the issue of abortion, we found a natural starting point in an article outlining the Supreme Court ruling of 1973:

> Women may obtain an abortion within the first six months of pregnancy and the states cannot prevent them from doing so, the U.S. Supreme Court ruled yesterday.
>   . . . the court balanced the personal "right of privacy" of women not to bear children with the states' "compelling interest . . . in the potentiality of life" on a scale calibrated to the length of the pregnancy. [*Boston Globe*, January 27, 1973]

We asked our students to agree or disagree, first with the decision itself, and then with the reasoning behind it. Should the Supreme Court have decided to legalize abortion? For any length of pregnancy? Would you base your decision on the woman's right to privacy? The overall reaction of the class to the Supreme Court ruling was one of affirmation of the woman's right to make decisions about her own body. "It's her life." "Nobody can tell her what to do with her body." Knowing many of our students to be of Catholic background and upbringing, we were somewhat surprised by the uniformity of this opinion.

To expose them to the opposing arguments, we gave out an article presenting statements issued by Cardinal Cooke, Roman Catholic Archbishop of New York, and John Cardinal Krol, Archbishop of Philadelphia:

> How many millions of children prior to their birth will never live to see the light of day because of the shocking action of the majority of the United States Supreme Court today? [Cardinal Cooke]

> The child in the womb has the right to life, to the life he already possesses, and this is a right no court has the authority to deny. [Cardinal Krol]

This time there was unanimity of response. Remembering personal experiences with Catholic morality, many students disagreed vehemently with the Cardinals' arguments. One student said she wanted to write a letter, "to tell those guys where they can go." When it seemed other people might be interested in expressing their views to the Cardinals, we made this a class writing project.

> Dear Cardinal:
>   In my personal opinion your article is over-exaggerated. While you ranted and raved about how drastically horrifying the abortion ruling was, people all over the world in lower classes or unwanted homes suffer all the time. Some of these children are born only to wish they were never born. [Cynthia Byrne]

> Dear Cardinal Krol:
>   Well as far as destroying lives go, just stop and think about all the people that are being killed anyway. For instance the men over in Viet Nam who are dead because of a war that never should of happened in the first place, or think about all the people who are dying or already dead of starvation because the Government won't give them any money to eat with . . . and then you have the nerve to say that us women are killing unborn children!" [Donna and Deborah L. Gillespie]

Most of the letters were as angry and eloquent as these. We suspected that this anger at the Cardinals and at Catholic morality was not leaving room for more ambivalent feelings about abortion, so we asked the students to do an additional, more personal writing assignment. "If you discovered tomorrow that you were pregnant, what would you do and how would you feel about it?"

The same girls who disagreed so vehemently with the Cardinals were equally strong in their conviction that they personally would not choose abortions. Almost everyone in the class expressed the feeling that she could not go through with an abortion; even knowing all the difficulties, they chose having the baby as the only choice possible.

Once again, we were caught off-guard. The class seemed to change overnight from pro- to anti-abortion. If we had stopped at the level of opinion, pros and cons, and opposing arguments, we would have had a grossly inaccurate impression of the students' total attitudes about abortion. This served as a powerful reminder of the importance of focusing on feelings, as well as reasoned opinion.

This is obviously only one example of how current issues can become part of the curriculum. The important thing is to give the students a chance to understand an issue through specific current events, and then give them ample opportunity to debate the issue and explore their feelings about it. In this way, the issue can really become "theirs," rather than some distant concern of remote spokespersons.

If there is time and interest, you might want to focus on the way the issue is being presented in various newspapers, as well as on the issue itself. Having discussed the possible range of opinions on the issue, students can more readily recognize media bias. They can see, for instance, that one newspaper tends toward presentation of a pro-abortion position, another toward a "right to life" position. They can see how the reporter's selection of sources determines the orientation of the article. "Where did the reporter get her/his information?" "Who didn't the reporter speak to?" "What would have happened if the reporter had spoken to those sources as well?"

The importance of news sources and points of view in determining the facts was very clear in the trial of Joan Little. In one of the daily newspapers, the issue was presented primarily as a murder trial, while in the entertainment and muckraking weekly, the jailor's state of undress at the time of the killing, and allegations by other prisoners about his sexual advances, were included. Obviously the stories of a reporter getting information from the District Attorney's office will differ from the stories of a reporter who interviews other prisoners. Going over these two articles gave our students a new and more critical way of looking at news.

3: Putting Out a Woman's Newspaper

Students have now tried their hands at producing news and have analyzed at least one current issue as it is presented in official news media. They are ready to return to the task of newsmaking and putting careful effort into a substantial news production. Depending on the interests and skills of members of your class, and the availability of equipment in your school, the production could either take the form of a women's newspaper or a video women's news show. For the sake of clarity here, we will describe the steps involved in putting out a woman's newspaper, and then, in Activity 5, describe differences in the preparation required to produce a news show.

What is "women's news"? Before the class can begin the production of a women's newspaper, they have to address themselves to this question. Does "women's news" mean any stories written by women, regardless of content? Or does it mean stories written about women, regardless of the sex of the author? Or does it mean stories about issues that concern women?

These questions will quickly lead to the question of the audience the students wish to reach, which may affect what they choose to include. Each class may arrive at a somewhat different decision on this point.

Most likely, students will want to distribute the newspaper to other young people in the school and to friends outside. This means that they can rely a great deal on their own interests and tastes in determining what to include. A good starting point is to think back over the stories included in the newscast. With a little effort, some of these might be appropriate for the first issue of the newspaper. The current issue (or issues) just explored may also provide good material for articles. Having formed opinions about a recent issue or event, students are in a good position to present these ideas to other young people.

Other sources of material are recent experiences of people in the class. Perhaps someone has had a run-in with the welfare department or has enjoyed a lively block party.

If the class has done any of the other units in the curriculum, the teacher should encourage people to draw story ideas from what they learned and experienced. A quick listing on the board of the topics explored, the interviews, surveys, questionnaires, speakers, and trips will remind everyone of the experiences that might be shared with their readers. "You know what would be good, a story telling about that nice lady at the counseling center." "We should include some of those interviews with the little kids." "I think we should put in our letters to Cardinal Krol." Even if the class has not taken up any of the other units, the teacher can refer to the activities in those units for investigations, surveys, or writing assignments students could do specifically for the newspaper. For instance, whether or not the class has done "Mean Streets," a student might be interested in visiting and reporting on a local service agency for young women (see Unit VI, p. 159).

Students can also look through their own and each other's previous writing assignments from this and other classes to find material. Fiction as well as nonfiction, poems as well as stories, can be considered. Often students will volunteer each other's writings, while denigrating their own—"I don't want to put *that* in there." One important by-product of this brainstorming is that students, hearing their work praised by others, are helped to recognize their own skills and talents: after just a little prodding, most students agree to contribute the requested article, story, or poem.

Finally, some system of editorial support and criticism must be developed. Most students have less trouble writing something than they have correcting and perfecting it. They are impatient to be finished; they are insecure about their skills. This is an excellent opportunity for the teacher to work individually with people on their writing skills. Because the newspaper will be distributed to a peer group audience, students will have a real investment in improving their writing—above all, they will not want to appear foolish before their friends.

Although the teacher plays a major role in the editing, a student can also learn a great deal from being involved. One system is to pair up the students, with each member of the pair serving as the other's assistant editor. They read one another's first drafts and make comments on content, style, and grammar. The improved copy then goes to the final editor, the teacher.

This kind of collaboration does not come easily to some students. They would often rather have a teacher go over their work than another student. For this reason, we provide a definite structure. Editing times are built into the class period, with students having specific questions to think about in reading one another's drafts:

1. Is the content clear?
2. Do you need or want to know more? If so, what might be added?
3. Should anything be cut?
4. Is it clearly written? Is the main point clear?
5. Are there spelling or punctuation mistakes?

Students tend to be uncritical of each other's writing; they are reluctant to make suggestions. If you use this editing system, you will probably want to do some of the writing and editing skills workshops suggested in the next activity.

It is important to set concrete and realizable goals for this first issue of the newspaper. During the initial brainstorming, some students may volunteer for interesting reporting assignments—like interviewing a probation officer—that they will have difficulty carrying through. The teacher can play a supportive role in helping students figure out how to get the material for articles. You can be with them when they make the first phone call, or you can suggest that two of them go together in a reporting team to undertake an investigation or to conduct an interview. More timid students can be encouraged to write about issues they have already investigated, places they have already visited, experiences they have already had.

It is best to allow a relatively short period (perhaps two weeks) for the production of this first issue of the newspaper. Production tasks—like mimeographing, or collating, or stapling—can be tedious, especially if they are drawn out over a long period of time. The pressure of immediate deadlines makes it all seem more exciting. Some students may even be willing to give extra-class time to speed along the process. Certainly, people are likely to complete their stories while there is still a great deal of enthusiasm about the project and curiosity as to what the audience's reactions will be.

4: Strengthening Writing Skills

During the couple of weeks that students are working on their articles for the newspaper, some class time can be devoted to exercises that strengthen writing and editing skills. Because students are working on a project that depends on these skills, they will have some investment in improving the quality of their writing. This is not the time to teach a whole grammar course, but a few quick exercises, combined with careful work on their articles, can result in real skill development. We focus on description and chronology, touching on topic sentences and sentence structure as well. (For our general approach to teaching writing, see "Techniques," p. 18.)

Describing People

The objective of this exercise is to learn to describe a person in a colorful way, by focusing on and exaggerating details. To begin, the teacher brings in a variety of small culinary tidbits—from peaches to ice cream. The messier the food, the better, for this assignment. The class divides into pairs, both members equipped with something to eat and with paper and pen. The assignment is to write a description of the other person, as she is eating her food.

The students are instructed to use as much detail and exaggeration of detail as is necessary to conjure up a distinct, even cartoon-like picture

in the reader's mind. Although there is much self-conscious laughter as students scrutinize each other, and more laughter when the papers are read aloud, the resulting paragraphs do reflect attention to detail.

Describing Places

A second writing exercise takes students out of the classroom to work on descriptive detail. If the class can go out during class time, you could take them to a nearby shopping district, where there are strong smells, colors, sounds, and generally much activity. (We use Harvard Square.) Everyone is assigned a different corner to stand on or store to go into. After twenty minutes, people return to class and write a description of their location, trying to pay attention to all senses; i.e., what did the place look like? smell like? taste like? sound like? feel like? If you cannot go outside the building, students could go to different areas within the school building, such as the lavatory or the kitchen.

Chronology

It is difficult to give someone the correct chronology of an event while highlighting the most interesting parts. In telling a story orally, most students will jump back and forth in time, imparting a lot of information, but not in a particularly organized way. When they are asked to write down a description of these events, they tend to lose much of the liveliness and spirit of the story in their attempt to be logical and sequential. "Then she did that." "Then I went . . ." etc. We do a series of short exercises with students to give them practice in putting events in chronological or logical order and in writing more interesting sentences.

In the first exercise, students are given a news story with the paragraphs jumbled out of order. The task is to create a coherent news story by rearranging the paragraphs. If there are disagreements among the students, they should be asked to argue the logic of their choices. Then, students check their results with the original, to see how the reporter intended the story to be read.

The same news story, or perhaps a longer

news feature, can be used for a brief review of topic sentences. After the class has been reminded about the definition of a topic sentence, they try to separate out the sentences that convey the main idea of the story from the sentences that provide additional details. The teacher should stress the importance of including both topic sentences and sentences with specific examples, quotations, or supporting evidence.

We usually follow this with a short exercise or two on how to vary sentence structure, giving students examples of three or four different ways in which the same thought or information can be expressed in writing.

5: Producing a Women's News Show

In some classes and school situations, you might choose producing a video women's news show over putting out a women's newspaper. Many of the same steps are involved in both ventures. The class starts by developing a common definition of "women's news." After brainstorming ideas for stories, students—with support from the teacher and each other—work on developing their investigative and reporting skills. Careful, sustained effort is required to create a finished project that the class will be proud to share with a wider audience.

Video is, however, a very different medium from print; and, to some extent, producing a video show reinforces and requires different skills and approaches. In working on their stories for a video production, students have to be concerned with the delivery as well as the content. They will need practice in reading their articles aloud; they may even want to memorize parts of their stories so that they can look up at the camera while giving their reports.

While requiring students to be more practiced in reading, and more familiar with what they have written, a news show may be less demanding of their writing and editing skills. When something is going to be in print, for all to see, there is more pressure to perfect it than when that same story is to be delivered orally. Because of the novelty of the medium, even somewhat su-

perficial or sloppy work can look flashy and exciting on a TV screen. The "hammy" students may be less inclined to put sustained effort into their stories, thinking that at the last minute they will come up with something interesting or amusing to say. Shier students may feel that no matter how hard they work on an article, they won't have the courage to give their reports in front of a camera. Their nervousness about delivering their stories may inhibit them from ever starting to work on them.

Both the "hams" and the "camera shy" will need structure, support, and encouragement from the teacher. Class time should be spent on speech skills as well as writing and editing skills. In pairs, students can help each other, not only with the content and writing style of their stories, but also with the oral presentation. The pairs can also spend time brainstorming on how to make the stories visually interesting. "Are there pictures or signs for the camera to pick up?" "Is there a way to dramatize an important point?"

Students will be able to think about visual aspects more productively, if early on in the production schedule, class time is spent becoming familiar and comfortable with the equipment. Video equipment is easy to operate; with minimal instructions, students in the class can learn to run it themselves. At least one class period should be given to letting the students pass around the camera, film each other, and film the classroom. One invariable result of this experience is that at least two or three students will volunteer to work on the production end of the news show. Students who have never imagined themselves as capable technicians are amazed to find that they can use video-tape successfully. Their new skills are accompanied by a new sense of competence.

A video production offers more entry points for students with different skills and learning styles than does a newspaper. Students whose writing skills are not on a level with their creativity are able to find in video an outlet for their ideas and energy. On the other hand, such students are not likely to improve their writing through doing a video show. Your teaching and learning priorities will have to determine which is the better choice for your class.

The issue of distribution might also be a consideration in deciding whether to produce a show or a newspaper. Only groups with access to equipment can see a video news show, which probably limits the audience to people within the school. A newspaper can be widely distributed to friends and relatives, and even sent to people out of town. Ultimately, however, the size of the audience is probably less important than the fact of producing something for other people. Students will gain self-confidence from successfully completing either project.

6: Audience Feedback

The publishing of the newspaper or completion of the video news show is a moment of accomplishment and let-down. The effort of several weeks has gone into producing something, but now it's over. Actually, however, another important aspect of the project is beginning—the audience's reaction to the material. Unfortunately, this reaction is largely private. Particularly in the case of the newspaper, where the audience consists of scattered individuals, there is little chance for the students producing the news to get a sense of how their work is being received. They may get general approving comments, but little specific feedback and support, especially from their peers.

To sustain the feelings of accomplishment, and acknowledge the importance of audience reaction, we conduct an audience survey. The class generates a survey questionnaire together, and then every student interviews at least two "typical" readers or viewers. The questionnaire can inclued items like:

1. Did you learn anything new from the newspaper or show?
2. Which articles interested you most? Why?
3. Are there other topics or events you would like to see included in future issues or shows?
4. Is there any article you have strong feelings about and would like to respond to?

5. Do you read other newspapers or watch TV news?
6. If so, how would you compare this one to those?

Interviewing people about their reactions to the newspaper or news show can be threatening. There is embarrassment about having produced something, and even more embarrassment about asking people to acknowledge it. "They aren't going to tell us what they really think." But, in spite of all this, people enjoy having an excuse to get feedback on their work.

Interpreting the survey results can also be interesting. "Was there any difference in the reaction of males and females?" This question has revealed certain patterns for us. The male readers of our newspaper expressed some resentment at the concept of "women's news," but also begrudgingly admired the results.

The class may want to do a second newspaper issue or news show, particularly after getting audience reactions. If there is time, it is a worthwhile activity. In the case of the video news show, you might want to add to and perfect what is already there rather than do a whole new production. For instance, some stories might benefit from outdoor footage, or new indoor visuals, or a new sound track; some students may want to retake their reports.

Audience feedback had some concrete effects on our second productions. In our second newspaper, the students asked males to submit things they had written for other classes; we did receive and print one of these articles. Another decision that came out of audience feedback was to make the second issue more personal, to include more articles directly from people's experiences. Feedback on the news show led to including more music and more neighborhood footage to go along with certain news reports.

With their self-confidence bolstered from successfully completing a first project, students are able to sustain their interest over a longer period. The second issue or show can thus be more ambitious, including more original research and writing, and resulting in a more careful and imaginative presentation.

NOTES TO THE TEACHER

Completing a Project

Producing a newspaper or news show is a difficult undertaking. Students may have extreme doubts about their ability to carry off such a project. They feel inadequate, both because of their limited writing skills and their limited knowledge of the world. The sustained effort required by this project can only be maintained if students develop a firm belief that the task can and will come to a successful completion. The teacher's task is to inspire students with this confidence.

Very few students feel good about their writing abilities. They are often reluctant to have things they have written read aloud in the classroom, much less shared with a wider audience. Sharing within the class is definitely an important step. The more help and approval they can get from each other and the teacher in the relatively safe classroom, the more confident they will feel about sharing their writing more widely. A definite editorial procedure, with the teacher available as a supporter and editor, will also reassure students that they will get help.

In helping students, however, it may be difficult to find the right balance of criticism and approval. Marking up a student's whole page with corrections can be very discouraging to her, reinforcing feelings of inadequacy. On the other hand, you don't want to encourage a student to submit an article that is really poorly written. A two- or three-step editorial process, including self-corrections and corrections by another student, provides a means of alleviating this problem, to some degree.

Students' feelings of inadequacy about skills are compounded by their feelings of ignorance with regard to the news. Their reactions to newspapers or news programs ("that's stupid"; "it's boring") while often expressed as hostility, may in fact be covering their shame at their own lack of understanding. Students who feel inadequate reading a newspaper or watching TV news may have trouble imagining themselves as "news-makers." In studying several current events together in class, students build confidence in their ability to understand and transmit the news. Depending on the class, you might want to spend several weeks on current issues before starting to produce a newspaper or news show. Or, you could get started on production, but take one day a week to keep up with the news.

Throughout the project, the teacher has to maintain a high level of enthusiasm, commitment, and confidence. This can be severely tested, when students are dragging their feet, or despairing at ever being finished, or demanding that the class forget the whole thing. We have found that in most cases it is best to take a deep breath and push on. Students want to be able to complain, but they do not really want us to give up, or agree with their pessimism. It is very important that someone believe in them and their capabilities to accomplish a difficult project.

Taking a Stand

"Are you one of them women's libbers?" In producing the newspaper or news show, students are publicly identifying themselves with a women's project. Regardless of the exact content of the articles, the very fact that a group of young women are producing "women's news" is a statement. And for some students, it may not be a statement they feel comfortable making.

It is very important that the newspaper or news show accurately reflect the views and feelings of the students in the class, even when these seem confused or contradictory. This may be hard for us as teachers to accept. Because the newspaper is *our* public statement as well, we feel under some pressure to have the content challenge traditional stereotypes and sex roles, to present new feminist perspectives and ideas. After all, what other justification is there for teaching a women's class?

If we are not careful, however, our concerns may influence students to write things that they do not really believe or feel. When challenged by friends, they will feel embarrassed and unable to defend themselves or the ways they are really changing. New ideas are threatening—particularly when they challenge old, accepted behavior patterns. In beginning to develop a consciousness about what it means to be a woman, students need time and space to think through the implications of this new perspective for their lives. For many students, there may be a tenuous period, when they know they are changing their perspectives, but are not quite ready to admit to or explain that change.

Producing the newspaper or news show can be a crucial, positive step. It can be a way for students to begin to identify themselves as people with ideas and understandings that they want to communicate to others. But when students are forced to defend ideas they themselves don't understand or agree with, they are in an impossible and vulnerable position. Our role should be to help students begin to articulate their ideas to the people around them, without becoming isolated or frustrated because of their differences.

BIBLIOGRAPHY

This is a listing of the books, articles, pamphlets, and films suggested in the curriculum. Almost all of the books are inexpensive paperback editions, available in local bookstores or libraries. The pamphlets can be ordered through the presses that publish them; the magazine articles obtained as reprints from the publishers. Some of the books listed are used in their entirety in the units, while others are useful for one short section or chapter. Descriptions of thematic content, ideas for classroom use, and information about page numbers are given within the units where the reading is suggested. In a few cases, we have included books in the bibliography that are mentioned only as supplementary material for the students or suggested as background information for the teacher.

Unit II: Early Socialization

Bethell, Jean. *When I Grow Up.* New York: Wonder Books, 1965.

Darrow, Whitney, Jr. *I'm Glad I'm a Boy, I'm Glad I'm a Girl.* New York: Simon & Schuster, 1970.

Gould, Lois. "X: A Fabulous Child's Story." *Ms.,* December 1972, p. 74. Reprints available from *Ms.,* 370 Lexington Ave., New York, NY 10017.

Additional References
for Nonsexist Children's Books:

The Feminist Press, Box 334, Old Westbury, NY 11568.

Lollipop Power, P. O. Box 1171, Chapel Hill, NC 27514.

Ms., 370 Lexington Ave., New York, NY 10017.

Unit III: Growing Up Female

Angelou, Maya. *I Know Why the Caged Bird Sings.* New York: Bantam Books, 1970.

Boston Women's Health Book Collective. *Our Bodies, Ourselves.* Rev. ed. New York: Simon & Schuster, 1976.

Delaney, Shelagh. *A Taste of Honey.* New York: Grove Press, 1959.

Frank, Anne. *Anne Frank: The Diary of a Young Girl.* New York: Pocket Books, 1952.

Howe, Florence, and Bass, Ellen, eds. *No More Masks.* New York: Doubleday Anchor, 1973.

Mead, Margaret. *Growing Up in New Guinea.* New York: William Morrow & Co., 1930.

_____. *Sex and Temperament in Three Primitive Societies.* New York: William Morrow & Co., 1935.

Meriwether, Louise. *Daddy Was a Number Runner.* New York: Pyramid Publications, 1970.

Olsen, Tillie. *Tell Me a Riddle.* Philadelphia: J. B. Lippincott Company, 1961.

Piercy, Marge. *To Be of Use.* Garden City, N.Y.: Doubleday & Co., 1973.

Singer, Frieda, ed. *Daughters in High School.* Plainfield, Vt.: Daughters, Inc., 1974.

Smith, Betty. *A Tree Grows in Brooklyn.* New York: Harper & Row, 1943.

Wasserman, Barbara Alson, ed. *The Bold New Women.* New York: Fawcett Books, 1970.

Records:
"Hang In There." Holly Near. Redwood Records.

Unit IV: Adult Sex Roles

Belden, Jack. "Gold Flower's Story." Pamphlet available from The New England Free Press,

60 Union Square, Somerville, MA 02143.

Boston Women's Health Book Collective. *Our Bodies, Ourselves.* Rev. ed. New York: Simon & Schuster, 1976.

Greene, Felix. "A Divorce Trial in China." Pamphlet available from The New England Free Press, 60 Union Square, Somerville, MA 02143.

Jensen, Oliver. *The Revolt of American Women.* New York: Harcourt Brace Jovanovich, 1971.

Mead, Margaret. *Sex and Temperament in Three Primtive Societies.* New York: William Morrow & Co., 1935.

Olsen, Tillie. *Tell Me a Riddle.* Philadelphia: J. B. Lippincott Company, 1961.

Singer, Frieda, ed. *Daughters in High School.* Plainfield, Vt.: Daughters, Inc., 1974.

Wakowski, Diane. *The Motorcycle Betrayal Poems.* New York: Simon & Schuster, 1971.

Unit V: Sexuality

Boston Women's Health Book Collective. *Our Bodies, Ourselves.* Rev. ed. New York: Simon & Schuster, 1976.

Demarest, Robert J., and Sciarra, John J. *Conception, Birth and Contraception, a Visual Presentation.* New York: McGraw-Hill, 1969.

Gray, Marian Johnson and Roger W. "How to Take the Worry Out of Being Close, An Egg and Sperm Handbook." 1971. Reprints available from P.O. Box 2822, Oakland, CA 94618.

Unit VI: Mean Streets

Chesney-Lind, Meda. "Juvenile Delinquency: The Sexualization of Female Crime." *Psychology Today,* July, 1974, p. 43.

"The Myth of Sexual Delinquency," *Women: A Journal of Liberation* 3. (Special issue: "Women Locked Up") Back copies available from 3028 Greenemount Ave., Baltimore, MD 21218.

Unit VII: Women and Work

Hullatt, Josephine. "Household Help Wanted, Female." *Ms.,* February 1973, p. 45. Reprints available from *Ms.,* 370 Lexington Ave., New York, NY 10017.

Jensen, Oliver. *The Revolt of American Women.* New York: Harcourt Brace Jovanovich, 1971.

Lerner, Gerda. *Black Women in White America.* New York: Vintage, 1973.

Maupin, Joyce. "Labor Heroines: Ten Women Who Led the Struggle." 1974. Pamphlet available from Union Wage, P.O. Box 462, Berkeley, CA 94701.

Meltzer, Milton. *Bread and Roses.* New York: Random House Vintage, 1967.

Merriam, Eve, ed. *Growing Up Female in America: Ten Lives.* New York: Dell Publishing Co., 1971.

Scott, Anne Firor, ed. *The American Woman: Who Was She?* Englewood Cliffs, N.J.: Prentice-Hall, 1971.

Tepperman, Jean. "Two Jobs: Women Who Work in Factories." In *Sisterhood Is Powerful.* Edited by Robin Morgan. New York: Random House, 1970.

Terkel, Studs. *Working.* New York: Avon Books, 1972.

Additional References:

Braverman, Harry. *Labor and Monopoly Capital.* New York: Monthly Review Press, 1974.

Davies, Margery. "A Woman's Place Is at the Typewriter. The Feminization of the Clerical Labor Force." *Radical America,* July–August, 1974, p. 7. Back copies available from *Radical America,* 5 Upland Road, Cambridge, MA 02140.

Huberman, Leo. *We, the People.* New York: Monthly Review Press, 1947.

Ingraham, Claire R. and Leonard W. *An Album of Women in American History.* New York: Franklin Watts, 1972.

Lens, Sidney. *Working Men, The Story of Labor.* New York: G.P. Putnam's Sons, 1960.

Seed, Susanne. *Saturday's Child.* New York: Bantam Books, 1974.

Seifer, Nancy. *Absent from the Majority*. Middle America Pamphlet Series, 1973. Available from The American Jewish Committee, 165 E. 56 St., New York, NY 10022.

Films:

"The Inheritance." Available from Contemporary/McGraw-Hill Films, 1221 Avenue of the Americas, New York, NY 10020.

Unit VIII: Women Organizing Themselves

Boston Women's Health Book Collective. *Our Bodies, Ourselves*. Rev. ed. New York: Simon & Schuster, 1976.

Gaines, Ernest J. *The Autobiography of Miss Jane Pittman*. New York: Bantam Books, 1972.

Galen, Marcy. "The Courage of Harriet Tubman." *Ms.*, August 1973, p. 16. Reprints available from *Ms.*, 370 Lexington Ave., New York, 10017.

Gluck, Sherna, ed. *From Parlor to Prison: Five American Suffragists Talk about Their Lives*. New York: Vintage, 1976.

Howe, Florence, and Bass, Ellen, eds. *No More Masks*. New York: Doubleday Anchor, 1973.

Jensen, Oliver. *The Revolt of American Women*. New York: Harcourt Brace Jovanovich, 1971.

MacKenzie, Midge. *Shoulder to Shoulder*. New York: Alfred A. Knopf, 1975.

Merriam, Eve, ed. *Growing Up Female in America: Ten Lives*. New York: Dell Publishing Co., 1971.

Moody, Anne. *Coming of Age in Mississippi*. New York: Dell Publishing Co., 1971.

Oakley, Mary. *Elizabeth Cady Stanton*. Old Westbury, New York: The Feminist Press, 1972.

Schneier, Miriam, ed. *Feminism: The Essential Historical Writings*. New York: Vintage, 1971.

Tremain, Rose. *The Fight for Freedom for Women*. New York: Random House Ballantine, 1973.

Van Gelder, Lindsy. "Coffee, Tea, or Fly Me." *Ms.*, January 1973, p. 86.

Films:

"Growing Up Female: As Six Become One." Available from New Day Films, P.O. Box 315, Franklin Lakes, NJ 06417.

"Men's Lives." Available from New Day Films (see above).

"Women on the March." Available from Contemporary/McGraw-Hill Films, 1221 Avenue of the Americas, New York, NY 10020.

ABOUT THE GROUP SCHOOL

The Group School is an alternative, certified high school for working-class youth in Cambridge, Massachusetts. In addition to academic instruction, the school offers personal counseling, vocational counseling and training, and advocacy assistance. Since 1969, when the school was founded, the staff has developed courses and materials geared to the special needs and interests of women students. This work has resulted in a comprehensive women's studies curriculum, *Changing Learning, Changing Lives.*

ABOUT THE AUTHORS

Barbara Gates, one of the organizers and founders of The Group School, has been recognized for her independent research on alternative schools in the United States. She has taught English in both high school and college and is author of two teaching guides for high school teachers on the subjects of women and sports and women working for social change.

Susan Klaw began teaching at The Group School in 1972, where she was primary fundraiser and co-director of the Youth Advocacy Program. Prior to joining The Group School staff, Ms. Klaw taught in Boston public and parochial schools.

Adria Steinberg, co-author of the *Vietnam Curriculum* and *Neighborhood Youth and Class,* joined The Group School in 1971 after teaching for five years in public schools in the Boston area. She has been academic coordinator of the school and is working with the Cambridge public schools on a federally-funded program for the inclusion of women in the curriculum.

ABOUT THE FEMINIST PRESS

The Feminist Press offers alternatives in education and in literature. Founded in 1970, this nonprofit, tax-exempt educational and publishing organization works to eliminate sexual stereotypes in books and schools, providing instead a new (or neglected) literature with a broader vision of human potential. Our books—high quality paperbacks—include reprints of important works about women, feminist biographies of women, and nonsexist children's books. Curricular materials, bibliographies, directories, and a newsletter provide information and support for women's studies at every educational level. Our inservice projects help teachers develop new methods to encourage students to become their best and freest selves. Through our publications and projects we can begin to recreate the forgotten history of women and begin to create a more humane and equitable society for the future. For a catalogue of all our publications, please write to The Feminist Press, Box 334, Old Westbury, New York 11568.

This book was made possible by the work of many people, including The Feminist Press Staff and Board. The Board, the decision-making body of the Press, includes all staff members and other individuals who have an ongoing relationship to The Feminist Press: Phyllis Arlow, Jeanne Bracken, Brenda Carter, Toni Cerutti, Ranice Crosby, Sue Davidson, Michelina Fitzmaurice, Shirley Frank, Merle Froschl, Barbara Gore, Brett Harvey, Ilene Hertz, Florence Howe, Paul Lauter, Carol Levin, Corrine Lucido, Mary Mulrooney, Dora Janeway Odarenko, Ethel J. Phelps, Elizabeth Phillips, Helen Schrader, Susan Trowbridge, Sandy Weinbaum, Sharon Wigutoff, Jane Williamson, Sophie Zimmerman.

CLEARINGHOUSE PUBLICATIONS: ELEMENTARY EDUCATION

Nonsexist Curricular Materials for Elementary Schools

Laurie Olsen Johnson, ed. (1974) A collection of materials for the elementary teacher and student, including quizzes, checklists, bibliographies, workbook, model units.

CLEARINGHOUSE PUBLICATIONS: SECONDARY EDUCATION

Changing Learning, Changing Lives

Barbara Gates, Susan Klaw, and Adria Steinberg. (1979) A comprehensive women's studies curriculum developed by The Group School, an alternative high school for working-class youth in Cambridge, Massachusetts. Includes nine thematic units plus suggestions for role plays, trips, interviewing, making a film, and publishing a newspaper.

High School Feminist Studies

Carol Ahlum and Jacqueline Fralley, compilers. Florence Howe, ed. (1976) A collection of curricular materials in women's studies for and from high schools including essays, bibliographies, teaching units.

Strong Women

Deborah Silverton Rosenfelt, ed. (1976) Annotated bibliography of widely available paperbacks to help the teacher supplement the male-biased curriculum: anthologies, autobiography, novels, short stories, drama, poetry.

CLEARINGHOUSE PUBLICATIONS: HIGHER EDUCATION

Who's Who and Where in Women's Studies

Tamar Berkowitz, Jean Mangi, and Jane Williamson, eds. (1974) Complete directory of women's studies programs, courses, and teachers, arranged by institution, department, and instructor.

Female Studies VI
Closer to the Ground: Women's Classes, Criticism, Programs—1972

Nancy Hoffman, Cynthia Secor, and Adrian Tinsley, eds., for the Commission on the Status of Women of the Modern Language Association. (1972) Essays on women's studies in the classroom, literary criticism from a feminist perspective, course materials.

Female Studies VII
Going Strong: New Courses/New Programs

Deborah Rosenfelt, ed. (1973) Syllabi for over sixty recent women's studies courses; descriptions of twelve new programs. Introductory essay assessing recent developments in women's studies.

Female Studies IX
Teaching about Women in the Foreign Languages

Sidonie Cassirer, ed., for the Commission on the Status of Women of the Modern Language Association. (1975) Listings and outlines of courses with a focus on women offered by departments of French, Spanish, and German in colleges and universities across the country.

Female Studies X
Student Work—Learning to Speak

Deborah Silverton Rosenfelt, ed. (1975) The fruits of some five years of undergraduate women's studies courses on campuses across the country: a first play, a "group autobiography," poems, short stories, papers.

CLEARINGHOUSE PUBLICATIONS: GENERAL EDUCATION

Feminist Resources for Schools and Colleges

Merle Froschl and Jane Williamson, eds. (Revised ed. 1977) A selective guide to curricular materials at every level from the elementary school to the university—for teachers, students, librarians, and parents who want to challenge sexism in education and create nonsexist and feminist curriculum.

Women's Studies Newsletter

A quarterly published by The Feminist Press and the National Women's Studies Association. Contains articles on women's studies at all levels of education: new programs, innovative courses, teaching techniques, curricular materials, book reviews, conference reports, bibliography, job information.